Sacred
Heart
School
♥ ♥ ♥

This book was generously donated by :

*The
Poggiolli Family
2009*

Sacred Heart School Library, 1095 Gage Street, Winnetka, IL 60093

Ancient Carpenters' Tools

*Illustrated and Explained, Together with
the Implements of the Lumberman,
Joiner and Cabinet-Maker in Use in
the Eighteenth Century*

Henry C. Mercer

DOVER PUBLICATIONS, INC.
Mineola, New York

Bibliographical Note

This Dover edition, first published in 2000, is an unabridged, unaltered
republication of the fifth edition (1975) of the work originally published in
1929 by The Bucks County Historical Society, Doylestown, Pennsylvania. More
than 250 illustrations are reproduced from the third edition (1960).

Library of Congress Cataloging-in-Publication Data

Mercer, Henry Chapman, 1856–1930.
    Ancient carpenters' tools : illustrated and explained, together with the
implements of the lumberman, joiner and cabinet-maker in use in the eighteenth century / Henry C. Mercer.
       p. cm.
    Originally published: Doylestown, Pa. : The Bucks County Historical
Society, 1929.
    Includes bibliographical references and index.
    ISBN 0-486-40958-9 (pbk.)
     1. Carpentry—Tools. I. Title.

TH5618 .M4 2000
694'.028'4—dc21
                                        99-086242

Manufactured in the United States of America
Dover Publications, Inc., 31 East 2nd Street, Mineola, N.Y. 11501

Contents

Foreword

In August, 1958, this writer was separated from the United States Army and returned to The Henry Francis du Pont Winterthur Museum in order to resume previous employment. At that time the Museum's South Wing was under construction and the writer was "permitted" to volunteer for a special project—the cataloguing and installation of the tools and shop equipment of the Dominy family of craftsmen who had lived in East Hampton, New York. It is an understatement to note that the first viewing of a great pile of more than 1,100 pieces of shop equipment and tools produced mixed feelings. There was certainly exhilaration with the challenge of arranging order from chaos and the prospect of learning a great deal about craft tools and techniques. Equally apparent was a definite feeling of panic at the thought of the enormous task represented by the material dumped into a large storeroom of the Museum's Gray Building.

It was not an accident that one of this writer's first thoughts was to turn to Henry Chapman Mercer's *Ancient Carpenters' Tools* for assistance. During two years of graduate study as a Fellow of the Winterthur Program in Early American Culture, the book was described as *the* standard and reliable work about woodworking tools. While the Museum's library was not fortunate enough to have the first edition of 1929, it did have a copy of the second edition of 1951. This writer reasoned that Mercer's book would be invaluable in sorting and identifying woodworking tools from the larger body of the Dominy artifacts.

It is not too simplistic to state that within a relatively short period of time "fair order reigned" and the task of cataloguing the Dominy Tool Collection was made more reasonable by the existence of *Ancient Carpenters' Tools*. In a very real sense, then, this foreword represents my appreciation to The Bucks County Historical Society not only for keeping this important book in print, but for publishing it in a form that will put it into more hands.

This pioneer contribution to the study of hand tools must continue to be acknowledged, for in many ways Mercer was "ahead of his time". Even he realized that in 1929 *Ancient Carpenters' Tools* was a book well in advance of general interest in the subject. In the July, 1936, issue of *The Chronicle* of the Early American Industries Association, dedicated to Henry C. Mercer, one of his closest associates, Frank Swain, is quoted as having stated: "I remember that he (Dr. Mercer) laid his first copy on the table, and said, 'Well that's a long job, done at last, but I am afraid it is all to no purpose'."

Heightened interest in the United States in the subject of hand tools did not begin until the late 1950's, and has continued unabated to the present. The study of tools became an unquestioned subject of academic respectability with the formation of The Society for the History of Technology and quarterly appearances of its fine journal, *Technology and Culture*.

The academic credentials possessed by Henry Chapman Mercer should not be overlooked. He studied law at Harvard, but began his career as an archaeologist, and held the position of Curator of American and Prehistoric Archaeology at the University Museum of the University of Pennsylvania, before beginning his own collection. Clearly, to Mercer, "tools" were equated with "artifacts".

In the fall of 1897 Mercer addressed The Bucks County Historical Society for the first time on the subject "Tools of the Nation Maker". Inspired by a visit to a dealer in "penny lots", he had begun to collect "obsolete utensils" that in many cases he found on trash heaps, consigned to oblivion by the advent of factory-made substitutes. He also spent some time at the Herstine pottery, Nockamixon Township, in northern Bucks County, and visited a number of sites where "potter's tools lay on abandoned work benches buried in dust". Suddenly he was made keenly aware of the significance of hand tools for America.

In 1910 Dr. Mercer became president of The Bucks County Historical Society and served in that office until 1930. His antiquarian collection, including large numbers of tools, was transferred from his own "Indian House" at the family home, Aldie, to the newly dedicated concrete museum which he built in 1916 adjoining The Society's building. The year prior to that, Mercer had first met Rudolph P. Hommel. By 1921, Mercer's thinking on the subject of hand tools was already crystallized, for in Hommel's own words, Mercer "planned, equipped and directed" an expedition to China in order to make a photographic and written description of the tools and implements of the Chinese people. Mercer had recognized that industry had already submerged the tools and techniques of the handcraft society that existed in the United States prior to 1850. He was convinced that primitive industries in foreign countries had to be systematically examined before they became submerged in modern processes and machinery.

A short statement by Dr. Mercer in the *Proceedings* of The Bucks County Historical Society dated January 17, 1925, says: "Among the tools of ancient type, and universal interest, exhibited in the Museum . . . those pertaining to the construction of the house may be regarded as of unusual importance . . ." Realizing that "any thorough presentation of the subject" would require extensive use of graphic material, he found it desirable to "utilize an opportunity then offered" to publish a series of profusely illustrated articles in *Old Time New England*, the bulletin of the Society for the Preservation of New England Antiquities.

It has been suggested that Mercer may have intended to write an updated version of Edward H. Knight's *American Mechanical Dictionary.* That is a moot question, but he certainly acknowledged his indebtedness to that work in a short preface to the series in *Old Time New England.*

In 1929, Henry C. Mercer paid the Southworth Press of Portland, Maine, to print an edition of over four hundred copies. The entire edition was given to The Bucks County Historical Society for sale. Despite Dr. Mercer's fear that his work had been to "no purpose", and despite its relatively high price of five dollars during depression times, the book did receive the acclaim it deserved. In the very first issue of *The Chronicle*, published in 1933, Mercer's tome headed the list of five books recommended to tool collectors and students. Amusingly, the central word of the title was incorrectly punctuated as "Carpenter's", a mistake that was to persist in the pages of *The Chronicle.*

For many years, the Early American Industries Association steadily beat drums for *Ancient Carpenters' Tools* in the pages of its quarterly. The July, 1936, issue was "respectfully dedicated to the memory of Dr. Henry C. Mercer". Readers were informed that his book "is, and always will be, the standard treatise on American woodworking tools of the 18th and 19th centuries". This sentiment was to be echoed by Eugene S. Ferguson in 1968 when he published his *Bibliography of The History of Technology* (Cambridge, Mass.: Society for the History of Technology and M.I.T. Press). In this important and useful study, Ferguson listed the 1929 and 1951 printings with the comments, "For long the only general work in English on hand tools" and "A standard work on hand tools through the nineteenth century". In a preface to an article about "The Cooper" in the June, 1938, issue of *The Chronicle*, William B. Sprague stated that anyone seriously interested in the subject "has, or will wish to acquire, a copy of Dr. Mercer's book". The Early American Industries Association's intensive interest in *Ancient Carpenters' Tools* is perhaps best illustrated by publication in *The Chronicle* (September, 1941, pp. 148, 150, 152) of Joseph E. Sandford's marginal notes to references in Mercer's book. Sandford's helpful comments were later published as part of the Addenda of subsequent editions of *Ancient Carpenters' Tools.*

Among the many encomiums delivered at the memorial services for Dr. Mercer, those of Rudolph Hommel and John T. Coolidge summarize this author's strong belief that there will be future editions of this book. Hommel believed that Henry Mercer's most important contribution to the world of learning was his systematic study of trades, domestic utensils, and activities.

In his studies, Mercer was able to break with "the old prejudice" that only the activities and artifacts "of the so-called 'upper' classes are worthy of investigation". Mercer's philosophy is quite evident in *Ancient Carpenters' Tools*.

Further, John Coolidge recognized that the contents of an important part of the collections of The Mercer Museum are recorded in *Ancient Carpenters' Tools*. As Mercer intended, and as Coolidge predicted, these collections have "become of increasing value to succeeding generations". In truth, the collections of The Mercer Museum are of national significance and it is to the credit of The Bucks County Historical Society that this fifth printing of *Ancient Carpenters' Tools* will continue to make the collection of woodworking tools available for use by this generation of students and collectors.

Charles F. Hummel
Curator,
Henry Francis Dupont
Winterthur Museum
Winterthur, Delaware

Preface to First Edition

HE woodworking tools by which man, since the beginning of the Iron Age, has helped himself to supply one of the most important and universal of his needs, namely shelter, are, and long have been, among the chief agents of his so-called civilization. Nevertheless, despite their great significance, they have been so generally overlooked by historians, travellers and antiquaries, and so imperfectly accounted for by technical writers, that the following attempt to illustrate and describe, as nearly as possible, all of them, seems justified.

Because the application of mechanical power to carpenters' tools in the nineteenth century has superseded many of them, and, while vastly increasing the efficiency, has obscured the construction of others, an artificial limit has been set to the following investigation, which for clearness sake does not attempt to deal with the woodworking machinery of the present day, but, stopping at the so-called industrial revolution, or soon after 1820, confines itself to the tools as they appear in the eighteenth century, in their simple and unchanged form.

Except for purposes of comparison, the specimens here shown have been collected in the United States, chiefly in Pennsylvania, but a short study of them will soon convince us, that though made in America, they were not invented there, but represent long-existing types of world-wide use, brought thither by the Colonists; hence, that the collection is neither local nor national, but international and of general ethnologic interest.

Still more surprising seems the fact that a large proportion of these continually-used implements of the eighteenth century, *have remained unchanged in construction since Roman times.*

Therefore, they are of far more extended industrial interest than the wood-working machines of today, which, despite their economic importance, have at most only been with us for about a hundred years.

To weigh the historic significance or universal distribution of these ancient tools, is to realize that all attempts to display them in order to glorify modern machinery can only distort history.

Because they are often identical in construction with the Roman, Greek, Assyrian, Egyptian and Chinese implements, they immediately throw a new light on the study of archaeology.

Yet, when the specimens here shown are compared with what ancient tools of like character remain to us in museums, an important oversight appears. Attention is again called to the fact that the evidence of these tools of the eighteenth century has been overlooked by archaeologists, who, concerned only with the past, often fail to account for the interval between it and the present, since many tools, once existing and very necessary to explain human effort, because made of or mounted with perishable materials, cannot be found or recognized in the excavations of Assyria, Italy, Greece and Egypt. If, therefore, in these specimens, the past has survived into the present, the more we study them the more certain it becomes that a gap of two thousand years can often be filled with implements in perfect condition, comparatively modern in date, but very old in type, not excavated or studied by the archaeologist, yet none the less the master-tools of ancient and extinct peoples.

In the preparation of the following pages, the writer gratefully acknowledges help given him by the Society for the Preservation of New England Antiquities, and its managing editor George Francis Dow and also for permission to reprint "Ancient Carpenters' Tools" from articles published in *Old-Time New England,* the Bulletin of the Society.

HENRY C. MERCER

Doylestown, Pennsylvania
August 4, 1928

Ancient Carpenters' Tools

THOUGH nearly all made in America, the tools of the house-builder of one hundred and fifty years ago, here described, including those used in felling trees, making and preparing boards, shingles, lumber, etc., for rough house construction by the carpenter, and for house finishing by the joiner and cabinet-maker, do not appear as American inventions but as European heirlooms, often in type two thousand years old, modified, rather than transformed, by a new environment. Because they pertain to no one district or even country, but to all countries, and to one of the most important and universal of human needs, namely shelter, the following imperfect notes, while often local in origin, are not limited in meaning, and might reasonably apply not alone to New England or Eastern Pennsylvania, but to the United States in general and also to England and Continental Europe. The specimens, shown chiefly by photographs from the originals, may be classified by using the terms employed in Moxon's *Mechanick Exercises* (ed. 1678), and Knight's *American Mechanical Dictionary* (ed. 1878), as follows, first:—

Tools for Felling, Splitting and Log Sawing

Among these, the first illustration shows two examples of the so-called

TRADE AXES (Fig. 1)

of the seventeenth century, first sold to the Indians by European traders; a heavy, rectangular, hafted blade about eight inches long, representing the original tree-felling axe long ago employed in Europe, brought by the pioneers to Canada, Plymouth and Jamestown, and used by them on the forests of North America.

The now rare instrument should consist of (*a*) the bit or blade,— (*b*) the poll, or face opposite the bit,— (*c*) the eye, generally with a pointed lower lip (here lacking) for inserting the handle,—and (*d*) the helve or handle. Apparently surviving in common use until *c.* 1720 or 1740, it differs, not only in appearance, from the common, comparatively square American axe of to-day, but also in construction; namely, though equipped with a very long, down-flaring, flat-topped bit, it has no poll; that is to say, the iron encircling the eye, as if bent around the handle, has not been thickened or squared, to make a pounding surface opposite the blade; hence, as always in old European, and never in modern American axes, the bit outweighs the poll.

W. H. Beauchamp ("Metallic Implements of New York Indians," in *New York State Museum Bulletin 55,* 1902) says of these heavy, long-bitted, tree-felling instruments, that thousands of them, dating from the early seventeenth century, smith-marked with little round, variously hatched stamps, as here shown; imported from Holland (Utrecht) and also made or mended by English and French blacksmiths employed by the Indians, have been found on Iroquois dwelling sites, in New York and Canada, and there can be no reasonable doubt, from their size,—eight to nine inches long, and

1

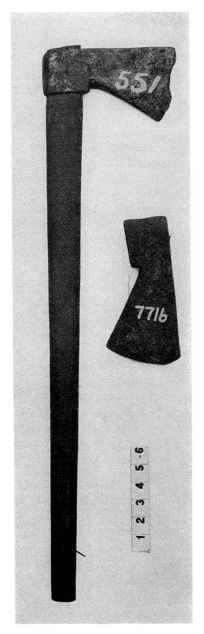

Fig. 1. Trade Axes

Two tree-felling axes of ancient European type sold
by European traders to the Indians at the time of the
earliest settlements. Flat-topped, long-bitted, lacking

weight.—three pounds, fifteen ounces
(Fig. 1, lower), that they were not used
by the Indians as tomahawks, and that
the small, light, and deadly iron tomahawk, so closely resembling them in
outline, was an afterthought, derived
from them, by white blacksmiths soon
after the settlement; before which
time, the Indian tomahawk had been
a stone or bone mounted club.

The absence of poll, observable in
these trade axes, though common, is
not invariable among old European
axes, since some have polls (*cf*. Figs. 2
and 4); nevertheless, where occurring,
it only adds to the overweight of the
bit, by which fixed characteristic these
early American tools are seen to be

poll and eye-lip, they are impressed on both sides with
duplicate groups of little circular smith stamps, faintly
seen in the photograph, as follows: on No. 551, a close
group of three half-inch stamped circles, enclosing two
raised bars forming crosses and appearing just left of
the eye, is repeated on the reverse. On No. 7716, the
stamps show three instead of two cross bars, and form
stars. As in all European axes, the bit greatly outweighs the poll. The handle of the hafted specimen is
not original. No. 7716 was ploughed up at an Indian
village site, at the Forks of Neshaminy, now Rushland,
Bucks Co., Pa., about 1870, by Joseph Warner. No.
551 was obtained in Chester Co., Pa.

There is a collection of these conspicuously flat-
topped, lipless, polless axes, at the New York State
Museum at Albany; another, at the Provincial Mu-
seum in Toronto, Canada; another of fourteen speci-
mens, exactly of this type, from Indian graves in the
Susquehanna Valley, in the possession of Mr. D. H.
Landis, of Windom, Lancaster Co., Pa.; and Mr.
Clarence B. Moore illustrates a replica, dug up, with a
skeleton, from an intrusive (later) Indian grave in the
Thursby Mound, Volusia Co., Fla. (*cf.* "Certain Sand
Mounds of St. Johns River, Florida." Phila., 1894).

A further study of trade axes may show a great
variety in their smith stamps and a divergence in
contour from the specimens here shown. But because
the French settlers came to North America before the
English, and because Capt. John Smith says that the
Indians already had iron axes, before his arrival in
1604, we may reasonably infer, that, although some
of these grave relics may be English, some Dutch and
some Swedish; in the Northern and Middle United
States, the oldest of them, as probably represented by
the type here shown, are French.

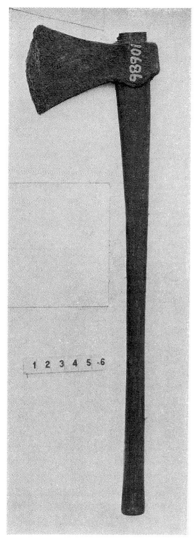

Fig. 2. Anglo-American Felling Axe

This axe represents the type brought over in the *Mayflower* and to Jamestown and surviving in England in 1897. (*cf. Fig. 4.*) The heavy, flaring bit greatly outweighs the very small, flat poll. It was ploughed up about 1890, by Mr. Grant, on the Grant farm on the left bank of the York River, near York Harbor, Me. The handle is not original.

identical with all the old trans-Atlantic tree-felling instruments.

Another early imported axe of the European type is shown in the greatly rusted, heavy-bitted

ANGLO-AMERICAN AXE (Fig. 2)

dug up *c.* 1890, by Mr. Grant, on the left bank of York River, Me., about one mile from its mouth. Though not positively dated and somewhat differing in the upward flare of its blade, slightly thickened and flattened poll, and lip under the eye, from the un-polled trade axes, above described, and lacking the smith stamp, this rusty master tool clearly shows the characteristic European and now utterly unfamiliar overweight of the bit, and certainly represents in construction the type of tree-felling axe brought over from Europe by the colonists in the *Mayflower,* and in use in Europe from prehistoric times to the present day. What can better prove the antiquity of these long-bitted tools in Britain than the next illustration of

PREHISTORIC IRISH AXES (Fig. 3)

for the very interesting specimens, now in the Dublin Museum, varying in blade-flare, but not in construction, are nearly two thousand years old. They were dug up from ancient crannogs or mounds, heaped up in County Antrim, before St. Patrick came to Ireland. To demonstrate the survival of this ancestral axe-form in modern Europe, the next illustrations show recent

ENGLISH AND IRISH FELLING AXES
(Fig. 4)

of similar shape and construction gathered by the writer in 1897, in scrap-iron heaps in Limerick and Chester; and a modern

GERMAN FELLING AXE (Fig. 5)

in its original handle, given to the writer in 1899, by William Hoffman, a

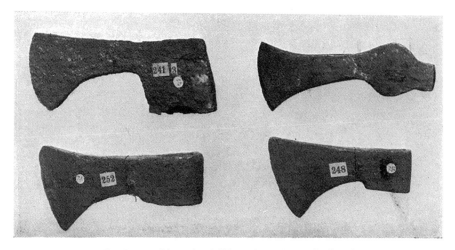

Fig. 3. Prehistoric Felling Axes from Ireland

These specimens were kindly photographed in 1897 from examples in the Dublin Science and Art Museum. Left, upper, from Dunschaughlin Crannog, Co. Meath. Left, lower, from Oldbridge, on the River Boyne, Co. Meath. Right, upper, Dunschaughlin Crannog. Right, lower, locality not recorded. These axes vary in contour and flare of blade, and all but the upper, right, specimen, lack poll and eye lip; nevertheless, in construction, namely, great overweight of bit, all are alike. Some kinds of iron, in some soils, rust more quickly in one hundred years, than these ancient axes (like the wrought-iron pillar at Delhi, also exposed in mother earth) have done in two thousand.

German emigrant, living in New Galena, Bucks County, Pa., who had used it in Halberstadt, East Prussia, and brought it with him to America, about 1890.

Sometime early in the eighteenth century, probably about 1740, — as meagre evidence, gathered with great difficulty, shows,—the unique instrument, unknown in other countries except by import from the United States, called in England, the

AMERICAN AXE (Fig. 6)

(*Chambers Encyclopedia*, 1897) began to appear in New England and the Middle States. The comparatively short-bitted, heavy-polled tool, here illustrated by old farm axes and Revolutionary camp-site specimens, had become well-established before 1776— by which time it differed from the ancient axes previously described, not

only conspicuously in appearance, but radically in construction; since, with the European ancestral instruments, the bit always outweighed the poll; in this new axe, the poll outweighed the bit.

Who knows when this happened? And why should book after book and dictionary after dictionary fail to account for the cause and origin of this change? As they do, we are left to deduce what we can from the scanty evidence. This shows, first, that the European emigrant continued to bring his Old World axes with him and use them, for a while (*cf.* Fig. 5), both before and after this new axe had superseded the European instrument, and such specimens as the very interesting

PERFORATED TRADE AXE (Fig. 7)

with blade greatly lightened by grinding, and its otherwise meaningless per-

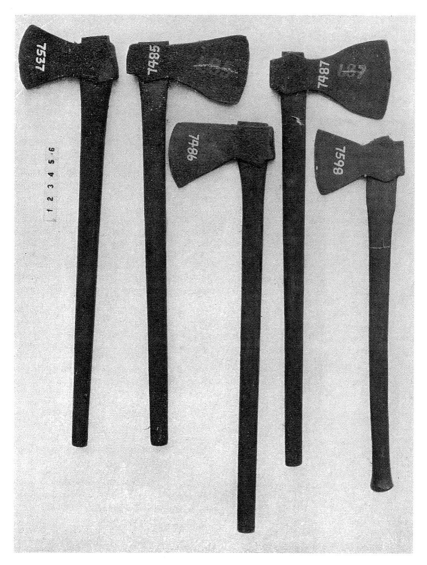

Fig. 4. British Felling Axes

These modern British axes were found by the writer in scrap-iron heaps of junk dealers, in England and Ireland, in 1898. With their flared bits and eye overlaps, all, save the flat-topped No. 7486, resemble the Anglo-American specimen, shown in Fig. 2. Although slightly flattened at the poll, all show the great overweight of the bit, characteristic of all European axes. The straight handles are not certainly original, except that of No. 7598. No. 7537 was bought from Robert Twyford at Limerick, in 1898, and is stamped F.S. No. 7598 came from Barbara Canker, at a sale at Hollidaysburg, Pa., in 1899. No. 7485, from Mr. Axton, Victoria Store, Radcliffe Road, Southampton, England, in 1898. No. 7486, ditto. No. 7487 is from Dobbin's Iron Yard, Chester, Eng., bought June 12, 1898.

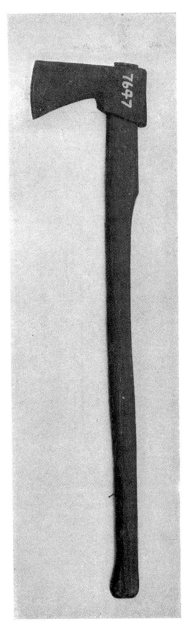

Fig. 5. German Felling Axe

This axe, in its original handle, was given to the
writer in March, 1899, by William Hoffman, who had
used it in Halberstadt, East Prussia, about 1880. He

foration; and the shorter-bitted, heavier polled axe (Fig. 9) of date *c.* 1740, from Salem, Mass., might indicate that the newcomer, unfamiliar with axes in the Old World and suddenly transformed into a woodman in the New, found that his long-bitted, Old-Country axe "wobbled" in the stroke, and the more he lightened the bit by grinding it down and the more he weighted the poll (Fig. 9) (not so much to pound with, since the woodman rarely pounds with his axe, but to over-balance the bit) the better it cut.

The above described axes, whether of the old European or late American type, though used by carpenters, were more particularly the tools of the woodman, and abundant evidence shows that until *c.* 1840 they were generally home-made, by local blacksmiths, of iron, with strips of steel inserted for the blade (*cf.* Fig 8), and that the latter continued to make them, on special occasions, long after 1840, both in America and Europe. This fact is vouched for by the unique photograph,

AXE MAKING (Fig. 8)

which shows, by two half-finished specimens, recently bought, that William Schaeffer, blacksmith, of Kutztown, Pa., still (1925) makes these axes by hand for sale. Jeremiah Fern of Doylestown, Pa., says that he made American axes, about 1864, at Edge Hill, near Quakertown, Pa., exactly in this manner, by welding together, over a handle pattern to form the eye, the sides of two blocks of iron, and then

brought it with him to New Galena, Bucks Co., and
used it there until about 1890. It is very slightly
thickened and flattened at the poll, flat-topped, smith-
stamped, and heavy-eyed, as in the ancient Irish axe,
Fig. 3, upper left; and like all European axes it shows
the very characteristic over-balance of the bit.

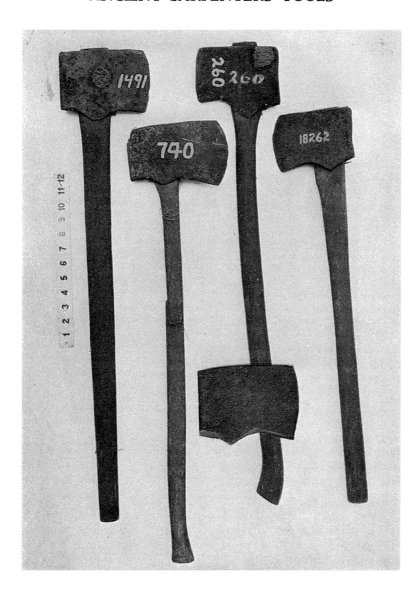

Fig. 6. The American Axe

These axes are of typical American construction, as developed in the American Colonies before about 1750; of a type unknown, except by importation, in other parts of the world. In the compact, almost square instrument, the heavy, squared poll, at variance with all Old World axes, outweighs the bit. The handles here shown, are not original. All the heads show lip extensions below the eye. None of the blades are basil edged. All except possibly No. 740 used by Barbara and Magdalena Landis, in the 19th century, at Grier's Corner, near Doylestown, Pa., are home-made. No. 18262 was dug up at the Revolutionary camp site at the Dyckman House, on Park and Prescott Avenue, New York City, by Mr. Reginald P. Bolton, and given to The Bucks County, Pa., Museum in May, 1922. The lower loose specimen (on a slightly larger scale) now in possession of The Berks County Histor-

Fig. 7. Altered European Axe

This interesting specimen was found at Jack's Reef, on the Seneca River, N. Y., and is in the New York State Museum, at Albany. It is illustrated in "Metallic Implements of the New York Indians," by William M. Beauchamp, *N. Y. State Museum Bull., No. 55,* pl. 21. Although the instrument, unlike the other trade axes shown, has an underlap on the eye, the author (Mr. B.) classes it with trade axes and says that the blade was evidently once longer than it now is. If so, it might well show the experiment of an early blacksmith to "Americanize" a European axe (of shape No. 7486, Fig. 4), by further lightening the ground-down blade, with the otherwise meaningless perforation, and weighting the poll by welding on a rim.

welding and hammering to an edge, a strip of steel as here shown (the blade), inserted into a split on the bit margin (*inf.* J. F. to Horace Mann, Aug. 9, 1924); and Karl Klemp, now of Doylestown, made axes of the long-bitted or trade-axe type, at Schneide-moll, near Dantzig, in *c.* 1896, by hammering one end of an iron block into a thin tongue, wrapping and welding the latter over a handle form, and inserting the steel blade as before (*inf.* K. K. to Horace Mann, Aug. 1924).

According to J. L. Bishop (*History of American Manufacturers,* Phila., 1864), the making of American axes in factories, beginning early in forges,

with water-run trip hammers (Hugh Orr, at Bridgewater, Conn., 1738-48)— (at Sutton, Mass., 1793)— (Collins, at Hartford, Conn., 1818) — (at Chambersburg, Pa., 1829); competing with imported European axes in Virginia, 1788; finally, by the use of cast steel, never employed by the local smith, 1846-59; (*cf.* J. M. Swank, *Iron and Coal,* in Pa., 1878) and the help of railroads, about 1840, generally superseded the home-made axe.

Omitting here the indispensable process of sharpening axes, when possible with a grindstone, when not, with a pocket whetstone, to be described later, the evidence derived from old

ical Society and photographed by their kind permission, was dug up on the site of a Revolutionary Fort, at Reading, Pa., where it had been probably used by one of the American guards or Hessian prisoners. The others were found in scrap-heaps, or on farms, in Eastern Pennsylvania, about 1890. Jeremiah Fern, blacksmith, of Doylestown, says that he made axes like these, near Doylestown, about 1870, by forging two iron blocks over a handle pattern and inserting a steel blade into a split on the bit edge. (See Fig. 8.) According to W. J. Phillips of McElhattan, Clinton County, Pa., axe helves in the Pennsylvania mountains, in the 19th century, were generally made of hickory but sometimes of white oak. The old helves were always straight. Curved helves, home-made, originated there shortly after the Civil War. *c.* 1868. (Information of Col. H. W. Shoemaker of McElhattan, to the writer, October, 1924.)

Fig. 8. Half-finished Home-made Axes

The blacksmith has roughly welded together two rectangular slabs of iron, over an iron handle-pattern (not shown) so as to leave the eye-hole. The thin steel blade, not yet placed, is shown loose with the left specimen. To the right, it has received its first rough weld, on insertion between the two slabs, where they meet at the bit's eye. These specimens were bought Jan., 1925, during their process of manufacture, from William Schaeffer, blacksmith, of Kutztown, Pa., who is still (1925) making axes for sale, by hand, in this old way.

axes found by the writer, and by tradition, shows that the ancient axe helves (or handles), still used in Europe in 1897, though often knobbed at the hand end, were always straight (Fig. 9), and the much-praised, very carefully curved, tremulous, American axe helve, made by the woodman himself from selected hickory, rarely white oak, with the draw knife (Fig. 6), did not come into general use before the mid-nineteenth century, in the North Pennsylvania lumber country (*inf.* W. J. Phillips of McElhattan, Clinton Co., Pa., to Col. H. W. Shoemaker to writer Oct. 1924); after which, *c.* 1860, cheap factory-made helves, of the same shape,

became so numerous, that to-day, a straight handle on a single-bitted, tree-felling axe is a thing unheard of.

Before leaving the subject of tree felling with the axe, let us glance at another picture which shows the highly interesting process of

CROSS-CUTTING LOGS BY FIRE.
(Fig. 11)

Here we see, according to information of Mr. F. K. Bowlby, how the inhabitants of Washington County, Pa., until about 1890, sometimes bi-sected freshly felled trees, dozens at a time, by "niggering" them, as they called it: namely, by burning downward upon

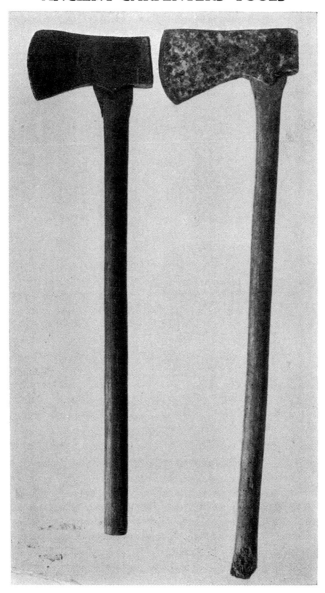

Fig. 9. Old Anglo-American Axes

Photographed by the kind permission of the Essex Institute, Salem, Mass. The right figure (Museum No. 101,137) shows a felling axe, of date 1725, of Anglo-American earliest type. It lacks a poll, and but for the eye overlap, exactly resembles the trade axe, Fig. 1. The characteristic straight helve (handle) is original. It was found where left by the house builders under the floor of a house erected in 1725. at Riverdade, Gloucester, Mass. The gift of L. R. Curtis. The left specimen (Museum No. 2559) is a felling axe, of inferred date about 1750. This remarkable axe is evidently of intermediate Anglo-American construction. The bit is still very long, but the poll has been considerably lengthened (weighted) so as to almost, if not quite, counter-balance it. Nevertheless, the final "American Axe," with its short bit, and over-balance of poll, has not yet been reached. The straight handle is original. The gift of Mrs. H. A. Brown.

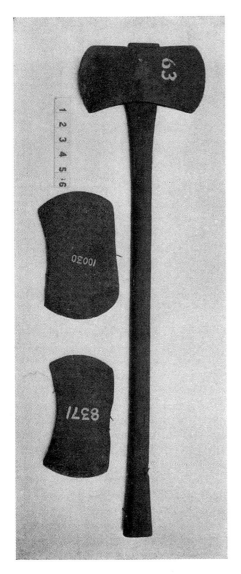

Fig. 10. The Double-Bitted Axe

The three factory-made specimens here shown come from Bucks Co., Pa., and illustrate a comparatively modern, 19th-century tool of the lumberman rather than the carpenter. They were used in extensive forest felling, where, minus a grindstone, they kept sharp twice as long as the single-bitted axe. The handle had to be straight, so as to work both ways.

them, with fires carefully watched, spaced and restricted from spreading by mud and water.

Who can estimate the immense historical importance, in felling trees and cross-cutting felled logs, of a steel instrument (the axe), two thousand years old in Europe, but which the primitive races of North America never heard of? And what of the hardly less valuable help given to would-be civilization by the tools used from time immemorial to split, or otherwise cut lengthwise, the prostrate tree?

As an example of the latter, a very important tool used by or for the old house-builder (rather for preparing the raw material than putting it together was

THE FROW (Fig. 12),

an ancient European instrument, referred to by Capt. John Smith to cleave pale at Jamestown in 1624,

---

The double-bitted war axe is as old as Rome and Egypt, but no 18th-century specimens of this deadly, tree-felling tool have been found by the writer. According to Seth Nelson, a mountaineer artificer, woodman and hunter, of Round Island, Clinton Co., Pa. (born 1838), this instrument, at first called "The Yankee Axe," and objected to as a back-wounder, was introduced into the Pennsylvania mountains about 1850, by lumbermen from Maine; after which (1860-1870) it became popular and widely home-made and superseded the old single-bitted tool in the Pennsylvania lumber country. One blade was kept very sharp, for felling; the other less so, for lopping knots. (Information Col. H. W. Shoemaker, of McElhattan, Pa., to the writer, Jan. 14, 1925.)

Two other specimens (not shown), home-made by Mr. Nelson, about 1880 and obtained by Colonel Shoemaker, are in The Bucks County Historical Society Museum. No. 10030, bought from Herman Bader, at the Elephant Tavern, Bedminster Township, Bucks Co., Pa., Nov., 1916, was found by him about 1911, while repairing his old log house, one-fourth mile east of "The Elephant," on the Ridge Road.

Fig. 11. "Niggering" Logs

This illustration shows a freshly felled log, cut by a small, regulated fire built upon it by F. K. Bowlby of Doylestown, Pa., to show the operation called "niggering," as practiced by him in Washington Co., Pa., about 1880.

(*New English Dictionary*), and frequently mentioned in the *Probate Records of Essex County, Massachusetts, 1635-1681, 3 vols., George Francis Dow, editor. Salem, Mass., the Essex Institute, 1916-1920.*) It is a thick-backed, rigid, dull-bladed steel knife, about fifteen inches long and three and a half inches wide, hafted at right angles upward from its blade, with which, by wriggling the short handle to maintain the thickness of the split, and clubbing the projecting knife end with

THE FROW CLUB (Fig. 13),

shingles, laths, barrel staves, and short, four to six foot long, clapboards, were split (riven) from squared or quartered logs.

Heavy planks, rafters, 16-foot floor boards, or fence rails, too thick for this light instrument, had to be sawn or hewn by wedge splitting (described later), but documentary evidence

shows that the frow made the short clapboards, above noted, for the old wooden houses, in New England and elsewhere, in the eighteenth century, and for the gables of log houses in Pennsylvania in the nineteenth century, and universally and exclusively was used to split house shingles and laths, everywhere in the United States until 1840, soon after which, sawed laths and later, sawed shingles, drove the instrument out of use.

Nevertheless, a few old riven shingle roofs still (1925) survive in Haycock Township, Bucks County, Pa., and we here show the home-made

SHINGLE HORSE (Fig. 14)

seated by which, with the oaken block leaned into its fork, Enos Lewis split shingles. near Hagersville, Bucks County, in 1890, and

THE SHAVING HORSE (Fig. 15)

in which the split shingle had always to be thinned with the draw knife at

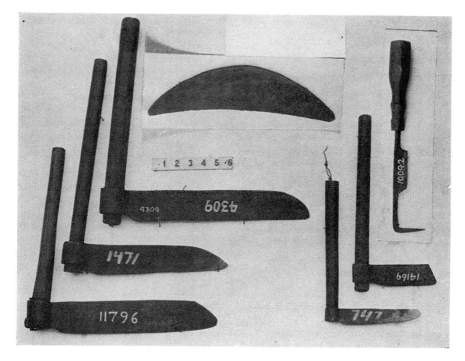

Fig. 12. The Frow

Having placed a block (red oak in Pennsylvania) about eighteen inches long and squared, or quartered from the log, to the required five-inch width, the worker, holding the handle vertically in the left hand, sets the heavy, wide-backed blade of the instrument, on the top of the block placed vertically in the tree fork frow horse, shown in Fig. 14. He then strikes the back of the blade, beyond its projecting end, continued blows with the club (Fig. 13), while he wriggles the handle, if necessary, so as to hurry the split, or regulate the depth of the cut, until a segment of the block,—the shingle, flies off. Brought to America by the first colonists in the 17th century (cf. *Probate Records of Essex County, Massachusetts, 1635-1681, 3 vols., George Francis Dow, editor.* Salem, Mass., the Essex Institute, 1916-1920.) the frow was ousted, for clapboards, by the up-and-down, water-run mill saw, in the 18th century (cf. Fig. 29) and for laths and shingles, by the circular saw, about 1830-1840; but survived, though rarely, for shingles, in Pennsylvania, until about 1890. Hand-riven shingles, imported from the South, were sold in competition with mill-sawed shingles, in Pennsylvania, in the late 19th century (*inf.* Lewis Treffinger, carpenter, of Doylestown, to the writer, 1924).

J. A. Rittenhouse of Philadelphia, in 1859, saw negroes in Nottaway Co., Va., splitting clapboards about six feet long, shingles about two and a half feet long, and laths for drying tobacco, with the frow and a horse, with two forks, otherwise like No. 11795 (Fig. 14). (*Inf.* of J. A. R. to the writer, Oct. 20, 1918.)

Fence palings were riven in northern Bucks Co., as observed by the writer, as late as 1890, and short boards, for "ash hoppers," in western Pennsylvania, until about 1800. (*Inf.* E. F. Bowlby to H. C. M.)

Mr. F. K. Swain of Doylestown, in January, 1917, saw a negro, ex-slave, splitting shingles near the cemetery at Vicksburg, Miss., from blocks about eighteen inches long, quartered from cypress logs. The workman worked across the quarter, so as to leave a triangular waste piece. He clubbed the blade into the wood and then either wriggled it to split off the shingle, or struck it further blows upon the protruding blade end and handle top. It took about three long-pull shaves (right, left and middle) of the draw knife, upon the shingle, clamped in the shaving horse, to thin its top surface and straighten its long sides. Numerous mis-splits were thrown away. The workman said that the shingles lasted about sixty years.

No. 11796 was in use by Anson Franklin, near Madison Co., N. C., in October, 1917, when Mr. Horace Mann bought it, with his whole apparatus, for two dollars.

No. 747 is a grafter's frow, given by Aaron Seifert of Springtown, Bucks Co., Pa., August, 1897, and used by him, until that year, for splitting the parent stock of fruit trees, to insert the graft. Nos. 10042 and 14169 are also grafters' frows. No. 19178 shows the semi-circular frow, minus handle, used in Korea, for making roof shingles. It was bought, in 1922, from a workman at Kang Kei, Korea, by the Rev. Clarence Hoffman.

one end (the upper) and on one of its sides, right or left, for overlapping.

THE SHINGLE BUTTER (Fig. 16) was employed for trimming, at a mitre, for looks' sake, the rough bottoms (butts) of shingles, and

THE SHINGLE PUNCH (FIG. 17) was sometimes used instead of a gimlet, for quickly making the preparatory nail holes (described later) in the exposed corners of riven shingles.

But the riving of shingles and clapboards was light work compared to the splitting of logs or segments of logs that the frow could not split. For this, a far stronger, wider-reaching tool was needed; namely, the

IRON WEDGE (Fig. 18),

an instrument of unknown antiquity, —the cuneus of the Romans. Look at the "Little Iron Giant," while the mists of ages gather about its triumphant shoulders; and also at the ringed maul or beetle, which is still used (1924) to drive it, in splitting firewood and which, until about 1890, was so employed in the Middle States to make the rails for the celebrated

WORM FENCE (Fig. 19)

As a great rarity and as a supposed (probably ancient German) improvement on the maul and wedges, we include

THE HOLZAXT (Fig. 20)

a heavy, iron, wedge-shaped, dullbladed, sledge axe, never used for felling, which will not only hammer wedges but split wood; and also the iron wedges, wood-topped, to prevent spreading under its blows, still (1925) sometimes used in Berks County, Pa.

Fig. 13. Frow Club

Used by the shingle maker to pound down the frow in splitting the shingle from the native block. When too much battered they were thrown away and replaced with fresh instruments. No. 743 was obtained from Aaron Seifert of Springtown, Bucks Co., Pa., in 1917.

But the wedge and beetle, rather than these rarities, did the great work. If they had only been used, as now, to split rails and firewood; if they were not associated with one of the oldest and greatest steps in human industry, namely, the first making of the board, we might dismiss them with a word; but Beckman (*History of Inventions*) quotes a writer to prove that the Norwegians were making boards with wedges, instead of saws, as late as about 1750; that is, wedge-splitting logs and thinning down the segments,

Fig. 14. The Frow Horse

In eastern Pennsylvania the squared or quartered block of red oak, about eighteen inches long by six inches wide, is stood in the fork of the lower homemade apparatus, and split by the workman, as described under Figs. 12, 13 and 14. The lower apparatus, No. 11843, was made by the late Enos Lewis, about 1890, and was often used by him for splitting shingles, until his death in 1916, when it was bought from his widow, at his log house, one and a half miles north of Churchill, Bucks Co., Pa.

The upper specimen (No. 11795) shows a simple tree-fork, without legs, used for the same purpose by Anson Franklin, near White Rock, Madison Co., N. C., in October, 1917. The fork, with a block nailed within the crotch, is laid, with its point on a rock or stump, its two prongs resting on the ground. The shingle block stands vertically in the crotch.

for the purpose; and he further says that Peter the Great introduced the pit saw (described later) into Russia about that time to prevent his subjects from thus wasting wood. We know further that the American pioneer certainly (*cf.* Joseph Doddridge, *Notes on the Settlement and Indian Wars*, Pittsburgh, 1912) hewed smooth the upper faces of split logs, called puncheons, on occasions, to ground floor his cabin, and we may suppose, though minus documentary proof, that he sometimes even split and hacked out floor boards and boat planks. But these instances of full-sized riven boards or planks (as distinguished from clapboards) or puncheons, were not steps in craftsmanship in the seventeenth and eighteenth centuries, but only makeshifts,

Fig. 15. Shaving Horse

The workman sits astride the bench, presses down the foot lever, so as to hold fast the freshly riven piece under the projecting clamp-block, and then shaves thin one of the ends of the shingle for top underlap, and trims and thins one of its sides, Pennsylvania style, if desired, for side underlap. Besides its use for shingles, this home-made apparatus was continually employed on Pennsylvania farms, until the late 19th century, for miscellaneous draw-knife work. The specimen here shown is from Buckingham Township, Bucks Co., Pa. The same type of horse may be found everywhere in New England and the Northern States.

for, as shown later, the far more efficient saw had been employed for board making for two thousand years.

Outranging the edged tools above mentioned, because potent in cutting metal and stone as well as wood, the all important saw, as a master tool of the wood worker, has outrivaled the axe and outclassed the wedge from the beginning of history. Some of its eighteenth-century forms still (1925) survive; others, masked or supplanted by machines, are seen or heard of no longer. In this latter class, the two-man saw, called pit saw in the eighteenth century produced (until *c.* 1720, in Pennsylvania) the chief raw material for carpentry,—namely boards, sawed directly from the log, and so outranks in historic interest and importance all other saws.

Save for the short, thin, frow-riven clapboards and the wedge-split, make-shift planks and puncheons, or the reversions to the wedge, in Norway and Russia, above noted; the evidence shows that this tool, inherited from the Romans, was continually used to make boards in historic Europe; and tenaciously and tyrannically held to as a breadwinner, by the sawyers, who kept on hand-sawing boards, in England until about 1820, and banded together in mobs, broke down saw mills there in 1663 and in 1768; and in Mississippi, in *c.* 1805, where they smashed the saw mill at Natchez, afterwards called the "riot mill," long after mill-sawing had been established; in Holland, *c.* 1596 (Disston); in Germany, 1322-1490 (Beckman); in Norway, 1530 (Beckman); and in New Eng-

Fig. 16. Shingle Butter

This home-made machine used to trim off or bevel (supposedly for looks' sake) the often uneven lower ends of riven shingles, was used in Bucks Co., Pa., until about 1890. By pressing the lever, the knife slides down upon the shingle thrust on its side, and at an angle, under it. No. 2091 was recently inherited by James Clark, of Ivyland, Bucks Co., Pa. Its probable date is about 1850.

land, *c.* 1634 (*Encyclopaedia Britannica.*)

By the seventeenth century, the evidence further shows that this great board-making tool had two forms, the older of which,

THE FRAMED PIT SAW (Fig. 21),

is here illustrated. Saw mills and saw factories, old and new, big and little, fade into the twilight of centuries, as we look at this thin, narrow, flexible blade, stretched in a rectangular frame,

—this ancestor of all carpenter work,— this most interesting of all saws. Here it is represented by a rare specimen in the Essex Institute, at Salem, Mass., which unfortunately lacks its original wide-toothed blade; and it is again illustrated by Figs. 22 and 23, from French engravings, appended to the article "Menusier," in Diderot's *Encyclopaedia,* of 1768. It was held vertically by two men, one the top man, standing on the log, laid horizontally on moveable cross pieces (transoms)

Fig. 17. The Shingle Punch

When that part of the riven shingle intended to be exposed to the weather on the roof is inserted into the guide, a down-push of the lever forces the chisel-shaped iron punch (always set across the grain) through the shingle at the lower corner where the needed corner nail, freshly driven into red oak, might split the wood. Otherwise a gimlet was used. Riven shingles were set in Pennsylvania, to overlap, not only at the top, but at the sides; hence these nails, to prevent upcurling at the exposed corners. Shingles were made of easily split red oak, hence the punch, not necessary with later imported cypress shingles. The punch or gimlet was probably not used in New England, with pine. Joseph N. Gross used this instrument near New Galena, Bucks Co., Pa., about 1880, as seen by his son, Henry Gross, of Doylestown, the writer's informant.

over a pit, or on a frame, and the other, the pitman, who stood in the pit, or below the log, to cut full-length, 16-foot boards, from the log. Another picture,

THE ANCIENT ITALIAN PIT SAW
(Fig. 24),

taken from a fresco of about 1350, at the Campo Santo, in Pisa, illustrates it in operation on a balk, set, not horizontally as described, but Chinese fashion, at an angle, and with the teeth of its blade raked all one way (described later) so as to cut only downward. The

KOREAN PIT SAW (Fig. 25)
and
THE CHINESE PIT SAW (Fig. 26)

show superior forms of the same instrument, for the same purpose.

How old in type are these latter tools? How long have they made boards, in Roman style, for these long-secluded nations who still use them? They are more efficient than our ancestral saws because their blades are adjustable sidewise, and if not so well balanced as the saw shown in Fig. 21, they are open sided; that is, framed like the buck saw (described later), so as to present less impediment to the log.

Besides the Pisan fresco, numerous old prints, wall paintings from Herculaneum, carved gems, etc., further recall the use by the Romans and in modern Europe of this ancient, framed, two-man, board-making instrument.

Why should Cescinsky assert (*English Furniture of 17th and 18th Cen-*

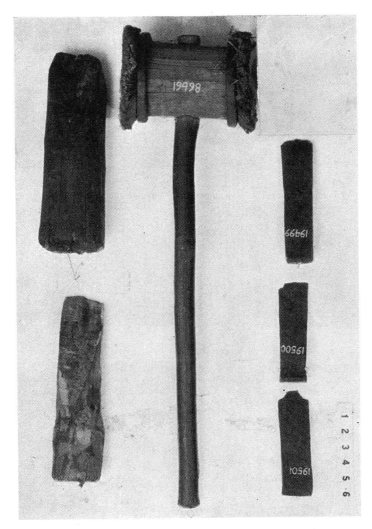

Fig. 18. The Maul or Beetle and Wedges

This heavy, home-made, iron-ringed maul,—a hickory block with a handle,—was bought Sept. 28, 1924, from John Wildonger of Plumstead Township, two miles north of Point Pleasant, Bucks Co., Pa. He had made and was still using it for splitting logs and excavated stumps for fire wood. The iron maul rings (called "beet'e rings" in the *Probate Records of Essex County, Massachusetts, 1635-1681, 3 vols., George Francis Dow, editor. Salem, Mass., the Essex Institute, 1916-1920,*) made by the blacksmith at Point Pleasant, were kept from coming off by the spreading (under repeated blows) of the wooden face, and also by pegging the face, to swell it around and outside the rings. When the face wore down to the rings, reringing or a new maul was necessary.

The rail splitter, who was ordered not to strike the iron wedge with an iron axe for fear of spreading the malleable wedge top, could work with two iron wedges (sometimes only with one), supplemented with a make-shift, axe cut, larger, wooden wedge, still called in Bucks Co., Pa., the "glut" (*cf.* quotation *New English Dictionary,* 1790) here shown at the left, and used to release its iron fellows (right) by widening the split.

These ancient tools were used by the pioneers to split logs for "puncheons" and house timbers; for rails and posts; for the post and rail entrances to walled or hedged fields; for the rails for the varied styles of wood-

Fig. 19. The "Worm" Fence

At an enormous expenditure of trees, this wood-wasting fence was very widely used for field enclosure, throughtout the Middle and Western States, in the 19th century and until about 1870, but rapidly fell out of use after the introduction of wire fences about 1885. Survivals continued until 1900, and very rarely in northern Bucks County, until the present time, 1925. No posts were necessary, except at the entrances, where two posts, often with double rows of holes, and four or five loose bars, namely rails with axe-sharpened ends, were employed. From six to ten, usually wedge-split rails, but sometimes poles, were laid zigzag under crossed poles set up at each angle of intersection, with a single rail, called a rider, on top. The lower rail, at every corner, rested on stones to prevent rotting. In the rebuilt or repaired specimen here shown, now (1924), standing on the north branch of the Neshaminy Creek, west of the Turnpike Bridge, about a mile north of Fountainville, Bucks Co., Pa., the first fork, not in its original, condition, has been clumsily over-loaded with riders. This ingenious device which, except at the barred field entrances mentioned, dispensed with holes hewn in the wood or dug in the ground and needed no nails or withe fastenings, probably originated in Scandinavia or Middle Europe. But the writer has failed to fix the date of its American introduction. A specimen was seen by Heinrich Partsch standing about 1897 at Bockstein, three miles west of Gastein, in the Austrian Tyrol. Information of H. P. to the writer, August 6, 1922.

turies, pp. 95 and 358, 1911 ed.) that the pit saw was not used in England until *c.* 1690 and that in England boards were hewn, not sawn, before that time, when the *New English Dictionary* shows (*cf.* sawyer) that the pit saw was in use in England in 1350-1415-1465-1497-1616 and 1640; and Moxon *(Mechanick Exercises)* describes and rudely illustrates it as a carpen-

---

mounted stone fences—for the "Swede fence," the "post and rail" fence (very common after 1803); and above all, until 1880, to make rails for the "worm fence" used widely in the Middle States until the introduction of wire about 1890 (*cf.* Fig. 19). According to Beckman's unrivalled treatise on the *History of Inventions*, the maul and wedges were used in the Middle Ages instead of, the pit saw, to split logs into sections, afterward hewn with the adze or broad axe into boards, rafters or planks. (*See a*lso Cescinsky, *English Furniture of the Seventeenth and Eighteenth Centuries.*)

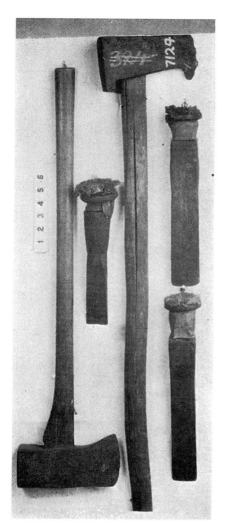

Fig. 20. Holzaxt or Split Axe

When all the woodman's wedges are fast in the log, his maul has become useless, and he cuts open the split, not with a felling axe, for fear of dulling its keen edge on underlying stones, but with this extra heavy, dull-edged, wedge-axe, perforated with an eye and mounted on a straight handle. Because, when thus used as a substitute for the maul, he dare not drive the iron wedges with it, for fear of spreading their malleable tops, he protects the latter, as here shown, with ferruled plugs of wood, socketed in their tops. The holzaxt is a rare tool which the writer, after years of search, has thus far failed to find anywhere in the United States except among the Pennsylvania Germans: or to trace to Europe. The specimen shown at the left (now in the

ter's and jointer's tool in 1677? The *Probate Records of Essex County, Massachusetts, 1635-1681* also prove that the Anglo - American pioneer brought it to Massachusetts before 1681.

The next illustration shows the other form of the great board-making tool, namely

THE OPEN PIT SAW (Fig. 27).

Here we see a thick, long, taper-bladed, two-man instrument, without a frame, with an upper handle, called the tiller, and a lower adjustable handle, called the box, surviving, *(a)* at J. S. Beacham's shipyard in Baltimore, in 1916; *(b)* still made by Disston, for export to Russia, in 1915, and *(c),* recently (about 1915) used at Snow's shipyard, Rockland, Me., for sawing ship's knuckles, and odd curved timbers that the power saws could not manage.

When and where this unframed variety of the ancient board saw first appeared; who, by calling it whip saw, first confused it with other saws, so-named, the writer has failed to learn. Dictionaries and books of reference break down one after another on this interesting subject. With one exception, the classic and later European pictures, thus far found by the writer, illustrate the framed saw and do not show the open pit saw. Moxon, in 1678, does not mention it. Neither does Diderot in 1768. Nevertheless, a

Museum of The Bucks County Historical Society) was owned and used by John Deisher, of Kutztown, Pa., from 1852 to 1885, and was bought from his grandson, Horace Deisher, of Kutztown, who used it until the present year (1925). The middle wedge, also in use, was obtained from Mr. F. Reimert of Kutztown, and belonged before 1904, to Samuel Smith of "Yammerthal," near Kutztown. The axe, No. 7124, is an old Bucks County farm relic, bought in 1897.

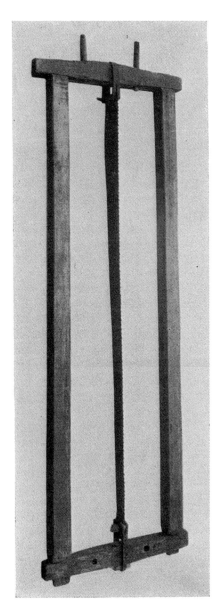

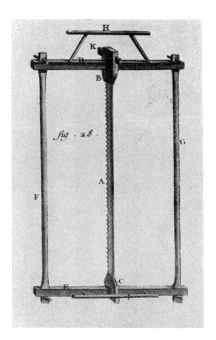

Fig. 22. French Pit Saw of 1768

From Diderot's *Encyclopaedia* article, "Menusier." The top and bottom handles, lacking in the joiner's frame saws (shown later) but appearing here and on Fig. 23 and betokened by pegs and peg holes in the unique Essex Institute specimen (Fig. 21), identify the latter, though lacking its original blade, as a true pit saw.

Fig. 21. Framed Pit Saw

Photographed by kind permission of the Essex Institute, Salem, Mass., Museum No. 101,451. This rare and very interesting instrument, four feet eleven inches long, showing a thin saw blade strained upon a rectangular oblong frame, is of the type universally used for sawing logs longitudinally into boards, before the 18th

century and surviving into the 19th century, after the introduction of the open pit saw (Fig. 27). The pegs for the top handle extension, and the peg holes for the bottom handle projecting at right angles, as illustrated by Diderot (Fig. 22) here show clearly. The large-toothed, adjustable blade, proper for board sawing, has here unfortunately been replaced by a smaller-toothed blade, for finer shipyard or joiner's work.

Charles Holtzapffel in his *Turning and Mechanical Manipulation*, London, 1846, Vol. 2. p. 703, while describing the English saw pits of the early 19th century, says that they were from 20 to 50 feet long, 4 to 6 feet wide, and 5 to 6 feet deep and were equipped with two stout timbers running their whole length, called side strakes, with transverse pieces, called head sills, at either end; and with one or more intermediate, loose, cross-pieces, shifted under the log or balk while sawing, called transoms. He also describes the chalk marking, for the saw, of timbers which must be stapled fast upon the head sill with dogs (described later), with one end on the head sill and the other on a transom. If crooked, the logs were laid with bend up-

Fig. 23. Framed Pit Saw at Work in 1768

This illustration from Diderot's *Encyclopaedia* (1768), article "Menusier," shows two French carpenters ripping a heavy plank, laid horizontally on trestles, with the framed pit saw. This instrument, equipped with an upper handle, resembles that shown in Fig. 21. While serving as an American soldier in France (1918-1919), William Labs saw, in a forest about four miles southeast of Montmorillon, Department of Vienne, peasants, sawing rough boards, by eye,—unmarked by chalk lines,—with a framed pit saw very generally resembling this (handles not noticed), about five feet long and four feet wide, thonged together at the corners and enlargeable by wedges to tighten the blade. The latter was wide and its teeth raked both ways. The log was sawed, not on trestles, as here shown, but chained longways upon, so as to protrude half its length beyond, the flat-hewn top of a single, long, under log, propped, head high, upon two X-shaped props, and with its bent-down, rear end, anchored in the ground. The top log was released, turned, rechained, and sawed end about, when the sawyers reached the under log.

rare engraving by Antonio Tempesta, 1555-1630 (Fig. 28) proves its existence in Italy in the sixteenth century, and such items in the *Probate Records of Essex County, Massachusetts, 1635-1681, 3 vols., George Francis Dow, editor. Salem, Mass., the Essex Institute, 1916-1920,* as "1 Whip Saw and 1 Cross

Cut Saw" (1647); "1 Whip Saw, 5 shillings, and 1 Cross Cut Saw, 3 shillings" (1654); "3 Saws of which 2 Whip Saws and 1 Cross Cut, 1 pound 4 shillings" (1655); and above all, "3 Whip Saws and Tillers, 16 shillings, 6 d." (1677), must refer to it.

By 1750 to 1760, the invention of rolled steel, replacing hammered steel, in the then water-run iron works (rolling mills), would have greatly facilitated its manufacture. As if oblivious to the lack of historical evidence on

wards. He speaks of sawing native English trees in log form, but says that for convenience of ship stowage, foreign timbers came to England already squared into balks, with axe or adze.

Fig. 24. Pit Saw of the Middle Ages

The picture represents Noah building the Ark and is from a fresco by Christofano Buffalmacco, in the Campo Santo at Pisa, painted about 1350. The tracing is from an engraving published in *Pitturi del Campo Santo di Pisa*, by C. Lasinio, Firenze, 1813.

The squared log, on which the topman stands, is shown as set, not horizontally over a pit or on a scaffold, as in the American shipyards of the 19th century, but, Chinese-fashion, on a trestle, with one end on the ground. (See Fig. 26.) The saw teeth are raked to cut downward and the pitman, on the ground, does all the cutting. The other two men in the picture are chalk-lining the next balk.

the subject, Charles Holtzapffel in 1846, in his *Turning and Mechanical Manipulations,* calls it the "long pit saw" or "whip saw," and illustrates and describes it, with its book-ignored, handle-names, "tiller" and "box." At that late day it was in use as a ship-wright's rather than a lumberman's tool, and in England and America (though probably not in Continental Europe), it had taken the place of the old framed tool.

Before considering further the work of board making, we should pause here to clearly realize that throughout the Colonial period, the man-saws above described, whether framed or open, were by no means universal tools, but rather superannuated survivals, used for odd work, such as

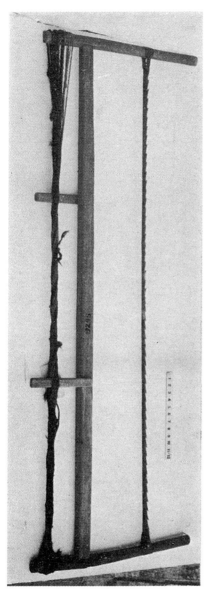

Fig. 25. Korean Pit or Board Saw

The thin, adjustable blade, set at right angles to the frame, with its large, acute-angled teeth very greatly raked both ways from the middle, is not, like the saw blades here shown, attached to the arms but simply strained tight upon them, by a rope (several strands of hemp cord) toggled against the centre brace,—as in the American buck-saw and Continental hand-saws shown

making special ship or bridge timbers or furniture boards, and at odd occasions or places, by slave labor, or where water power failed; and that ever since the first settlement of the American colonies, the grand demand for boards, planks, rafters, etc., was supplied by another apparatus which had been doing the same work in Europe before the discovery of America, namely

THE SAW MILL (Figs. 29 and 30)

in which a frame saw, with one or more blades, was worked vertically up and down by a crank revolving on the end of the horizontal axle of a water wheel.

Old pictures, imperfect descriptions, obscure hints in old books, and the writer's personal observations, show a considerable difference in the style and manipulation of this ancient apparatus namely, in its old log carriage, whether moving on rollers, impelled by cog-wheels (as described with the illustrations) or on greased channels, or by windlass ropes or suspended weights; and we find further that owing to variations in the force and volume of water, and in order to get the required velocity, the waterwheels ("overshot," "undershot," "tubwheel," "flutterwheel," "turbine," etc.) varied in size, construction and name; and in the gear, direct or indirect, of the axled crank above mentioned. But

later. Here, two toggle-pegs are used and the central brace, notched at either end against the arms, is also loose. This very clever, light instrument, if not so well balanced as the old American framed pit saw, lacks the outer frame obstruction, and by its adjustable blade and brace, better meets the varying thickness of logs. It is worked, not up and down, but nearly horizontally, on logs set at an angle, as in the Pisan fresco (Fig. 24); hence each sawyer cuts on the pull. It was bought by the Rev. Clarence Hoffman, from the Young Sil Academy, at Kang Kei, Korea, in the summer of 1923.

Fig. 26. Pit Sawing in China

From a photograph taken in April, 1922, by Mr. R. P. Hommel, at Cha Tsuen Chekiang, China. The sawyers are working (like the Italians in Fig. 20) on an oblique, propped log. Their open-sided saw, with a loose adjustable blade and loose central prop, resembles the Korean saw (Fig. 25). Its teeth are also set to work both ways so that each man does half the work.

the principle of construction of the machine, whether working in Europe in the Middle Ages, or in the American forests in the seventeenth, eighteenth and nineteenth centuries, was always the same. It is not necessary to confuse the mind by examining the modern log carriages or power applications of recent circular or band-saw mills, where the gearing has changed and where the log is often clamped or dogged so as to overhang the side of the carriage; or to climb down into damp, ruinous cellars and wonder at rotting waterwheels; or to lose ourselves in the picturesque maze of ancient wooden machinery which often confuses this masterful device with flour mills. The important point always is, that until the early nine-

teenth century, a framed pit saw was moved, as here shown, not by men but by water, and that the moving carriage took the place of the long strips ("side strakes") and cross-pieces ("head sills" and "transoms," etc.) laid over the hand sawyer's pit; and that the log moved against the saw and not the saw against the log.

Beckman, in his delightful *History of Inventions,* follows the history of this immensely important, labor-saving apparatus, far back into the Middle Ages, in Central and Southern Europe and Scandinavia. Half a dozen highly interesting pictures, showing it mounted with more than one blade (*i. e.,* as "gang saws") appear in the *Theatrum Machinarum Novum,* by George Andreas Bockler, Cologne, 1662; and

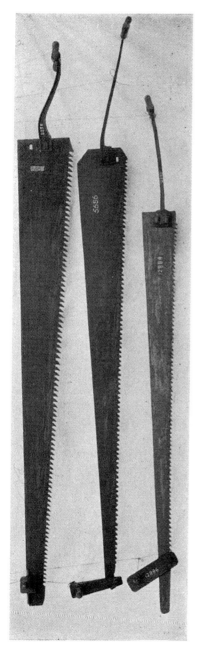

Fig. 27. Open Pit Saw

This factory-made, two-man saw was used for the special sawing of ship timbers, knuckles, etc., at ship-

although we gather from Charles Holtzapffel *(Turning and Mechanical Manipulations,* vol. 2, p. 703) and elsewhere, that it was kept out of England or was little used there until *c.* 1820, and boards were generally sawed from imported trunks already squared up into balks; yet Bishop *(History of American Manufactures),* proves that it appeared at the Newichewannock Falls, on the Piscataqua River, above Portsmouth, N. H., before 1635; at Scituate, Mass., in 1656; at Plymouth, Mass., in 1654; in Connecticut in 1661

yards in the Eastern United States until about 1900. The large teeth of the wide, tapering blade are all raked downward. The upper handle, called the tiller, is fast; the lower, called the box, is slid, loose, over the blade's end, so that on its removal the blade can be pulled out of the kerf. In Maine shipyards, as observed in 1920, the log or balk was set horizontally not over a pit, but on a scaffold built against the side of a bank, and after being chalk-lined, was sawed longitudinally by the top man, standing on the log, who lifted but did not cut, and the pit man, standing under the log, who cut on the down-pull.

The writer's brother, in February, 1921, near Mandeville, Jamaica, observed negroes sawing boards, with one of these saws, from a log about sixteen feet long, adzefaced on top and bottom, and placed on a trestle, constructed as follows:

Five feet from the ground, a cross-piece was laid on the top forks of two four-inch, propped posts, from which two parallel poles, about fourteen feet long, extending to the ground, formed an inclined plane, up which the log was rolled, wedged to its face level, and staked, at its intersection with the poles, to prevent down-sliding. The log seen was marked to cut eleven boards and two slabs. It was slightly lifted and the poles shuffled, when, in sawing, the saw had to clear the poles.

The old Italian engraving (Fig. 28), by Antonio Tempesta (1555-1630), proves that this instrument existed in Italy in the 16th century, but it seems probable that it was not so widely used, as the framed pit saw (Fig. 21), until rolling mills (about 1760-1780), facilitated the making of its requisite smooth, broad steel plates.

No. 5686, bought from J. S. Beacham, Baltimore, Md., July, 1916, was then, though rarely, used in his shipyard. No. 8338 was bought March, 1918, for $7, from Henry Disston and Son, of Philadelphia, who had recently revived the manufacture of these pit saws for their Russian trade. No. 12884 was bought in 1918, from Martin Scanlan, of Thomaston, Me., an employe at Snow's Shipyard, Rockland, Me. Scanlan, who sold it with No. 12890 (not shown) and two other similar saws, and kept two for shipyard use, had used it in Snow's yard, a short time before.

Fig. 28. The Open Pit Saw of the 16th Century

This illustration reproduces a copper engraving by Antonio Tempesta, born at Florence, 1555, and died there 1630, satirizing (as explained by the Latin legend and a crowing cock) the house builders of the "Age of Brass." It shows at the left, two sawyers, one of whom is seated on the ground, sawing longitudinally a log, with an open, unframed pit saw. The log is lifted at one end on a cross-piece laid upon two forked posts; and the handles (tillers) of the saw are both fixed. The saw teeth are raked to cut only downward.

and soon after in Maine; in Pennsylvania in 1662 (built by the Swedes); and frequently after 1675; in New York by the Dutch, with wind-power, about the same time; and on the Chamblee River, near Montreal, Canada, in 1706. It was in frequent use in New England and the Middle States throughout the eighteenth century, and in 1790, a hundred to two hundred and fifty mill-saw blades were manufactured per year at Canton, Mass., for this apparatus, by which, according to Douglass (*British Settlements in North America*, vol. 2, p. 54, quoted by Bishop), a man and a boy in New England, in 1750, could saw in ten hours, four thousand feet of white pine boards, fifteen to twenty feet long, and one inch thick.

But its day is gone. Because cheaply built and cheaply run (by water) in this, its ancient form, it held its own on American farms, and in the backwoods, long after the introduction of steam in the early nineteenth century. Yet, for the vast general board supply, it failed. The circular saw (1825 to 1840) followed by the band saw, more quickly exhausted the forests and gradually supplanted it, until by the twentieth century, the lumberman forgot it, and like the one here shown it had become a curiosity.

We will conclude the subject of raw-material sawing by illustrating the

Fig. 29. The Saw Mill

This illustration shows a part of a typical 18th century water-run saw mill, found and bought by W. H. Labs, near Saltillo, Huntington Co., Pa., and now in the Museum of The Bucks County Historical Society. It was made about 1800, bought in 1864 from Henry Hudson, by the Weaver family, and worked by H. T. Weaver, until 1902, on the main branch of Roaring Run, a stream rising on Jacks Mountain.

The saw mill appears here in its simplest form. A single saw blade (A), strained in a frame (BB), works vertically in an upright channel (CC), by means (not shown) of a staff (the pitman) operated by a crank, revolving directly on the end of the horizontal shaft of a water wheel. The saw blade (A) works inside the log carriage (DD), while the saw frame (BB) encloses the latter, which, as here shown, is a long, heavy, narrow, horizontal frame, cross-mortised at either end and moving backward and forward by impulse of a cogged axle (E) engaging cogs (F) under it.

At either extreme end of the carriage, a heavy cross-piece, the tail block (Fig. 30), (fixed) and the head-block (G) (adjustable), rest upon its frame, and before the freshly-felled log, cross-sawed at both ends and notched underneath to lie flat, is set before the saw; the carriage is pushed toward the back of the latter until the saw blade enters a deep slot (H) in the head-block. The log is then rolled with cant hooks and pried with crowbars upon the carriage, so that its lower end rests on the inner rim of the head-block (Fig. 30) and its upper end, now clear of the saw, on the inner rim (I) of the head-block. The felled tree is then spiked fast, with two dogs on the tail block, and with one dog on the head block. To further stiffen the log, the long, iron, slotted strip (J)

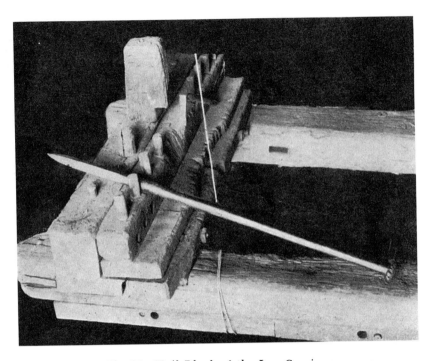

Fig. 30. Tail Block of the Log Carriage

Upon the mid, inner ledge of the tail block, here shown (the heavy crosspiece, with upward projecting pins, fixed upon the end of the log carriage), the smooth-sawed end of the log is pushed into position by means of the pointed crowbar (shown), when the latter, spiked into the log end, is pried sideways against the pegs. The much battered upper end of the crowbar has been used to pound down the log dogs, one of which is here seen attached to the block.

---

stapled down to straddle the wooden slot, is next driven forward so that its two gouge-shaped, reversed prongs spike into and hold fast the log end, on either side of the proposed kerf. The saw then starts, while the action of the carriage pushing the log against the saw begins by the forward movement of the carriage. This is caused by four elbowed sticks not here seen, harnessed to the saw frame, the first of which, attached to its top, rises with every up-stroke of the saw, while the last, thrust downward thereby, upon the toothed circumference of a large, peg-handled ratchet wheel (K), here seen, causes the latter to revolve with intermittent stops when the saw goes down.

As the cogged axle (E) of this wheel engages the under cogs (F) of one side of the carriage, the carriage otherwise resting on a greased roller track, then moves forward until the log is bisected longitudinally as far as the tail block, at which the saw stops and the carriage, by backward, man-turning of the handle pins (not seen) projecting from the ratchet wheel above mentioned, backs to its position at the start. When the saw is thus again out of the way, in the head-block slot, the log is undogged, pried sideways with crowbars (Fig. 30) at either end, to the desired width for the next kerf whereupon the carriage push and saw cut are repeated. (Information of William Young, mill sawyer of raft logs at Point Pleasant, on the Delaware River, c. 1870 to 1890, to the writer, February 22, 1925.)

Until replaced in 1882 by a so-called rosewheel of cast iron, the water wheel, called a flutterwheel, belonging to this saw, was about three feet in diameter and five feet long and consisted of a series of about eight open, flat paddles in no way angled or hollowed which were bolted on wooden arms running through the shaft. The water, conducted upon the wheel, through a chute, overshot its paddles. Old flutterwheels, seen by the owner of this one, varied in length from four to eight feet, with a diameter of from two and a half to never more than five feet. In some of them (undershot), the water passed under the paddles.

In man-pushing back the log carriage as above mentioned, the ratchet wheel was reversed, not by hand, but

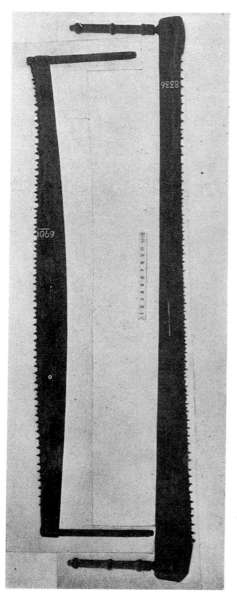

Fig. 31. The "Cross Cut" or Thwart Saw

From the earliest period of the American settlements this saw was used, as now, by two men, each holding

ancient but still familiar, two-man instrument, with rigid vertical handles, broad unframed, flexible, down-curved blade, and very wide-set teeth, known as the

CROSS CUT OR THWART SAW (Fig. 31)

Far less important and fundamental than the pit saw, because it did not make boards; this long, tremulous tool, was nevertheless, sometimes used by the carpenter for cross-cutting heavy timber and instead of the axe,

one of the verticle handles, to cross-cut logs and sometimes to saw down trees (*cf.* numerous mention of the name in the *Probate Records of Essex County, Massachusetts, 1635-1681, 3 vols., George Francis Dow,* editor. *Salem, Mass., the Essex Institute, 1916-1920*). The very characteristic, wide-set teeth, showing stubbed-intervals, are not raked, so that the instrument cuts both ways. Long before rolling mills facilitated its manufacture, by rolling iron or steel into sheets, this wide, open, saw-blade, forged by blacksmiths or trip-hammered by water-power, was used in Europe, as shown in the old German engraving (Fig. 32) of date about 1500, where the Emperor Maximilian is seen holding one under his arm; or, in another print of the 15th century, shown later, where the end of another appears with modern doubled-teeth, interspaced with the usual very characteristic blunt intervals. The specimens here shown, are 19th century relics of Bucks Co., Pa., with probably home-made blades.

About 1880, Pennsylvania lumbermen began felling hemlock trees with the cross-cut saw, before which time all trees had been axe-felled, though cross-cut into lengths and butted (*i.e.,* axe-cut butts sawed off) with this factory-made saw (*inf.* John C. French, of Roulette, Potter Co., Pa., to the writer, Feb. 24, 1925). Until the end of lumber rafting on the Delaware, *c.* 1890, all raft logs received at the Point Pleasant saw mill, had had their axe-butts sawed off before reaching the mill (*inf.* Wm. Young, of Point Pleasant, to the writer, Feb. 22, 1925).

Colonel Shoemaker of McElhattan, says, "It is true that the chopped butts were always sawed off the logs (by lumbermen with the cross-cut saw) before the logs were floated or made into rafts. Twenty-five years ago, when I was a boy, the mountain-sides (in Clinton Co., Pa.) were covered with these butts; and although now many of these have rotted or been destroyed in forest fires, there are many still lying about in the old slashings. This was done long after the old saw mills were superseded by more modern ones. But the custom originated, as Mr. Young stated, because the early saw mills could not accept the axe-cut butts" (Letter of Col. Henry W. Shoemaker to the writer, Feb. 26, 1925).

by foot pressure against the wheel pegs, by a man standing to the right of the saw, outside of the carriage, steadied by grasping two pins, one of which, projecting from the saw frame, may be seen in the picture. Information of the former owner, H. T. Weaver, by letter to the writer, March 6 and 13, 1925.

Fig. 32. Cross-Cut Saw of the 16th Century

From a wood-cut, possibly by Hans Schaufflein of Nuremburg, b. 1492, d. 1540. The picture shows a pile of undressed logs; several squared balks; two small hand-saws, with straight handles in the workmen's belts; the broad axe; the mortising axe; the line and reel with ink or chalk pot; and the cross-cut saw, held under the arm of the Emperor Maximilian. *Monographen zur Deutsche Kultur Geschichte,* G. Steinhaufen, Leipsig, 1900. Vol. 8, der Handwerker, p. 29.

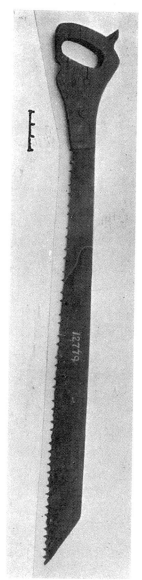

Fig. 33. One-Man Cross-Cut Saw

With home-made, hollow-grasp handle and wide-spaced unraked-teeth, with rough-rounded intervals, like the two-man instrument, Fig. 31.

by the farmer or lumbermen, for cross-cutting the trunks or butts of axe-felled trees, and gradually, after c.

1880, for felling trees.

Besides its general construction, one of its most important and conspicuous characteristics is the shape of its teeth, which, though greatly diversified by recent factory patents, are here shown only in their old inherited European form.

In most saws, the angles of the teeth are never made at right angles, but always at acute angles, and always raked away from the hand, hence cut on the thrust, and not on the pull of the sawyer.

But in this horizontal, two-man saw, where both sawyers should do equal work, the teeth are not raked at all, so that they cut both ways.

We further learn that in order to check the clogging of sawdust in a wide back and forth cut through heavy timber, the teeth of the cross-cut saw are extra wide spaced, and unlike those of any other saw, show jagged or rude shaped intervals between the teeth, as if every other tooth had been broken off or filed down.

In the specimens here shown (Fig. 31), these teeth are single and equi-sided. In others (not shown) the teeth are double, and appear in close set pairs, raked contrariwise, which latter device, though frequently reproduced in modern factory saws, is no modern idea, since it appears in an old German engraving (shown later) by Veit Stoss of the fifteenth century, in the Dresden Print Collection.

The *New English Dictionary* proves that the thwart saw was in use in England between 1404 and 1612, and the *Probate Records of Essex County, Massachusetts, 1635 - 1681, 3 vols., George Francis Dow, editor. Salem, Mass., the Essex Institute, 1916-1920,* show by numerous entries, that the

Fig. 34. Tree Sawyer's Props

A heavy stick, penetrating the top of a downward-forked branch through a hole above the fork, forms a tripod, with an upper fork, upon which branches of felled trees were raised off the ground for convenient sawing with the cross-cut saw. The specimen No. 11827, was used by Enos Lewis of Richlandtown, Bucks Co., Pa., about 1900. It was bought from his widow in 1917.

early New England settlers employed it between 1635 and 1681. Because of its size, it must have been hard to forge and polish; but as blacksmiths had made it since the sixteenth century in Europe, it seems probable, though lacking direct proof, that they made it before the factories made it in America; and if we are right in supposing that the open pit saw (Fig. 27) was not extensively made until about 1760, then for centuries this remarkable saw, again shown in Fig. 32, from an old German print of about 1500, with its characteristic widespread teeth at blunt intervals, was the chief open, two-man saw in use.

The next figure shows an old example, with home-made handle, of the comparatively modern and now very common

ONE-MAN CROSS-CUT SAW (Fig. 33)

and the above illustration pictures two home-made

SAW PROPS (Fig. 34)

used about 1890 by Pennsylvania woodmen, to hold up, in sawing off, the branches of felled trees.

Tools for Moving and Measuring

THUS obtained or prepared by axe, frow, wedge, or saw, the wooden material had to be further dealt with by the tools for moving and measuring it, either at the start, or later in the wood-making process.

As the destruction of the magnificent North American forest proceeded, lumber was always necessary, and the evidence shows that some of the methods for its preliminary transport, whether by the pioneer, while exterminating trees for house room; by the later farmer, in supplying local saw mills; or the organized lumbermen, helped by river, railroad and canal, in meeting the voracious national demand for building material, have remained unchanged, until the end of the 19th century. The important but overlooked tools, that served these uses, are here shown, beginning with

THE DRAG SHACKLE (Fig. 35)

a short chain, which, when its spurs are driven into the opposite sides of the log end, dragged the log out of the woods by means of horses attached to its ring. Otherwise a common chain would do the work with more friction.

The apparatus is called span dogs by Knight's *American Mechanical Dictionary*, 1878, also, in the *New English Dictionary* quoting 1867 for the earliest use of the word, and probably the name drag prongs of 1662, listed in the *Probate Records of Essex County, Massachusetts, 1635-1681, 3 vols., George Francis Dow, editor. Salem, Mass., the Essex Institute, 1916-1920*, Vol. 1, p. 395, and the word

span shackle, frequently there mentioned (1635 to 1681, refer to it, though neither word appears in the *New English Dictionary*.

A similar chain with similar claws was found by the writer in 1924, in use by John Wildonger, near Point Pleasant, Bucks County, Pa., and another, used c. 1880, by Lewis Treffinger, a carpenter of Doylestown, was given by him to the Museum there in 1925. This specimen, No. 20256, was presented by Col. H. W. Shoemaker, of McElhattan, Pa., and was made by Seth Nelson, Jr., a mountaineer woodsman, hunter and artificer of Round Island, Clinton County, Pa., about 1885.

For the pioneer or the farmer of the 18th century, the drag shackle sufficed to drag logs, one by one, or, if small, laid sidewise two by two; but when later at the final funeral of the forest, organized bands of lumbermen strung dozens of logs together and dragged them wholesale with horses or oxen down the mountain sides, variations of the tool became necessary. These fatal spurs, together with the more common harness chains for directly pulling the felled tree, or fastening it upon the wagons and sleds, shown later, are herewith grouped together and illustrated as

LOG GRABS AND LOG CHAINS (Fig. 36)

Mr. A. J. Marschner, mill owner, of Roulette, Pa., and lumberman of the 80's, explains them as follows: namely, the single and double trailer grab—a short two- or four-clawed swivelled chain for dragging logs by the dozen

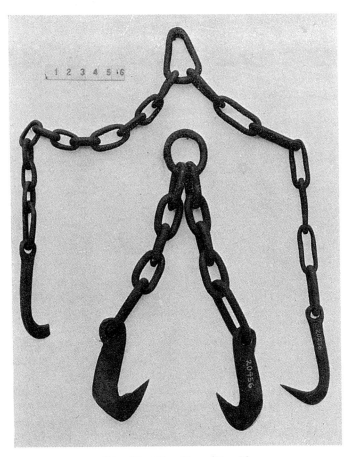

Fig. 35. The Drag Shackle

Called crotch grabs by Pennsylvania mountain lumbermen in the nineteenth century. For dragging logs out of the woods, the iron spurs were driven into the opposite sides of the log and horses harnessed to the ring. The more the pull, the tighter the clench. Lewis Treffinger, above noted, says that he sometimes used four horses for heavy logs with his heavy, hooked shackles here shown (middle). The other specimen, Museum No. 20256, was made about 1885, in Clinton Co., Pa.

or more yoked together in a single string or laid side by side in a double string; the log chain or ox chain, with a ring or a large coupling hook at one end and a small chain hook at the other for dragging lengthwise or rolling sidewise a log, when noosed or wrapped around it; the log hook spiked into the log side for the same purpose; and the growser or brake chain for wrapping around a log to retard its down plunge, dangerous to men and oxen, on the mountain side. Look twice at these suggestive chains, so little known, so rarely seen, forged and spurred for the forest's doom. No boast, no excuse, no exaggeration in the stern story they tell of the crash of trees, the shouts of lumbermen, and the fatal song of the saw.

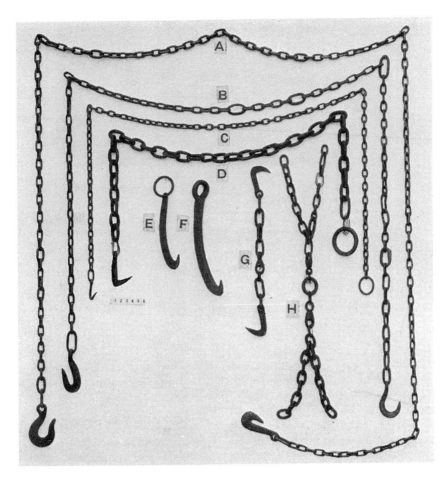

Fig. 36. Log Grabs and Log Chains

These little observed tools except A, C, and F, were obtained in June, 1925, from Mr. A. J. Marschner, saw mill owner of Roulette, Potter County, Pa., who as a lumberman of the 1880's describes and explains them for this illustration as follows:

(*G*)—shows the single trailer grab, a short chain spurred at each end, exactly resembling the log shackle (Fig. 35) except that the chain is swivelled, to prevent twisting, when a dozen or more logs are dragged in a string by this instrument, spurred longitudinally from the rear end of one log to the front end of the following log.

(*H*)—the double trailer, consisting of two log shackles (Fig. 35) swivelled together on a central chain which repeats the operation on two strings of logs, set side by side, when pulled, wriggling, rolling and twisting down the mountain side. The four spurs on the four chain ends are missing on this imperfect specimen.

(*A*)—the log chain, ten to fifteen feet long, terminates at one end either in a large ring, not here shown, through which the chain easily passes, or as here illustrated, in a large open hook, ditto. Its other end is mounted with a smaller narrow mouthed chain hook, through which a link will pass flat, but not sideways, hence the latter hook will clasp the chain on any link against the alternate turned link without penetrating the link hole. The log chain is thus easily noosed or grappled upon itself and meets many emergencies. It serves as a binding chain, to secure logs to the wagon or sled as shown in Fig. 38. As a shorter pulling chain, ox chain (*B*) for oxen or horses, or a makeshift brake chain for sleds or wagons, etc. It will also drag a log forward, if noosed around its end, or roll it sideways if properly wrapped or hooked around its middle.

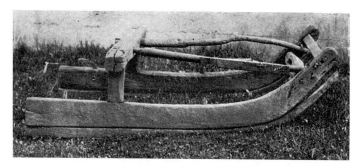

Fig. 37. Log Sled

A massive home-made wooden sled, with wooden runners unshod with iron, which, when backed under the pried up log end, reduces friction in the winter transport of a log thus lifted at one end, while its other end drags on the snow. Single, modern sled sections of the so-called "bob sled,"—a long sled composed of two similarly shaped iron--shod sleds, coupled together longitudinally, are still so used (1925) at Hohlefelder's lumber yard, in New Britain, Bucks Co., Pa., where also, as in Potter Co., Pa., the whole log, supported at both ends, is sometimes transported on the complete "bob sled." Information of the lumber merchant, W. J. Hohlefelder, New Britain, and A. J. Marschner, Roulette, Potter Co., Pa. Specimen No. 9992 was obtained in Bucks County about 1900. One like it was found May, 1925, stored in Youngkin's disused saw mill near Haycock Mountain, Bucks Co., Pa.

For long distances in winter time

THE LOG SLED (Fig. 37)

a heavy, low, home-made wooden sled, minus iron runners, served the same purpose. One end of the felled and trimmed tree having been pried up on blocks or stones with crow bars, and the sled pushed under and chained fast to it, the log was pulled by horses or oxen harnessed to the runners, out of the woods and along the roads over the snow to the saw mill. In its progress its fore end was thus lifted to reduce friction and its rear end dragged. Employed since the settlement of Pennsylvania, this ancient transport apparatus fell gradually out of use after about 1885. Nevertheless, Wil-

liam J. Hohlefelder says that he still thus uses one of the sections of a modern double runner sled in transporting logs in winter to his saw mill in New Britain. But far more effective than the sled, for distant road transport was

THE LOG WAGON (Fig. 38)

as here shown; upon the high frame of which, logs were, and still are, loaded by dragging them sideways on "skids" over the wheel tops. According to information given to the writer by Charles Hohlefelder, Jr., April 25, 1925, the felled tree, lopped of its branches and cross-cut at both ends with the cross-cut saw, is rolled with cant hooks if possible, or if not, in

The log hook (E) if spurred into the log side, and caught by its ring to the log chain hooked to horses or oxen, will serve the same purpose.

(F)—is a special log hook of similar construction but with rigid ring, found with the log wheels (Fig. 46) and used with a similar hook to shackle logs under the axle of that apparatus as described.

The short heavy growser chain (D) noosed through its ring around a log, and with its end spur grab spiked fast thereto, acts as a brake to retard the down slip of the log on muddy or icy slopes (trails).

The binding chain (A) and boom chain (C) now (1925) in use at W. G. Hohlefelder's lumber yard at New Britain, Bucks Co., Pa., were kindly loaned for the illustration by the latter.

Fig. 38. Log Wagon

The logs here shown, laid upon a log wagon of century-old type, have been dragged upon its high frame on two stout, ten to twelve foot long poles, called skids, over the wheel tops. Photographed March, 1925, as still, with six other similar wagons, in use at the wood-yard of Wm. J. Hohlefelder, at New Britain, Bucks Co., Pa. The wagon, made by a country wheelwright about 1895, is wooden axled (old style), but very high framed, forming the log rests called bolsters level with the wheel tops. It is equipped with a brake and is extensible on its long coupling pole, extending from axle to axle, to fit varying log lengths.

The chaining of the logs to the wagon appears too faintly here to b' understood at sight. Two log chains, ten to fifteen feet long, with a chain hook at one end and a ring, or ring hook, at the other (*cf.* Fig. 36), first wrapped around the coupling pole, are passed loosely and caught with their chain hooks over the logs at either end thereof. Under these chains, so wrapped, two hickory saplings called booms are thrust at right angles to the logs, from the log-end or outside of each chain wrap, and then toggled or twisted inwards over the middle of the log to tighten said chain wrap. To hold fast these booms, thus twisted, the light three to four feet long boom chains (*cf.* Fig 36) are noosed over the boom ends, by slipping the boom chain hooks through the boom chain rings, drawn tight, and hooked around the coupling pole.

A log placed on the ground parallel to the wagon, is loaded as follows: Two stout, ten to twelve foot poles, called skids, hewn flat at the top, are laid, at right angles to the wagon, from the wheel tops to the ground against the log side. A log chain is then hooked to a ring on the inner face of one of the bolsters, wrapped through the wheel top over the skid, again back through the wheel and down under and over the log. This log chain is then fastened by its chain hook to another log chain, similarly placed, extending from the other bolster, via the other wheel top, etc., and under and around the log as before, so as to form a loop to the middle of which the horses standing on the opposite side of the wagon are attached by a third log chain. As they pull, the log rolls up the skids, over the wheel top, and on to the bolsters.

The writer saw two cedar skids, laid from axle to axle, on one of these log wagons, as it brought a heavy log to Overholt's Deep Run saw mill in Bedminster, Bucks Co., Pa., in May, 1925. The log was unloaded by one man, who rolled it easily with a cant hook over the wheel top, without the slightest injury to the wheels.

"tight places," chain-dragged with horses directly, or with tackle guyed to trees, to the side of, and parallel with, the wagon. Two heavy ten to twelve foot fresh-cut poles (skids) are then chained from each wheel-top, (*i.e.* the chains wrapped through the spokes and over the skid) so that the pole ends reach the ground close to the log. Whereupon, when two wide-spaced chains are looped under, and hooked over the log, the horses standing on the opposite side of the wagon, are harnessed to the middle of the loop and pull the log up the skids, over the wheel-tops and on to the wagon. Other chains are then wrapped around the loaded log under the

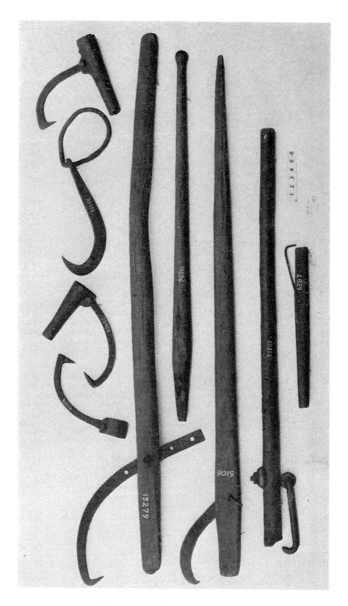

Fig. 39. The Cant Hook

The German "Kanthaken" and French "Renard." This particular pattern, Nos. 13279 and 9019 (centre), probably originated in Germany. The spur, either extensible or non-extensible, works loosely on a pin through a handle-slot, grasping or releasing a log by the pull or back push of the handle. The instrument works both ways. It rolls a log away from the workman on a handle push, if the spur points towards him. If the spur points away from him, the log rolls toward him on the pull. Sometimes, though rarely, according to John Overholt, mill sawyer of Bedminster, Bucks Co., Pa., the workman must stoop to release the hook with his left hand.

wagon framework and these are tightened by saplings, (toggle sticks) called booms, thrust under said chains, more or less twisted and chained to the wagon frame. During this operation the vertical axle posts are moved from their sockets and replaced, after which the horses are reharnessed to the pole, and the wagon loaded with one, two, or more logs, begins its slow journey to the saw mill.

For rolling rather than dragging logs, the next two illustrations show a far more ingenious one-man master tool,

THE CANT HOOK (Fig. 39)

called "Kanthacken," in Myer's *Konversations Lexikon,* and "Renard," in Diderot's unrivalled *Encyclopedia,* of 1768. The wooden staves shown are mounted with spurred iron hooks (one of them, No. 13279, adjustable through four holes) loosely hinged on iron pins through mortise holes, and forming jaws, which, opening around the log, grasp it with the spur, and roll it by a back pull of the staff. As we see, the grasp of this hook can be enlarged, but the non-adjustable, No.

5106, cannot be used on logs too big for its spur.

Both specimens show the common type used on farms and at country and riverside saw mills in the Delaware Valley in the 19th century.

The writer has failed as yet to find evidence for the origin or antiquity of this remarkable tool, which Mr. Herman Muller, of Trenton, says he saw thus constructed and in use about 1863 at the "Hirschmuhle" saw mill at Rodach, near Coburg, Germany. It does not appear in the *Essex County Probate Records,* 1635-81. Moxon does not mention it in 1678. The *New English Dictionary* does not quote any use of the word "cant hook" in the English language earlier than 1848, but Diderot, who calls it "Renard" (fox), describes without illustrating it in 1768, and the sentence, "Jemand beim Kanthaken nehman," (to take him with a Kanthook) quoted as used in 1695 in Germany, in Kluge's *Etymological Dictionary of the German Language* (information R. P. Hommel), proves that the tool was in use in Germany two hundred years ago.

Without considering factory-made or patented cant hooks, other home-made types of the instrument, with hook greatly varying in curve and with square or round point, appear in eastern Pennsylvania, as the ring dog cant hook (Fig. 40), now generally obsolete, and in the Pennsylvania lumber region, a third form, not shown, in which the spur is hinged on a wide clasp (as in the peavey, Fig. 42), which clasp, meeting a bolt upon which the claw is hinged, is riveted upon the handle.

In the home-made cant hooks now (May, 1925)) used at John Overholt's saw mill, above noted, the non-adjustable spur hinges, not on a clasp, but on a bolt penetrating the handle; while some of the farmers bringing logs to the mill, still use the ring dog form (Fig. 40) also here shown, second downward, left side.

According to the information of Arthur J. Marschner, lumberman of Roulette, Potter Co., Pa., and Mr. J. C. French, to the writer, a fourth variety with a short iron beak, not here shown, set at right angles to the base of the handle, was used in the 1880's in the Pennsylvania mountains, where and when any cant hook, minus a pike point, was called a "muley" cant hook. Col. H. W. Shoemaker, on the authority of W. J. Phillips, of McElhattan, Pa., informs the writer that the handles of the old cant hooks in the lumber period c. 1850 to 1890, were made of ash.

The non-adjustable specimen, No. 5106, was loaned by Christian Myers, 1916, and was used at Stover's grist and saw mill on Tohickon Creek, Bucks Co, Pa., in the late nineteenth century, and the adjustable No. 13279 was given July, 1918, by E. S. Lovett, of Taylorsville, Bucks County. In the unhandled No. 20408 and its fellow (upper left) from Clinton County, the hook hinges on a rivet in a wrought iron pointless socket.

No. 20392, from Colonel Shoemaker, made by Seth Nelson in Clinton Co., Pa. (right), shows the blacksmith's similar instrument for squeezing hot iron wagon tires upon the wooden wheel rims.

No. 6387 is a cooper's tool, from New Bedford, Mass., working on the same principle.

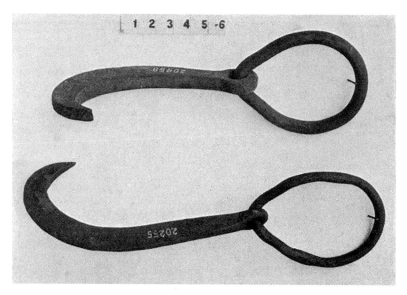

Fig. 40. The Ring Dog or Ring Dog Cant Hook

Another pattern of the highly effective and indispensable cant hook is here shown in its old Anglo-American and also German form, namely, a curved, iron arm with a spur at one end, and a ring into which a handle is pushed at the other.

No. 20255 was obtained, 1925, by Col. H. W. Shoemaker from Seth Nelson, Jr., of Round Island, Clinton Co., Pa., whose father made it about 1840. The other specimen, probably of about the same date, was found May, 1925, at Youngkin's abandoned saw mill on Haycock Run, Bucks Co., Pa.

John Overholt, mill sawyer and owner, of Bedminster Township, Bucks Co., Pa., tells the writer that some farmers bringing logs to his mill, still (1925) use the ring dog, one great advantage of which, he says, is the unattached handle easily replaceable if broken, by a sapling cut in the woods. Hence these tools can be carried about minus handles on log wagons. The ring should fit reasonably on the handle and not slip too easily. If too loose, a twig or splint wedge will tighten it.

Kluge describes it as used at seaports for the tilting and turning over of barrels and boxes. Hence, the twenty patents under the word "cant hook," in the United States Patent Records (first 1856, to Allicott, of Hancock, N. H., and last, in 1873, one in New Hampshire, and one in Maine) are not inventions of its principle, but only attempts to adjust or strengthen its powerful grasp.

The next illustration shows the instrument in simpler if not older form, as used previously in the forests of eastern Pennsylvania, namely the

RING DOG (Fig. 40)

in which the hook is not pivoted through the staff, but equipped with a loose ring, through which the staff is thrust. While in Figure 39 the spur is lengthened by shifting the spur-pin, so as to grasp a larger log; here the grasp of the instrument is less efficiently increased by a deeper thrust of the handle into the ring.

David Angeny, carpenter, of Danboro, Pa., tells the writer March, 1925 that he saw logs rolled in Bucks County, in the late 19th century, without cant hooks, by the extra leverage of crow bars thrust through chains wrapped around them.

In the right specimen shown, No. 20255, the ring is twisted to the proper

angle for handle insertion. It was
made by Seth Nelson, Sr., about 1840,
near Keating, Pa., and represents, as
noted, the older type of cant hook frequently used in Clinton and Berks
Counties, Pa. in the 19th century to
roll logs.

Meyer's *Konversations Lexikon*, edition 1894, *cf.* "Kanthaken," omitting
all reference to the type shown in
Figure 39, also German, describes this
ringed spur only, as if no other form
of cant hook existed in Germany; and
Mr. George Sturt, of Farnham, Surrey,
England, in more than thirty years'
experience in England as a wagon
manufacturer, tells the writer in
April, 1925, that he has never seen the
form shown in Figure 39, and that
this ringed form, called in England
ring dog, is the only English cant hook
known to him.

Besides the above ancient tools and
apparatus adapted to the shift of the
raw material (logs) by summer and
winter on land, several others, as part
of the equipment, rather of later organized bands of lumbermen, than of
the individual farmer or pioneer, re-
late to log and lumber transport by
water, namely,

THE JAM PIKE (Fig. 41)

an important special tool of the lumberman used in deforesting the mountains of Pennsylvania, in the 19th
century, as here shown, a stout pole,
ferruled upon a home-made iron
point, used by the lumberman in the
dangerous operation of prying free
single logs, wedged or caught fast, or
heavy masses of floating logs, jammed
fast, in their water transport down the
freshet-swollen mountain streams.
With its restored handle it was kindly
obtained for this illustration May,

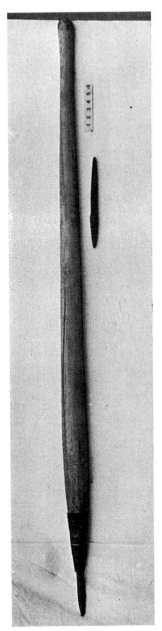

Fig. 41. The Jam Pike

An iron spike, here also shown loose in duplicate, is
inserted and fixed with iron bands (ferrules) into the
end of a stout pole, by which, worked with one or two

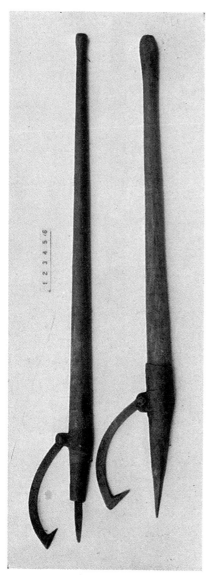

med or caught logs, not only by prying up but by rolling them. According to Mr. J. C. French, of Roulette,
to the writer, May, 1925, it was devised by John
Peavey, a blacksmith at Bolivar, Allegheny Co., N. Y.,
about 1872; and according to A. J. Marschner, mill
sawyer, of Roulette, Potter Co., Pa., is still in use in
slightly modernized form in Potter County.

The rare and very interesting specimen shown at the
left, of date soon after its invention in the 1870's,
shows the original make of the tool, as a combination of
the jam pike (Fig. 41) and of the so-called "muley,"
or old, variously made, but unspiked cant hook (Fig.
39). The hook is held by a clasp. The stock somewhat
thinner than the usual 2⅝ inches at thickest peavey
stock, is of iron wood (*Carpinus Caroliniana*). It was
obtained May, 1925, from Mr. Marschner, who found
it at his saw mill in Roulette, among the old tools used
forty years ago and earlier, by himself and his father.
Mr. Marschner says: "The peavey I sent you (left) is
a real old one, and does not conform to the latest style
now in use at our mill chiefly because the clasp is old
style, while our modern clasps are solid with projections
beneath, which hold the hook a little away from the
pike and above the clasp, and a bolt to stop the hook
from coming close to the handle, and possibly pinching
the lumberjack's fingers (*i. e.*, in releasing the hook by
a hand pull.—H. C. M.)."

The peavey (right) of somewhat later make, is another of Mr. Marschner's mill relics, in which the spike
enlarges into a socket, into which the handle is inserted
and riveted, hence when the handle breaks it is more
easily repaired than the older peavey which, in that case,
had to be respiked and re-ringed by a blacksmith. When
bought, about 1890, by Mr. Marschner, it was originally mounted with a five and a half foot maple handle,
which was broken and replaced by the present ash
handle, also broken close to the pike and re-inserted, as
noted, in the socket.

Mr. French describes the best make of the peavey, in
the height of the lumber period, *c.* 1880, to the writer,
May, 1925, as follows:

---

to rivers, or saw mills, on freshet-swollen mountain
streams. Made before 1870, it was used by the father
and grandfather of Arthur J. Marschner, lumberman, of
Roulette, Potter Co., Pa.; also by the latter, from
whom it was bought May 20, 1925, and who says that
it went out of use in Potter County in the 1880's when
it was supplanted by the peavey (Fig. 42). The handle
has been restored by Mr. Marschner and lacks one, if
not two, of the original iron ferrules over the pike point.

Mr. Marschner writes May 28, 1925: "I only have a
dim recollection of the jam pike, and remember that it
was large and heavy and that it was further used for
prying and lifting, punching holes into the ground; also
for pulling grabs (*i.e.*, prying up tight-driven shackle
points). Mr. French states that (before the invention
of the peavey—H. C. M.) two men, one with a cant
hook and the other with a jam pike, worked together
on roll ways (not described) or floating logs, as above
noted.

Fig. 42. The Peavey

Here, a cant hook has been attached to the pike end
of a jam pike (Fig. 41), forming an effective combination of two lumbermen's tools in one. It releases jam-

---

men, the lumberman shifts the position of heavy logs,
or pries loose single, floating logs, caught fast, or floating masses of logs, jammed, in their downward passage

1925, by Mr. John C. French, of Roulette, Clinton County, Pa.

But the day of the jam pike has passed with that of the primeval forest and the adventurous lumberman so that now, 1925, in the bared mountains of Pennsylvania, the tool has become no less a rarity than the celebrated

PEAVEY (Fig. 42)

a still more efficient modern combination lumberman's tool for the same purpose, by which a cant hook attached to a jam pike above the pike point enables the daring lumberjack to roll towards him, as well as pry away from him, the key log, and so release with a crash the congested log mass upon the dammed-up roaring waters.

When, about 1870, at Bolivar, N. Y., according to the information of Mr. John C. French, the blacksmith John Peavey thus added to the efficiency of the jam pike by attaching a cant hook to it, he never sought to patent his apparatus, and his name does not appear among the grantees in any of the twenty United States patents for cant hooks between 1856 and 1873, nor

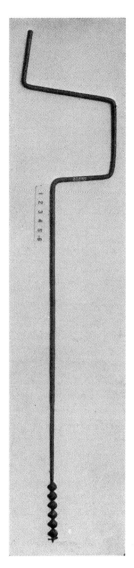

Fig. 43. The Raft Auger

"The maple stock is white, short-grained and flawless. The hook of best cast steel, with the proper curve and point,—the pick of tool steel. The clasp and bands of the toughest Swedish or Norway iron. Many imitations of the peavey lever and hook have been made since 1872,—useful tools,—but not equal to the original."

When used to pry logs up, sidewise, or endwise, the peavey had to be turned on its side, or under, to get the hook out of the way. Mr. French dramatically describes its dangerous use in holding back (on the back pull) logs rolling down hill; and Mr. Marschner, its further efficiency in prying up grabs (shackle hooks) (Fig. 35), trailer and growser chains (Fig. 36), and log hooks (Fig. 36), etc.; also in pushing, with the pike point only, or pulling, with pike and spur together, floating logs, for which latter purpose, and general log running in freshets, a special light, slim long-handled, so-called driving-peavey was used.

With this instrument held vertically in his left hand, while turning the crank with his right, the raftsman bores holes, two by two, into the tops of the ends of logs, floating side by side, so as to yoke them together into rafts, by means of wooden staples, pegged over cross-laid saplings, as explained in the text. Mr. J. C. French, of Roulette, Potter Co., Pa., informs the writer, May, 1925, that the raftsman found it easier to stand erect on the log when boring these holes,—hence he preferred this long instrument to the common short,

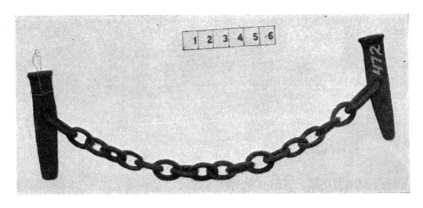

Fig. 44. The Raft Shackle

In this instrument, the two straight spikes driven into two floating logs or two dislocated parts of log rafts on the Delaware River, chained them together, until abandonment of log rafting, *c.* 1890. Information of Dr. Cooper of Point Pleasant, September, 1924, and John Young, ditto, May, 1925. This specimen, No. 472, was given by Frank Preston, of Carversville, on the Delaware in 1897. The spike-points are not round but wedge-shaped (*cf.* Fig. 45).

under the reference to the word cant hook, ahead of patents in *Harper's Magazine* in 1948. But he immortalized his name, and added a word to the language, for his new fore and back action tool, as illustrated in *Webster's Dictionary,* supplement (edition 1906), was named "peavey," and becoming at first popular in Northern Pennsylvania, soon grew famous as part of the equipment of lumbermen throughout the United States. In its early home in Clinton County, Penna., the short-lived master tool went out of common use when the forests failed and lumbering ceased, about 1900.

It is only after the loose logs have finished their wild and obstructed

dash down the mountain stream, and reached the river, that

THE RAFT AUGER (Fig. 43)

explains their assembling and construction into the tremendous rafts that, after 1840, helped by canals and railroads, carried them at high water to their destination at river-side saw mills or distant cities.

This eccentric, home-made spiral auger, with long iron shank, hand-crank elbow, and lacking the wooden cross-handle, was obtained March 3, 1925, by Col. H. W. Shoemaker from Seth Nelson, Jr., born about 1838, lumberman, mountaineer, hunter, trapper, maker of axes, lumber tools, hunting knives, bear traps, and general artificer, who had forged it for the raftsmen in his younger days, at Round Island, Clinton Co., Pa.

At that time rafting was in full swing, and the great floating islands went down the Susquehanna and Delaware in season, often dozens per day. The prehistoric mantle of Poco-

---

cross-handled auger, which would have required him to stoop.

Mr. David Baird, president of the David Baird Lumber Co., of Camden, N. J., remembering the rafting days, writes June 2, 1925, that the tool called "crank auger," is not now obsolete, but still employed by wharf builders, ship builders, and contractors; that it enabled the raftsman to stand erect at his work, and that it is a very rapid instrument for boring holes in pine and hemlock lumber.

no Mountain was going or gone when John Young was employed in sawing raft logs at Stover's Mill, Point Pleasant, Bucks County, Pa., who informs the writer May, 1925, that the Delaware rafts floated down from the mountains in his time, were constructed as follows: across either end of a group of logs floated side by side, a thin two to four-inch pole generally of ironwood (according to T. S. Kenderdine, see illustration) was laid and fastened by steamed and bent ash splints stapled across them, one staple per log. These staples, called bows, were pegged into auger holes, two holes per log, bored on either side of the pole with the raft auger as here shown.

Because, adds Mr. J. C. French of Roulette ,Potter Co., Pa., the raftsman balanced on a single log, found it easier to stand, rather than stoop, at his work, he preferred this high-action instrument, held at its top with his left and cranked with his right hand, to the common short, cross-handled auger, which Mr. Young says he never saw used on a raft.

As also connected with the rafting of logs, and an epoch of adventure which still haunts the memory of old men, the next two illustrations show

THE RAFT SHACKLE (Fig. 44)

a short chain, ringed at either end upon straight spikes, which if driven into the tops of adjacent floating logs, or disrupted raft sections, will shackle them together, and

THE SNUB RING (Fig. 45)

a ring-mounted, wedge-shaped, iron spike, which, when driven with the grain into the end of a lost log, and

Fig. 45. The Snub Ring

A ring-mounted, wedge-shaped iron spike, which, when driven into the top of a floating log at its end and roped through the ring, will moor the log to the shore, or fasten it to a raft or other logs, or draw it to the log wheels. According to the information of Mr. J. C. French, to the writer, May 1925 "The log was caught by driving the wedge into one end passing the rope through the ring, then with another log, and another so caught, towed like a string of suckers to an eddy or a cover and tied to a tree or a stump, until the owner called with a tug boat, paid one doller per log to the scavengers and took the salvaged logs to a saw mill beyond to be sawed into lumber."

Besides this use, on the Susquehanna and its branches, Mr. French says, that, "Mr. Benjamin Burt, of Potter Co., Pa., now (1925) aged eighty, and his father, Benjamin Burt, Sr., born 1811, on Lake George, N. Y., used these ring wedges to drag logs out of the woods. In that case, the wedges were chained together as with the drag shackle (Fig. 35), one being driven into each side of the log end, and horses attached by a chain and hooked to the middle of the wedge chain."

Charles Robbins of Potter County, aged seventy-five, says that his father dragged logs with a single one of these instruments, barbed on its sides and corners, driven not into the side or top, but into the sawed face of the log end.

The wedge point was preferred to the spike point, for this instrument, because easily driven in with the grain, it was easily pulled out, without risk of leaving a broken iron point in the wood to rupture a mill saw.

roped through the ring to a boat, will salvage the log, otherwise it will moor a raft to the shore, or fasten it to other rafts or logs, or draw a log to the wheels.

Fig. 46. The Log Wheels

For pulling raft logs out of the river. The two gigantic whee's were rol'ed if possible into the water on a hard shallow beach over a floating log. Then horses, attached to the very long tongue, dragged the log, shackled with two log hooks (Fig. 36), and chained to the under-axle hooks of the hand screw, here plainly seen, out of the water and up the bank to the neighboring saw mill.

According to the information of John Young, mill sawyer, c. 1870-90, of Point Pleasant, to the writer in May, 1925, the more mid-balance the log got, the easier its rear end dragged, hence the length (22 feet 6 inches, from axle) of the tongue of these whee's, to get the horses out of the way of their burden.

Similar wheels were seen in use by Patrick Trainor of Philadelphia, in c. 1867, hau'ing logs out of the pine woods in Ocean County, New Jersey, and in c. 1861, drawn by about twenty white horses, hauling a stone for Col. Ellsworth's grave in Brooklyn, N. Y. (Information of P. T. to the writer June, 1925.)

The wheels and one of these log hooks were presented in April, 1925, by Mrs. Elizabeth B. Troemner, owner of the now obsolete saw mill, at Point Pleasant, Bucks Co., Pa., where they had been kept in a shed since the disuse of the mill about 1890.

The log hooks, save for their rings, too small for a handle, resemble the ring dog (Fig. 40) minus its staff. Through these rings, when the spurs were driven in the opposite sides of the log-end, a loose chain was thrust and hooked to the under-axle hooks seen in the picture.

This last far more conspicuous and now forgotten apparatus, connected with the water transport of the carpenter's raw material, appears in the next illustration as the

LOG WHEELS (Fig. 46)

for hauling raft-logs out of the water to river-side saw mills. A gigantic cart, disused on the Delaware River in the nineties, when forests failed and rafting stopped, it was wheeled where possible, into the river, on a hard, shallow beach, near the moored log raft. Whereupon, a detached log, clutched at its end by two loose, ring-topped hooks (see Fig. 36) was chained through the rings of the latter, to the lower forks of the heavy iron turn-screw penetrating the axle. Otherwise, a common chain wrapped around the log would serve the purpose. The turn-screw was then cranked up to lift the log end, and horses pulled the wheels and suspended log, with its dragging rear end, out of the

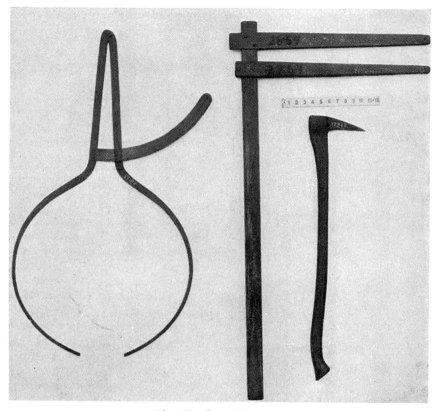

Fig. 47. Log Measures

The illustration shows the lumberman's calipers (left) from Vermont, and sliding scale (right) from Pennsylvania, for finding the diameter of trees or logs. Another home-made specimen, generally resembling the latter, was found by the writer June 2, 1925, among the discarded tools at the disused water-run, frame saw mill of the late Christian Myers on Tohickon Creek, Bedminster Township, Bucks Co., Pa.

water and up the bank to the saw mill. Where the bank formation prevented, the wheels remained on shore and the loosened logs were dragged to them out of the river by ropes tied to the snub rings (Figure 45) or common chains, wrapped or tightened on slip rings around the log ends.

Who remembers these details today, except John Young, above quoted, who in the 1880's used the historic apparatus presented to The Bucks

County Historical Society Museum in April, 1925, by Mrs. Elizabeth B. Troemner, owner of the long closed, riverside saw mill, at Point Pleasant, Bucks County, Pa., where it had been stored in a shed since the saw stopped working about 1890.

This brings us to another group of tools concerning the sale rather than the transport of the raw material, and pertaining to the lumberman owner or lumber merchant, who used them in the measuring, buying, and selling

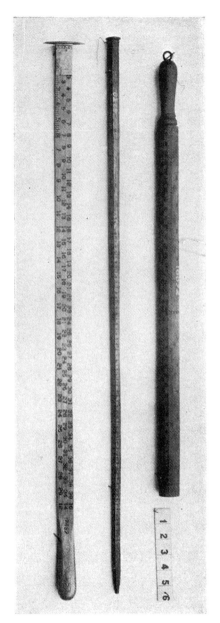

Fig. 48. The Lumber Stick

The lumber merchant's log measure, a polygonal, scaled staff of wood, used to measure the diameter and length, and hence to calculate from its scale, the cubic contents of logs, employed in Pennsylvania until *c.* 1840. As now

of standing trees, logs, rafts, balks, boards, sawed lumber, etc., namely

THE LOG MEASURES (Fig. 47) ‾ here shown as an iron calliper, No. 17182, from Vermont (left), opening upon the log, which measures its thickness on the scaled arm; and the old scaled stick with its sliding arm adjustable against the diameter of the log, from Bucks County, which serves the same purpose. The next illustration

THE LUMBER STICK (Fig. 48) shows (right) two polygonal sticks, long out of use, for ascertaining the cubic contents of logs or lumber, by calculation, according to known rules, from the varying scales marked on each of their facets. No. 19489 (left) is a flat stick, still used by lumber dealers in Eastern Pennsylvania, for the same purpose, or for measuring the cubic contents of piles of boards or squared lumber. It was bought August, 1924, from T. C. Ulmer Co., Lumber Supply Store, Philadelphia, Pa.

Next is shown

THE RACE KNIFE (Fig. 49) the lumberman's little two- or three-pronged timber scribe or scorer used to register tallies, numerals, crosses, circles, etc., on log ends, balks or boards for selling them, or otherwise to mark the parts of worked-up material in assembling it into framework.

The fixed iron point of this tool will form the centre of a circle inscribed with its hinged, scoop point, while the fixed scoop, also used singly, cuts hollow channels. The race knife

in use in its modern form, the left specimen was bought by the writer in 1925, at a lumber supply store in Philadelphia.

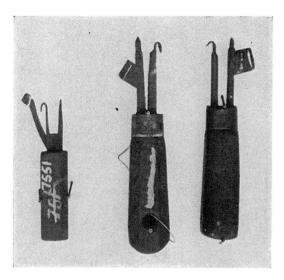

Fig. 49. The Race Knife

The vertical iron prong of this tool will form the centre of a circle inscribed with its fixed scoop-knife. Another scoop-knife, fixed to the side of the prong of the right and middle specimens, if held singly with the tool handle pressed against the wood, cuts straight hollowed channels. In the lefthand specimen this extra scoop-knife is on a hinge. Used by coopers to mark barrels or barrel parts; by lumbermen to tally or number with Roman numerals balks or log ends; and by carpenters to register junctions for heavy frame work, in the latter case accounting for the numerous Vs Xs and multiplied I's seen at the mortised beam and rafterfittings of old barns and sheds.

T. S. Kenderdine, in "Lumbering Days on the Delaware," *Bucks County Historica' Society Proceedings,* Vol. IV, p. 247, says concerning the marking of sawed lumber with this instrument: "When formed into rafts, chalk or lead pencils would not do for noting dimensions, as the water would wash the marks out, so the knife-edged hook was used, which gouged them out in Roman characters, some of them modified; thus, a perpendicular under the cross of an X made a 9, and under that of the last of a double X a 19. An upstroke from the cross of an X made 15; from the last cross of a double X—25, a down stroke under an upset V—4, etc.

"These were the days of large pine logs, when boards and planks came from the mills two feet and more wide, which at first were set aside at the yards for coffin-case boards."

The specimens illustrated here have been used by coopers. No. 7551 was bought at York Harbor, Me., in 1898. The others are from New Bedford, Mass.

was used by coopers to mark barrels or barrel parts, or by lumbermen to scribe or number balk or log ends, or by carpenters to register junctions for heavy framework.

A simpler form of this tool (see "Race Knife," *Knight)* consists of a single, steel scoop-point fixed in a wooden handle. At best it works slowly compared with the more restricted but instantaneous

MARKING AXE (Fig. 50)

an axe-shaped block of iron or steel still used for stamping the owner's initials, etc., on logs or lumber. When struck by its wooden handle against the sawed log or balk end, the initial *F* for the owner's name, and the number *2*, here seen worked in relief on its poll, are stamped against the wood.

Both specimens were obtained in 1924, by Col. H. W. Shoemaker, from Seth Nelson, Jr., of Round Island, Clinton County, Pa., born 1838, who made them about 1900.

Thus far the tools described, many of them rarely seen and generally overlooked in books, pertain to the felling, transport, and preliminary

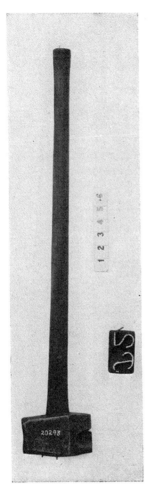

Fig. 50. The Marking Axe

This heavy block of iron, mounted like an axe on a wooden handle and faced with the initial "T" and number 2 in high relief, was used to stamp the owner's initial and number, on the end of a log at a single blow. By means of these marks, according to Dr. B. F. Fackenthal, Jr., of Riegelsville, on the Delaware, Bucks Co., Pa., log waifs, lost or disrupted from wrecked rafts, were identified and salvaged by boatmen along the river shores (*cf.* snub rings, Fig. 45). Obtained by Col. H. W. Shoemaker, in Clinton Co., Pa., where the tool is still (1925) in use.

shaping of the raw material. Now, at last, the tree, whether still unshaped, or transformed into boards or balks, has reached the carpenter, and his work upon it begins with

THE CROW (Fig. 51)

which, unlike the special straight, round-pointed, saw mill crow bar, shown in Figure 30, is an iron bar whose leverage is increased by a very characteristic claw, used either to pry up heavy timber or pull spikes. This master tool, the Roman "vectis," the German "waltze," or "hebel," was probably not called "crow bar," in England, before the 19th century, *cf. New English Dictionary,* quotation 1400-1458-1590 for Shakespeare, etc., and Rees' Cyclopaedia. In the picture we see it as illustrated and described by Moxon, in 1678, Croker's *Complete Dictionary of Arts and Sciences, in* 1764, and *The Circle of Mechanical Arts,* in 1813. It consists of (*a*) the shank, (*b*) the very noticeable flat curved lower notched end, the claw, and (*c*) the round-pointed upper end, the "pike end." The bent claw clearly distinguishing it from the common crow bar and saw mill crow bar, illustrated in Figure 30, puts it at the head of its class. Up comes the beam or out the spike when this mighty prong is pried under it, often on an underplaced block or fulcrum. In the upper comparatively modern specimen of date about 1880, the claw is reinforced with a ring clutch.

THE DRUG (Fig. 52)

is a home-made carpenter's truck on wooden cylindrical rollers, used for shifting heavy pieces of timber pried up upon one or more of these easily under-placed wagons, as here shown and as illustrated by Moxon in 1678. But the drug, dependent upon the

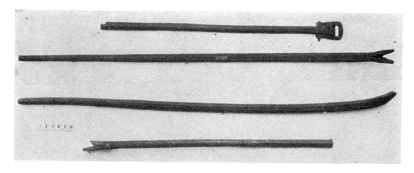

Fig. 51. The Crow

The typical carpenter's crow bar, distinguished from the other forms of the instrument by its bent claw, is here shown as described and illustrated by Moxon in 1678. In the top and bottom (front and side view) of the comparatively modern specimen, of date about 1880, the claw is equipped with a ring clutch. The middle specimen, also here duplicated in side view (No. 20400), was obtained March 3, 1925, from Col. H. W. Shoemaker. It was made by Seth Nelson, Sr., near Keating, Pa., about 1870, and reforged by his son about 1885. The ringed crow was obtained April 17, 1925, from David Angeny, of Danboro Pa.

crow, dwindles into insignificance when compared with the all-powerful

JACK (Fig. 53)

the French "crick," a compact, boxed, cogged crank, with a top fork, to push up ponderous weights. The crank, axled on a small cog wheel, engages a larger cog wheel which, with tremendous power, elevates a vertical iron bar (rack). This raises the weight resting on its upper fork or sometimes suspended on an extra side projection.

Fortunately Moxon, in 1678, and Diderot, in 1768, illustrate this herculean tool in its old form, here shown as surviving in the United States until about 1840, by no means confined to the carpenter, but a general mechanics' tool and common as a weight-lifting apparatus on farms, when, for instance, heavy or loaded wagons, like the Conestoga, had to be jacked up to grease their axles.

The specimens are all old 19th century farm relics, obtained between 1897 and 1922, from Bucks, Berks and Montgomery Counties, Pa.

Having thus reached the carpenter's workshop we pass from the tools and apparatus used by him for moving, to those employed in marking, measuring and correctly placing his material. Look next at

THE CHALK LINE (Fig. 54)

a chalked string, previously referred to (Figs. 21 and 24) as stretched along and twanged against a log, to straighten it for the saw or axe, therefore a preliminary lumberman's tool, but also a carpenter's implement, used to mark out long saw kerfs on planks, boards and balks.

As here shown, the string is wound on a home-made rectangular frame-spool turning on a pivot. When stretched along a log top for pit sawing, or board or balk, for ripping, or frame for cross cutting, whitened by pulling against it a lump of chalk, and twanged, it white marks the necessary guide line for the cut. Black ink (judging from Figure 32)instead of dry chalk, must have been used in the 16th century in Germany for this purpose as according to the informa-

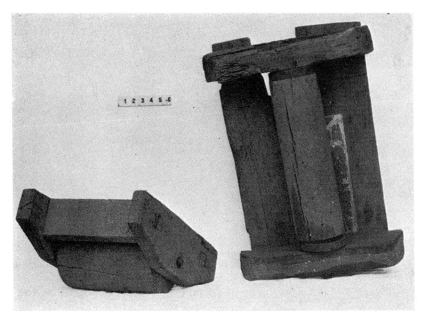

Fig. 52. The Drug

A home-made carpenter's truck on wooden cylindrical rollers, used for shifting timber. Both specimens are old Bucks County relics. No. 5276 (left) was bought July, 1916, among a shed-full of old carpenter's tools, from Miss A. H. Swartz, of Point Pleasant, Pa.

tion of Mr. R. P. Hommel, to the writer in 1924, it is now used at Chang Sei, China. No. 4171 was found in Atlantic City, N. J., No. 5096 in Philadelphia. The other specimens are old Bucks County relics, except No. 19244, which was obtained October 4, 1923, by the Rev. Clarence Hoffman, at Kang Kei, Korea. Here, as in China, fluid black ink contained in the hollow, right side of the apparatus, serves for chalk. The string, fastened to the loose pegs shown, is wound through the ink on the spool (left,) and twanged wet and black, upon the stuff.

Another carpenter's instrument in continual use and of the highest importance, is the

PLUMB LINE (Fig. 55)

to establish vertical lines. When unwound from its ball and suspended from a fixed point, the string ending in a leaden plummet (plumb bob) fixes a true vertical line for the accurate erection of framework, joists, corner overhangs, etc., as described by Moxon in 1678. This applies to vertical construction only, not to the correct horizontal lines, continually needed by the carpenter. For two thousand years these have been established by means of

THE SQUARE (Fig. 56)

the Roman norma, with which straight lines can be scratched or pencilled at right angles to each other or to a fixed margin, provided this

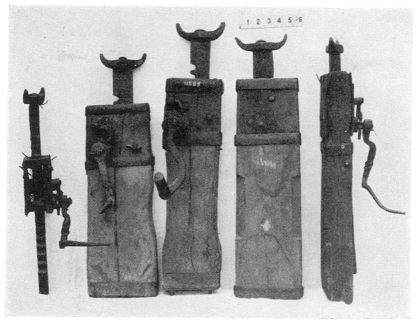

Fig. 53. The Jack

This compact apparatus, boxed in two slabs of hollowed plank, and exactly resembling that illustrated by Moxon in 1678, consists of a crank with a back-stop ratchet, axled on a small, forged cog wheel, engaging a larger, forged, wheel-on-wheel cog wheel, which with overpowering force lifts a vertical, forged, toothed iron bar. The boxes formed by two oaken plank sections, hollowed into troughs, are held together by three rectangular iron sleeves, slipped over and bolted upon them, and also top-faced on both sides with iron plates bolted upon the wheel work.

None of these remarkable old farm relics, obtained between 1897 and 1922, from Bucks, Berks and Montgomery Counties, Pa., are factory made. All their cranks, racks, single and double cog wheels have been hammered out with variations and decorative touches by country blacksmiths. All the specimens show chisel-cut dates on the rack face just below the fork as follows, from left to right: (1) 1807, (2) 1809, with the initials F N, (3) 1790, H. Z., (4) 1800, (5) 1793.

Not only as a carpenter's but as a general mechanic's tool, this ancient, home-made jack survived until the late nineteenth century, on farms, for miscellaneous weight lifting.

ancient instrument is properly placed upon or against the carpenter's work. It here appears in two forms (a) in which one arm much thicker than the other forms a shoulder or fence, intended to be set against the straight side of the stuff, while the thin arm projects at an angle of 90 degrees across its surface; and (b) in which both arms are of equal thickness and the whole instrument may lie flat on the work. We also see that the arms are generally scaled to inches in class

(b) but not so scaled in class (a), and further, that while the instruments of class (b) are all either of iron or wood, some of those in class (a) show a thin iron arm projecting from a thick arm of wood.

This omnipresent and highly important tool is described by *Vitruvius, 7.3,* and *Pliny, 36.51,* and frequently also mentioned in the *Probate Records of Essex County, Massachusetts, 1635-1681, 3 vols., George Francis Dow, editor. Salem, Mass., the Essex Institute,*

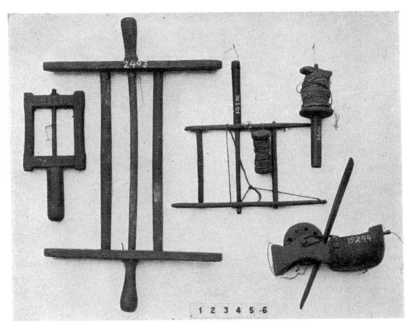

Fig. 54. The Chalk Line

The carpenter's chalk lines as here shown, in the four upper specimens, are wound on home-made spools. When stretched along a log top for pit sawing, or board or balk for ripping, or frame for cross cutting, and whitened by pulling against them a lump of chalk, and twanged, they white-mark the necessary guide line for the cut. The specimens are all old Pennsylvania relics, except No. 19244, which was obtained October 4, 1923, by the Rev. Clarence Hoffman, at Kang Kei, Korea. Here fluid or pith-soaked black ink contained in the hollow, right side of the apparatus, serves for chalk. The string, fastened to its loose peg (shown) is wound through the ink upon the wheel-spool (left), and twanged wet and black (as in China) upon the stuff.

1916-1920. As pictured and explained by Moxon in 1678, the ancient carpenter's square, like some of the old Bucks County specimens here shown, and also like No. 19254, bought by the Rev. Clarence Hoffman at Kang Kei, Korea, in 1923, was thus generally home-made of wood before 1800. Moxon says nothing of metal or half metal (steel or iron) squares, Nos. 19436 and 2514. Neither does Diderot in 1768. But the square melted "at 2 corners" in a thunder storm at Rutland, Mass., in 1732, according to the *Boston News Letter* of July 6 to 13, of that year, must have been home-

made entirely of iron, by a blacksmith. All-steel squares appear in 1813, in *The Circle of Mechanical Arts,* Plate 1, Fig. 9, and as factory-made in the United States in 1834 (imported and domestic, *cf. Bishop,* Vol. 2, p. 389). They were also sold at a store in Wilmington, Del., in 1814 (Tryon, *Household Manufacturers in United States,* p. 271).

Besides this familiar form Diderot shows a makeshift French carpenter's square, not found by the writer, made by sawing out a rectangle in the end of a board, and the noble little masterpiece of unhonored and forgotten scholarship, Rich's *Companion to the Latin Dictionary and Greek Lexicon,* London, 1849, illustrates exactly this latter tool as one form of the Roman norma. All the specimens here shown, except the Korean square No. 19254, bought by Rev. Clarence Hoffman, at Kang Kei, Korea, are old Pennsylvania relics.

Another form of this invaluable instrument is the

MITRE OR MITRE SQUARE (Fig. 57)

A mitred wooden block into which a flat blade is vertically fixed which, when set against a straight edge, throws the unscaled blade for pencilling or scribing at an angle of 45 degrees across the carpenter's work. Since repeated correspondence, searches of shop rubbish and questionings of old carpenters, have failed to find a true example of this now forgotten little tool, we here illustrate it in its old form by a model (middle) from Moxon's picture of 1678. We also photograph from an existing specimen at the Essex Institute, Salem, Mass., a double-armed form of the same tool entirely of wood with its thin arm fixed at the required mitre angle, and finally show the equally effective present form, a common L shaped square in which the end of the thick wooden arm has been mitred at its rectangular junction with its thin steel arm, so that the instrument may be held to line either at 45 or 90 degrees across the work.

But these two angles though the commonest of all, are not enough for the carpenter. Hence the still more effective

BEVEL OR BEVEL SQUARE
(Fig. 58)

in which the thin, movable, unscaled

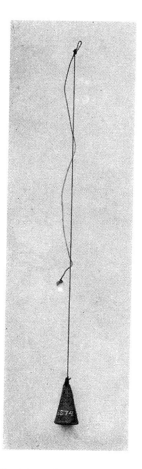

Fig. 55. The Plumb Line

When thus suspended from a fixed point, the string, ending in a leaden plummet, establishes a true vertical line by which the carpenter erects framework, joists, corner overhangs, etc., as described by Moxon in 1678. This specimen, with old home-cast plummet, was bought October, 1897, from Enos B. Loux, of Hilltown, Pa.

wooden arm, here made as Moxon illustrates it, moves stiffly on a rivet in the slotted end of its thick arm. Therefore, when the latter is set against a straight margin, the instrument can throw a line at any desired angle across the wood worked upon.

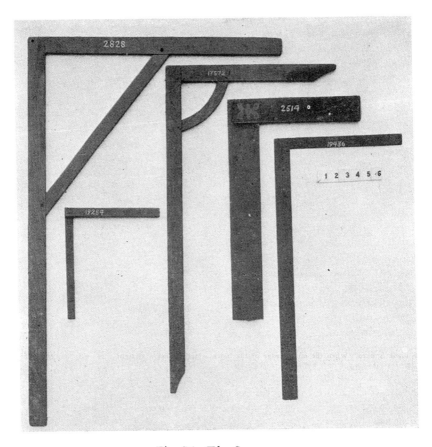

Fig. 56. The Square

The Roman norma, as described by Vitruvius and Pliny. The instrument here appears in two forms, class (a),
No. 2514, with one arm thicker than the other, in which case a straight line can be pencilled with the pencil (Fig.
62) or scratched with the scratch awl (Fig. 61) at right angles to the carpenter's work, along the thin, generally
unscaled instrument, when its thick arm is set against a straight margin. In this specimen, the thin, unscaled arm,
is of iron. In older specimens (not here shown) it appears of wood, and in recent modern examples the iron arm
is sometimes scaled. In the other specimens, class (b), both arms, scaled to inches, etc., are of equal thickness,
when not only the same thing can be done by holding one arm, at a tilt, along the said margin, but also two lines
can be drawn at right angles, following both arms of the instrument laid flat on the work. In older specimens of
class (b), both arms as here shown and as described by Moxon are of wood. In No. 19346, representing nineteenth century examples of this class, both arms are of iron.

The bevel and mitre may yield in
antiquity to the common square, but
the
COMPASS (Figs. 59 A and B)
is the circinus of the Romans. This
widely used, many-sized metal tool, by
no means confined to the carpenter,
consists of two sharp-pointed legs
stiffly hinged together on a rivet at
their tops, so that one loose point may
scratch a circle around the other centred as a pivot. No aesthetic thrill
stirs the modern collector, as he looks
at this little undecorated instrument,

Fig. 57. The Mitre or Mitre Square

For marking woodwork (at a mitre), *i.e.* at an angle of 45 degrees to a fixed margin. The instrument is here shown in three forms.

(*a*) Middle example as illustrated and described by Moxon in 1678, a mitred, wooden block in which a flat, wooden blade is fixed. When the mitred edge of the block is set against a straight edge, the instrument throws the blade for pencilling or scribing at the desired angle of 45 degrees across the carpenter's work. The specimen is shown in a model made from Moxon's description and picture.

(*b*) Left example—a T shaped, old, home-made, all-wood specimen, kindly loaned for illustration by the Essex Institute of Salem, Mass. It shows a thin wooden arm, mortised and pegged into the thick wooden arm at an angle of 45 degrees. The thick arm, just above the hole for suspension, is stamped on both sides with the initials J. L.; also, on the side shown, the marks 3 x 1 x H J S appear on a narrow strip of surface, left slightly above the face level. The Essex Institute has no definite information as to the origin of this old Salem tool.

(*Ac*) Right example—a rectangular factory-made square now (1925) in use in which the thick wooden arm is mitred at its junction with the iron arm.

If in this ingenious modern tool, the thick arm is laid full-length against an established margin, the iron arm casts a right angle—if only the mitred shoulder at the junction is used, it casts a mitre.

hoary with age—one of the "real things that have no show' 'in the large pamphlet *Piccoli Bronzi del Real Museo Borbonico*, Carlo Cici, Napoli, 1858, which pictures it in two specimens in bronze, dug up at Herculaneum. Durer's celebrated engraving, "Melancholia," illustrates it in metal, as does Moxon in 1678, Diderot, for France, in 1768, and *The Circle of Mechanical Arts*, for England, in 1813.

By the kind permission of the Rijks Museum at Amsterdam, we here show it again in metal from a store of tools left more than three hundred years ago (in 1596) on the desolate Island of Nova Zembla, and brought back to Amsterdam in 1885. Some of the other specimens here shown in wood (Fig 59B) were used by Eastern Pennsylvania carpenters in the 18th century, some by Pennsylvania German farmer - carpenters in the last fifty years to decorate wooden barns with ornamental circles, swastikas, etc.

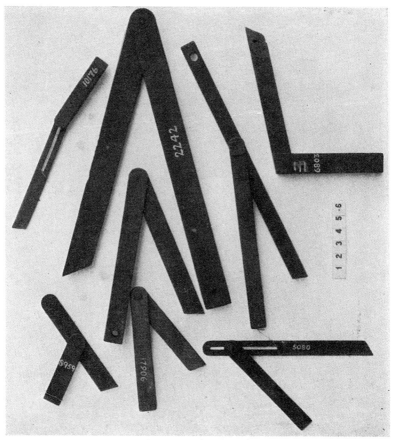

Fig. 58. The Bevel

The thin arm of this old instrument, whether home-made of wood, here shown as Moxon illustrates it, or in its later nineteenth century types (Nos. 10176 and 5080, of iron), whether moving stiffly on rivet, or fixed by a thumb screw, is adjustable to any angle which the carpenter wants, to pencil or scratch along it when he holds the thick arm against the margin of his work.

The next illustration shows

The Gauge (Fig. 60)

for scratching lines spaced from a fixed margin. From one side of one end of a squared stick, upon which a perforated wooden block slides tightly, a little steel point projects. When the block, moved as far as need be from the point, and fixed by a wedge or thumb screw, is held against

and pushed along a straight edge, the down turned point scratches a parallel line at the desired inner distance upon the carpenter's work. The old instruments here shown, one of which, No. 16373 was bought in June, 1919, of John Trumbaur, of Gardenville, Bucks County, Pa., and was used by his father Philip, early in the 19th century, do not differ in construction from the present factory-made tool.

But as the ancient predecessor of the now common carpenter's pencil, another line marking tool has gone out of use in the last twenty years. This is

THE SCRATCH AWL OR SCRIBE AWL OR SCRIBER (Fig. 61)

A thin steel shank with a round point, inserted on a tang in a wooden handle, used not for puncturing wood but for scratching lines established by the rule, square, bevel, etc., on its surface. Whoever confuses it with the brad awl, which superficially resembles it, does not notice or know that its round point will not, like the chisel point of the brad awl, penetrate wood.

The single word "awl," appearing in the *Probate Records of Essex County, Massachusetts, 1635-1681, 3 vols., George Francis Dow, editor. Salem, Mass., the Essex Institute, 1916-1920,* may refer to either this tool or the brad awl. The *New English Dictionary* quotes the first use of "scribe" in 1875. Moxon, who speaks of it as a "pricker" and of scratching lines with the compass point and brad awl, does not take the trouble to describe this special scratching instrument. But at last the word "scratch awl" appears in an American hardware list of 1834—*cf.* Bishop, Vol. 2, p. 88. Today the never well observed tool is obsolete among carpenters in Eastern Pennsylvania, but survives among cabinet-makers. No. 20269 from Clinton County, Pa., obtained January, 1925, by Col. H. W. Shoemaker, was made by the old mountaineer Seth Nelson, Jr., about 1885, by which time

THE CARPENTER'S PENCIL (Fig. 62)

a strip of sawed native black lead, or

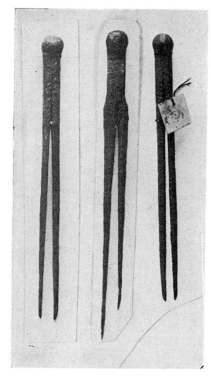

Fig. 59A. The Compass

The three metal specimens (Fig. 59A) of the sixteenth century, now in the Rijks Museum at Amsterdam, were found in 1885, on Nova Zembla, where they had been stored by a Dutch expedition in 1596.

later cast powdered lead, alias plumbago, alias, graphite, glued between two strips of wood, was rapidly taking its place. This latter, now universal marking tool, is here shown in its older unpainted, and its later, after *c.* 1900, painted form. It differs conspicuously in its much larger flat lead and broad flat stick, from the common small, round, lead pencil, which must have preceded it; *cf. New English Dictionary,* 1612 and 1683, also *Complete Dictionary of Arts and Sciences,* 1764, and Rees, *c.* 1800.

In an old inventory of 1677 in the

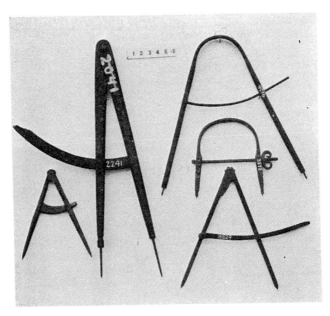

Fig. 59B. The Compass

The circinus of the Romans. Besides its chief purposes in scratching circles and spacing geometrical patterns, etc., the compass is used to close-fit irregular board margins by "scribing" them. In the latter case, one point of the partially opened tool, held close to and pulled along the rough or waved margin, follows its irregularities, while the other point scratches (scribes) a duplicate, waved line on the close-pushed board. When worked down to this line the board must fit the crooked margin.

The wooden compasses (Fig. 59B), adjustable on sliding arms, are old Bucks County and eastern Pennsylvania specimens. They are often found on farms as heir'ooms of farmer-carpenters, and are sometimes still used by the latter, if Pennsylvania Germans, to outline the decorative painted circles, stars, swastikas, etc., conspicuous since the mid-nineteenth century on their wooden barn fronts.

Among these, No. 16565 (lower left), presented by Dr. B. F. Fackenthal, Jr., was bought at the sale of George W. Laubach, 88 years old, in 1919, at Riegelsville, Pa.

Probate Records of Essex County, Mass., 1635-1681, vol. 2, the words "27 pensills at 8 d. p .doz.—1 s. 6 d.," seem to refer to it. Nevertheless, Moxon does not mention it. It appears in the *American Hardware List* of 1834, above noted, as of domestic and imported make (Bishop, Vol. 2, p. 388), and must have gradually thereafter rivalled without ousting the scratch awl. Lewis Treffinger, a carpenter of Doylestown, Pa., informed the writer in April, 1925, that his father, a carpenter in the 1880's, refused to replace his scratch awl with the pencil, and we learn from David Angeny, carpen-

ter, of Danboro, Pa. (1925) that because the older unpainted pencils were easily lost in the shavings and litter of carpenter's shop, the present brightly painted instrument, gradually replaced the paintless in the 1890's.

Another now very familiar instrument of the wood-worker is

THE RULE (Fig. 63)

a pocket instrument scaled in inches, half inches, quarters, and eighths, which, though in general use among mechanics, was and is incessantly employed by the carpenter for measuring and line ruling his work. Moxon in

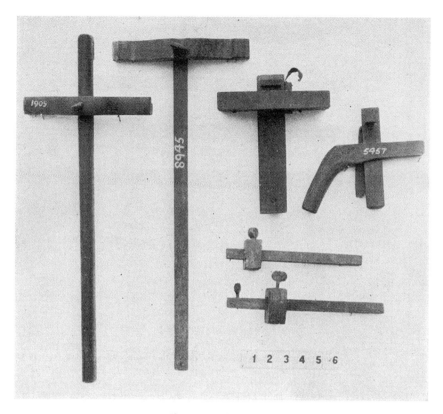

Fig. 60. The Gauge

When this block or strip, adjustable by a thumb screw and sliding back and forth on a square stick, is held against an established margin, an iron pin set at the end of the stick scratches a line parallel to said margin on the carpenter's work. It is often used to mark mortise holes. These wooden tools are all home-made and represent the pre-factory (c. 1840) period. In all, the block is fixed by a thumb screw of brass (left) or of iron (lower right), otherwise of wood, except in the two upper right specimens, in which it is tightened, as Moxon describes, with a wedge. Sometimes the blocks are round or oval. No. 5457, included by mistake, is not a gauge, but a knife,shiftable by a wedge, probably used for slicing leather.

1678 illustrates it in its old form as a single foot-long stick; *The Circle of Mechanical Arts* in 1813, as brass tipped and brass hinged in two six inch arms; and the evidence shows that the present factory-made joint rule of box or hard wood, 24 inches long, in four folding, brass-tipped arms, at first imported and later American made, appeared about 1840.

Besides this tool the carpenter continually makes for himself now, as he did in Colonial times, a thin wooden strip for long measurements notched or marked into ten foot long divisions, not here shown, called

The Ten Foot Rule

described but not illustrated by Moxon.

This brings us to another instrument which, if not more important, is

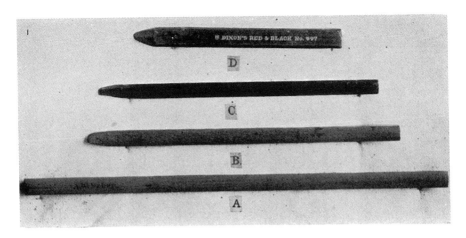

Fig. 62. The Carpenter's Pencil

A strip of sawed native, or later cast, block lead, alias plumbago, alias graphite, glued between two strips of wood.

*Fig. 61. The Scratch Awl or Scribe
Awl or Scribe*

As the ancient predecessor of the carpenter's pencil, this now obsolete, thin, steel shank, inserted on a tang, in a wooden handle, which but for its round point resembles the brad awl, was used for scratching lines,

established by the rule, square, bevel, etc., on wood work, until the mid-nineteenth century, after which, except rarely with cabinetmakers, the pencil superseded it.

(A) kindly loaned for this illustration by the Essex Institute, of Salem, Mass., Museum No. 108860, blue stamped "A. W. Faber," on one side, with the red stamped words "Bleistift Manufactur" on the other side, here shows the carpenter's pencil in its early, unpainted, imported German form.

(B) also unpainted, marked "Eagle, pat. 1862-1867-1876" is from Manheim, Pa.

(C) varnished, stamped, "Eagle, pat. Apr. 3, 1860," was found *c.* 1914, in an old workshop at 2512 N. Hancock St., Philadelphia, Pa.

(D) painted red with black corners, stamped in reverse "E. W. Foster, Frankford Avenue, Philadelphia."

The dictionaries do not tell us when the lead pencil was first specially made for carpenters' use, but only that the modern lead pencil, in general, was first made of sawed strips of native graphite from the Borrowdale (Cumberland, England) mines, discovered 1664 and exhausted *c.* 1850. That the cast graphite, powder-mixed-with-clay-process, discovered by Conté in 1795, revolutionized the industry. That the Fabers started pencil manufacturing at Nuremberg and vicinity in 1760, and in 1847 began the use of Siberian graphite at the Bogodolsk mine in Eastern Siberia, some of which raw material was sawed native. That Faber founded a branch in New York in 1861, after which the Eagle and American Pencil Cos., were established in 1865, and the Dixon Co. in 1872.

certainly far more ingenious than the rule, namely

THE LEVEL (Fig. 64)

all the more interesting because, as the libella of the Romans, it is one of those tools which maintained their ancient form for two thousand years and then suddenly changed it when the so called "Industrial Revolution" modernized industries in the 19th century.

When this home-made semi-circle is set upright on a piece of carpenter's work, so that the string on its leaden plummet, suspended from its top centre, coincides with a vertical line or crack marked on its centre piece, the work is level. From two to ten feet long, these primeval tools vary in construction as semicircles or triangles, or L's or T's. As illustrated by Moxon they exactly resemble the Roman libella of Lucretius, Pliny and Varro, and must have been universally used by carpenters throughout the Middle Ages. They survived, as above noted, until early in the 19th century, when the spirit level (Figure 66, cf. Rees) was at last sufficiently cheapened by factories to take their place. The specimen shown was presented August 1, 1924, by Howard Cope, of Sellersville, and had been sold by his father's estate, after the latter's death about 1915. Another example of the same tool appears in

THE LEVEL (Fig. 65)

which in the form of a wooden T differs in shape, but not in principle, from the preceding. It was bought from Miss A. H. Swartz, Point Pleasant, Bucks County, Pa., in 1916, and was found among her father's old shop

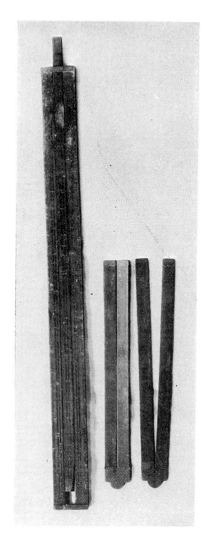

Fig. 63. The Carpenter's Rule

In the seventeenth century, a flat, home-made, straight-edged wooden strip, either one or two feet long, scaled to inches, halves, quarters and eighths. Factory-made in the nineteenth century, it became hinged, first in two, and later, as now, into four brass-tipped, box-wood sections.

The two twelve-inch long (when extended), double-armed specimens, kindly loaned for this illustration by David Angeny, carpenter, of Danboro, Bucks Co., Pa., are still in use by him. The rule at the left, with a central sliding arm, extensible to twenty-four inches, is an eccentric American instrument, not typical of its class and without record in the Museum.

Fig. 64. The Level

The libella of the Romans, the predecessor, before *c.* 1830-1840, of the present carpenter's spirit level. When the suspended string with its leaden plummet, of this home-made, wooden semi-circle set upright on a piece of carpenter's work, coincides with a vertical line or crack marked on its cross piece, above the swing-hole, the work is level. These home-made instruments, in universal use in the eighteenth century, from two to ten feet long, vary in construction as triangles or L's or T's.

This specimen, No. 19469, was presented to the Museum of The Bucks County Historical Society, August 1, 1924, by Howard Cope, of Sellersville, Bucks Co., Pa. It was sold by his father's estate after the latter's death about 1915, and later repurchased by Howard Cope to present to the Museum. Pointed wood screws used in its construction date it after 1846.

relics. Long before this, as above noted, it and its predecessor (Fig. 64) had been superseded by the

SPIRIT LEVEL (Fig. 66)

This is a glass tube partly filled with spirits (alcohol) set horizontally in a strip of wood, which, if laid on the carpenter's work, levels the latter when the confined bubble rests at the marked middle of the tube. Delicate, expensive, and at first somewhat inaccurate, the device, invented as before mentioned, according to Rees, by Thevenot in 1666, or Dr. Hooke, *c.* 1680, and sometimes used in the 18th century by surveyors, etc., is not classed as a carpenter's tool by Rees, *c.* 1800, and not illustrated as such by *The Circle of Mechanical Arts* in 1813, which shows only the old plumb level (*see* Fig. 62). Moreover, as the very exact making, filling, sealing and setting of its glass tube put it beyond the

home craft of the carpenter, the evidence shows that it was factory made from the start and not adopted by carpenters until its manufacture had been, as above noted, simplified and cheapened by factories in the middle 19th century.

At this point two makeshift levelling instruments, not here illustrated, ought to be described, namely,

THE STRAIGHT EDGE

a long narrow board, still continually used, with one level-planed edge, or with its two straight planed edges exactly parallel, used to ascertain surface irregularities, establish elevations from point to point, and to project the line of the carpenter's level set upon or under it, and

THE TRYING STICKS

two or more, now obsolete, smaller, shorter, makeshift strips, similarly double straight-edged, used as Rees

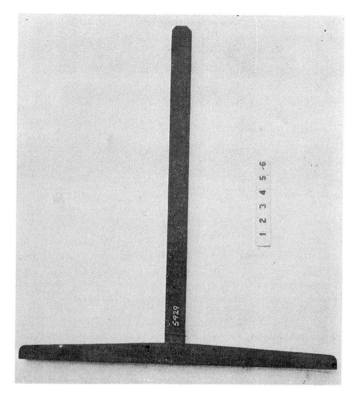

Fig. 65. The Level

In this old Bucks County specimen, No. 5429, which differs in shape, but not in principle, from the preceding, the plummet is suspended from the top of the vertical arm. It was bought in 1916, from Miss A. H. Swartz, of Point Pleasant, Bucks Co., Pa., when found in an old carpenter and wheelwright shop among the many obsolete tools of her deceased father.

describes, as sights, to detect the so-called "windings," namely twists, warpings, etc., on supposed levels, for which purpose they were laid parallel at several feet apart, across planed board surfaces, and top-sighted by the carpenter.

This brings us to the end of a group of tools here classed as devoted to the measuring and adjustment of the carpenter's work, which though insignificant in appearance, are most important in fact, and appear everywhere about a carpenter's shop and bench, stock his chest, and follow his work from one end of a new building to another.

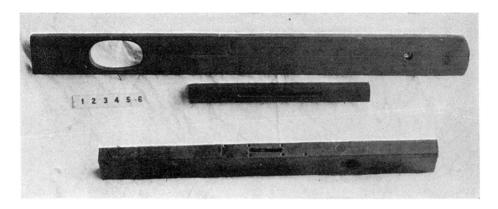

Fig. 66. The Spirit Level

A glass tube partly filled with spirits (alcohol) is set lengthwise on the narrow side of a long strip of wood. When the strip is laid edgewise, horizontally on the carpenter's work, and the confined bubble rests at the marked middle of the tube, the work is level. The lower brass-mounted specimen is a factory-made instrument, about fifty years old, kindly loaned for the illustration and now in use (1925) by Lewis Treffinger, carpenter of Doylestown, Pa.

The very interesting, apparently home-made small level (middle), kindly loaned by the Essex Institute, Salem, Mass., Museum No. 101227, entirely lacking marks or mid-score, consists of a glass tube, now dry, showing the remains of an enclosed red fluid. The tube is tightly inserted in a top slot, here turned sideways to be seen, in a 15 in. by 1⅜ by 1⅜ in. strip of dark, heavy wood. The glass, deeply underset in the slot at either end, contains a loose, black plug, apparently tipped with red sealing wax. It came from an old house in East Lexington, Mass., belonging to Miss Ellen M. Stone, there found with a store of old household relics. If the instrument is a carpenter's level at all, it probably represents an early 19th century experimental attempt to produce the tool.

The upper specimen with a bubble glass, faintly seen, inserted on its narrow side, shows on its wide face a centered, vertical scratch above a swing-hole to clear the plummet, and ending in a notch for the string. Hence the instrument is a spirit level, if held horizontally, if vertically, a plumb level. A brass plate over the bubble glass, loaned for the illustration by Mr. H. M. Mann, of Doylestown. It was found at No. 2512 N. Hancock St., Philadelphia, among a store of old inherited tools, probably bought about 1875. According to information just received from Mr. S. Horace Disston of the firm of Henry Disston and Sons of Philadelphia, the level is a bricklayer's level, "not used by the carpenter at all," and must have been made by his firm, then under the name of Disston and Morss, between 1868 and 1901.

Tools for Holding and Gripping

EXCEPT that the old wooden square of Moxon turned to iron in the 18th century, that the carpenter's rule multiplied its joints, that the pencil largely replaced the scribe, and above all that the ancient level, the Roman libella, gave way to the spirit level about 1830, no great change has taken place in these measuring and marking tools in two hundred years. But the same thing may not be said of the tools for holding and gripping the carpenter's material, among which the following most important four have slowly varied their shape or fallen out of use in the late 19th century, beginning with the ancient

WORK BENCH (Fig. 67)

here shown from one of Moxon's illustrations.

Unfortunately the writer has been unable to find an example of one of these now obsolete benches, common towards the middle of the 19th century, until superseded in Eastern Pennsylvania by the sliding catch bench shown in Figure 70.

But in Moxon's celebrated picture of 1678 from *Mechanick Exercises,* 1703 edition, Plate 4, here reproduced, probably the earliest known systematic grouped illustration of English carpenter's tools, the old work bench is shown in the upper right corner. It consists of a waist high table for the standing workman and is equipped with the wooden vise

(right), never projecting above the bench top, namely, two turn screws which compress or release a wooden jaw against the bench corner; and the peg holes in the left bench leg, by which the opposite end of the board, held sideways in the vise, is supported at a desired level on adjustable pegs.

Look at the two little instruments driven into the table top. For two hundred years at least, next to the vise, they (namely, the hold fast and catch) were the chief characteristics of the apparatus.

THE HOLD FAST (Fig. 68)

is a stout angle of iron flattened on the inside of its short arm. When its long arm is driven loose into a hole on the bench top, it binds upon the hole, and squeezes fast the board or stuff thrust under its projecting upper arm. But as the instrument, described and illustrated by Moxon, does not, like the catch, clear the top of the work, it was used rather for sawing, tenoning or mortising, than planing. The sliding catch bench (shown in Figure 70) gradually displaced it in Pennsylvania in the 19th century. No. 5533 is an old shop relic, bought in 1916, from Miss Mary H. Swartz of Point Pleasant, Pa.

In the next picture we see

THE CATCH (Fig. 69)

here photographed exactly as pictured by Moxon; an adjustable iron plug, topped with a flaring, saw-toothed, over-bent lip, which is fixed into a hole at one end of the bench top, so as to

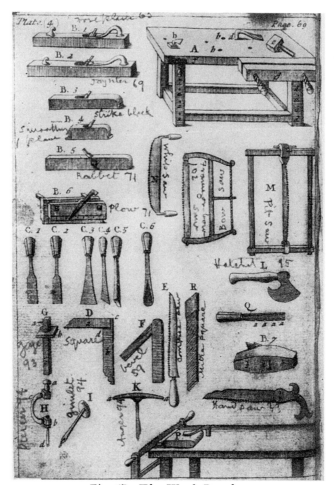

Fig. 67. The Work Bench

The now obselete, ancient carpenter's work bench, as described in the text, is here seen, upper right corner, from Moxon's unique picture of carpenter's tools, in his *Mechanik Exercises*, edition 1703, plate 4. Driven into the bench top, (d) shows the hold fast (Fig. 68), and (b) catch (Fig. 69) holes for adjusting which (bb) with the peg holes in the bench legs, for holding up the end of the side-clamped board, also appear; (g) at the right hand corner is the vise.

Unfortunately Moxon does not tell us how this old vise, "bench screw" as he calls it, was constructed. But Charles Holtzapffel, in his *Turning and Mechanical Manipulations*, London, 1846, Vol. 2, p. 494, with Roman brevity describes a similar apparatus as a thick strip of plank—a chop block, fixed horizontally by two wooden hand screws against the top outer corner of the bench, forming a jaw, with its chops turned sidewise to the bench-front, which jaw shuts or opens by the right or left turn of the hand screws. As these hand screws, here shown, ending in simple hand grasps, are only threaded where they penetrate the fixed bench side, and turn loosely in the chop block, they would only loosen and not pull back (open) the latter, if one of them were not ingeniously keyed to the said chop block, by a so-called garter, namely, a wooden strip ending in a round notch, mortised through the chop block, so as to engage a circular groove in the unthreaded, loose-turning neck of the screw, and so pull out the chop block on a back twist of the handle. Another little one-screw vise, which Moxon does not refer to, dimly appears on the left corner of the bench top.

That this, the old form of carpenter's bench, had not yet gone out of use in England in 1846, appears by inference from Holtzapffel's further observations.

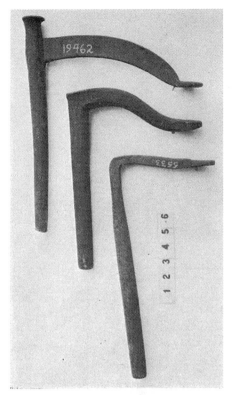

Fig. 69. The Catch

A small, flaring-toothed blade of iron, also illustrated by Moxon, mounted on a vertical, square shank, which, driven tight and deep into a bench-top hole, nips the under side, while clearing the top of a board pushed flat against it for planing.

According to Holtzapffel, above cited, where its iron teeth might injure fine work, the catch, or "bench hook," as he calls it, was replaced by a square wooden plug.

Not shown here, but as figured in Knight's *American Mechanical Dictionary* (ed. 1876), cf. "Bench Clamp," a common, modern makeshift device for catching boards set on edge, so as to plane their top edge, is a sawed, wooden notch, nailed on the bench top, into which notch, the under edge of the board is slid and wedged. Charles Holtzapffel in *Mechanical Manipulations* (ed. 1846), Vol. 2, p. 980, illustrates this later device, as invented by Mr. S. Nicholls of England, who was rewarded for it by the Society of Arts in 1843.

Fig. 68. The Hold Fast

An L-shaped iron, illustrated by Moxon (*cf.* Fig. 67) which dropped into a hole on the bench top, and hammered down upon a board-end thrust under it, by side pressure of its vertical arm in the hole, squeezes tight the board or stuff, though without clearing its top. Hence it is adapted for chiseling, mortising, etc., rather than for planing.

The upper specimen is from Berks County, Pa.; the others were found in 1916, in Miss Mary H. Swartz's remarkable store of shop relics, previously noted, at Point Pleasant, Bucks Co., Pa.

CARPENTER'S SLIDING CATCH BENCH
(Fig. 70)

project about half an inch above it. It thus catches, near its under edge, the board or stuff slid against it and so resists the regular forward push of the workman's plane.

But today (1925) the hold fast and catch are superannuated shop relics, almost forgotten and very hard to find, for, superseding them, as previously noted, the later

had appeared in Eastern Pennsylvania in the middle and late 19th century. The specimen here illustrated was photographed, August, 1925, in the workshop of David Angeny, in Danboro, Bucks County, Pa. It shows as surviving features of the older bench (Figure 67) the ancient vise (left), the peg holes, thirty-three of them, no longer in the bench leg, but in a more adaptable b o a r d sliding in the grooved frame along the bench front, and (right corner) as its modern characteristic, the sliding catch, a wooden

Fig. 70. Modern Carpenter's Bench and Vise

This bench, as described in the text, superseded the old bench (Fig. 67) in the early nineteenth century and is still in use in eastern Pennsylvania. Here the wooden bench-saw or vise, unlike Moxon's in Fig. 67, is set vertically, but does not project (like the wheelwright's vise) above the bench top. It is equipped with a turn screw, which by the right or left twist of a handle, freely sliding in a hole at its enlarged outer end, opens or shuts against the bench leg a heavy, top-rounded plank section forming the jaw or chop block of the vise. By no means as simple as it looks, this turnscrew is threaded where it enters the bench leg, but not threaded and turns loose at its neck where it penetrates the chop block, hence, at this latter point, the screw is ingeniously "keyed" to the chop block, as in Moxon's vise (Fig. 67) by a wooden strip called a garter, round-notched at its inner end, which, penetrating a square mortise in the chop block, engages a groove in the unthreaded screw neck. As a result, a back turn of the screw not only loosen but pulls open the jaw of the vise. It further appears that because an object pinched above the screw would push the chop block outward at its top and hence inward at its bottom, so as to bind the screw, another equipment is necessary. This is a long, thin, wooden strip, punctured with peg holes, extending at right angles from the bottom of the chop block. It slides loosely into a slot in the bench leg and can be pegged outside the latter to stop the obstructive bottom inpush of the chop block.

Whoever breaks up a carpenter's vise to discover the secret of its concealed garter, or examines or uses it long enough to understand the purpose of this perforated arm, will excuse this lengthy description.

So much for the vise, the peg holes for which, *ie.* for holding up the board-end clamped in it, are faintly seen in the sliding board pushed against the right leg. As distinguished from the vise, the box turn-screw is seen screwed tight into place on the right corner. The chief purpose of this apparatus, *ie.* to grip a flat-laid board at both ends, appears in the square-shanked, rough-faced catch pin, which protrudes from a square hole on its top, to nip the underside of said board, and which catch pin can be raised or depressed for the purpose on a compressible side spring. Its duplicate catch pin appears at the left end of the row of square catch-pin holes along the front bench margin.

No holes for the old hold fast (Fig. 68) or old catch (Fig. 69) appear on the bench top. Holtzapffel, as noted, illustrates and describes the main features of this bench in *Turning and Mechanical Manipulations,* Vol. 2, p. 494, copied by Knight's *American Mechanical Dictionary, cf.* bench. His statement that in his time there were other bench constructions, some of which retained the old hold fast and catch, and were not equipped with this sliding-catch apparatus at all, proves tht Moxon's bench (Fig. 67) had not yet gone out of use in 1846.

turn screw, enclosed in a box, mounted with an iron catch pin. This latter catch pin which takes the place of the old catch (Figure 69) is square and raised or lowered in its square hole on a compressible steel spring. By turning the screw the box, with this, its top catch pin, is approached or withdrawn from a duplicate catch pin, adjustable in the row of holes along the bench edge, so as to nip, at both ends, the under sides of a board laid flat in the interval. Notice carefully this latter apparatus, which gripped

the board both ways and in all cases
cleared its top, for it is this which did
away, as noted, not only with the old
catch (Figure 69), but also with the
hold fast (Figure 68), no holes for
which here show in the bench top.

Look next at another ancient tool
used upon, though not attached to the
bench, namely

THE SIDE REST (Fig. 71)

a short, makeshift board, sawed into
opposing shoulders, for cross-sawing
boards and mouldings, etc., when laid
flat along the outer edge of the work
bench. It is here shown exactly as
Moxon illustrates it about two hundred and fifty years ago, and as
Diderot shows it in 1768. The board
has been cut down on either broad
side, so as to leave projecting, square
offsets at either end, and when set at
right angles to the edge of the bench
top, with one of its offsets turned
down outside and pushed against the
corner, and the other offset turned up,
forms a stop or catch, against which,
when a second board or side rest, so
set at a proper distance from the first
is used, a piece of long stuff laid from
rest to rest, parallel to the bench corner and pressed down and forward by
the carpenter's left hand, can be cross-
sawed without scoring the bench. No.
6668 is an old shop relic from Lancaster, Pa. The other specimens are
from Bucks County.

Without a carpenter's explanation
it is hard to grasp the purpose of the
side rest, but anybody can understand

THE CLAMP (Fig. 72)

a still familiar and variously adjustable apparatus, by which, where a

Fig. 71. The Side Rest

Is a short, makeshift board sawed into opposite
shoulders, which, when spaced apart from a duplicate
side rest, and pushed with its under shoulder against
the top, front edge of the bench, catches a board laid
flat upon it, and from it to its companion. When thus
placed and pushed against the two upper back shoulders
of the two side rests, the board is lifted and held off
the bench top for convenient bisection with the saw.
This ancient tool is still found necessary by the
carpenter. The middle specimen, bought October, 1916,
of Amos Scheetz, farmer-carpenter, near the Irish
Meeting House, Bucks Co., Pa., had been used by him
in the late nineteenth century. No. 5450 came from
Miss Swartz's store of a carpenter relics at Point
Pleasant. No. 6668 came from Lancaster, Pa.

fixed vise will not reach, two wooden
arms tightened by two wooden hand
screws, hold fast the carpenter's or
cabinetmaker's material for various
purposes, but chiefly for glueing.

Another variety of this instrument
is shown in

THE CLAMP (Fig. 73)

where the wooden hand-screw penetrating a block, fixed at the end of a
long strip perforated for pegs, holds
fast an object on the strip by forcing
it against an inserted peg. And a third
form appears in

Fig. 72. The Clamp

Two wooden arms, tightened by two wooden hand-screws, hold fast the carpenter's or cabinet maker's material for various purposes, but chiefly for glueing. The threads of one screw, *i. e.* that in the middle of the apparatus, turn loosely in an enlarged, smooth hole in the arm nearest its handle, and only engage the opposite arm. Hence this screw pulls the arms together at their jaws. The other screw only engages the arm next its handle, and loosely meets a shallow socket in the opposite arm; hence it pushes the arms apart, at their rear end where it works, but since the centre screw acts as a fulcrum, this end screw, by leverage, forces them still tighter together at their other or jaw end.

Both screws, therefore, help to tighten the clutch, and in working them they should be turned together, keeping the arms reasonably parallel to prevent binding. Both specimens were obtained (1922) from George Reed, at Castle Valley Mill, Bucks Co., Pa.

THE CLAMP (Fig. 74)

consisting of two stout strips loosely tenoned together forming two rectangular openings in which inserted material is compressed by a single hand screw.

The next illustration, resembling a miniature turning lathe,

THE TOOL HANDLE CLAMP (Fig. 75) shows a much rarer variety of the device.

In this, two posts, one of which sometimes slides in a slot, and is fixable by a wedge, rise vertically from a stout wooden strip. Both posts are mounted at their tops with iron pivot-points, one of which, in the left post, terminates a hand screw. When the instrument is fixed in a carpenter's vise, a stick set longitudinally and screwed tight on the pivots, can be twisted about by the workman, as he rounds it into a tool handle with the draw knife. The apparatus might be mistaken for a carpenter's version of the small portable hand lathe, turned with a bow by metal workers, and described by Moxon as the *Turn Bench*. But the evidence shows that numerous examples of it found by the writer were not used by carpenters as makeshift turning lathes, but as described.

Another ancient holding tool illustrated by Moxon, which survived longer than the hold fast and catch, but which now (1925), has almost entirely gone out of use in Eastern Pennsylvania, is

THE HOOK (Fig. 76)

a stout, variously-sized pin, first of iron, and later a makeshift of wood, as here shown, loosened by up-hammering its figure 4 top, used for the preliminary or test-pegging together, of wooden framework, through junction peg holes, before final wood pegging. To conclude our examination of tools of this class, look at the

DOGS (Fig. 77)

here shown, namely the heavy iron staples, often hinged, used for centuries to hold logs or balks in place, as previously described in saw mills, or over saw pits, but also sometimes by the carpenter for log hewing, when the log was not heavy enough to lie still of its own weight.

In that case the light rafter, or bracket, or post, or brace, often hand hewn until the late 19th century, in framing Pennsylvania barns, was laid like the heavier rafter-log upon blocks or cross pieces placed at right angles under it upon the ground. The dog was either (*a*) a heavy solid iron staple, with its wedge-shaped spurs (Fig. 77, No. 5836) or (*b*) a spike with a similarly spurred arm hinged upon it (ditto No. 3617). In the first case, one spur of the staple was driven into the underplaced cross piece, and the other at an upward tilt into the log side. In the second, the spike was driven into the under piece, and the spur lifted up, and driven down into the log as before. A single dog sufficed

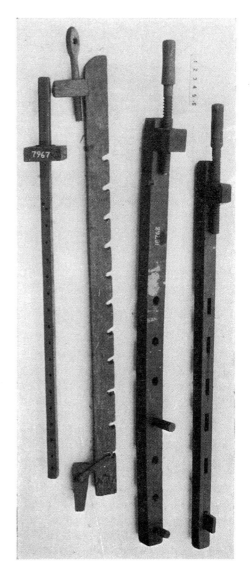

Fig. 73. The Clamp

The wooden hand-screw penetrating a block fixed at the end of a long strip, which latter is perforated for pegs, or notched for a sliding block, holds fast an object on the strip by forcing it against the inserted peg or adjustable block.

In the left clamp, No. 7967, the sliding hand-pushed block is fixed by a thumb-screw not seen.

The specimens are old Bucks County relics of the nineteenth century.

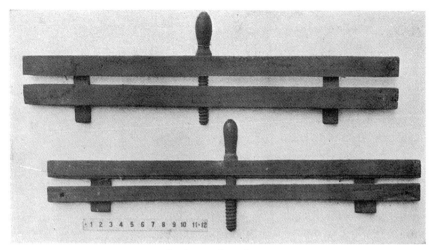

Fig. 74. The Clamp

In this old nineteenth century apparatus two stout strips opening and closing upon each other by a hand-screw, are kept parallel by two tenons projecting downward from the upper strip through loose mortise holes in the lower strip. The wooden home-turned screw-threads only engage the lower strip, and turn free in a large unthreaded hole in the upper strip.

for the hewing operation in both cases. But because the lighter timbers for barn framework were more and more often supplied, ready cut, by the saw mills, and because therefore the carpenter more and more generally confined his hewing operation to heavy rafters, etc., which required no dogs, his modern successors have almost forgotten the use of these instruments. Nevertheless, evidence gathered with difficulty, clearly proves that he used them whenever thus needed in the early 19th century, and that after his need for them ceased, the farmer so continually employed the spurred variety for hewing the posts for the increasingly popular post and rail fence, that the instruments thenceforth became as now, only known as "post dogs." There can be little doubt that these tools, particularly the solid stapled variety, resemble the dogs which Charles Holtzapffel says were used by the pit sawyers to hold fast their logs upon the sawing trestles, or over the old saw pits, while a letter from Mr. R. P. Hommel, July 15, 1924, informed the writer that the Chinese board sawyers in the Kiang Sei province, then, using framed pit saws (*cf.* Fig. 26) upon trestles, not shown in the picture, employed a similar solid wedge-pointed staple, with arms set at right angles to each other, for the same purpose.

The *Theatrum Machinarum Novum* by George Andreas Bockler, Cologne, 1662, shows the solid double spurred staple (Fig. 77, No. 5836) driven at a tilt from the log carriage to the log, in German water-run saw mills, of the 17th century. On the other hand we find that the instrument has been transformed in the 19th century Pennsylvania saw mills into the variety shown in Figure 77, (second specimen down from right,) in which

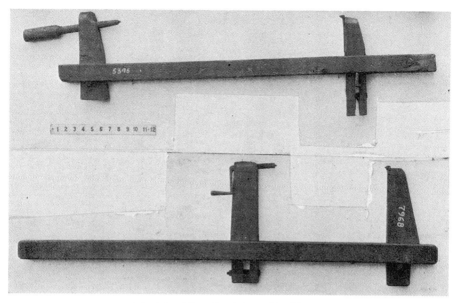

Fig. 75. The Tool Handle Clamp

As described in the text, this apparatus no longer holds the object—a single wooden stick—in a fixed position but, as in the lathe, pivoted between two points, one of which is set upon a handscrew. When tightened thereby, the stick revolves conveniently in the workman's hand, while he rounds it into a tool-handle with the draw knife. (Information June, 1925, of Charles Snyder, carpenter and mechanic, of Plumstead township, Bucks Co., Penna., derived from his own still used specimens, inherited from his father a carpenter of the middle nineteenth century.)

one arm of the instrument is no longer a spur, but a round blunt elbow, at right angles to the spur, which latter when pushed into a hole in the tail block of the log carriage, forms a hinged spike which fixes the log on its side, close to its end, while the double spurred staple is now only retained as described in the label, for straight edging bark-edged board slabs with the mill saw.

Having examined the dogs, look finally at

THE MITRE BOX (Fig. 78)

which in construction closely resembles that illustrated by Moxon and is still in universal use among carpenters, as it has been since the 17th century. The piece of stuff, moulding, picture frame, etc., is laid in the trough, held firmly against the side, and the saw, namely the rigid mitre or tenant saw (for fine work) is drawn through one of the transverse 45 degree saw cuts in the trough. Two operations on two pieces at two reversed angles produce two mitre strips, which fit at right angles.

From a world wide point of view, and compared with some of the master tools previously noticed, the last class of instruments here described, might seem of secondary importance, until attempting to experiment in carpenter work, we try to get along without them, or on realizing the necessity of devices of this kind, for holding

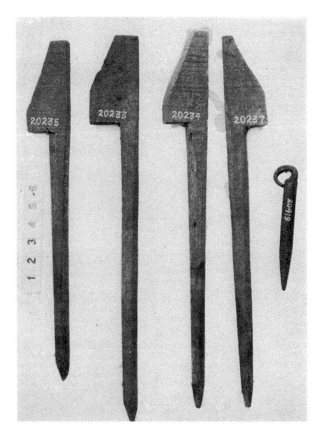

Fig. 76. The Hook Pin or Drift Hook

This ancient tool, here appearing as a makeshift of wood, loosened by up-hammering its figure 4 top, was used for the preliminary or test-pegging together of wooden framework, through the peg holes in the latter, before final wood-pegging. It was preceded, in the nineteenth century, by a similar instrument, variously sized, of iron, as illustrated by Moxon. (See *Mechanick Exercises*, plate 8.F.)

The four wooden specimens presented to the Museum in 1924, by Lewis Treffinger, carpenter, of Doylestown, were made by him from an oak plank about 1905.

The small, iron hook pin, lacking the characteristic figure 4 top, was obtained in 1925, by Col. H. W. Shoemaker. It was made by Seth Nelson, mountaineer-artificer, of Round Island, Clinton Co., Pa., about 1880.

fast the material worked upon, we seek to trace their history or compare them with similar inventions used in other parts of the world. Who has seen or cited the authorities that will enable us to follow back the work bench into the Middle Ages, date the origin of the hold fast or catch, or explain how the Chinese, who appear to be ignorant of the use of the screw, supply themselves with the vise and clamp?

Beyond the mining tools shown in the famous work of Georgius Agricola, (*De Re Metallica*, Basel, 1556, translated by Herbert Clark Hoover, London; *The Mining Magazine*, Salisbury House, 1912); the milling apparatus

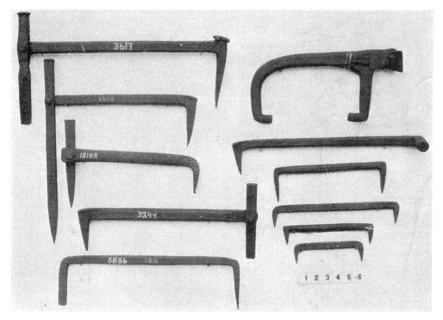

Fig. 77. Dogs

The five wrought-iron instruments on the left, four of which are equipped with spurred arms, hinged on spikes, are hewing dogs. When the piece to be hewn is laid at right angles across two underplaced supporting timbers, the workman uplifting the hinged arm, drives the vertical spike into one of the underplaced timbers. He next drives the overhanging spur into the top or side of the cross-laid upper piece to be worked upon. Whereupon, standing astride or at the side of the latter, thus dogged, he hews it with his broad axe away from the dog. The bottom staple-shaped specimen, minus the hinge, if driven in at an up tilt, serves the same purpose.

The tools are now known as "post dogs," because, until c. 1905, very commonly used by farmers for hewing fence posts when a single dog at the post-butt, sufficed to hold the otherwise shaky post. They were also used until c. 1860-70, by country carpenters for hewing barn and house beams, rafters, braces, etc., too light to lie steady by their own weight under the broad axe. (Information of Ely T. Utz, carpenter, of Telford, Bucks Co., Pa., to the writer June, 1925.) Harvey Johnson of Doylestown, also informs the writer that he saw carpenters hewing barn timbers with dogs like these, near Hinkletown, Bucks Co., Pa., about 1886. But the modern carpenter, abundantly supplied with mill-sawed lumber, and who now no longer hews beams, has discarded and almost forgotten these tools of his ancestors.

The spur points of hewing dogs are never round but always wedge-shaped and set at right-angles to their arms, so as to enter the hewn log with the grain.

The spike points, as here shown, are sometimes round, sometimes wedge-shaped, and in the latter case, always set parallel with the arm of the instrument, and at right-angles to the spur point, so as similarly to enter the under-placed log with the grain.

The right specimens are all saw mill dogs. No. 1 (top, badly shown) is a spurred bracket hinged on its two hinge hooks (through two ringed bolts not shown) at the inner shoulder or log-rest of the head block of the log carriage, so as to turn against, spur fast, and so steady, the vertical face of the log-end close to the saw. (See the specimen at H. Fig. 29.) No. 2 is an adjustable, spurred arm ending in a round right-angled elbow. It steadies the log-end resting on the tail-block, when, by means of the round elbow, pushed into one of the holes in the vertical face of the log rest, and acting as a hinge, the instrument is swung over and spurred into the log-side. (See the faintly visible specimen in place, and the holes for its insertion, in Fig. 30.)

The lower four, staple-shaped dogs were used at old water power sawmills to straight-edge the bark-margined boards or planks, sawed off the four rounded sides of a log, during its preliminary squaring into a rectangular balk. For this purpose the bark-rimmed board is laid flat upon the balk-top, so that its bark-edge overlaps the next pro-posed cut. Whereupon the board is stapled fast to the balk at either end, by one of these dogs spurred into the board-end and balk face. When the saw then starts again, it bisects the balk and trims the board at a single cut. All the latter (right) six, sawmill dogs, loaned (except the top specimen) for the illustration by John Overholt, are still in use at his water-power "muley" sawmill, one of the last of its kind, on Deep Run, in Bedminster Township, Bucks Co., Pa.

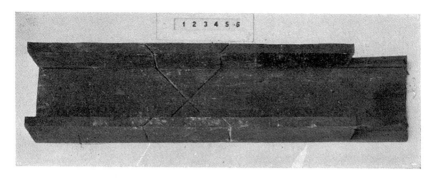

Fig. 78. The Mitre Box

A square, home-made, wooden trough, crossed diagonally with saw kerfs at 45 degrees, to hold the saw blade for mitre cutting. Still in universal use as described by Moxon, in 1678, and *The Circle of Mechanical Arts*, in 1813. The specimen shown was used in building the new Museum of The Bucks County Historical Society, in 1914.

in Bockler's *Theatrum Machinarum Novum;* the comparatively modern illustrations of Diderot, for France, 1768, and the two little pictures of Moxon in 1678, one of which we here show, the books with few exceptions devoted to these things, fail us; and as if Art had preferred to belittle and obscure the subject, a few German and Dutch Masters since the 16th century, Jost Amman, Jan Joris Van Vliet, Christolph Weigel, Jan and Casper Luiken and Johan Amos Comenius, who, always from a pictorial point of view, have illustrated the trades in several noted series of engravings or wood cuts, have neglected the tools. Antiquaries delight in endless descriptions of statues, decorations, tombs, gems, pottery, costumes, arms, pageantry, and bric-a-brac, but for clues to the history of the tools, which underlie all forms of human endeavor, we are left to chance references in early printed volumes, or a hopeless search in picture galleries, among architectural carvings or the painted miniatures bordering illuminated missals.

Tools for Surfacing, Chopping and Paring

HAVING reached the point where the old house builder (carpenter-joiner) begins his work, let us next consider the tools for surfacing, chopping and paring the raw material, which, except in the case of laths and shingles, has reached him either in the form of the board or the beam.

From the first, the evidence shows, that while the board (exclusive of the early restricted hand-sawing noted), was universally machine-sawed in a saw mill, the beam, though sometimes so sawed, was a far less invariable and marketable mill product; hence, because of the abundance and varied size, etc., of trees adapted to house and barn framework, the carpenter continued, until late in the 19th century, to hew and dress beams, rafters, trusses, purlins, girders, plates, etc., from the native log. For this purpose he used the broad axe, a ponderous, broad-bladed, short-handled instrument, more than twice the size and weight of the felling axe, which, compared with the saw and plane, more clearly hand-marks the wooden surface. It was employed generally with two hands, rarely with one, not to cross cut timber, but to hew smooth, vertically placed sides of logs, previously rough-squared ("scored in") with the felling axe.

Common opinion and the definition in Knight's *Mechanical Dictionary*, restrict the tool to a single form, but the evidence here presented proves that it had two definite forms one hundred and fifty years ago, the first of which is shown in the next illustration as

THE CHISEL-EDGED BROAD AXE WITH BENT HANDLE (Fig. 79)

Many specimens found among the rubbish of old farms and mills and in the scrap iron of the junk dealer, show that this instrument, used in colonial times for fine surfacing of house framework, was chamfered to an edge on one side only, that its blade was also levelled on one side only, that it often had, but sometimes lacked, a rectangular poll for pounding, and that it was always mounted with a conspicuously bent handle.

When axes of this class are held by the workman with handle toward him and blade downward, the blade appears sharpened at a chamfer or basil on the right side only, so that the sharp edge coincides with the left side or face of the blade, as shown in outline in Figure 83.

If the eye orifice sometimes swells beyond the level of the blade, said swell is always and only on the right or chamfered side of the blade, throwing that side out of level, while the left, opposite side remains flat, unless, as in some cases, the axe has been constructed, mounted and sharpened in reverse, for a left-handed man.

Old carpenters tell the writer that all broad axes were held with both hands, right hand foremost, and that the log face was set against the workman's left side, since, if set against his right side, his right or guiding arm, from knuckle to elbow, would intervene between the axe handle and log face. When thus held, it is only the workman's righthand fingers that so intervene between the log and the axe handle, while his left hand, grasping the latter at its widest divergence, is

81

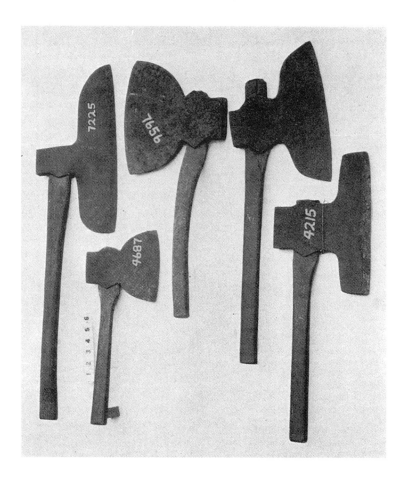

Fig. 79. The Chisel-Edged Broad Axe with Bent Handle

As described in the text, these axes differ importantly in construction from those illustrated under Figure 82. The photograph does not clearly show that, unlike the latter, all are sharpened on the right side of the blade and that the handles, as in broad axes of this type, are all bent to the right, except one abnormal axe, No. 7656, here imperfectly shown in the photograph, basilled, eye-swollen, and handled in reverse, which has been made for a left-handed man.

According to Mr. Wilson Woodman, who, at the building of his barn near Wycombe, Bucks County, Pa., in c. 1860, helped hew the timbers, the fresh-felled tree, laid about knee high above the ground on underplaced cross strips, was first pared to the brown under-bark with the draw knife, then white chalk-lined on the brown for the hewing line. Thereupon, the workman standing on the log "scored it in," preferably for ease and speed, with a common felling axe, i. e., hacked into the log side with a succession of deep cuts, and split off the intervals nearly to the chalk line. Standing then on the ground with the log on his left hand and close to his left knee, he held the axe right-hand foremost with its flat side against the vertical log face, and hewed with both hands, not longways with the grain but diagonally downward across it.

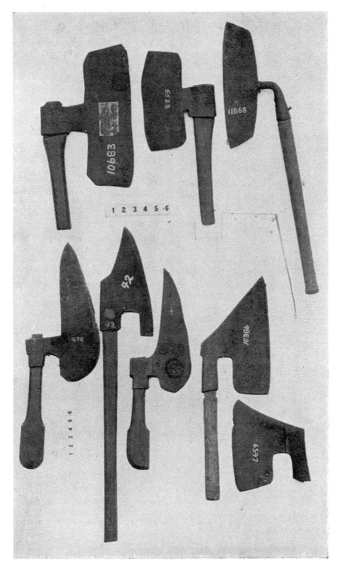

Fig. 80. The Polless Broad Axe

The basilled forms here shown, as varieties of Class I (Fig. 79), have become forgotten by carpenters in the last fifty years. All the specimens, except No. 42, retain their original right-bent handles. All are basilled on the right blade side, and flat bladed on the left. All also lack polls and hence are true hewing tools, not well adapted to pounding.

Square-bladed specimens, like No. 10683, were found by the writer at York Harbor, Maine; among ship carpenter's tools at New Bedford, Mass.; and in Pennsylvania; and appear illustrated in Diderot as cooper s axes. The very thin No. 11868, with its extraordinary socket mount, is probably too rare to have any historic or typical significance. The five lower specimens, of which No. 16315 and the middle axe are very typical, show the extraordinary so-called goose wing, brought to America by the Pennsylvania Germans, in use in Bucks Co., Pennsylvania, until the mid-19th century, and known in Germany in the 16th century, as proved by the old German woodcut, Figure 81.

Fig. 81. Goose Wing Broad Axe of the 16th Century

The picture, a section of a satirical German woodcut of about the 16th century, called the "Triumph of Maximilian," in the Berlin Kupferstich-Kabinet (reproduced as Fig. 88, in *Die fahrenden Leute in der Deutschen-Vergangenheit*, Diederichs, Leipsic, 1902), shows the goose wing axe (Fig. 80) carried as a weapon by one of the camp followers.

For another illustration of this type of axe in use during the 16th century see Fig. 249, p. 302.

well cleared of the wood worked upon. Constructed for accurate cutting upon a chalked line, the whole left face of these chisel-edged axes must slide flat over the wood, hence the blade, which, if double-side-sharpened would turn outward, evade the line and over-ride protuberances, had to be edged, as noted, upon the inner left face and therefore basilled on its right side. It is to prevent the chafing of the workman's knuckles against the

No. 10386, stamped "F. Hemerby" and "N. B. F.," was inherited by Erwin Kramer of Bucksville, Haycock Township, Bucks Co., Pa., from his wife's grandfather, Mr. Weitzel, a carpenter of Haycock Township, who, in the early 19th century, built several log cabins, still standing there in 1917, when the axe was obtained.

No. 6547 is almost an exact duplicate of the tool, now painted out by restoration, but originally in the lower, right corner of a picture of the Nativity, by Albert Durer, of date about 1504, in the Alte Pinakotheck, at Munich.

log face that the handles of these tools are always bent to the right or outward from the plane of the blade, while many of them, as here shown, are mounted with heavy, rectangular polls, adapted for heavy hammering and the pounding together of the mortised and tenoned framework of buildings. Though the basilled hewing axe is ascribed by Moxon, not to the carpenter but to the joiner, the evidence shows that in America, in the country where the two trades merged, the carpenter continually used these special tools for fine beam and rafter hewing in dwellings and mills, etc., until wood planing machinery superseded such work, toward the middle of the 19th century.

As a variety of this instrument, proving that it was by no means always equipped with a poll for pounding, as above noticed, the next illustration shows

THE POLLESS BROAD AXE (Fig. 80)

which, though differing in blade contour and the more marked upswell of its eye or handle-orifice, is constructed exactly in the same way, except that it lacks a poll, and hence, that it was not adapted for the pounding together of framework, where, according to Moxon, the double-handed, heavy carpenter's mallet, called the commander, could have been used for that purpose without scoring the wood. As superficially the unique contours of some of these latter axes would attract attention anywhere, they are here shown, either with narrow, rectangular blades, or as the remarkable so-called goose wing, brought to America by the Pennsylvania Germans and here again illustrated in the next picture as

THE GOOSE WING AXE OF THE 16TH CENTURY (Fig. 81)

from a woodcut of that time, called "The Triumph of Maximilian," in the Berlin Print Gallery, where this tool is seen held in the hand of one of the miserable recruits satirized by the engraver.

Unless we carefully examine broad axes, another type, here illustrated, might easily be confused with the instruments above described and escape us. But because it is constructed differently; because it cuts differently; and because Knight does not notice it, it is here shown as

THE KNIFE-EDGED BROAD AXE WITH STRAIGHT HANDLE (Fig. 82)

Numerous variously shaped examples, ancient, and comparatively modern, show that the blade of this latter axe is not basilled, but sharpened on both sides; that it is equally flat on both sides and lacks the lopsided eye swell, so characteristic of Class I; that, as thus far found, it is equipped with a heavy, square poll; and that its handle generally, though not always, is set straight. The evidence thus gathered from collected specimens and the opinion of old carpenters, shows that after the general disuse of the basilled broad axe (Figs. 79 and 80), above illustrated, in the middle of the 19th century, these latter less specialized hewing instruments, here classed as Type 2, as the last of their kind, survived until about 1900, among country carpenters for rough beam facing in barns, sheds, cabins and outbuildings.

The next illustration shows a now far more rarely found hewing tool, once part of the house builder's equip-

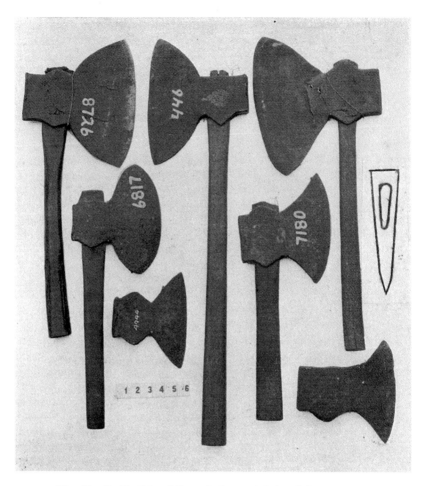

Fig. 82. Knife-Edged Broad Axe, with Straight Handle

Differing in construction from the instruments illustrated in Figures 79 and 80, this particular axe was sharpened, not on one side only, like the chisel, but on both sides, like a knife, as shown in the outline added. The instrument is not swollen out of level on one side by the eye orifice, but is equally level on both sides. The blade does not slide flat, but cuts at a slight tilt. The handles, here original, sometimes appear bent to the right but are generally, as here shown, straight. These instruments should represent the ancient carpenter's axe as distinguished from the joiner's hatchet, according to Moxon, who describes the former tool as thus sharpened on both sides, while the latter is basilled.

ment, too small to be called anything but a hatchet, namely the true

CARPENTER'S HEWING HATCHET
(Fig. 83)

generally found with a poll, but sometimes without it. It is a small, one-hand variety of the broad axe, used originally by the joiner to smooth-surface wood and not to split it or to drive nails, hence, basilled, *i. e.,* chamfer-sharpened, on one side only.

While the larger broad axe held its own through the 19th century, this

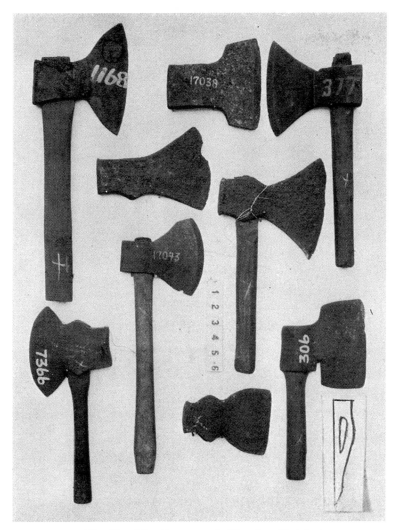

Fig. 83. The Carpenter's Hewing Hatchet

These little instruments used by the old American carpenter-joiner to smooth-surface odd joints, faces, corners, etc., are, as here shown, certainly one-hand tools. Nos. 377 and 7366 are basilled and swollen at the eye on the left side of the blade. All the others are basilled and eye swollen on the right side (see outline, lower right corner), and flattened on their left side so that their handles (original in Nos. 7366 and 306, and probably 377, though not set at an angle like the larger axes) still rise above the centre of the blade and hence frequently clear the wood. Therefore they are all hewing tools. On the other hand, all except the polless, square-bladed No. 306, show well-forged rectangular pounding polls.

In contour the lower unnumbered specimen, probably from York Harbor, Maine, resembles the shingling hatchets, described later, but unlike them it has the right side basilled and the eye bulged. The remarkable No. 17043, also basilled, notwithstanding its rectangular, inefficient poll, must be associated with iron nail driving, because it shows the nail pull on its lower blade margin. On the other hand, No. 7366 has a poll altogether too big for nailing, and the square-bladed No. 306, resembling two larger broad axes of the shape shown in Figure 80, conspicuously basilled,

Fig. 84. The Carpenter's Shingling Hatchet

These tools, bought since 1897, from farmers and at junk yards in eastern Pennsylvania, were made by country blacksmiths. They were used by the carpenter for splitting, trimming, nailing, and unnailing roof shingles and otherwise widely employed as household implements. Factories produced them after c. 1840. None are flat topped like the lathing hatchets, next shown, but all show flaring bits, well developed, contracted polls for nailing, and all but one have double-lipped eyes. All but the unnumbered specimen, and No. 13864, and No. 1493, show notches for the nail pull, which latter device is not an American invention but appears in Moxon (1678) on the lathing hatchet. (*Mechanick Exercises* [1703 ed.], Bricklayer's Work, Plate 2.)

little, basilled, one-hand hewing tool, with or without a pounding poll, owing to the increased abundance of ready-prepared lumber dressed in the planing mills, fell out of use after about 1830, while two other forms of hatchet, used for rough-surfacing, splitting, chopping and nailing, became more and more the continual companions of the carpenter. Of these, notice first

The Carpenter's Shingling Hatchet (Fig. 84)

This, as here shown by old and late specimens, was and is a one-hand tool of miniature, broad-axe shape, with blade not basilled, but always with an elongated or rounded poll for driving nails, and a straight, ten to twelve inch handle, generally with, rarely without, a notch in the lower rim of

eye-bulged, and side-flattened, with no poll at all, can in no way be reasonably associated with lathing, roof shingling or any kind of nail driving. Diderot illustrates the form as a cooper's hatchet, and an exactly similar tool was bought by the writer, with a set of carpenter-cooper's tools, from one of J. & W. R. Wing's whale ships, at New Bedford, Mass., in 1907. As the only polless hatchet here shown, it duplicates in construction Moxon's joiner's hatchet in Figure 67, an instrument, according to him, devoted not to pounding or nail driving, but entirely to hewing.

To infer, however, fom Moxon's cheap little picture, that all joiner's hewing hatchets, in his time, lacked polls, might be going too far. Diderot (1768) shows two hatchets for the carpenter (menuisier), one polless and the other, called "hache a marteu" (hatchet hammer), polled.

Fig. 85. The Lathing Hatchet

These home-made tools, as used before 1840 in eastern Pennsylvania, are flat-topped for clearing ceilings in nailing on upper partition laths for the plasterer. All show a contracted hammer poll and the old English nail pull notched on the lower rim of the bit, as shown in Moxon in 1678. (*Mechanick Exercises*, Bricklayer's Work, Plates 2. Fig. 1.) Many of the hatches are in their handles as found.

No. 17685 was given by Theodore Holcomb, Doylestown, in 1921, and had been used by his grandfather when learning his trade of carpenter about 1820. No. 8646 was owned and used about 1800 by Job Hallet, of Cape Cod, great-grandfather of Mrs. Combs, 98 Charles Street, Boston, who sold it to the writer in 1897.

Two small hatchets, not here shown, possibly British Army hatchets of 1776, minus the nail pull and hafted on riveted plate-extensions of the lower eye, like the hammer in Durer's *Melancholia* (shown later), were dug up in 1923, by Mr. R. P. Bolton of New York, at the site of the Cortwright house, built 1763 at Sherman Avenue and Arden Streets, New York City, and at Bear Mountain, N. Y.

the bit for nail pulling, and hence particularly adapted for the use of the worker, who, in shingling a house roof, could trim, split to fit, and nail on shingles with this single instrument.

Though probably not much used in England, where slate and thatch precluded it throughout the 18th century and where it appears (in Moxon) as a bricklayer's lathing tool, nail-notch and all; the evidence shows that in the United States, owing to the superabundance of shingled house roofs, it had replaced the old hewing hatchet and become a typical carpenter's tool by the end of the 18th century.

The same thing may be said of

THE LATHING HATCHET (Fig. 85) here shown in some of its varying

smith-forged types which, in all respects, as a small, one-hand cutting, nail pulling and driving instrument, resembles the shingling hatchet except that it is flat-topped, *i. e.,* lacks the upper projection of the eye and bit, and hence clears the ceiling in nailing on the top-plastering laths for room partitions. Handier for nail driving though less so, because narrower in the blade, for surface dressing than the former hatchet, this flat-topped tool, in its latest machine-made forms, seems to have become more and more the carpenter's favorite, since about 1890.

The evidence of collected specimens shows that these two old Anglo-American shingling and lathing hat-

Fig. 86. Special Factory-made Hatchets

These specimens, showing early factory experiments with the hatchet, were found in eastern Pennsylvania between 1897 and 1900. All except No. 16891, lack the notched nail pull on the blade, and all except No. 305, have substituted claws for the purpose, either on the poll or, in No. 14405, on the top of the eye. All are factory-made, probably after 1840, exce t No. 7649 and No. 17705, which appear to be hand forged. No. 305 was given, in 1897, by Mr. Huffert, of New Galena, Bucks Co., Pa., and used by him for labelling logs. It is factory-made and trade stamped on the side of the bit, "Horton & Arno, N. Y." The log stamp on the face of the poll, "K. G. & Co." was hammered on the log end. The extra long handle is original.

chets were invariably home-made, as here illustrated, until about 1840, after which the factories, neglecting the ancient, true hewing hatchet (Fig. 83), then nearly obsolete, took up their manufacture, and at last, after about 1870, slowly forced the country blacksmith, who had been forging them by hand, to give up the unprofitable job. Originally carpenter's tools, the instruments in these forms, thus cheapened, widely scattered and well adapted for domestic use, soon became, as now, the universal rough and ready cutting, splitting and hammering tools of every household.

But as the Patent Office records show, there was not much room for patent improvement in the shape of hatchets. The eleven patents listed as simply for "Hatchets," resulting in various attempts to remodel them, failed to win the market, as appears in the next illustration showing

SPECIAL FACTORY-MADE HATCHETS
(Fig. 86)

in which several ingenious but unsuccessful and now rare machine-made devices, attempt to substitute a claw for the notched nail-pull of the old tool.

At this point we risk taxing the reader's patience by calling attention to another class of old home-made hatchets, probably not used by the carpenter at all, but still as significant scrap iron relics here classified as

DOMESTIC AND SPECIAL HATCHETS

That small hand axes, probably called hatchets, were long ago used in Europe by soldiers and workmen other than carpenters, as by the mason (Moxon, 1678), and the slater (Diderot, 1768); as belt tools for the British grenadiers, and saddle pendants for the French dragoons before 1800 (Rees, *Cyclopaedia*, 1807), there can be no doubt. And if it were not too great a digression we might pause here to illustrate a selection of the various forms of little light iron and steel hatchets called tomahawks, at first made in Europe and imported by the colonists to sell to the Indians with trade axes above described under Figure 1, and later forged by country blacksmiths a l o n g the enlarging American frontier, for the same purpose.

Derived from the axes and hatchets here described, numerous examples of these deadly little skull-wounding weapons are exhibited in North American Indian collections, as found throughout the eastern seaboard region and in Canada. They appear in outlines resembling miniature trade axes, lathing hatchets, shingling hatchets and hatchets of the domestic types described later. A few are forged with a tang to be driven into the handle, but most are perforated with an eye for mounting. Some with the usual characteristic cutting bit, have polls ending in long, murderous points either straight or curved. Some have hammer polls, and in some the poll is replaced by the bowl of a peaceful tobacco pipe connected with a smoke perforation in the wooden handle. Not a few of these latter pipe-tomahawks are made of brass, and some, useless as weapons, but still retaining the blade, are cast in pewter. One illustrated by Beauchamp, without mentioning its material ("Metallic Implements of the New York Indians", *N. Y. State Museum Bulletin 55*, 1902, plate 23), shows a pipe at one end and a dagger at the other.

More relevant to our subject are several remarkable hatchets found by Mr. Reginald P. Bolton, and Mr. W. L. Calver, at British Revolutionary camp sites in New York, and hence of date *c.* 1776, or earlier. In one of these found at Fort Ticonderoga, the poll is replaced by an adze blade, and in two others discovered, one at a British camp site at Bear Mountain, New York, and another at the site of the Kortright House, Sherman Avenue and Arden Street, New York City, the form is that of the lathing hatchet, lacking a nail pull. In both these cases the mounting is effected not only by the usual perforation or eye, but by two long, semi-cylindrical plates projecting from the lower eye-lip, which enclose the handle and are riveted upon it with two or more rivets, as in the recent tack hammer, or as shown in the hammer seen among the discarded tools in the engraving by Albert Durer, called "Melancholia," shown later. A third specimen thus constructed, found at Fort Ticonderoga and of similar date, lacks the hammer poll and unlike the others, is equipped with a double-notched nail pull on the lower bit-margin.

Without considering further these irrelevant or eccentric or military forms, the evidence of old (if not definitely dated) hatchets found about farms in Pennsylvania, abundantly shows that the country blacksmith in the 18th century and before c. 1840, supplied not only the carpenter with the two kinds of special (shingling and lathing) hatchets, above described, but also the farmer, with at least two other forms of this useful tool, for general hacking, splitting and pounding.

These very peculiar looking, little one-hand axes or hatchets are shown in their early, long-bitted form as

AXE HATCHETS OF EUROPEAN TYPE
(Fig. 87)
and in their later, short-bitted American shape, as

AXE HATCHETS OF AMERICAN TYPE
(Fig. 88)
Though adapted to rough and ready household use, they all lack the specialized hammer poll and nail pull. If the carpenter used them at all, he must have done so for hacking and pounding. If for shingling and lathing, he must have carried a claw hammer with him to draw, when necessary, the ill-driven, wrought nails which were too valuable to waste.

Another once famous surfacing and hewing tool, now out of use among carpenters and passing away (1925) with the cooper and shipwright, is the very ancient

ADZE (Fig. 89)
the ascia of the Romans, brought to America by the pioneers (cf. Probate

Records of Essex County, Massachusetts, 1635-1681, 3 vols., George Francis Dow, editor. Salem, Mass., the Essex Institute, 1916-1920), homemade until c. 1840, and still (1925) surviving as a factory-made instrument. It was a two-hand, long bladed, hoe-shaped axe, with a bit generally down-curved, rarely flat-topped, bladed at right angles to its straight, deep-hafted helve (handle), and which, because basilled on the inner bit curve, had to be unhafted for grindstone sharpening. Hence, its very large eye, sometimes rectangular, is slightly funnel-shaped, as in the pickaxe, so that the helve can be driven out upward.

The tool, though part of the equipment of the carpenter, was far more generally and conspicuously used by the shipwright, a fact which helps to explain the striking variations in its form, as first, with a very peculiar, peg-shaped hammer poll; second, with a heavy, rectangular block-poll; and third, with no poll at all.

As if no other type of adze existed, the peg-poll variety is alone illustrated in The Circle of Mechanical Arts, 1813; by Holtzapffel, 1846; in Knight's American Mechanical Dictionary, 1878; and in Webster's Dictionary, 1891. But neither Moxon nor Diderot show it, and the writer has thus far failed to find it in the background of any pre-17th century pictures or woodcuts. But whatever its history and date, it had become a very important shipyard tool in the 18th century, and has continued so until now (1925), when the building of the wooden ship in England and America nears its end.

According to the information of Mr. Israel Snow, shipbuilder, of Rockland, Maine (August, 1925), gangs of workmen called "dubbers," standing

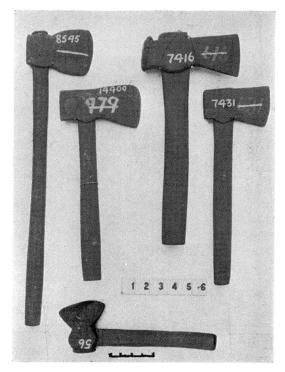

Fig. 87. Axe Hatchets of European Type

These diminutive, one-hand, chopping and pounding tools, found as farm relics in eastern Pennsylvania and Massachusetts, resemble the long-bitted, short-polled, European tree-felling axes previously described (see Fig. 4). All are home-made and differ greatly in contour from the shingling and lathing hatchets already described. None show devices for pulling or driving nails, but all, with rectangular flat polls, are meant to rough-pound as well as to cut. About one-half the size of the tree-felling axe, they were probably used less by the carpenters than for domestic purposes. The handles appear as found, but are probably not original. No. 8545 is smith stamped, and was bought with its handle from Franklin Bigelow, Fall River, Mass., in 1897.

upon scaffolds nailed or spiked against the open ship framework, adzed down the latter to proper level and contour, for receiving the inside and outside ship's planking, which latter, called the "skin," had to be again adze-levelled, before the joiners planed it to a finish. Because in this process, nails whole or broken, often remained in the ship's ribs, after aforesaid scaffolds were wrenched off, and because these nails, etc., not easily pulled out, had to be driven in by the "dubber," the small peg poll, which in hammer-ing the hostile projections followed them below adze-level into the wood, so as to clear his adze blade, became a highly efficient feature of the instrument.

For this special purpose the block poll adze would not serve, but otherwise, the latter tool, here shown (Fig. 89) was used, according to Mr. Snow, by shipwrights, not only to hew, but to drive spikes, in marine railways, and to spike and hew timber work. Further than this, the evidence of the photographs here reproduced and also of collected specimens, abundantly shows that not only the shipwright but the common carpenter, in the early 19th century, used both the first and second forms of the great marine instrument when, as described by Moxon, he adzed away projections in vertical house framework or levelled handhewn floor rafters before flooring. But he dressed his loose logs with the broad axe and not with the adze, and we find that as sawed house rafters came more and more into use, he more and more confined his adze operations to the overflooring of sagged or rotted house floors, or to the levelling for floors, of hand-hewn rafters in barns. The blades of the two above noted adzes (here illustrated) thus used by him and as found by the writer, are, as a rule, not saucered as is often supposed, but flat, and their concealed work rarely appears in old houses. The cuts at right angles to the grain that we sometimes see on the sides of rafters in barns and house lofts, etc., are the make-ready scorings-in of the felling axe above referred to, and not of the broad axe, much less of the adze, and whoever confuses them with the work of the latter tool is as mistaken as he who applies the name adze to both instruments. According to Cescinsky, we must go back to old furniture of the 16th century to see the work of the adze, otherwise we may look for it in the unplanked bilge troughs in the holds of wooden ships, where the ship carpenter last used the tool.

Besides this use of the adze among shipwrights and carpenters, abundant further evidence shows that in the new forest environment of the Anglo-American Colonies, the employment

Fig. 88. Axe Hatchets of American Type

In this group of little old one-hand tools in which the poll outweighs or nearly outweighs the bit, we see half-sized variations of the American tree-felling axe. (See Fig. 6.) The three left-hand specimens, if not the others, were made by local blacksmiths in Bucks Co., Pa., before 1840. They were used for various purposes on the farm, such as brush and kindling cutting, etc. If by the carpenter, not probably for shingling or lathing, since they lack the nail pull and modified nailing poll. The handle of the right specimen is not original. No. 13356, given by Mathias Hall, in 1918, is a farm relic of the old Hampton family, of Bucks Co., Pa.

of the tool was greatly extended among farmers to excavate the

Log Troughs (Fig. 90)

for feeding or watering horses, cows, chickens, etc., and also

The Dugout Canoe (Fig. 91)

Then the need for pounding nails out of adze-reach, or driving spikes, no longer existed and we find adzes of irregular home-made form, sometimes two-handed, of the third class mentioned with no poll at all, or sometimes for excavating large bread

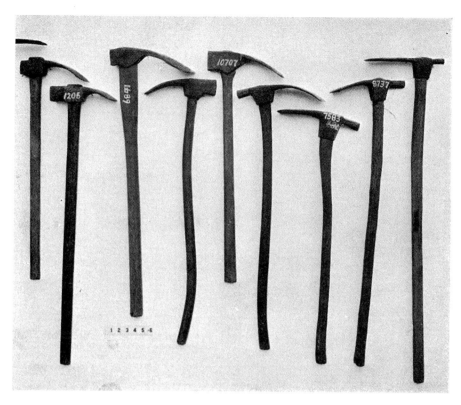

Fig. 89. The Carpenter's Adze

These old, home-made, two-hand instruments vary considerably in the shape of (*a*) the bit set at right angles to the handle, generally single, but sometimes (not here shown) double, generally curved toward the handle, but sometimes straight; (*b*) the cutting edge, always basilled on the lower (inner) side, generally flat, but sometimes very slightly saucered; (*c*) the eye, generally wedge-shaped, funneling upward inside for handle release, as with the grubbing hoe or pick, but sometimes straight-sided inside, and hence with fixed handle (No. 6841 and No. 10707); (*d*) the poll, sometimes peg-shaped (four specimens to right) and sometimes a heavy rectangular block face; sometimes (not here shown) polless.

As illustrated by these specimens the evidence shows that this celebrated tool, though sometimes saucer-bladed, by no means always cut a rippled surface; that the handle was not always releasable, for grindstone sharpening, as Moxon describes it; that when not free of its handle, it must be sharpened either on the side of the grindstone, or, particularly if saucered, with a whetstone.

The three right-hand specimens with their noticeable rectangular eye, wedge-shaped inside, for upward handle release, and still more noticeable peg-shaped poll, represents a conspicuous if not ancient type of the instrument, which neither Moxon (1678) nor Diderot (1768) show. But *The Circle of Mechanical Arts*, 1813; Holtzapffel, 1846; Knight's *Mechanical Dictionary*, 1878; and *Webster*, 1891; illustrate this particular shape as the adze par excellence. No. 7583 was bought at York Harbor, Maine, in 1898 and another, not shown, of J. & W. R. Wing, ship owners of New Bedford, Mass., among the carpenter's tools of one of their whale ships; and the evidence indicates, if it does not prove, that the type was developed in the 18th century, probably in England, among ship's carpenters, who chiefly used the adze.

As noted in the text, Mr. Israel Snow, ship-builder, of Rockland, Maine, informs the writer (August, 1925), that adzes are thus peg-polled and continually used at shipyards to drive down-broken nails, spikes, etc., in the ship's timbers, so as to clear the adze blade when adzing the ship's framework for inner and outer planking. He also says that some of the ship yard adzes, called line adzes, preceding the flat-bladed adzes, in rough-hewing sections of the framework called lines, are saucer-bladed. Also that the saucer or gouge adze is used in cutting the waterways under the floor timbers, down near the keel of vessels, in what is called the limbers.

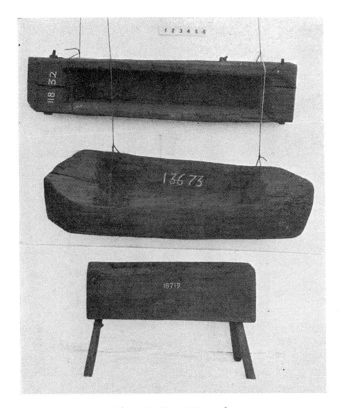

Fig. 90. Log Troughs

In these comparatively small specimens of a very large class of home-made troughs, used on farms until the late 19th century, to feed and water fowls and animals, axe-cut sections of logs, often left unfinished on the outside, have been, according to the information (1925) of farmers, excavated on the inside, downwards, with the adze, and sometimes retouched on the inner sides and ends with the felling axe.

troughs, bowls, etc., of the small, single-handed type, here shown as the

COOPER'S ADZE (Fig. 92)

It is this latter tool, thus used, that often shows the saucered blade sometimes erroneously supposed to be characteristic of all adzes but which, as noted, rarely appears on the large, standardized instrument of the shipwright and carpenter; and it is this saucered blade which ripples the wooden surface of the board trough, bowl or canoe with a pleasing sheen

of faint light and shadow compared with which the long, side shave of the broad axe and the drag of the plane and saw, are monotonous, so much so, that the modern architect now (1925), as did Mrs. J. L. Gardner at "Fenway Court" in Boston, sometimes deliberately orders his machine-made board and beam to be resurfaced "for Art's sake," in a deliberate manner unknown to the old-time carpenter, with saucered varieties of the once famous tool.

For comparative purposes and as of

Fig. 91. Dugout Canoe

Made by excavating a cypress log with an adze, helped on the inner and outer sides with a felling axe. Bought by Frank K. Swain in 1917 for the Bucks County Historical Society, at Learned's saw mill at Natchez, Miss. One of about fifty dugouts used there to obtain floating logs.

great historical and ethnological interest, the next illustration shows

THE KOREAN ADZE (Fig. 93)
used from time immemorial in the Far East, and bought from a carpenter at Kang Kei, Korea, in 1923.

Another important one-man paring or surfacing tool is the

DRAW KNIFE (Fig. 94)
also used in other trades (cooper, wheelwright, etc.,) and noted as "Shave," "Draft Shave," "Round Shave," "Hollow Shave," and "Shaving Knife," in the old New England records (Probate Records of Essex County, Massachusetts, 1635-1681, 3 vols., George Francis Dow, editor. Salem, Mass., the Essex Institute, 1916-1920). It was used in 1678, says Moxon, to round-shave ladder rungs, tool handles, etc., when the latter were held between the workman's breast and the bench or, as later evidence shows, on the tool handle clamp (Fig. 75), but more universally to shave thin the tops and sides of riven shingles when the split pieces were gripped by pressure of a foot lever, in the shaving horse (Fig. 15).

As a variety of the draw knife the

ROUND SHAVE OR SCORPER
(Fig. 95)
a one handled circular iron knife, here shown, was used not only by coopers for shaving to a level the joints between freshly set staves inside tubs, etc., but also by farmer artificers one hundred years ago for excavating the concave surfaces of home-made wooden bowls, butter ladles, etc.

Still another tool, too rare to be very significant, in the form of a funnel-shaped cylinder, knife-edged on its top rim, is here shown as the

PEG CUTTER (Fig. 96)
used for perfecting pegs and treenails, driven down through its sharpened, circular orifice, while the

WITCHET OR ROUNDING PLANE
(Fig. 97)
which has two blades projecting into an orifice, expansible on hand screws, is used to round-shave a stick into a tool handle. The draw knife in more regulated form appears as the

SPOKE SHAVE (Fig. 98)
in which the blade no longer works free but is reduced to a narrow cutter set in a narrow slit or mouth, which restricts the depth of the cut and regu-

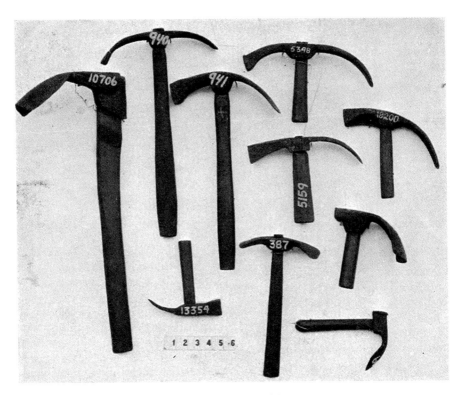

Fig. 92. Cooper's Adzes

These small, one-hand adzes, used by coopers for hewing down barrel staves, show the characteristic, curved, transversely set, single (rarely double. No. 940) bit and pounding poll of the two-handed carpenters' tools, shown in Figure 89, but differ from the latter in the following particulars: (*a*) their bits are more curved; (*b*) their cutting edges generally basilled on the inside; but sometimes on the outside and sometimes flat, are often saucered far more conspicuously than on the other tool; (*c*) their eyes are not wedge-shaped inside and hence their handles are not releasable by updriving, and would be always in the way for sharpening the inner basil on the grindstone. If saucered and so basilled, the blade would have to be sharpened on a file, or the whet-stone, or one of the oil-stone strips mentioned by Holtzapffel, Vol. 3, p. 1138.

The evidence shows that the tools were widely adopted by the pioneer carpenter and farmer in the 17th and 18th centuries, for hollowing large bowls, bread troughs, dugout canoes, gum tree boxes, bee hives, etc. As here illustrated, the specimens, including the exceptional polless No. 10706, are old Bucks Co., Pa., farm, mill and shop relics.

lates the thickness of the shaving. This latter tool, which has ceased to be a draw knife, may be said to form an intermediate link between the open blade driven by percussion (*i. e.* broad axe), and another celebrated instrument far more commonly associated in the popular mind with the carpenter.

THE PLANE

the runcina of the Romans. It is a wooden, rectangular block, called the stock, perforated by a central, upward-expanding slit, through which the flat, steel, basil-edged blade called the iron, is inserted downward at an angle and tightened with a thin wedge, notched for the upward escape of shavings.

The iron projects through the lower orifice of the slot, called the mouth, a little below the bottom of the stock, called the sole. The fore end of the plane or stock, is that in which the handle, called the tote, is inserted and towards which the top of the blade leans. The britch is the other end of the stock, away from the carpenter, when grasping the tote with his right hand, he pushes forward the instrument.

Who has ever fully described this ancient tool, in its 18th century varieties? Owing to the confusing and non-descriptive names given to it, it is hard to understand until we overlook the endless variations in its make and shape and grasp the three purposes of its construction, as devoted, first, to levelling; second, to 'fitting, i. e., cutting the i m p o r t a n t rectangular-notched channels and ridges, called rabbets, or rebates, needed to fit pieces of wood together; and third, to ornamenting, i.e., making d e c o r a t i v e mouldings.

The first of these purposes is served by the so-called · bench planes, of which there still are, and for at least three hundred years, have been, three kinds; namely, the so-called jack planes, trying planes, and finishing planes.

THE JACK PLANE OR FORE PLANE
(Fig. 99)

used, not for smoothing but for preliminary rough surfacing, superficially resembles all the other bench planes but differs noticeably from them all, in the curvature of its steel blade. This blade, the so-called iron, usually mitred or basilled like a chisel on the underside of the cutting edge, and set rank, i.e., projecting farther than

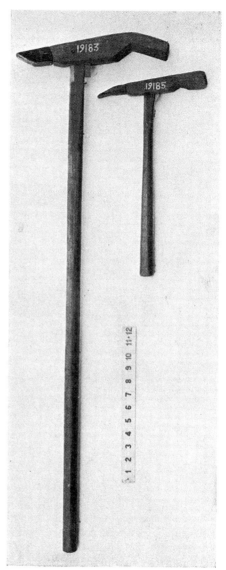

Fig. 93. The Korean Adze

The Korean adzes here shown are of great comparative interest, as coming recently from one of the most conservative countries of the world. The Far Eastern tool is represented by a two-hand large, and one-hand smaller example, which except that the blades, invisible in the photograph, widen transversely at the cutting edge in general shape and construction, resemble the American adze. Otherwise, not only the handles, side-pegged for easy removal when sharpening the blades, but also the heads are of wood, into which the straight-

Fig. 94. Draw Knife

A narrow steel blade basilled on its upper side (*i. e.*, away from the wood) with two wooden handles tanged upon it at right angles, pulled with both hands to thin the sides and tops of shingles held in the shaving horse (Fig. 15), or to round-off tool handles, wagon spokes, stool legs, ladder staves, etc., grasped for it in the vise. Much employed by coopers and in other trades, it is illustrated by Moxon as a carpenter's tool and called by him "Draw Knife." It appears in the *Essex County* (*Mass.*) *Court Records* from 1635 to 1681, frequently as "Draw Knife," "Drawing Knife," "Shave," "Draft Shave," "Shaving Knife," and when called "Round Shave," and "Hollow Shave," was probably used as a cooper's tool.

usual below the sole, so as to cut deep and quick, unlike all other bench plane irons, is slightly convexed, so as to perceptibly trough-cut the surface, as is sometimes proved by the unfinished, rippled, under sides of old drawers, or the backs of cupboards

THE TRYING PLANE (Fig. 100) is constructed for more perfect level-

edged, steel bits, basilled on the lower side as usual, are mortised, with a shoulder. The specimens were bought from a Korean carpenter, Kim Mok Sow, for six yen, in Kang Kei, Korea, in 1923, by the Rev. Clarence Hoffman.

ling ("shooting") of edges and smoothing of surfaces. This tool superficially resembles the jack plane, but its accurately-flat sole, 20 to 22 inches long, is longer and its blade is not convexed, but flat. Following the jack plane, it finally smoothes the surface of a board, laid flat on the work bench, against the catch (Fig. 69), or "shoots," *i.e.*, accurately levels, the edge of a board held upward in a vise. It varies in fineness and angle of blade and in size, but its construction,

Fig. 95. The Round Shave or Scorper

Though these old home-made, one-handled, circular-bladed iron or steel knives, inserted on a tang at a right or obtuse angle, into short, wooden handles, are not illustrated in Diderot (under *Boisellier or Tonellier*), the evidence gathered by the writer with many collected specimens, proves that like one of them (No. 14225 not shown) bought from J. & W. R. Wing, of New Bedford, Mass. (with an outfit of cooper's tools belonging to one of their whale ships), they were used by coopers to reach down into barrels, buckets, tubs, etc., and shave level the joints between the staves. For this purpose Diderot illustrates a similar, open-sided, one-handled, semi-circular knife, not shown here.

According to the information of Matthias Hall, of Wrightstown, Bucks Co., Pa., who gave another specimen to the Museum, these circular-bladed knives were also used by farmers, sixty years ago, to cut the concave surfaces of home-made, solid, wooden bowls, butter ladles, etc. Knight figures Diderot's semi-circular knife, calls it a "Scorper" and says it was also thus used to hollow bowls and ladles. In the double-handled, draw knife form, the tool, now factory-made and on sale at hardware stores, is universally used in mercantile transport for erasing paint, addresses, etc., on packing boxes and barrel heads.

accounting for its purpose, *i.e.*, final smoothing, is always the same. The irons in the old specimens seen by the writer are all set at right angles to the sole, and in the two examples here shown (left), are single, and in the two right-hand specimens doubled, *i.e.*, a duplicate blade, with reversed basil, is screw-bolted through a slot upon the cutting blade just above its edge. This device, to quicken the up-curl of shavings, unknown in the 18th century but now universal on bench planes, was introduced in England, according to Charles Holtzapffel, early in the 19th century.

The next illustration

VARIETIES OF THE TRYING PLANE
(Fig. 101)

illustrates long examples of the same instrument, which by reason of their varying lengths have special names, *i.e.*, according to Holtzapffel, common

Fig. 96. Peg Cutter

Two slightly funnelled iron cylinders, the sharpened top rims of which form circular knives, are set over two holes penetrating a heavy wooden block standing on pegged legs. When slips of wood, rough-rounded to approximate size, are driven down and punched through the cylinders, they fall through the block as rake teeth. Mrs. Jacob Hahn of Point Pleasant, now about 82 years old, remembers seeing a similar but larger apparatus, employed in a neighboring wood, in 1846, to make the large trenails, illustrated and described later, used by the hundreds in building the wooden covered bridge over the Tohicken Creek, at Point Pleasant, Bucks Co., Pa. (Information of Mrs. William R. Cooper of Point Pleasant, to the writer, August, 1925).

trying plane 20 to 22 inches, long plane 24 to 26 inches, jointer, for smoothing to close-fit board edges, 28 to 30 inches. We learn also that the adjustable blades, released by hammering either the britch, or the front sole-top, are, by means of their wedges, set "rank" or fine, *i.e.,* so as to project more or less below the sole, and therefore cut deep or shallow, and also, from Holtzapffel, that they are pitched at varying angles called "common pitch," at 45 degrees, for soft woods, "York pitch," 50 degrees and "middle pitch," 55 degrees, for mahogany, and hard woods; also, that they are sometimes set perpendicularly or with a forward tilt, for boxwood, etc., in which latter case the plane is called a scraping plane. Moxon mentions and illustrates (Fig. 67.B.3) a short variety of the trying plane,

Fig. 97. The Witchet or Rounding Plane

In this instrument (right), two plane stocks, bladed as usual, and with notched soles, are set adjustably sole to sole, on hand screws. When a rough-rounded stick, clamped in a vise, is thrust through the rectangular orifice between the stocks, and the stocks are tightened upon it and twisted around it by the handles, the opposed, plane blades, protruding from the notches, round-shave the stick into a tool handle, etc. One blade in only one of the stocks does the same work in the left-hand instrument.

called the "strike block," for smoothing at short quarters, and often when used for mitre edges in framing, worked upside down, in which case the workman held the little plane in his left hand, fore-end towards him, and pushed the mitred edge along its upturned blade.

Besides this Holtzapffel briefly describes, as used in 1846, a method for working a trying plane sideways along an apparatus called a shooting board, or shooting block, first dated in the *New English Dictionary*, by a quotation for 1812, and described in improved form, by Knight, in 1878. It consists of a straight-edged board mounted on a side channel in which the plane when held sideways slides (so as to clear said channel with its blade). The apparatus was variously blocked or tilted to permit the plane,

thus fenced, to straight-edge or bevel longways, or cross-edge or mitre the wooden strips worked upon.

All the plane handles shown in Figure 101 show the hollow grasp, not illustrated by Moxon or Diderot, nor found by the writer in ancient pictures, and apparently unknown before the later 18th century, soon after which it appears in an illustration from *The Circle of Mechanical Arts,* by Thomas Martin, London, 1813.

A still longer variety of the trying plane is

THE FLOOR PLANE (Fig. 102)

conspicuous for its extra length (here about three feet) and used especially for the surface-levelling of floors, thus exceeding the ordinary length of the longest common bench plane, which, according to Holtzapffel, was thirty

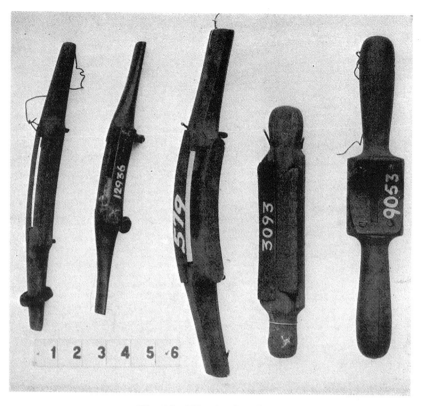

Fig. 98. The Spoke Shave

A restricted draw knife used by carpenters for smoothing tool handles and by wheelwrights for wagon spokes, also variously, on barrel staves, by coopers. It is handled at both ends upon a short, straight or slightly curved stock. The shortened blade is adjustably stapled or thumb screwed so as to project very slightly below the wooden, or metal-faced sole of the instrument, which thus halts the cut while the shavings escape into a widened orifice under the blade. The depth of the cut is increased by twisting the thumb screws or pounding the projecting staple ends, to raise the knife. In No. 9053, made after 1846, as proved by its pointed wood screws, the blade takes the form of a plane iron, wedged through a slot in the stock as described with the witchet (Fig. 97). Moxon does not mention the ancient tool, but it is named in an old Salem inventory of 1644 in the *Probate Records of Essex County, Massachusetts, 1635-1681*, 3 vols., George Francis Dow, editor. Salem, Mass., the Essex Institute, 1916-1920, and in the vast lore of quotations in the *New English Dictionary*, in references cited for 1510, 1572, 1688, 1794, 1837, and 1846.

inches. But the floor plane dwindles into insignificance in contrast with the great cooper's plane called

THE COOPER'S LONG JOINTER (Fig. 103)

worked upside down and here shown for comparison, from a specimen in the Museum of The Bucks County Historical Society at Doylestown, Pa.

The little known tool seems well worth illustrating again as

THE COOPER'S LONG JOINTER OF THE 16TH CENTURY (Fig. 104)

from one of the old German woodcuts of 1568 by the engraver Jost Amman (born 1539, died 1591), picturing workmen at work in the various trades.

Fig. 99. The Jack Plane or Fore Plane

The first so-called bench plane used by the carpenter. The basilled blade, unlike that of all other bench planes, is slightly convex-edged for quick, preliminary levelling. In the right-hand specimen the iron (blade), in ancient pre-19th century style (described under Fig. 100), is single; in the other two specimens (left), double. The hollow-grasp handle only appears in the middle plane.

To complete the list of so-called bench planes, the next illustration shows

THE SMOOTHING PLANE (Fig. 105)

This little, boat-shaped block plane, poorly named smoothing plane, is and was used, not like the trying plane to smoothlevel boards, but to wriggle about into corners, over ill-fitted joints, etc., and so put the last levelling touch upon finished work.

In No. 445 which may called a scraping plane as above described, the iron is set almost vertically for planing over hardwood, like apple or box, and rather scrapes than planes the wood. When used in Colonial America these little instruments were grasped in the workman's hands, without handles. But as an exception, No. 12799 is equipped with a handle, called the horn, at the fore-end of the stock. Moxon's "smoothing plane" (Fig. 67), shows no such grasp, but smoothing planes, thus horned, have long been in use in Continental Europe, as is shown by the

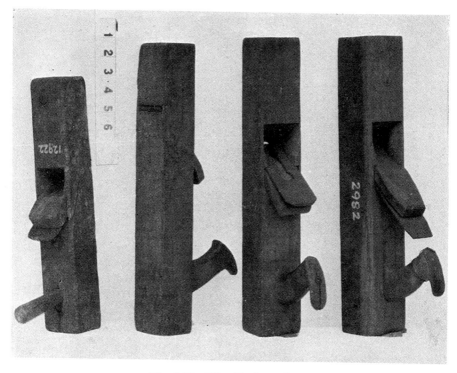

Fig. 100.   The Trying Plane

The second bench plane used by the carpenter. Longer than the jack plane, with flat sole and flat-blade edge for more perfect smoothing. None of these old, home-made specimens show the hollow grasp. Two of them (left) have single irons (blades) in pre-19th century style, as noted in the text. The other two (right) are double-ironed, *i.e.*, equipped each with a double iron or blade, basilled in reverse. A bolt headed rigidly in the latter, penetrating a long slot in the lower or cutting iron is tightened flat and upside down by a threaded nut, upon the said lower, cutting iron, just above its blade, to help the upcurl of shavings. Extra notches in the wooden wedge above, and plane stock below, clear the bolt head and bolt nut.

SMOOTHING PLANE OF 1596 (Fig. 106) here illustrated from a relic of the ill-fated Dutch expedition sent to Nova Zembla, in 1596. After two hundred and fifty years, it was recovered and brought back to the Rijks Museum, at Amsterdam, in 1871.

Let us pause here to follow this smallest of bench planes farther back into the past,: and wonder whether acting also as the jack plane, it did not serve the carpenter of the Middle Ages, for most purposes, whether he used the trying plane at all, and why Albert Dürer, in 1514, chose to represent this little instrument as the type of its class, in his celebrated engraving known as

THE MELANCHOLIA (Fig. 107)

There we see it plainly, horn and all. It lies in the foreground of the great masterpiece, along with the open handsaw of its day, the carpenter's rule, some wrought nails, and a very remarkable claw hammer, to be described later, among the tools thrown down for a moment by the Genius which "by searching" has failed to "find out God."

Fig. 101. Varieties of the Trying Plane

Still longer than the common trying plane. (No. 5261, 26 inches, No. 2515, 24½ inches long) hence adapted for still truer levelling and edging of boards. All the specimens show the hollow grasp, "tote" or handle: probably not earlier than the mid-18th century. The irons are all doubled in post-19th century style, as noted in the text.

In connection with these and other carpenters' planes, described later, we may suppose that the planes frequently mentioned in the *Probate Records of Essex County, Massachusetts, 1635-1681, 3 vols., George Francis Dow, editor. Salem, Mass., the Essex Institute, 1916-1920,* were sometimes homemade, of stocks cut by the carpenter himself, and mounted with irons forged by local blacksmiths, and sometimes bought ready-made from cutlers or tool-makers also, that they were sometimes made in Massachusetts, and sometimes brought from England.

The evidence of planes used in the late 18th and early 19th centuries, seen by the writer, also shows that some of the latter were thus homemade, while many others, toward the middle of the 19th century, show the names of makers or early factories stamped on the stock, or having smith stamps on the blade, often with the added words "cast steel" (first made in the United States, in 1850-1859, according to J. M. Swank, *Iron and Coal in Pennsylvania,* 1878, p. 80)

J. L. Bishop in his *History of American Manufacturers,* Philadelphia, 1864, Vol. 1, p. 568, refers to "one cutler" and tool-maker in Pittsburgh in 1808: the "Lemnos edge" tool factory in Chambersburg, Penna., in 1828; and the Lamson and Goodnow Cutlery works, near Springfie'd, Mass., in 1842-44. He also says in a unique hardware list (Vol. 2, p. 387), that he learns from John W. Quincy of Boston and Mr. Hand of Philadelphia, that American hardware, including carpenters' planes, first imported from England in the early 19th century, began to be manufactured and extensively sold in the United States, between 1829 and 1834.

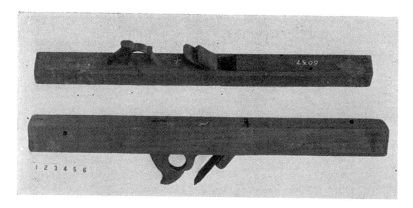

Fig. 102. The Floor Plane

These extra long planes, the longer of which is 34¾ inches, and hence longer than the longest of the carpenters' trying planes (30 inches) listed by Holtzapffel, were used possibly for special accurate "trying" *i.e.*, straight edging of framework, but chiefly, as old carpenters say, for the surface levelling of floors.

Fig. 103. Cooper's Long Jointer Plane

The chief feature of this longest of planes, which in construction exactly resembles a common carpenters' trying plane, except that it lacks a handle, is its extraordinary length (here 5 feet 6 inches long) and the fact that, unlike all carpenters' planes, it is always used upside down.

The framed legs, socketed loosely into a mortise in one end, elevate the britch of the plane towards the workman, thus enabling him to smooth-edge a barrel-stave, which he slides downward over the blade of the upturned sole. An underplaced block lifting the instrument at the lower end would extend the range of his push. The mouth is wide and the blade, basilled as usual, is not convex-sharpened but flat edged, not slotted to bolt upon a reversed double blade, as in modern carpenters' bench planes, but single.

Fig. 104. Cooper's Long Jointer Plane of the 16th Century

An old German cooper of the 16th century is using his long jointer plane as described under Figure 103. The lower end of the plane rests on a block thus extending its range. Below it lies a wooden compass with a stop arm (Fig. 59B), while in the background another cooper releases a barrel hoop with the lever hook, resembling the cant hook, Figure 39, No. 6387. From a wood cut by the German engraver, Jost Amman, b. 1539, d. 1591.

The specimen here shown with stock of very heavy wood had been made and used by a maker of turpentine barrels for turpentine gatherers, and was bought by Dr. Wm. S. Erdman, from J. H. McGhee, of Cumberland, N. C., in December, 1923.

Charles Holtzapffel says in 1843 (*Turning and Mechanical Exercises*, Vol. 2, page 483), that the Chinese were then using planes like this for a purpose which he does not specify.

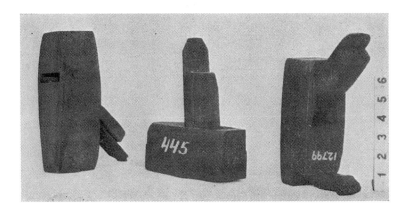

Fig. 105. The Smoothing Plane

The last bench plane used by the carpenter, not for smoothing the raw material (boards) but to put the last levelling touch across ill-fitted joints, etc., on finished work. No. 12799 is equipped with a continental European handle. called the horn. at the fore end of the stock, as in Fig. 106, and in Durer's *Melancholia*, of 1514 (Fig. 107). The other instruments were clasped in the workman's hands, minus handles. The iron stands up almost vertically in No. 445, for planing hard woods.

In general, as to the angle or rake of plane irons adapted to soft or hard or ill-grained woods, Holtzapffel, *Turning and Mechanical Manipulations*, Vol. 2, p. 482, notes, for bench planes, common pitch, 45 degrees from the horizontal, for soft woods; York pitch, 50 degrees, for mahogany and hard or stringy woods; middle pitch, 55 degrees, for moulding planes for soft wood, and for finishing planes for mahogany, etc.; and half pitch, 60 degrees, for moulding planes, for mahogany and ill-grained woods, such as bird's-eye-maple.

Fig. 106. The Smoothing Plane of 1596

The little stock, lacking its original blade and wedge, is not coffin-or boat-shaped, but rectangular, and like many of the continental European instruments now in use. and seen in old pictures, has a handle, the so-called horn. at its far end. The instrument is a relic of the Dutch Expedition to Nova Zembla in 1596. It was found in an ancient store of implements then left on the island and brought back to the Rijks Museum at Amsterdam. Photographed by the kind permission of the latter.

Fig. 107. The "Melancholia" of Albert Dürer

In this famous picture of date *c.* 1514, the seated figure holds the metal compass (Fig. 59-A) in her right hand, while the horned smoothing plane (Fig. 105), the iron pincers, the rule, the open handsaw (as seen in the carpenters' belts in Fig. 32), four wrought nails, and the claw hammer with riveted eye-projection (to be described later) appear among the scattered tools.

This disposes of the so-called bench planes of the carpenter and joiner, as strictly defined by the name, which are only referred to when we speak of levelling wooden surfaces. But their horizontal work is flat and we are not done with the subject until we consider the rarer, free-working instruments which smooth down convex and concave surfaces in the same way. One of these, Holtzapffel, in 1846, in *Turning and Mechanical Manipulations*, Vol. 2, p. 475, speaks of as the

COMPASS PLANE (right) (Fig. 108)

In this rare tool, here shown to the right of the picture, not mentioned by Moxon or Diderot, but used sometimes (according to Rees, *c.* 1800) by the old carpenter-joiner for the free smoothing of concave furniture surfaces or wall curves, the sole is convexed, not in cross-section like the round plane (Fig. 123), but longitudinally, like the rocker of a child's cradle. The blade is convex-edged and protrudes from an extra wide mouth, and the shavings, as with the jack plane, are discharged u p w a r d s through the middle of the stock. But as the construction of such a plane, and not its size, should classify it, we may, despite the difference of name, regard the little, so-called

MODELLING PLANE (left) (Fig. 108)

imperfectly described by Knight, who says nothing of its curved sole (here shown), as only a miniature variety of the compass plane. In this slightly flatter-soled, little home-made specimen, decorated with corner groovings, dotted scallops, two floral scrolls, and the date 1771, the blade is missing. The instrument also once had a horn,

as proved by an empty mortise hole in the fore stock.

By way of comparison with these bench and levelling tools, so typical, in their common types, of the carpenter's plane in general, let us here pause to glance at other forms of similar planes, used in other trades or by carpenters in other parts of the world, or as rare and highly prized relics, excavated by archaeologists. Two of these now rapidly becoming obsolete, owing to the transformation of cooperage by modern machinery, are shown in the next illustration as among the typical instruments used in the ancient process of making barrels by hand, namely

THE HOWEL AND THE SUN PLANE
(Fig. 109)

At first sight, the extraordinary howel (lower specimen), with its convexed blade, appears to be nothing more than the compass plane (Fig. 108) bolted against a flat, semi-circular fence; and so it is, except that its sole is convex, not only longitudinally, but also in cross-section. If placed horizontally and pushed around inside the top of a barrel previously levelled with the sun plane, it will smooth, across the grain, the inner circumference at about one to one-and-a-half inches below the rim, where the croze (described later) must cut the channel to hold the barrel head. If fenced and pushed at an outward tilt, it will cut the familiar chamfer, called the chine, between the head and rim top. This chamfer could also be cut with the loose compass plane.

The unique sun plane (upper two specimens), with flat blade and central-shaving discharge, may be said to

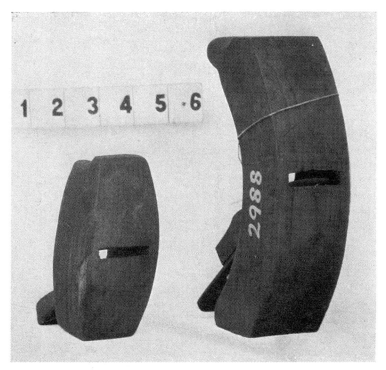

Fig. 108. The Compass Plane and the Modelling Plane

The rare compass plane, here shown to the right of the picture was used sometimes by the old carpenter-joiner for the free smoothing of concave furniture surfaces, or wall curves. Its sole is convexed, not in cross-section, like the round plane (Fig. 123), but longitudinally, like the rocker of a child's cradle. The little so-called modelling plane (left) in which the blade is missing, imperfectly described by Knight, who says nothing of its curved sole, here shown, may be regarded as only a miniature variety of the compass plane.

  Neither Moxon nor Diderot, nor *The Circle of Mechanical Arts,* mention the compass plane, but Rees describes it. *c.* 1800. Holtzapffel, *Turning and Mechanical Manipulations,* Vol. 2, p. 475, refers to it in 1846, and the *New English Dictionary* quotes W. Halfpenny, *Sound Building,* 1725, and Weale's *Dictionary of Terms,* in 1850, as its only citations of the word "compass plane."

resemble the carpenter's trying plane, both in construction and purpose, *i.e.,* to level the top rims of freshly staved barrels, except that, to conquer the narrow, circular margin worked upon, which a straight-soled plane would tilt over, the stock is semicircular while the sole is flat.

Concerning the history of levelling planes and of planes in general, we might well regret the lack of information here presented. Whoever investi-gates the matter will soon find that writers, earlier than the 18th century, have little to say about planes, and that the variations of the tool, in different parts of the world, have been overlooked by travellers.

According to Rich, Pliny *(Hist. Nat. 16, 42),* describes the smoothing plane, and Tertullian (2d century), *Apologia,* 12; and St. Augustine (4th century), *De civitate Dei,* 4, 8, mention the rabbet plane; but, except the

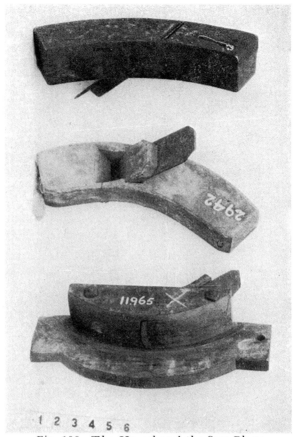

Fig. 109. The Howel and the Sun Plane

Because of its similar large semi-circular fence the cooper's howel (lower specimen) looks like the cooper's croze (Fig. 121). But it differs therefrom in blade construction. Closer examination shows that while the sole of the howel is equipped with a broad blade for surface levelling, that of the croze is mounted with a channel cutting tooth.

As described in the text, the howel is a compass plane with sole convexed both longitudinally and in cross-section and equipped with a semi-circular fence, used by coopers to chamfer the inner barrel top above the head with the familiar bevel called the chine.

The sun plane, (upper two specimens) with semi-circular stock and flat sole, levels the top rim of freshly-staved barrels.

ROMAN CARPENTER'S PLANE (Figs. 110 A and B)

excavated at Silchester, England, and here illustrated from photographs kindly furnished by the Reading Public Museum and Art Gallery, the only ancient Roman planes known to the writer, appear first, as illustrated by a sepulchral stone carving found at Rastadt, Germany, and shown in Rich's *Companion to the Latin Dictionary and Greek Lexicon,* and second, as a bronze plane, lithographed in *Piccoli Bronzi del Real Museo Borbonico,* Carlo Ceci, Napoli, 1858, plate X, Figure I.

This latter relic, two thousand

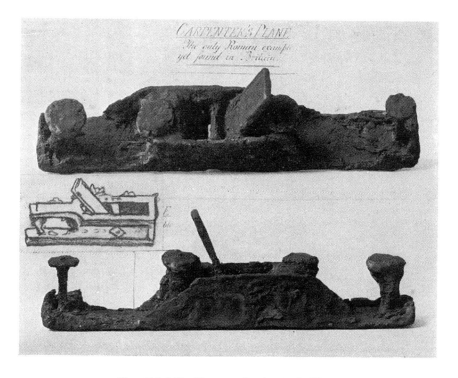

Fig. 110 (A). Roman Carpenter's Plane

Found in excavating the ruins of the Roman town of Calleva, near Silchester, ten miles southwest of Reading, Hampshire, England, and according to *A Short Guide to the Silchester Collection*, by G. E. Fox and Mill Stephenson, Honorary Curators, is of date earlier than the 4th century, A.D. It was found in 1890 among about sixty objects, mostly of iron "pitched hastily into a well" into a part of the excavations called by the explorers "Insula I."

The much rusted stock 13½ inches long, here shown on its top and right side, consists of an open topped box made of iron plates in which two wooden blocks leaving a central opening for the blade, have been fastened by four much rusted vertical iron rivets. The single blade set at a high pitch slides down in the wide mouth, not in side channels as in the modern plane, but under a cross rivet. Its method of sharpening is not described. The wedge, probably necessary for adjustment, is gone. The added sketch shows a similarly constructed Roman plane of bronze, found at Pompeii, and illustrated in lithograph in *Piccoli Bronzi de' Real Museo Borbonico* by Carlo Ceci, Naples, 1858, Plate 10. Figure I, very miserably described as "Rabot Avec Sa Doloire." W. M. Flinders Petrie, who hastily describes it and illustrates it with a dissimilar outlined sketch in *Tools and Weapons*, Constable & Co., London, 1917, says that three other similar planes were found at Pompeii.

Carpenters planes with iron stocks and patented adjustments have become common in the United States since about 1890, but the writer has seen no such instrument of the 18th or early 19th centuries, with one unique exception, namely a plane now in The Museum of the Bucks County Historical Society, here shown in Fig. 111, in which two wooden blocks enclosed on their sides and bottom with iron plates—are held in place by horizontal wood screws penetrating the sides—pointless and hence earlier than 1846. The original blade is missing, but the narrow mouth would only permit a shaving of extreme fineness. The writer has been able to learn nothing from books or living carpenters of this modern iron duplicate of the Silchester plane, which was probably imported from England, certainly made before 1846, and perhaps used for very fine cabinetmaker's work, such as planing out scratches on furniture veneering, etc.

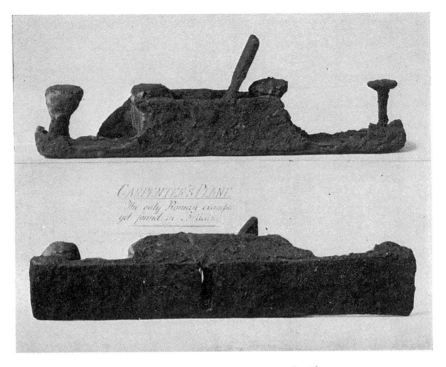

Fig. 110 (B). Roman Carpenter's Plane

The photo-engraving shows the sole and left side of the Silchester plane, Fig. 110(A).

years old, is again apparently represented in an outline drawing by W. M. Flinders-Petrie, in *Tools and Weapons,* London, 1917, who says that four planes resembling his dissimilar drawing, found at Pompeii, consist of wooden "bodies" (stocks) iron plated on the bottom (sole), and on the front, back and top, but not on the sides; that the wooden "body," or stock, is perforated with a "back hole," for a handle; and that the "top opening" (shaving discharge) is cut through the top iron plate, and that "a cross bolt [as in the Silchester specimen], runs through the wooden body serving to block the wedge which holds the cutter in place." He also speaks, without illustrating it, of a plane found at Cologne "which has only an iron body without wood block." He adds "there is also a broken one from the Saalburg *(Archaeologia,* 1894, p. 139)" and finally illustrates a Roman "plane iron for shooting mouldings," found at Newstead, England.

That the soles of Anglo-American carpenters' or coopers' planes of the 18th and early 19th centuries were sometimes plated with iron or other metal, is shown by several specimens of plow and tongue planes and of coopers' sun planes and howels (Fig. 109) in the Bucks County Museum, also by a fork staff plane of the type

Fig. 111. Iron Plated Joiner's Plane

This bench plane of date about 1800 in construction resembles the Roman plane from Silchester (Fig. 110 A and B). Like the latter its stock consists of two wooden blocks plated on the sides and bottom with iron, and its wedge is held down in the shaving discharge hole, not in side channels, but under an iron cross piece. With its extremely narrow blade opening (mouth), and blade set upside down, it was probably used for very fine joiner's work, such as smoothing veneers, etc. It was found in 1925, with many other tools used in an amateur workshop, *c.* 1820 to 1860, by Charles J. Wister of Germantown, Pennsylvania, and given to the Bucks County Historical Museum by his heirs.

shown in Figure 122, shod with brass, and in the cooper's short jointer or pull plane (Fig. 114) shod with iron. But by way of much closer comparison with the Silchester plane, we here show the very remarkable

Iron Plated Joiner's Plane
(Fig. 111)

found October, 1925, among the tools long preserved in the amateur workshop *(c.* 1820 to 1860) of Charles J. Wister of Germantown, Pennsylvania.

In this plane, unnoticed by Holtzapffel and Knight, but probably made in England about 1800, two wooden blocks, entirely plated with iron on the sole and sides, but not on the top, form the stock. The top-opening between these blocks, forms the shaving discharge, and the wedge is held down exactly as in the Silchester specimen, except that a flat iron plate takes the place of the round cross bar. The slotted blade (originally single) is a replacement, and on

Fig. 112. Ancient Dutch Plane Irons

These are relics of the ancient Dutch Nova Zembla Expedition of 1596, *cf.* Fig. 106. The rusty irons (blades) are all basilled on the bottom only, to cut downward. The first to the left, with curved edge, belonged to a moulding plane the second and third with slightly convexed blades, to jack planes. The rest were probably used in trying planes. None are slotted or mounted with bolts for adjustment upon the "double iron" of modern times. Photographed by the kind permission of the Rijks Museum, Amsterdam.

account of the extreme fineness of the mouth, is set upside down (basil upwards). The wedge is not notched.

Of sixteenth century date, the

ANCIENT DUTCH PLANE IRONS
(Fig. 112)

here illustrated, are of interest, as showing that the jack plane and the moulding plane were used in Holland in 1596; that the plane irons were basilled then as now; and that the device of doubling them, *i. e.,* bolting two together, face to face to facilitate the upcurl of shavings, does not appear on any of the specimens. As proved by photographs seen by the writer, the Chinese have the plow plane, the spoke shave and the saw-toothed croze; also rabbet and bench planes resembling the

KOREAN PLANES (Fig. 113)

now in use in Korea and recently bought there by a missionary at Kang

Kei for the Doylestown Museum. But how long the plane has been in use in Korea and whether the Koreans got it from the Chinese, and finally, whether the Chinese invented it or borrowed it from Europe, in ancient or modern times, the writer has failed to learn.

Mr. Stewart Culin of The Brooklyn Institute Museum, quoting the evidence of relics found by him, and the *Wa-Kan-San-Sai-Dsue,* or *Chinese-Japanese Encyclopedia* of the 18th century, believes that the plane in Japan, which was there preceded by a one-hand draw-knife, called the "yariganna," is probably not older than the 16th or early 17th century.

Of considerable historic interest is the fact, that all the Anglo-American and continental European planes thus far considered have been pushed by the workman. But whoever supposes that all planes in all parts of the

Fig. 113. Korean Planes

In construction, the Korean rabbet plane (left) exactly resembles the Western instrument, with left-side shaving discharge. The fence (not seen) is a solid offset along the right side of the sole. The flat-basilled blade, sharpened only on the bottom, not shouldered, is set at right angles to the stock and not doubled ironed.

The blade of the right, lower plane, is convexed as with Western jack planes. In the other two little planes it is flat. In the upper specimen the sole has been reduced to a flat, circular protuberance. A little peg, utterly unlike the thin side-pronged plane-wedge of Europe, flattened on its upper side and driven not over, but under the iron, forces the latter upward against side shoulders in the discharge hole. This peg also wedges down the projecting handles into their open cross-cut sockets in the stock. In the two upper specimens, the handle, otherwise loose in the lower plane, has been extra fastened with little iron nails.

The lower plane has a square mortise (not seen) in the upper fore-end of the stock as if for the insertion of a horn (handle) now missing.

world are and always have been pushed, is mistaken.

Unfortunately the buyer of the Korean planes here illustrated, neglected to notice whether they were pulled or pushed. But Mr. Culin and Knight's *American Mechanical Dictionary,* tell us that the Japanese workman pulls the instrument towards him, and the next illustration

THE COOPER'S SHORT JOINTER OR PULL PLANE (Fig. 114)

shows a plane operated by the European and American cooper in the same comparatively unheard-of reversed fashion. Here, on working the little iron-soled instrument to smooth the edges of tank staves 14 to 22 feet long and too long for the cooper's

Fig. 114. Cooper's Short Jointer or Pull Plane

This little iron-soled plane is worked by two men, one holding the handles and pulling it towards him, the other bearing down upon the stock, with his thumbs inserted into the hole of the shaving discharge and pushing it. It is used on very long staves employed in constructing tanks, which staves may be from 14 to 22 feet long and therefore too long to be smoothed upon the cooper's long jointer plane (Fig. 103) which is adapted to barrel staves the longest of which would be about 8 feet in length. The tank stave is held in a vise or clamp for the purpose. Information given the writer November 18, 1925, by Charles Lynch, cooper, of 115 North Water Street, Philadelphia, and repeated by his Jewish workman, Abraham Ackovitz, who learned his trade at Kief, Russia. The picture shows the top and bottom of the same plane.

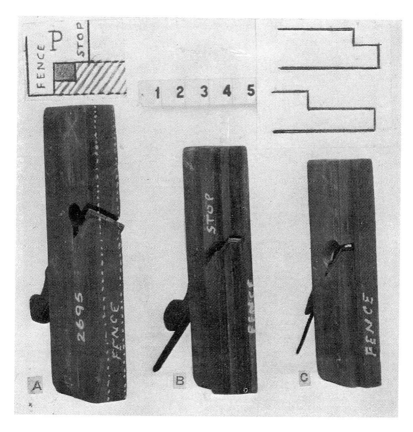

Fig. 115. The Rabbet Plane

This plane is here shown in its simplest, home-made, early 19th century, narrow form for notching board margins.

In (A), the blade is set, not at right angles to the stock, but slightly askew ("skew rabbet"). The fence was a rigid, longitudinal shoulder, now missing, originally nailed along the left side of the sole, within the dotted lines, to regulate the width and accuracy of the cut and its distance from a fixed margin. As this instrument lacks a stop, the depth of the excavation is left to the judgment of the workman. The plane, if pushed with its fence pressed against the free edge of a board, will notch the latter longitudinally, either downward on its narrow edge, or, if the board is laid flat, at right angles to its breadth, as in the enlarged outlines shown.

In (B), with a solid side stop, the blade is set at right angles to the stock, and the fence, an overlapping strip, is screwed fast upon the left side of the sole (right side in the picture).

In (C), the fence is a solid offset of the sole. But as this instrument also lacks a stop, the depth of its cut is again left to the workman's judgment.

In (A) and (B), the blade is basilled only to cut on the bottom (bottom rabbet); in (C) to cut on the forward side and bottom. In all three instruments the shavings are discharged where the blades are partly exposed at the side of the stock, and not upward through its middle as in the bench plane, and these discharge holes which penetrate the stock horizontally in (B) (C), open only on its right side in (A).

Fig. 116. The Moving Fillister

This much larger plane, in construction and purpose, exactly resembles the common rabbet (Fig. 115) except that the fence, instead of being rigid, *i.e.*, nailed fast, or a solid, down-extending shoulder of the sole, is an adjustable strip, sliding on slotted grooves, to increase or diminish the breadth of the cut by its distances from a fixed margin. The stop, also adjustable in (A) and (C), is a similarly slotted strip on the right sole side and in (B) is a down-sliding slotted peg. In (C) a small, cutting tooth, vertically penetrating the stock called the "router," incises the inner corner of the notch, just ahead of the blade, to prevent tearing the wood when the plane is worked, as sometimes, across the grain, *i.e.*, around the corner of a board or door panel. All these and all other rabbet planes have fences, either fixed or adjustable on the stock, or as loose, makeshift strips nailed on the stuff since, without a fence, the instrument would wriggle and cut falsely.

long jointer (Fig. 103), one workman pulls the plane towards him by its side-projecting peg handles, while another, bearing down upon it with thumbs inserted into its shaving discharge hole, pushes it forward. Whether this pull plane explains the construction and working of the Korean planes (Fig. 115) we are unable to say. But it is not the only pull plane used in the West, since the carpenter's moulding plane (Fig. 125) is pulled in the same way.

But to return to our subject. A few experiments with any of the levelling bench planes will show that they all work freely and in all directions across the wooden surface, while one of the chief characteristics of the next class of planes, namely the

FITTING PLANES

above mentioned, is that they do not work freely, *i. e.*, in order to produce the exact rectangular notches, made therewith, they are required to move by means of a so-called "fence," against an established margin. They vary greatly in construction, but their simple purpose, namely to enable one board to overlap and so fit or join upon another, is at the bottom of all carpentry and joinery. It appears first in

THE RABBET PLANE (Fig. 115) here shown in three samples of its simplest, narrowest form, with its blade set, not as usual at right angles to the stock, but askew, to avoid tearing soft woods. It is so narrow that it must discharge its shavings through side holes, and its fence is a downstep of the sole, which clears the board edge, slides along outside it, and so regulates the width of the cut.

A large group of these little, narrow, corner-cutting planes, identical in purpose, vary considerably in make. In some, the blade, as an exception, is set at right angles. In some, a shoulder (the stop), appears on the stock side to halt the downcut; but as others lack such stops, the depth of the cut is then left to the judgment of the workman. In many, the blades are sharpened to cut only downward; in others, also on one (the forward side); or, both ways; while the shavings in some escape from the right, in some from the left, and in others from both sides of the stock.

Another variety of the rabbet plane appears in the

MOVING FILLISTER (Fig. 116) a name, according to the *New English Dictionary,* of unknown origin. It is used for cutting wider notches, overlaps and panel inserts. The blade is set askew and sharpened on both side and bottom, and as the stock is much wider, the shavings escape through its middle. T h e conspicuous fence moves, *i.e.,* it is not fast upon the sole, but adjustable on slotted screws so as to widen or diminish the breadth of the cut, and an adjustable stop on the right side of the stock, regulates the depth excavated, while also some-

times an iron tooth scores the wood just ahead of the blade, to prevent tearing in cross-grain rabbeting.

Very different in appearance from the common little side-hole rabbets (Fig. 115) and used for special extra-wide or extra-placed notches, whether constructive or ornamental, these latter, heavy fillister planes, often home-made in the 18th century, also vary among themselves in outward appearance and plan of adjustment. Many stop on the sole, some on sliding pegs. Others lack stops altogether, and some, as if to puzzle the student and contradict the name, have no fences, in which case, straight strips must be nailed upon the stuff to guide them. Many lack the routing teeth, above mentioned, and though most are sharpened (basilled) to cut on the side as well as bottom, some cut only on the bottom. Nevertheless, these differences among themselves, and between them and the common rabbet (Fig. 115), are secondary variations adapted to the grain, wood, position, etc. To attempt to illustrate them in detail would not help matters, but rather confuse the subject. Their principle of construction is always explained by their purpose, which is to plane an accurate notch, of fixed depth and width, on or near the edge of a board.

While these notch-cutting or rabbet planes, as above mentioned, enable one board to overlap at a level upon another board, similarly notched, two boards may also fit together, if a tongued edge on one, enters a grooved edge or channel on the other, hence two other ancient fitting planes, called the plow and the tongue, were well known, according to Moxon, in the 17th century.

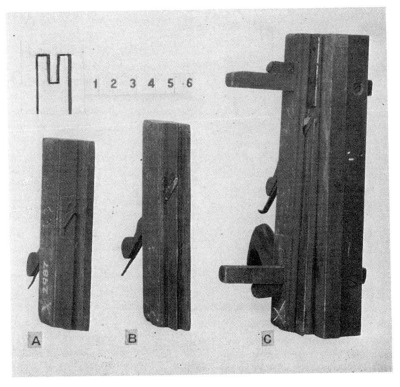

Fig. 117. The Plow

Illustrated as a very important plane in Moxon (1678), Diderot (1768), and in *The Circle of Mechanical Arts* (1813), for cutting the narrow fitting-channel (shown in outline above (A),) on the edges of boards. (A) and (B) show its simplest varieties in which the very narrow blade extending like a tooth for the entire depth of its cut is "shouldered," *i.e.*, thickened at its cutting end for strength, and further protected from back-bending, by a thin, iron plate fixed upon the stock to prop it from behind. In all three instruments the breadth of the tooth (11-16 inch in (B) to ¼ inch in (A) and (C) establishes the width of the cut, and the sole of the plane, acting as a stop, the normal depth of about ¾ of an inch. The offset in (A) and (B) on the left side of the sole (right side in the picture), which is held against the board edge, for the plane to slide upon, is the very important so-called fence, which exactly spaces the distance of the excavation from the said edge; and while in (A) and (B) this fence is an immovable solid shoulder on the sole, in (C) it is a heavy adjustable strip moving on wedged pegs penetrating the stock, and hence prepared to vary the distance of the channel from a fixed margin, as, for instance, in grooving the flat surface of boards for drawer bottoms, rather than their narrow edges for floor fitting.

THE PLOW (Fig. 117)

is here shown with its tooth-like projecting blade, "shouldered" for strength, that is, increasing to extra thickness at bottom, and with a fence as an offset of its sole. It was adapted to excavate the familiar normalized channels on board edges for floor and partition fitting, while in

THE TONGUE (Fig. 118)

the deeply notched blade, also shouldered, and enclosing a notch in the stock, gauged to its work by a fence—offset in the sole, and stopped by the bottom of the above mentioned notch, cuts away the board edge on either side of a thin, remaining ridge or tongue measured to fit into the cor-

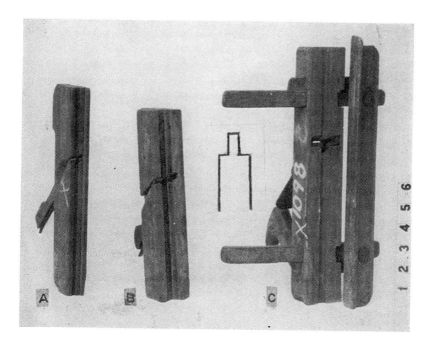

Fig. 118. The Tongue

In this plane the deeply-notched, shouldered blade, enclosing a corresponding longitudinal channel in the sole, cuts away the board edge on either side of a thin, remaining ridge, called the tongue (see enlarged outline), intended to fit a corresponding channel called the groove, made by the plow (Fig. 117), in flooring, partition boards, etc. In the smaller, simpler type (A) and (B), as in the plow, a solid shoulder on the left side of the sole (right side in the picture), forms an immovable fence, while the bottom of the channel, above mentioned, stops the cut. In (C), with similar stop, the adjustable fence is a heavy side strip moving to and from the blade, on pegs, tightened by wedges penetrating the stock. The blades of all three instruments are single, set at right angles to the sole, and basilled to cut only downward. (A) and (B) discharge their shavings only on the right side of the stock; (C) upward through its middle, as in the bench planes. As if to save wear, regardless of weight, some of the tongue planes have their soles and their channelled bottoms and even their fences, side-faced with iron.

responding groove cut by the plow (Fig. 117), as previously described.

Both of these planes are shown in their simple, narrow forms and also as larger, more adjustable instruments, in which the depth of the cut is regulated as above, while the fence, movable on wedges or hand screws, permits the tool to operate on the edge of wider boards or planks, at various distances from their margins. Both were continually used when the wooden-latched battened door, was tongued

and grooved to be hinged on its "H L" hinges, or when the kitchen table was topped with poplar, or when white pine floor boards, fourteen or more inches wide, were nailed down over ceiling or floor rafters with wrought nails.

As a variety of the plow, a still more comprehensive instrument called

THE BANDING PLANE (Fig. 119) was adapted by shifting fences or stops, or extra, nailed-on fences, and routing teeth, etc., to cut much broader chan-

Fig. 119. The Banding Plane

These grooving planes differ from the plow, not in purpose but in cutting a much wider groove. Not for tongue- and groove-fitting along the narrow margins of a board, but for special purposes upon its flat surface; hence their wider blades no longer need the long, iron back-prop, so conspicuous in the common plow (Fig. 117). The little specimen (A) probably intended to cut grooves at odd places for shelf inserts in cabinets, etc., lacks a stop, so that the depth of the groove is left to the workman's judgment. Moreover, as it might be required to cut across the grain, the blade is preceded by a little, double-toothed, vertically-set, iron blade, the router (here missing), to scrape out the channel corner and prevent tearing. The similar plane (B) shows the router in place, and is equipped with a sliding peg stop, entering the offset on its sole, adjustable on a transverse screw (not seen). In the heavy (C), probably intended for the insertion of heavy shelves, the single, router tooth precedes the blade on the left side only of the instrument, while offsets in the sole, on either side of the blade, effectively stop the depth of the cut. In (A) and (B), the shavings are discharged through the sides; in (C) upward, through the middle of the stock. In (A), the narrow blade is set at right angles to the sole; in (B) and (C), askew. In (C), the wide iron is not shouldered for strength, like the narrow blades of (B) and (C). All three instruments lack fences, hence, to guide them, a strip must be tacked at the right place upon the surface worked upon.

The enlarged outlines illustrate the grooves cut.

nels on the surface of the board, at greater distances from its narrow edge, either with or across the grain, for the insertion of book shelves, drawer bottoms, etc., or more rarely for ornament. But we are not done yet with the plow, for a still further peculiar

variety of the same channeling instrument (not shown) in use in England in 1850, was known as

THE OLD WOMAN'S TOOTH

in which a wide block, fenced to slide over a mortise hole, leveled the bot-

Fig. 120. The Toothing Plane

This little 6¾ inch long instrument is constructed and shaped like the smoothing plane (Fig. 105). The very long single and shouldered iron, smith-stamped "Newbould," is "pitched" about 22 degrees higher than usual, or more than 65 degrees above the horizontal. This basilled iron, 1½ inches wide, is notched with 33 minute side-raked notches, each notch coinciding with a groove on the flat surface, as shown in the enlarged outline. The wedge is notched as usual, and held in side channels. The front of the wooden stock is stamped "Butler Philad." The plane constructed to roughen wooden surfaces for glueing veneers thereon, was used between 1820 and 1860, by Charles J. Wister of Germantown.

tom of the latter by means of a deep, projecting, prong-like blade. A still further and now rare variety of the same tool, which the writer has found with difficulty for illustration, was known as

THE TOOTHING PLANE (Fig. 120)

in which the serrated blade scratches the surface of a slab of veneer to help the glue to stick, and in the

GAUGE PLANES

not shown, a knife or scoup "router," set in a stick and fenced by a sliding block like the carpenter's gauge, enabled the joiner to slice veneers or cut notches for marquetry inlay, at given distances from fixed margins. They

are best typified by an extraordinary cooper's plane known as

THE CROZE (Fig. 121)

in which instrument, a very large semi-circular fence, distorting the tool almost beyond recognition, holds the blade to its work when the cooper uses it, to ream out the semi-circular channel for barrel heads.

To end the subject of fitting planes, it may be said in general or repeated for the sake of clearness, that the notches, etc., which they cut, generally appearing on the narrow edges of boards, always required some kind of a fence, whether rigid or adjustable upon the plane, or nailed upon the

Fig. 121. The Croze

For comparison with the carpenter's plow, this celebrated instrument of the cooper, for plowing out the channel for barrel heads (itself called the croze), is here shown in three of its variations. In (A), the movable wooden stock, V-shaped in cross-section and convexed longitudinally, is iron-rimmed at its apex. It is adjustable on wooden hand screws penetrating the remarkable fence, a large, flat, semi-circle of wood, which latter is held horizontally on the barrel rim, as the instrument, pushed around the close-set stave tops, across the grain, cuts the needed circular groove to receive the barrel head. The triple blade, consisting of two routing teeth preceding a plow tooth, would not finish the job, for it would only cut a rectangular notch too narrow for the purpose, hence the croze (B). In this variety, the iron stock, shaped and fenced as before, is immovable. It is equipped with a single V-shaped blade which would open the channel already cut to the required size and wedge shape. (C) is a primitive version of (A) in which a little toothed saw, protruding from a single sliding peg, fenced as before, makes a preliminary channel which must be afterwards widened by the instrument (B).

stuff, to regulate their distance from a fixed margin, and that the irons were not doubled as in the bench plane. Furthermore, that sometimes, where the cut is far removed from a corner, no fence appears on the plane, in which case the fence must always be nailed down across the stuff in the form of a separate strip; and finally, that because of the varying grains of different woods and because some of these planes must cut not only with, but across the grain and on the side, as well as the bottom of the blade, many of the said blades, unlike those of the bench planes, are set askew or, to fur-

Fig. 122. The Fork Staff or Hollow Plane

This instrument, with its sole concaved (in cross-section) and enclosing a blade curved to match (in its larger size above) will round off a tool handle, or a small post, or banister rail, etc. In its smaller size, as the little, extra wide-mouthed specimen (lower), worked in all directions, it will smooth down rotundities in furniture, etc., for the cabinetmaker. The middle plane, by means of its rounded-corner blade-extension, would reduce and flute on either side an already rounded cylinder or bead moulding. All three planes lack stops and all, except the latter, will work freely, longwise with the grain, on cylindrical surfaces.

A small fork staff plane bought by the writer with some whaleship cooper's tools in New Bedford, Mass., in 1897, has its sole covered with a sheet of copper or brass bent upward and held fast under wooden strips rivetted against its sides.

ther prevent tearing, preceded by vertical teeth that "rout" the notched corner ahead of the blade.

Thus far the planes examined appear as constructive tools only. The next pictures illustrate a very large and varied group, no longer absolutely necessary for the builder's purpose, but interesting to house decorators and furniture collectors as having produced the grooved fillets and ornamental mouldings of colonial times.

These are known as the

MOULDING PLANES

which in their simpler form appear in the next two illustrations as

THE FORK STAFF OR HOLLOW PLANE
(Fig. 122)

with the sole concave in cross-section and with concave, hollow blade to match, used to round longitudinal, convex surfaces, such as stair rails, etc., and as its ill-named complement

Fig. 123. The Convex or Round Plane

This rarely used plane, with central shaving discharge, sole-convexed in cross-section and with blade to match, works freely, lengthwise with the grain, to round the inside of wooden gutters or to deepen mouldings already cut. With its reverse, the fork staff or hollow plane (Fig. 122), it illustrates the class of planes called hollows and rounds.

THE CONVEX OR ROUND PLANE (Fig. 123)

with its sole convex in cross-section, enclosing a convex blade, which reverses the work of the fork staff by cutting or widening large cylinderical, concave grooves, or, if ever used for practical purposes, the inside of wooden troughs.

But far beyond the simple work of these so-called hollows and rounds, moulding planes for pure ornament, appear in a vast number of elaborate forms. They are reasonably typified by

THE MOULDING PLANE (Fig. 124)

a little instrument with a variously grooved blade which, dicharging its shavings on the side, and fenced and stopped by offsets in its sole, moulds the edge of a table top, etc., or beads the corner of a ceiling rafter or beautifies a door panel.

THE MOULDING PLANE (Fig. 125)

a larger instrument, with central shaving discharge, fenced and stopped as before, either pushed by one man, or pushed by one and pulled by another, puts the would-be classic touch along the board edge in wider mouldings for wall, fireplace or cornice.

At this point we halt before a vast, collected variety of decorative instruments, which in make, adjustment and blade contour, seem to have no end. Many of them may be dated reasonably by the changing fashion in house and furniture mouldings, revealed by their blades. Sometimes, to the confusion of the student, it appears that one plane will not finish the cut. Then one or more others must follow it to perfect imperfect curves, or, like the "snipe's bill," with side-curved tooth, to undercut them. Without attempting to examine or discuss their endless

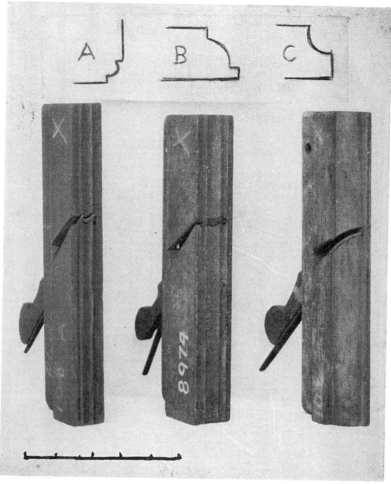

Fig. 124. The Moulding Plane

In these three small examples of the moulding plane, the curved, basilled blades, sharpened with files and special whetstones, conform to the flutings of the sole, which flutings, at their thinnest projections, are often reinforced by inserted strips of box or hard wood. Offsets in the sole (to the left in the pictures) form the stop; to the right, the fence. The familiar outlines, next above each plane, show the mouldings it produces.

variations or names (ogee, ovolo, cavetta, astragal, etc., etc.), or fence or stop equipment, we can understand all and explain any of them, if we fix our attention upon their purpose rather than their shape.

To conclude the subject of planes, the next illustration shows a cele-brated instrument far outrivaling in prevalence all other tools of its class, which may be said to be not only ornamental but constructive, namely

THE SASH FILLISTER OR SASH PLANE
(Fig. 126)

in which a rabbet plane, cutting a corner notch, and a moulding plane, cut-

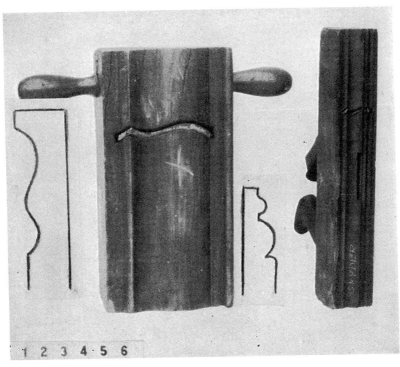

Fig. 125. The Moulding Plane

While the little moulding planes shown in Fig. 122 decorate often only the narrow edge of boards when edged up in the vise, these wide and often heavy instruments cut broad mouldings on the flat face of boards. In the cumbersome, two-man instrument (left), a second workman pulls the transverse peg handles, while the first pushes the "tote" (not seen). The offset, screwed fast on the side of the stock, is the fence, and the right sole margin, beyond the blade (left in the picture), the stop. The plane cuts the out-line next it on the flat side of a board. The smaller, one-man plane (right), fenced by the solid, left offset in its sole (right in the picture) and stopped as before, cuts the smaller outline.

Both instruments, like others of their variety, discharge their shavings not sideways, but upward, through a central hole in the stock. To save wear or breakage, many of the wooden ridges following the blade curvature of these planes, have been replaced or reinforced with entire strips, or as in the right plane, by inserts of boxwood, one of which has fallen out.

ting a "quarter round," are adjustably held together by handscrews, so as to straddle and double-corner a strip of wood on both sides and by two planing operations at once, thereby shaping it into the well-known, glass-holding framework of the common colonial window sash which, to this day, has preserved its contour of two hundred years ago.

From an artistic point of view, the old moulding planes claim attention as having by means of decorative cornices, chair rails, door, wall and fireplaces, so greatly beautified the houses and furniture of the 18th century. Diderot illustrates (1768) French mouldings, often undercut and far more elaborate than any seen by the writer in old American houses, or which could have been produced by observed planes.

Fig. 126. The Sash Fillister or Sash Plane

Two planes, namely, the rabbet (upper) and the ovolo moulding (lower), are set together on hand screws forming a single instrument, which, when pushed along the edge of a board, clamped edge-upward in the carpenter's vise, will cut the outline A B C thereupon. Then, when the board is released and ripped into a long strip on the line of E, and replaned in reverse into the outline A E D in cross section, the strip becomes the style or muntin of a common window sash in which the outline B A E faces indoors, with the opposite side notched for the glass and putty at C D, fronting the weather.

But the day of the moulding plane passed seventy years ago. The evidence shows that it reached its climax at the beginning of the 19th century, when, as listed by *The Circle of Mechanical Arts* (1813), and Rees' *Cyclopaedia,* and as shown by collected examples, a far greater variety of these hand instruments existed, whether home-made or factory-made, imported or domestic, or improved by English or American patents, than Moxon pretends to describe or mention. It was between 1830 and 1860, that wood-working machinery (planing mills) put them all out of general use.

By a reasonable number of photographs, we have hoped, not to illustrate their endless variations, but to save the reader a headache by explaining their purpose, which is a key to their construction in every case.

As a supplement to the great surfacing tools above mentioned, consider last

THE WOOD RASP (Fig. 127)

the scobina of the Romans, mentioned in 1678 in the *Probate Records of Essex County, Massachusetts, 1635-1681, 3 vols., George Francis Dow, editor. Salem, Mass., the Essex Institute, 1916-1920,* a heavy, steel file,

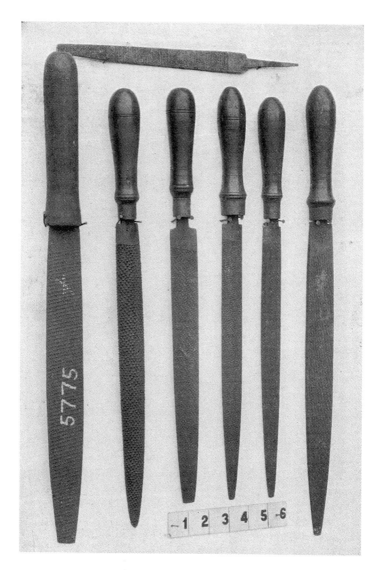

Fig. 127. The Wood Rasp

Mounted with a wooden handle driven upon its tang or thin, pointed haft-end, the ancient radula of the Romans, overlooked by Moxon, resembles in appearance a common, metal worker's file, though it often differs in the make of its teeth. These, though sometimes (two right specimens) cut by the blacksmith in close parallel lines, as in files, to file metal, are generally, as in all the other specimens here shown, punched up into burrs to reduce or round off the rough edges of tool handles, etc., in wood. The handled files of date *c.* 1830 are from the large store of tools, preserved by the Wister family, at their colonial house, known as "Grumblethorpe" in Germantown, Pa., as amateur relics of Charles J. Wister (born 1782, d. 1865). They were presented to the Doylestown Museum, July, 1925, by his descendants, Owen Wister and Alexander W. Wister. The upper rasp was made by Seth Nelson, mountaineer artificer of Clinton County, Pa., about 1880.

Fig. 128. The Scraper

The sharp-edged tablet of steel, here illustrated by five examples, and now (1925) sold as a factory-made tool at hardware stores, is the *radula* of the Romans, though neither Moxon nor Diderot mention it. It must have survived through the Middle Ages as a joiner's and carpenter's tool, to remove paint or varnish and to follow the plane over rough places in knot holes, etc. J. Stokes, *Complete Cabinetmakers' and Upholsterers' Guide*, London, 1829, says that the English carpenter made it for himself with the cold chisel, out of broken saw blades held in a vise, square-edged on a grindstone and then sharpened on a turkey stone. The four rectangular specimens were loaned for this illustration by Oliver Hohlbain, cabinetmaker of Doylestown, and were made by him and used about 1905 to 1910.

often surfaced with round burrs punched upon it by the blacksmith, for finishing round-surfaced tool handles, etc., and the very effective

SCRAPER (Fig. 128)

This is the Roman radula. A hundred years ago, according to J. Stokes, *Complete Cabinet Maker's Guide,* London, 1829, it was cut with a cold chisel out of saw blades and made sharp on a turkey stone (oiled whetstone), and is sometimes still so made and used by the joiner to follow the plane over knotty surfaces. The common

SAND PAPER

otherwise called glass or emery paper, not found in home-made form by the writer, and not here shown, is now a factory-made, store-bought product and as part of the shop stock of every carpenter, is a universal and very efficient agent for smoothing all kinds of woodwork. Yet, Moxon (1678), who describes the smoothing and polishing of wood and iron in the turning lathe, with a piece of seal skin or the frayed end of a Dutch reed, does not mention it. Neither does Dr. Johnson's *Dictionary* (1754). But Martin's *The Circle of Mechanical Arts,* London, 1813, speaks of "glass paper" seal skin and Dutch reed as used with the turning lathe; the *New English Dictionary* quotes "emery paper," in 1772, and J. Stokes' *Complete Cabinetmaker's and Upholsterer's Guide,* London, 1829, tells the joiner how to make "glass paper" by sprinkling glass on glued cartridge paper.

Tools for Shaping and Fitting

U P TO this point, the tools of the carpenter, however indispensable, may be looked upon as preparatory to his final work, namely, the perfected adjustment of pieces of wood. Hence, all the instruments which form to a desired size the previously prepared wooden material for that final purpose, whether by cutting it into shape and over- or underlapping it with or without a framework, or fastening it together with the help of mortise, tenon, dovetail, mitre, nails, bolts, pegs, glue, etc., may be regarded as the final master tools of the woodworker, among which, for fear of confusion, though at the risk of describing some instruments out of place, we venture to distinguish in a series, Tools for Shaping and Fitting, beginning with one of the most conspicuous and important of them all, namely

THE OPEN HAND SAW (Fig. 129) a wide, c. 2 ft. by 10 in. smooth-ground steel blade, with triangular-shaped, pointed teeth notched at a slant (raked), away from the hand, so as to cut chiefly on the push of the workman.

The picture shows three of these open saws of Anglo-American type, and probably of English factory make, imported into the United States before 1830 to 1840. All are decorated on their upper blade margins with the minute ornamental knobs, not shown by Moxon but appearing in pictures of the 18th century, still used to adorn saw blades. The upper, a rare tool, found in a gravedigger's shed at the

old (1763) Buckingham Friends Meeting House, near Doylestown, Pa., shows the earliest type of this widebladed, unframed Anglo-American carpenter's hand saw, as described and illustrated by Moxon. In construction it resembles the carpenter's hand saw of today, except in the shape and set of its handle, which lacks the now invariable hollow grasp and is not riveted upon the blade, through a slot, but set on a tang. This hollow grasp, which Moxon does not show, and the earliest example of which, found by the writer, appears in Hogarth's engraving of "Gin Lane," dated 1756, appears upon the two lower saws, mounted with homemade handles by American carpenters before the establishment of American saw factories, c. 1840, while the greater antiquity of the upper saw, the teeth of which are very roughly filed and now show no "set," is proved, not only by this now utterly forgotten tanged handle and open grasp, but also by the following old Dutch copper engraving of 1718,

THE CARPENTER'S OPEN HAND SAW OF THE 17TH CENTURY (Fig. 130) where the same saw is clearly represented lying on the ground. It also appears carried under the arm of a house building carpenter, in a little pictured title page of the rare *Exact Dealer Refined*, 5th edition, enlarged, by J. H. Rhodes, London, 1702.

In no other resting place except the secluded and rarely visited out house of the dead, where this relic was found, can we reasonably suppose that

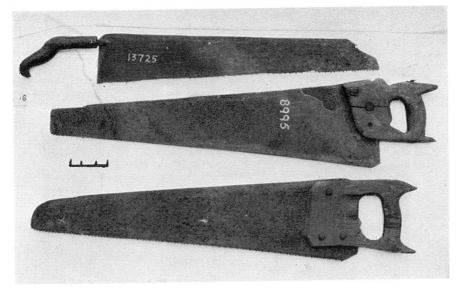

Fig. 129. The Open Hand Saw

The two lower specimens are old Bucks Co., Pa., carpenter's relics. Their factory-made blades are riveted in a slot upon homemade handles, which latter show the now universal hollow grasp, not appearing on Anglo-American saws before about 1750. The very rare upper specimen, found in a grave digger's shed at the Buckingham Friends Meeting House, Bucks Co., Pa., and doubtless used for cutting off tree roots in freshly dug graves, is of date probably before 1768, and shows the earlier type of open handle, mounted on a tang, as used in Holland, England, and the American Colonies in the 17th and 18th centuries. The rudely filed, irregular teeth of this saw have lost their set, and a down-cut with ornamental knob, partly rusted away, decorates the end of the blade on its top corner margin, which trivial and curious silhouette noted by Disston, without explanation of its origin, in *The Saw in History* (Henry Disston & Sons, Philadelphia, 1916), and now appearing on many American open hand saws, appears clearly on the two lower specimens.

such a saw would so long have escaped the innumerable chances which elsewhere would have destroyed or lost it. One hundred and eighty years ago, or about 1740, when the original meeting house was built, we may reasonably suppose that the first gravedigger used the tool to saw off grave-obstructing tree roots in the freshly cleared graveyard, which is still surrounded by woods. But the once omnipresent roots have long since rotted away; generations have come and gone since the old meeting house burnt down, in 1768, to be then replaced by the present building, while the saw, never lost, broken, worn out, or rusted away, remains.

A small variety of the one-man, open hand saw is shown in two of its smaller forms in the next illustration as

THE COMPASS AND KEYHOLE SAW
(Fig. 131)

with teeth unset, as Moxon says, and with blades extra thick for strength, but extra narrow, and thin at the back, to avoid friction in cutting short circular kerfs, as for key or latch or lock holes in doors.

The blade of the old homemade, upper specimen, as with modern factory-made types, used for fine keyhole work, is riveted in a slot on a straight handle, not mounted on a tang like

De TIMMERMAN.

Het minder word betracht, Het meerder niet bedacht.

Fig. 130. The Carpenter's Open Hand Saw of the 18th Century

The picture called *De Timmerman* (The Carpenter), is one of a hundred copper engravings, representing workmen at their trades, from *"Spiegel Van Het Mense'yk Bedryf*, Van Kornelis Van Der Lys and J & K Luyken, Amsterdam, 1718." The hand saw lying on the ground with its broad blade decorated with the still surviving ornamental knob at the upper end margin, and tanged, not riveted, to the handle, and with its small, down-curved open hand grasp, is almost an exact duplicate of the ancient hand saw found in 1920, by Mr. R. P. Hommel, in the grave digger's shed at the old Quaker Meeting House at Buckingham, Bucks Co., Pa., shown in Fig. 129.

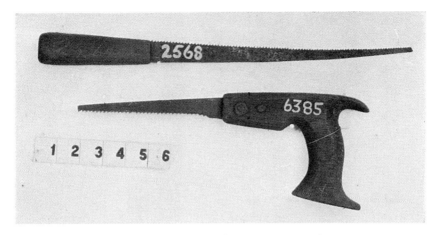

Fig. 131. The Keyhole and Compass Saw

The very narrow-bladed keyhole saw is here shown in the upper specimen, No. 2568, and illustrated by Moxon in 1678. Its old-style handle, not formed to the hand, and riveted on the blade, is straight like the handle of a chisel. The teeth, in this case, five to the inch, unlike those of other saws, are not set at all, and the blade, tapering from one to one-quarter of an inch, thins towards the top or back, so as to run easily in a wide kerf, when the instrument, following a more or less curved line, cuts around a corner, and where, but for the frame, which is always in the way, the much thinner strained blade of the Buhl saw (Fig. 144) would do the work better. The instrument thus shaped appears as carried in the carpenter's pocket in the old engraving of date about 1500 (Fig. 32), and also as the hand saw in Durer's *Melancholia*, and in the *Annunciation*, c. 1438, by the unknown Flemish painter called the Master of Flemalle in the Merode Gallery, Brussels.

The compass saw (lower specimen), No. 6385, also with thin back and unset teeth, called "fret saw" and "lock saw" by Knight (*cf. American Mechanical Dictionary*, 1878), differs from the above in its modelled block handle grasp also riveted upon the blade; otherwise ,it is only a large variety of the keyhole saw.

Fig. 132. The Tenon Saw

The short, rectangular blade of this fine-toothed instrument, briefly described, but not illustrated, by Moxon, in 1678, and named, in the *New English Dictionary*, first for 1549, is so thin that to keep it from buckling, it is stiffened with a metal rib along its top. Hence, the blade never entirely penetrates the wood. With its slightly set teeth (8 to the inch in 1878, according to Knight) it was used one hundred years ago, as now, to smooth-cut the edges of tenons, dovetails, or mitre fittings, sawed in the mitre box. Open hand saws, stiffened with metal back ribs, are used in Japan (*cf.* Fig. 133), and a small form of similar instrument, with hollow-grasp handle, and stiffened with a wooden back rib, as an extension of its handle, is shown in Fig 134, as used by cabinetmakers in China.

Modern varieties, with metal back ribs, are described by Knight as the "dovetail saw," for cutting dovetails, with 15 teeth to the inch and about 9 inches long (also illustrated with a straight handle in Disston's *The Saw in History*), the "carcass saw," with 11 teeth to the inch, and the "sash saw," backed with brass instead of iron, with 13 teeth to the inch.

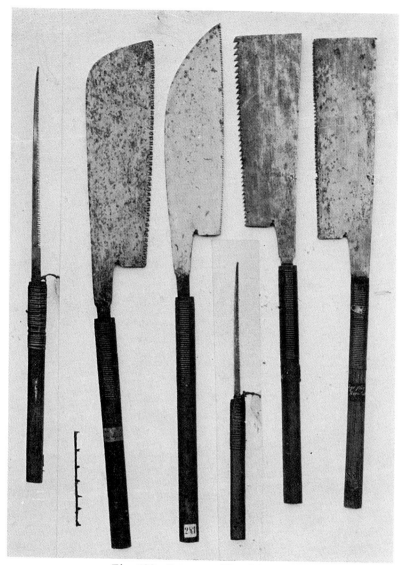

Fig. 133. Japanese Hand Saws

These saws were collected in Japan, before 1873, and were exhibited in the Vienna World's Fair of that year. They are now (1926) in the Commercial Museum of Philadelphia, and were photographed by kind permission of the Director, Dr. William P. Wilson.

Though ignorant of the history of Japanese saws, we learn from a Japanese sawyer, now working at Kuling, China, questioned by Mr. R. P. Hommel, in 1925, that specimen No. 2, counting to right with very long, paired, and slightly raked teeth, is used for cross-cutting; No. 5, with large, sharply raked teeth, diminishing in size towards the handle, is used for ripping, that other varieties, not shown, stiffened by back ribs, are used as tenon saws. Some Japanese saws are double, *i.e.*, toothed on both sides of the blade, and a large variety of No. 5 is used for tree felling, by sawing off cleared roots and then roping the tree top and pulling over the trunk to break the tap root. All these saws cut on the pull of the workman, and all are tanged upon straight wooden handles wrapped with bamboo. Nos. 1 and 4, counting to right, which are keyhole saws, are constructed like ours, with unset

the example illustrated by Moxon (Fig. 67E). The lower saw, probably much reduced by sharpening, also shows the slotted block handle with open grasp riveted upon the blade, still in use.

Look next at another ancient variety of the one-man, open hand instrument, namely

THE TENON SAW (Fig. 132)

Here the extra-thin, fine-toothed rectangular blade with hollow-grasp handle slotted and riveted upon it, intended for very exact mitring or otherwise cross-cutting of comparatively small flat wooden strips, is stiffened to prevent buckling or wavering, by a steel rib upon its back margin. Therefore the entire blade can never penetrate a piece of wood.

Moxon illustrates a variety of the mitre box (Fig. 78) in which these back-ribbed hand saws have been continually used since his time; but though he imperfectly describes, he unfortunately does not illustrate the saw itself. Nevertheless, as here shown, it is clearly pictured in *The Circle of Mechanical Arts,* of 1813.

From a world-wide and historical point of view, the comparatively short, open, one-man hand saws, in their three ancient types, as thus described, form a distinct class by themselves, while their varieties in size, handle and blade construction, adapted to several purposes of fine or coarse or straight or curved cutting, seem minor considerations, compared to the two

following facts, in their construction, namely: first, that as distinct from some of the preparatory saws (pit saws), already described, none of their blades are strained upon a frame, but all cut with the open blade; while, as here shown, in their American and Continental European types, they are all extra strong, or wide or stiff, to prevent buckling; and second, that all are equipped with teeth raking away from the workman, and hence, as described later, designed to cut on the push, while the Chinese and Japanese open hand saws, and (as Disston asserts) the Turkish hand saws, tooth-raked contrariwise, cut on the pull.

Supplementing Disston's interesting illustrations (*cf.* his valuable pamphlet *The Saw in History*, Henry Disston & Sons, Phila., 1916) we, by help of photographs from originals, here illustrate several

JAPANESE HAND SAWS (Fig. 133)

thus pulled by the workman, originally collected in Japan for the Vienna World's Fair of 1873, and kindly loaned for illustration by the Commercial Museum of Philadelphia.

In comparing these beautiful and delicate pull saws made of finely wrought steel, with our own old push saws, we find that though less effectively grasped, in their straight handles wrapped with bamboo, their teeth, in one case diminishing in size towards the handle, are far more varied, elaborate, and effective, than those of our pre-factory instruments of

---

teeth and blades thickened on the toothed edge to widen the kerf. Otherwise, the teeth of all of them are not only carefully sharpened, but set, *i.e.,* bent to the right and left to prevent blade friction by enlarging the kerf.

Owing to their straight handles they are less firmly grasped than our saws, but they cut, according to Mr. Hommel, more easily. Their far more delicate and varied teeth require much greater care and skill in sharpening with very fine, knife-edged files.

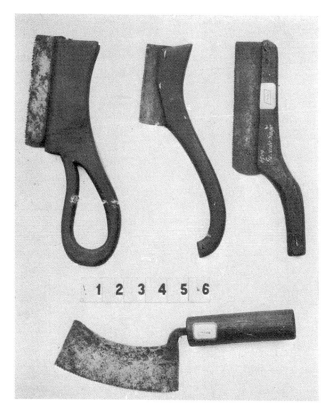

Fig. 134. Chinese Cabinet and Coffinmakers' Saws

Photographed by kind permission of the Commercial Museum of Philadelphia, from specimens in their collection. According to information received in 1925 from Mr. R. P. Hommel, at Kuling, China, the three little upper saws, in which the blade is stiffened by inserting it in a slot in the wooden handle, are used by cabinetmakers for sawing tenons or dovetails, or channels for the insertion of key-blocks (described later) in furniture. The lower saw, without this back stiffening, mounted on a tang, is employed by all coffinmakers in sawing the grooves for the insertion of the end panels in the remarkable Chinese coffins, the four long sides of which consist of four log-slabs thus boxed together at either end. Though the tooth-rake of these little open hand saws does not show clearly in the photo-engraving, they all cut on the pull, according to Mr. Hommel. Hollow hand grasps, as on the upper left-hand specimen, appear sometimes, but not always on these Chinese cabinetmakers' saws.

A modern factory-made variety of the three upper saws, *i.e.*, in which the blade is slotted into an extension of the wooden handle called the stair builders' saw, appears in recent price lists, and is illustrated in Disston's *The Saw in History.*

Disston also shows two small, fine-toothed, modern forms of the lower specimen, minus back stiffening, with blades riveted upon open wooden hand grasps, called the pattern-maker's saw and the joiner's saw.

one hundred years ago, and therefore must have required much greater care and skill in sharpening, wth far finer knife-edged files, than ours. As related to these, the next picture shows several.

CHINESE CABINETMAKERS' AND COFFIN-MAKERS' SAWS (Fig. 134)

which also, as one-man, open hand saws, generally contradict our saws in action and, like the Japanese speci-

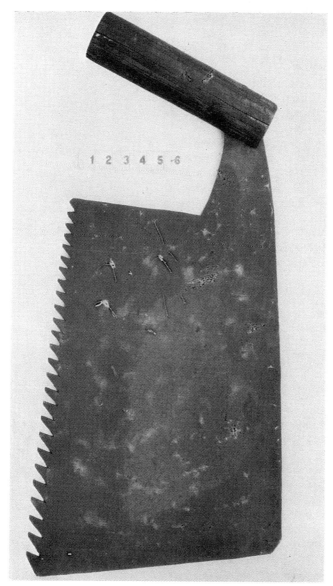

Fig. 135. Japanese Rip Saw or Board Saw

In this remarkable one-man rip saw, with blade 21 inches long tanged into its wooden handle, the teeth are raked to cut on the pull as in the smaller hand saw shown in Fig. 133 and decrease in size towards the workman, according to Disston, *The Saw in History,* p. 10, which shows a picture of the saw in use. The single Japanese workman, standing upon a small log, propped up at one end on a large log, cuts the former longitudinally into one or more planks or strips with this saw. Photographed by kind permission of Dr. W. P. Wilson, Director of the Commercial Museum, Philadelphia. The specimen there on exhibition had been shown at the Paris Exposition in 1900. With teeth apparently never sharpened or set, it seems never to have been used.

mens, cut on the pull; while the cumbrous

JAPANESE RIP SAW OR BOARD SAW
(Fig. 135)

illustrates the remarkable instrument, not used in China, by which a single Japanese workman, standing on a tilted log, saws it into boards.

Though in general the bronze or iron or steel saws of pre-historic times, or of Greece, Rome, or Egypt, however constructed have long since rusted, or lost their mounting, a few ancient and very rare specimens of this open-unframed type, much overlooked by antiquaries, have been preserved in museums, such as the

EGYPTIAN HAND SAW (Fig. 136)

found by Mr. James Burton, in a basket of carpenter's tools in an ancient tomb of the 18th Dynasty (c. 1450 B.C.) at Thebes, and here illustrated by the kind permission of the British Museum.

A celebrated wall picture from Thebes, showing a man ripping downwards a vertically set board with one of these open saws, but much longer than the specimen here shown, published in Wilkinson's *Ancient Egyptians,* John Murray, London, 1854, p. 118; several moulds for casting bronze saws, found in Scandinavia, and illustrated by Disston; saw blade fragments found in Assyria, or at prehistoric Swiss lake dwellings, shown in

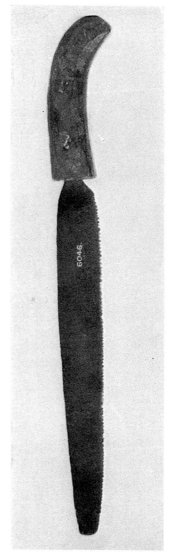

Fig. 136. Egyptian Hand Saw

This saw, now in the British Museum, was found in 1853, in a dry and dusty tomb of the 18th Dynasty, or about 1450 B.C., at Thebes, by Mr. James Burton. It was in a basket, along with drills, a drill bow, chisels, an oil horn, a nail bag, and a short wooden club mallet, swelling at one end into a heavy conical cylinder, shaped like the modern sculptor's mallet, but made, not with an extra wooden handle inserted in a bored hole, but of a single stick, like the frow club shown in Fig. 13. The saw-blade is of bronze or hardened copper, mounted on a tang, in a handle of wood. The teeth are not set, and are V-shaped, without rake. Hence the instrument would cut both ways. Its blade is 10½ inches, and its handle 4⅝ inches long. Photographed by kind permission of the British Museum.

outline or photograph by Sir W. M. Flinders-Petrie in *Tools and Weapons*, Constable, London, 1917, conclusively prove that these short one-man, open blades, as distinct from framed saws, were in use from the beginning of history. Hence, we may reasonably infer that they continued in use in various shapes and forms throughout the Middle Ages. But in an effort to trace them backwards from Moxon's time, books and pictures fail us. As filling the historic gap of two thousand years, we have been unable to here illustrate anything older or more interesting than the little tanged instruments, of compass saw shape, in Dürer's *Melancholia* (Fig. 107), or in the pockets of carpenters in the German print shown in Fig. 32, or finally the large, swordlike specimen

AN ITALIAN HAND SAW OF THE 17TH
CENTURY (Fig. 137)
here reproduced from an unidentified Italian print probably engraved before 1700.

So much for the open, one-made hand saw, but as a little reflection tells us not only that a saw blade, if thin and narrow, will cut better than if thick and wide, but also that a thin and narrow blade will buckle or bend, even if made of steel, unless it is either pulled toward the workman, or strained upon a frame, we find, as we might expect, that a considerable variety of thin-bladed saws, mounted in frames, were used either by one or two men for various woodworking purposes a hundred years ago. One of the most familiar of these was and still is

THE WOOD CUTTER'S SAW OR BUCK
SAW (Fig. 138)
Let us look closely at this ancient framed saw and in order to escape the confusion that has followed the history of saws in general, observe clearly, first, that the thin, flexible blade is strained, not in the middle, but along the margin of its frame, by means of a rope twisted tight between its side arms, upon a stick caught against its central brace, and second, above all, that its blade is rigid. It is this latter important fact which greatly limits the use and scope of the instrument. You cannot rip, *i.e.*, cut longitudinally, a board, nor cross-cut a large log, with the buck saw, because the central brace is continually in the way. Hence, the buck saw is, and always has been, confined to the cross-cutting of comparatively thin or narrow wooden pieces. Although frequently shown by Diderot, as used by French carpenters and woodworkers in the 18th century, the old Anglo-American carpenter seems to have rejected it. As here illustrated, in a homemade frame, it is still used, not by carpenters and joiners, but by farmers, when holding the long frame-side of the saw, left hand uppermost, and right hand on its lower extension, they cross-cut fire wood sticks on

THE SAW BUCK OR WOOD HORSE
(Fig. 139)
another still familiar apparatus described by Moxon, consisting of two wooden crotches, pegged together on a cross bar.

Having noticed the rigid blade of the wood saw, let us look carefully at the next saw, here illustrated, superficially resembling it, often confused with it, but which, by a slight difference in construction, far outclasses it in efficiency. This is

THE BOW SAW (Fig. 140)

Fig. 137. Italian Hand Saw of the 17th Century

From an unidentified copper engraving, in the Italian style of the 17th century, representing *The Downfall of Paganism*, in which St. Simon is shown (as usual by the Old Masters) with a saw,—this time a large, long-bladed open hand saw, in his left hand, as he reads a book.

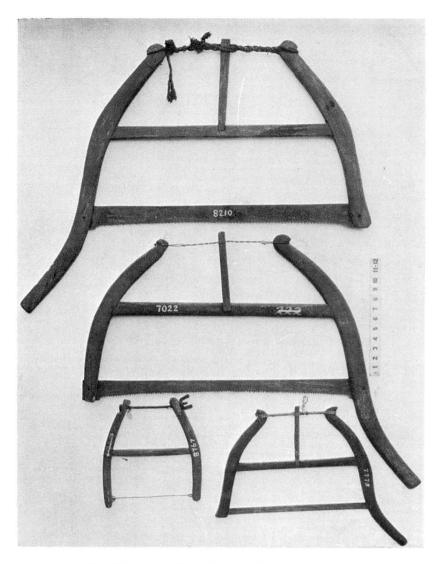

Fig. 138. The Wood Cutter's Saw or Buck Saw

This saw of ancient European type, in construction, resembles Fig. 110, except that the blade is wider and therefore stronger, and not adjustable to various angles, but rigid. It is still widely used among farmers, etc., who grease the blade with a piece of hog fat, kept hung on a nail in the wood shed, and crosscut firewood sticks laid on the wood horse (Fig 139). The specimens shown are from Bucks County, with blades probably factory made, but in frames constructed by the farmer or village carpenter or wheelwright.

Out of place here, the small saw, No. 8767, tightened with a thumb screw, bought from C. E. Osburn, Philadelphia, in October, 1907, was used for cutting cheese.

The writer has been unable to learn whether this device of the rope-twist and twist-stick was known in ancient Rome or Egypt. W. M. Flinders-Petrie in the series of classified groups of outline drawings and photo engravings of ancient implements, now exhibited in European museums, in his *Tools and Weapons*, Constable, London, 1910, shows

Fig. 139. The Saw Buck or Wood Horse

As represented by Moxon in 1698, each end of the apparatus (left) consists of two heavy wooden sticks mortised together in the form of a diagonal cross. These crosses are pegged together in the middle on a stout longitudinal stick, so as to form a double crotch, upon which the farmer, having placed the long firewood stick, whereon he rests his left knee, saws off the stick inside or outside the crotch, with the buck saw. This specimen, fifty or more years old, now owned and loaned for the picture, by Mr. B. H. Barnes, was used by his father and grandfather on a farm about a mile and a half north of Doylestown, Pa.

The *New English Dictionary*, quoting 1860 for its earliest use of the American name "saw buck," derives it from the Dutch . Zaag-boc, and German Saegebock,—Zaag, Saege = saw, and boc, bok=goat. In New England it is known as a "saw horse," in the vernacular of the 19th century.

The right specimen is one of a curious class of tree sawyer's props, used in pairs, and pushed close together from opposite sides under the uplifted heavy bough of a freshly felled tree, as shown in the appended outline, whereupon the bough is sawed off with the buck saw or cross-cut saw. Bought from William Giles, on Buckingham Mountain, Bucks Co., Pa., in 1926.

---

an old Egyptian frame saw "from the Fayum." as if it might be the only ancient frame saw thus far found in its original frame. But it is stretched on a bent staff, lacks the rope and twist stick, and is therefore constructed, not like the buck saw, here described, or the bow saw, but like the Buhl saw, Fig. 144.

One of these instruments. thus tightened with the twist-stick and with the long handle-extension on one side of the frame, though not clearly showing whether its *blade* is twistable or rigid, appears in a French manuscript miniature of the middle 15th century, *Valeur Maxime*, by Simon de Hesledin de Nicholas de Coiresse (British Museum, Harl. 4375, fol. 123, *cf.* also *The Guilds of Florence* by Edgecumbe Staley, Methuen, London, 1906), kindly shown the writer by Mr. Joseph E. Sanford, and a photograph recently received from Mr. R. P. Hommel proves that an exactly similar saw. with rigid blade, though lacking the long handle-extension, is now (1926) in general use among the carpenters of China.

otherwise called by Holtzapffel, in 1846, "Continental Frame Saw;" by Knight, in 1878, "Turning Saw," "Sweep Saw," "Frame Saw;" and by Disston, in 1916, "Web Saw;" which, as the great rival of the open, hand saw described (Fig. 129) and preferred thereto in some parts of the world, may be considered as one of the most interesting and important tools of the ancient carpenter.

In this one-man instrument, the blade is again strained, not in the middle of a frame, but along its margin by means of a rope twisted tight between its side arms with a stick caught against its centre brace or frame-fulcrum, so as to pry open the side arms upon the saw blade, and which brace, in all the old homemade specimens here shown, is loose and shiftable, in its end mortises, like the Korean pit saw (Fig. 25). But its great superiority lies in the fact that its blade is no longer rigid, but adjustable. That is, it can be turned by means of projecting handles, so as to cut not only on the plane of the frame, but at any other desired angle. Hence, within the range of its frame construction, it will cross-cut a board, or "rip" it longitudinally, cut straight, or, if thin enough, cut at a curve, when sometimes the blade, releasable at one end, could be inserted or withdrawn through a previously bored start hole. The instrument unmistakably drawn with its twisted rope, twist stick, and blade handles, appears among the old woodcuts as one of the letters of a pictorial alphabet in the *Oratoriae Artis Epitomata,* of the Florentine Jacopo Publicio, published by Erhard Ratdolt at Venice in 1482-1485, kindly shown the writer by Mr. Joseph E. Sandford. Two hundred years later, in 1678, Moxon describes

and pictures this master saw (*cf.* Fig. 67) and Holtzapffel, in his unique and indispensable description of saws in *Turning and Mechanical Manipulations,* illustrates and carefully describes it as used in England in 1846. But the evidence indicates, that though employed, as he says, for special and curvilinear cutting, it was never popular with the Anglo-American carpenter in the 17th and 18th centuries, or used by him as a substitute for the common, open, unframed hand saw. Not so, however, in France, where Diderot, in 1768, illustrates an example of it, rather than the open-hand saw, under discussion, as one of the typical bench instruments of the French carpenter and joiner.

In spite of its awkward shape and the fact that the frame is often in the way, we learn from Disston, Mr. R. P. Hommel, and personal observation in museums, that in Germany, Switzerland, Austria and Eastern and Northern Europe, the open hand saw has never rivalled or superseded it among carpenters, as the favorite instrument of its class, while in Korea and China, (though not in Japan), for no one knows how long, an exactly similar instrument has entirely displaced the open hand saw, to prove which, the next illustration

THE CHINESE BOW SAW (Fig. 141)

shows the same saw, now (1926) preferred for one-man sawing by the carpenters of China. Here, the toggle stick, in familiar American style, as above noted, is twisted against the rigid centre brace through several strands of hemp rope, while the blade, with teeth raked all one way, pinned upon wooden pegs penetrating the side arms, can be turned to any desired angle by the workman.

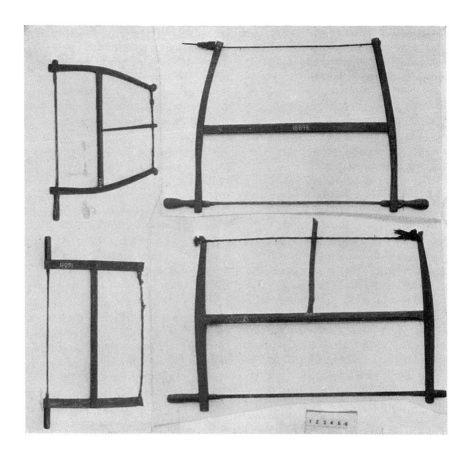

Fig. 140. The Bow Saw

The very thin blades with their teeth slightly raked to cut one way, and which can be turned by means of the handles to any desired angle, are strained between the lower arm ends of the instrument, by twisting a stick through strands of cord connecting its upper arm ends, and then, to prevent back twist, catching the lower end of the stick upon the central brace.

In No. 18,848, a threaded wire, tightened with a screw instead of a cord, is used. The central brace, like that of the Chinese bow saw, Fig. 141, rests in a loose mortise. The handles (single in the upper left-hand specimen) end in round pegs penetrating the side arms, slotted inside the frame to receive the blade. Loose iron pins (not seen in the dark picture), penetrating the slots through end-holes in the blade, hold the blade in place, or release it, when said pins are easily driven out, after unstraining the instrument. In spite of its awkward shape, the carpenters of France and Germany, like the workmen of Korea and China, still prefer this instrument to the open, Anglo-American hand saw, and turn its blade at various angles to cross-cut and rip boards. The frames, if not the blades of these specimens, surviving among Pennsylvania-German cabinet-makers until about 1890, are home-made.

Gruter's little picture (*cf.* No. A, under Fig. 142), misrepresented as explained later, in many dictionaries, and the little outline drawings in Flinders-Petrie's *Tools and Weapons,* copied from Roman stone carvings, certainly represent frame saws with a central brace and blades strained on their outer margin, but none except Montfaucon show the twist stick, and none represent any sign of the handles for turning the blade. The little blade fragments with rivet holes, shown in *Tools and Weapons,* might belong to any kind of frame saw. In his brief references to museum specimens of ancient frame saws, Flinders-Petrie fails to note the difference, owing to this adjustability of the blade, between the buck saw and the bow saw, and we are left to wonder how long the Chinese have used the bow saw, whether they invented it or copied it from western nations, and whether the Roman or Egyptian carpenters could have ripped boards, with its shifting blade, twenty centuries ago.

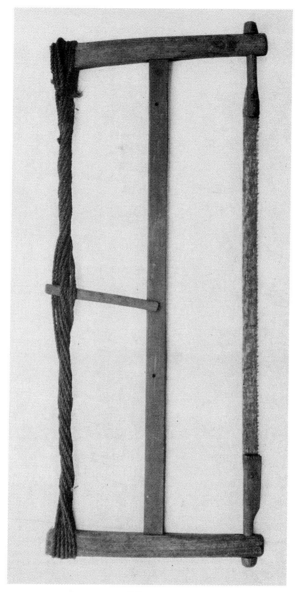

Fig. 141. Chinese Bow Saw

This instrument now at the Commercial Museum in Philadelphia, and photographed by the kind permission

Knight, *American Mechanical Dictionary*, edition 1878, calls it the bow saw, also the "turning saw," "sweep saw," "frame saw," and "web saw." Disston, *The Saw in History*, 1916, prefers to name it only "web saw."

A bow saw very clearly shown with rope-twist, toggle-stick, and turn handles for the blade, appears in a wood-cut alphabet of 1482, representing the letter E (by reason of the toggle stick) in an edition of the *Oratoriae Artis Epitomata* of Jacopo Publicio, published in 1482-5, at Venice, by the printer Erhard Ratdolt, (cf. *Early Venetian Printing*, New York, Charles Scribner's Sons, 1895). Kindly found and drawn for the writer by Mr. Joseph E. Sandford, 1925.

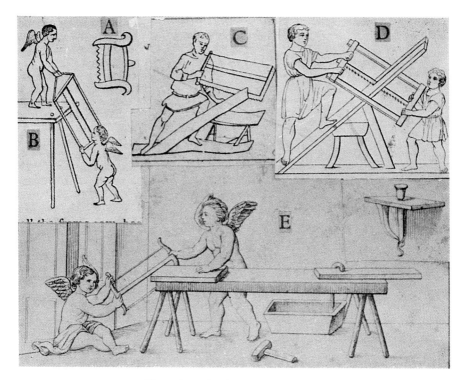

Fig. 142. Ancient Frame Saws

The illustrations show—(A) An outline drawing of a frame saw with marginal blade, but lacking turn handles, rope and twist stick, from Smith's *Dictionary of Classical Antiquities* (Anthon's N. Y. edition, 1843) there acknowledged as "from a funereal monument published by Gruter." Knight's *American Mechanical Dictionary* copies Smith, in 1897, as does Disston in *The Saw in History*, in 1916. Rich shows the same saw, with ornamental cuts on the teeth, in 1843, as "from a sepulchral bas-relief", without mentioning Gruter or naming the bas-relief. Neuberger, *Technik des Altherthums*, Leipzig, 1919, copies Rich. A similar drawing, but clearly showing the twist stick, appears in a minute corner plate showing eleven "joyner's tools", labelled "Gruter", by Father Montfaucon, in the English translation of his *Monuments of Antiquity Explained and Represented in Sculptures*, 5 Vols., Tonson and Watts, London, 1722.

(B) Two genii ripping a board with a pit saw. According to Anthon's *Classical Dictionary*, article "Serra", the picture is from a manuscript of Discorides of the 6th century, sometimes called the *Codex Cantacuzene*. Knight (*cf. American Mechanical Dictionary*) who confuses it with (E), here shown, says it was found at Herculaneum.

(C) A man ripping a board with a frame saw of questionable pattern without toggle stick or turn handles for the blade. From a painted glass vase from the Catacombs at Rome in the Vatican Library (*cf. Die Technik des Altherthums*, Neuberger, Leipzig, 1919, p. 77).

---

of Dr. W. P. Wilson, was obtained in China and exhibited at the Vienna World's Fair of 1873. It represents the carpenter's one-man framed hand saw, not only of China, but of Korea, being constructed like two others now in the Bucks County Museum, bought from a Korean carpenter by the Rev. Clarence Hoffman, missionary at Kangsi, Korea, in 1923. With a stick twisted through several strands of hemp cord, and locked against the central brace, which latter is loosely mortised into the side arms, it is in construction an exact duplicate of the old Pennsylvania-German bow saws shown in Fig. 140. The marginal blade is fastened through holes therein, by loose iron pins pushed through the slotted inner ends of wooden pegs penetrating the side arms, and is set at any angle by turning the pegs, not by means of handles projecting therefrom outside this frame, as in the American saws, but by the inner ends of the pegs within the frame. The left peg, with widened inner end is released through an upward slot-extension of its peg hole, not seen.

Whatever the history or origin of this tool of the Far East, we learn from Mr. R. P. Hommel, that the instrument today (1926) replacing for all important Chinese purposes, the little open-hand pull saws shown in Fig. 134, cuts not on the pull but on the push, and from the Rev. Clarence Hoffman, that an exactly similar saw is now preferred and used by the carpenters of Korea.

Reasonable evidence shows that both the buck and the bow saw must have existed together throughout the Middle Ages, but they so closely resemble each other that it is difficult to distinguish them in old prints, while as we go back still farther, the confusion increases. The celebrated little engraving here marked A in the next illustration

ANCIENT FRAME SAWS (Fig. 142)

which has long figured in classical dictionaries to show that the Romans used the frame saw, has been so distorted and misdrawn, that it is almost as curious for what it does not, as for what it does prove.

It probably first appeared in *Inscriptiones Antiquae totius orbis romani* by the philologist Janus Gruter or Gruytere, Heidelberg, 1602-3 (2 vols.) 2d ed. with plates, Amsterdam, 1707 (4 vols.) The learned Father Montfaucon copies it with a twist stick, in a microscopic corner plate showing eleven "joyners tools," labeled "Gruter," in his *Monuments of Antiquity Explained and Represented in Sculptures,* English translation (5 vols.), J. Tonson and J. Watts, London, 1722. Smith's *Dictionary of Greek and Roman Antiquities,* edited by Charles Anthon, N. Y., 1843, there briefly acknowledges the same picture as "from a funereal monument, published by Gruter." Rich, above quoted, shows it again in 1849, "from a sepulchral bas-relief," whereabouts unnamed, without mentioning Gruter. Neuburger, 1919, copies Rich, without comment. Knight's *American Mechanical Dictionary,* 1877, copies Smith-Anthon, and Disston, 1916, copies the latter or Knight. The little outline certainly does not represent a pit saw, for the blade is set on the frame margin. But is it a buck saw? Or is it a bow saw? Is the blade rigid so that it will only cross-cut, or adjustable, so that it will rip a board? Why does Montfaucon illustrate it with a twist stick, and Smith without one?

Fortunately, with the kind help of the Librarian of Congress, at Wash-

---

(D) Two young men ripping a plank with a pit saw, from a remarkable illustration to the word Prista, in Rich's *Companion to the Latin Dictionary.* etc., London, 1843. Of the very important picture, Rich unfortunately says nothing more definite than that he has taken it "from a painted vase of early Etruscan or Roman make."

(E) The celebrated picture found painted on the walls of a house at Herculaneum, from the outline engraving in *Herculaneum and Pompeii,* by H. Roux Aine, ser. 10, plate 146, vol. 3. By an open, panelled door, a genius seated on the floor holds with both hands a frame saw, as if in the act of sawing across the end of a short board laid flat on an eight-legged table. Another standing winged figure, holds the other end of the saw frame in its right hand. An unclawed hammer in the foreground, another board on the bench under a hook, a bowl on a shelf, and a box on the floor complete the picture. In this case, the saw blade, like that of the buck or bow saw is strained on the margin of the instrument. But as the cross brace rests on the board, with the blade far below it, the blade cuts nothing. Rich, above noted, escapes this error, by making a frame saw of the instrument, *i.e.,* he transforms the central brace, as here shown, into a notched saw blade. In any case, the saw here represented lacks the turn handles of the bow saw, and the twist stick of both it and the buck saw. Knight's *American Mechanical Dictionary* still further obscures the subject by confusing this picture with that from Discorides, here shown (B).

*Roma in Sanćto Georgio, Velabro, sub monte Palatino, est ara quadrata
sacrorum quinquennaliciorum collegii fabrum, quæ forsan Quinquatria,
habens in superiori circumferentia titulos undique, sed adeo rasos, ut col-
ligi omnino nequeant.*

*In fronte, ubi sacrificium, bovem immolant, adsunt camilli & cætera
sacrificantium turba.* MINISTRI. LVSTRI. SECVNDI

*In dextro latere, ubi statua Palladis in ara, clypeata, galeata & hasta-
ta, in medio multorum tenetur.* ∴∵∴∴∴∵∴ MILONIS

∴∵∴∴∴∵∴ AMPHIONIS

*In sinistro latere sunt instrumenta
hæc fabrilia & sacra, &
inscriptio.*

∷∷∷∷ ERILIS.M.ANTONI.ANDROMIS
∷∷∷∷ VTILIS. FICTORI. FLACCI

*In quarto latere instrumenta sacra
sunt: videlicet patera, calix, cape-
duncula: at litera legi nequeunt.*
MAR.∴∵∴∴∵∴∵∴∵∴

Vidit Smetius, & è Pighiano exemplari descripsit.

Fig. 143. Gruter's Roman Saw

As described in the text, this engraving from a page of *Inscriptiones Antiquae totius orbis Romani*, by Janus Gruter, Heidelberg, 1602-3, 2 vols.; Amsterdam, 1707, 4 vols., shows in a miniature group of eleven tools briefly and only described by Gruter as "fabrilia et sacra," from the side of a Roman sacrificial altar on the Palatine Hill at Rome the celebrated bow saw under discussion, continually misrepresented in books and dictionaries. The toggle stick, here clearly represented, appears also in Montfaucon's copy, but is omitted in all the other versions of the saw seen by the writer.

ington, D. C., the writer has been able to show as a literary and historical curiosity

GRUTER'S ROMAN SAW (Fig. 143) in a half-tone engraving copying the original page in Gruter, above noted, which is the starting point of these contradictions. The little group of instruments with Gruter's statement that it is taken from the left side of a rectangular sacrificial altar at St. Georgio, under the Palatine Hill at Rome, shows eleven tools which he refers to without describing, as "Instrumenta fabrilia et sacra," and there, in the upper right corner, the much misrepresented saw in question, appears with the toggle stick, which Montfaucon has copied correctly, but which all the other authors quoted have omitted.

Returning to Fig. 142 and the little pattern C shown from a painted glass vase from the Catacombs in the

Vatican Library, illustrated in *Die Technik des Alterthums* by Albert Neuberger, Leipzig, 1918, p. 77, which is certainly a one-man frame saw, a workman appears to be ripping a board laid end-up, on a stool, with what should therefore be a bow rather than a buck saw, though the instrument lacks the turn handles and twist stick. Another old picture B, described as from Herculaneum in Knight's *American Mechanical Dictionary*, but really from a miniature in the so-called *Codex Cantacuzene*, a manuscript of the Roman physician Discorides, written at the beginning of the 6th century (*cf.* Smith's *Dictionary of Greek and Roman Antiquities*, edited by Charles Anthon, New York, 1843, article "Serra"), showing genii at work as wood sawyers, represents neither a bow nor buck saw, but rather a pit saw, as previously described, because the blade is strained, not on the edge, but in the middle of the frame.

Fig. 142 D, showing two men ripping a plank with a pit saw, illustrates the word Prista in the *Companion to the Latin Dictionary and Greek Lexicon*, by Anthony Rich, Jun. B.A., London, Longmans, 1849, in which Rich poorly describes it as painted upon a Roman or Etruscan vase, whereabouts unnamed.

Several ancient saw blade fragments, of bronze or iron, perforated with rivet holes, in various European museums might belong to any of the several kinds of frame saws, while in the most interesting pictorial relic of all, namely the dimmed fresco, found at Herculaneum (Fig. 142, E) the published engravings contradict each other, as when Rich pictures the blade set in the middle, and Barre (*cf.* H. Roux Aine and M. L. Barre, *Herculaneum and Pompeii*, Paris, Firmin Didot, 1870, plate 146) as here shown, on the edge of the frame, as if the instrument were sawing air.

A very much smaller and differently constructed one-man hand saw, with strained marginal blade, hardly thicker than a wire, was known one hundred and fifty years ago as

THE BUHL SAW (Fig. 144) named from Boule, an Italian inlayer of brass and tortoise shell, who worked in France in the time of Louis XIV. As we have failed to find an old specimen, we here show one of the modern factory-made varieties, constructed in exactly the same way, which still survive for special wooden scroll or fretwork among cabinetmakers, or as playthings for boys. They were generally superseded in the middle and late 19th century by foot-turned machines working vertically with strained saw blades, too modern to be described here. In its old wooden framed form, the instrument is shown in an outline drawing by Holtzapffel, as used continually in the late 18th century, not to make veneers, but to saw out marquetry patterns therefrom. T h e tightly strained blade, easily working at various curves, and screwed upon the ends of a wooden elbow from 12 to 20 inches deep, would saw in counterpart several duplicate silhouette patterns at once, from several slabs of veneer, pasted together for the purpose, and held in the quickly released chops of a treadle clamp, also shown by Holtzapffel, in outline. Then, the workman sitting astride this latter apparatus, held the saw in his right hand, and worked it horizontally at right angles to the veneer, but at various tilts, swaying the frame to turn corners, describe circles, etc., and so suit the marked pattern.

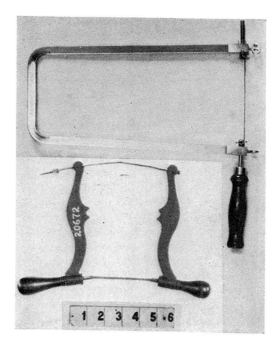

Fig. 144. The Buhl Saw

As explained in the text, the upper specimen, now called bracket saw and scroll saw in a hardware price list of 1925, with its fine, adjustable blade fastened by thumb screws, is a modern, metal, factory-made counterpart of the wooden instrument as used in marquetry sawing, illustrated by Holtzapffel, *Turning and Mechanical Exercises*, vol. 2, p. 733. It is now employed by cabinet makers for special scroll or fret work or wood inlaying. The smaller saw, constructed like a bow saw, with centre brace (lost), may have been used in a similar manner for small wood inlays in clock making. It was found among the tools used between 1820 and 1860, in the amateur workshop of C. J. Wister of Germantown.

William G. Thomson of 249 N. Hobart Street, Philadelphia, draughtsman, in Cramp's shipyard, and amateur wood-inlayer, informed the writer, May 30, 1926 that on inquiry among Philadelphia wood-inlayers, including an English workman. he had found none who had seen or heard of a wooden buhl saw, except a single Swedish inlayer who had used one. as described by Holtzapffel, in Sweden, about 1880. He also learned that in the early 19th century most of the wooden inlay work seen in the United States, and preceding such work produced here, had been imported from France, where it had been done in prison by convicts.

So much for the one-man frame saws and the varied work which one man could do, and in many parts of the world has done, for centuries, with this often preferred master tool, held in one or both hands, when its blade is strained upon the margin of the frame. But to conclude the subject of saw construction, it is necessary to examine two other interesting, generally larger, instruments—with blades fixed not on the margin, but in the middle of the frame, and one of which, generally too heavy for one man, had to be worked by two. This was

THE VENEER SAW (Fig. 145)

The homemade examples of this now disused form of saw, in which the long flexible blade strained in the middle of the frame, by means of wedges or hand screws, cuts at right angles to the frame, looks like a pit saw and might easily be confused with

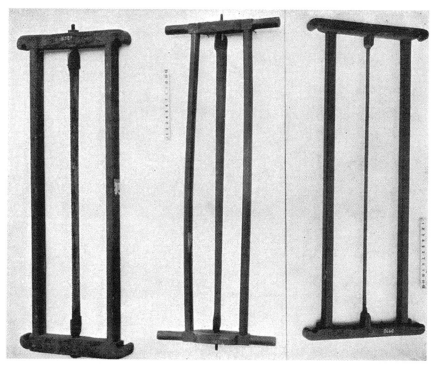

Fig. 145. The Veneer Saw

In these long obsolete, interesting, two-man frame saws, the narrow, flexible steel blade is strained, not as in the buck and bow saws, on the margin, but in the middle of a rather heavy wooden frame, about 4½ feet long, and not by means of the familiar rope and toggle, but by corner wedges as in No. 8490 (right) or by tightly screwed bolts. The teeth, varying greatly in size in these and other specimens found by the writer, always much too fine for pit saws, are raked to cut one way, except in No. 16,989 (left) where they are raked both ways. Though light examples of this type of saw were, according to Holtzapffel, sometimes used vertically, by one man, for ripping boards and planks, they were commonly used horizontally, by two men, to saw veneers from balks of mahogany or to cut off boards about 6 to 8 feet long from quartered logs set vertically in a clamp or against the table in the workroom. (See Fig. 146.) This latter fact would account for the comparative heaviness of the frames, which in horizontal sawing would help, and not as in vertical sawing, exhaust the sawyer. No. 8490 (right) was used by a Moravian missionary and carpenter about 1830 to 1840, among the Cherokee Indians in the Indian Territory to make door boards in log houses, and was brought back by him as a relic to Bethlehem, Pa., and descended to a carpenter in whose possession Mr. R. P. Hommel found and bought it in 1918.

A similar instrument, not shown, No. 17,474, was owned and used by Jacob Clewell, carpenter, of Nazareth, Pa. (born 1799, died 1871). From him it descended to his son, Christian Henry Clewell, undertaker of Nazareth (born 1826, died 1897), and from him to his son, Mr. Clewell, who sold it to Mr. Gieringer, who sold it to Mr. A. H. Rice, in December, 1920.

the latter. Nevertheless, the blades here shown, are too fine for board sawing from the log and they alone, as replacements, would not identify these old instruments. The frames also are too heavy for up and down pit work, and lack the extra protecting frame handles characteristic of the true pit saw, as described under Figs. 21 and 22.

In the hasty description of carpenter tools by Peter Nicholson in his *Mechanics Companion*, American Edition, Philadelphia, Lacken, 1832, this

Fig. 146. French Veneer Saws

This illustration from Diderot's *Encyclopedia*, of 1768, article "Ebeniste," shows one of the veneer saws, shown in Fig. 145, on the floor, and another in use by two men.

Disston, *The Saw in History*, does not describe these ancient two-man framed saws, about 4 feet 6 inches long, in which the thin blade is strained upon and entirely encircled by a rectangular frame of varying width, resembling the framed pit saw (Figs. 21 and 22), but comparatively heavier and shorter and with much smaller teeth. Diderot, however, in 1768, illustrates and describes these now obsolete relics of the old woodworker, and according to information from Jacob Reptsik, cabinetmaker, of Lansdale, Pa., who used them at Gross Lomnitz, in Northern Hungary, in 1885, they were there employed by cabinetmakers to cut short boards, veneer strips, etc., from timbers, set up vertically in a frame, as appears in the above picture, or against the work bench where the two men, standing on either side of the timber, worked the saws, not up and down like the true pit saw, but horizontally, and where the comparatively extra weight of the frame would be helpful.

In some of the instruments the teeth are raked in opposite directions from the middle of the blade, so that each man would have to do half the cutting, while in others, with a single rake, one man does it all. For veneering, the instruments would slowly cut about twelve veneers to the inch, and for that purpose they must have gone rapidly out of use after about 1820-30, when, by help of the newly perfected steam power, the power-run circular veneer-saw (invented by Isambard M. Brunel, in 1805-8) cut fifteen to twenty veneers to the inch and made veneering cheap and popular. The latter fact is proved by the once common machine-made veneers glued upon mitred mirror frames, nailed together with post-1820 cut nails, which became fashionable about 1840 to 1860.

forgotten and obsolete instrument is not noticed, but fortunately Charles Holtzapffel clearly describes it as used by cabinetmakers, rather than pit sawyers, one hundred years ago. Then, two workmen held the saw, not vertically, but horizontally, to cut veneers, about six per inch, from balks set upright in a clamp. But the instrument would also cut out little boards in the same way and J. M. Reptsik, cabinetmaker, of Lansdale, Montgomery County, Pa., informed the writer in 1922, that he had seen similar saws used at Gross Lomnitz, in Northern Hungary, about 1880, by cabinetmakers, to cut special short boards used in furniture making, in which case the balk, sometimes penetrating the floor of the shop, was fastened vertically against the sides of the work bench or clamped in a frame. An illustration in Diderot's great *Encyclopaedia*, here reproduced as

THE FRENCH VENEER SAW (Fig. 146) still further explains the instrument as in use in France, in 1768, by two parquetry makers (ebenists) who are sawing veneers, as noted, not up and down, as with the pit saw, but horizontally from a balk set upright in a clamp.

As additional proof of the purposes and use of these two-man frame saws, which are not pit saws, we learn from the descendants of a cabinetmaker of Bethlehem, Pa., that one of the instruments now in the museum collection of The Bucks County Historical Society. No. 8490, had been taken *c.* 1830, by their ancestor, a Moravian missionary, to the Indian Territory, and there used by him to saw short boards to build log-cabin doors for the Cherokee Indians. On his return to Bethlehem he brought back the old saw as a relic of his pioneer life at a time when the unfortunate Cherokees had just been driven from their ancestral home across the Mississippi.

THE FELLOE SAW OR CHAIRMAKER'S

SAW (Fig. 147)

ends our list of saws, with still another of the now forgotten and almost obsolete handmade tools of the old woodworker. This shows a much lighter and generally one-man variety of the frame saw, which, by reason of its smaller size, unhandled frame, and much lighter teeth, is again not to be confused with the pit saws already described—Figs. 21 and 22. As the last of its class, it has survived until late in the 19th century, among wheelwrights, to cut felloes or segments of tires of wagon or wheelbarrow wheels from pieces of timber, wide enough for two felloes, held in a vise. Holtzapffel says that the same light instrument was used in 1846, in England, by chairmakers, for cutting straight or slightly curved pieces used in their work. We learn from old wheelwrights that the stuff was fixed at an upward slant or

horizontally in the bench vise, or projected from the bench, and one workman, standing erect and grasping the saw by its side rails, sawed up and down, or at a down slant, with the teeth held away from him.

To classify and describe saws, as we have done, or even to see them in use, fails to get to the bottom of the subject, unless we answer two or three final but highly important general questions concerning the construction and history of this great master tool, usually overlooked in the books, but which any child might ask. First, that unless the slot or kerf cut by a saw is somewhat wider than the blade, the blade will stick or clog in the kerf. Hence, that either the kerf must be expanded with wedges, or the blade must be thinned above the teeth, as in the compass saw, or the teeth must be "set," that is, alternately bent to the right and left, as described later, so as to cut a kerf wider than the blade.

This difficulty of sawing in a kerf too narrow for the blade, which must have beset the saw from the beginning of its history hampers it still. To meet it, the old pit sawyer continually opened his kerf with wedges, and no one knows better than the modern tree sawyer, that when the fallen trunk or bough worked upon, sags upon the kerf, and squeezes the blade of his crosscut saw, he must either open the kerf with iron wedges, or stop work.

When, therefore, Flinders-Petrie (*cf. Tools and Weapons,* Constable, London, 1917) says that the teeth of the earlier saws found in Egypt, were not set, we pause for a moment to wonder at what unrecorded moment in man's history, one of the most important of all tools, first became effi-

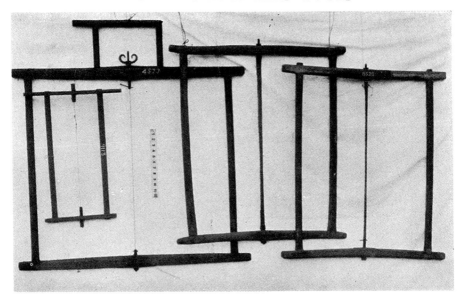

Fig. 147. Felloe Saw or Chairmaker's Saw

These instruments are constructed like the veneer saws (Fig. 145), but are slight'y shorter and comparatively wider. The adjustable blades and teeth found in them are much finer and adapted for curvilinear rather than straight cutting. Whether constructed for one or two men, they were used until about 1890, by wheelwrights for hand sawing the circular wood sections of the tires of wagon or wheelbarrow wheels, called felloes.

As with the veneer saws, it is easy to confuse large varieties of this felloe saw, particularly when equipped with extra frame handles, as in No. 4577 (left), with the pit saw already described, Figs. 21 and 22. But the veneer saw lacks projecting handles, and the felloe saw is too short, while the teeth of both, showing great variety in the specimens here shown, are never coarse enough for common pit-sawing of boards from the log.

cient by this process of setting its teeth, requiring a special set of instruments to be shown later? We are left to infer that the older Egyptian sawyers, when working with unset saws, must have continually greased their saw blades, and wedged the kerfs, in order to do any such otherwise impossible work as is vouched for in the celebrated picture published in Wilkinson's *The Ancient Egyptians,* where we see represented in a sepulchral wall painting at Thebes, one man ripping a vertically clamped plank, with an open hand saw. But if the early Egyptians did not set their saws, there is no doubt according to the last named author that the Romans did set them, and we know that

since their time saws have not only had to be set, as described later, but as now, continually reset, as the teeth bend back into their original position by use.

Hardly less important than the set of saw teeth is the fact that their generally triangular notches, by a process explained later, must be continually sharpened—that is sharp-pointed and sharp-edged, by application of a triangular or narrow file made for the purpose.

Besides this, the shape of saw teeth has always been of great importance in varying the thrust and power of the instrument. If the saw teeth are straight pointed, that is, with equal sides, they will cut both ways equally well. But if raked, that is, with one side very nearly vertical, or shorter than the other, they will cut only on the short side. Hence, if the short side is faced towards the handle, the saw cuts on the pull, and if away from it, on the push of the workman.

What must also be a very important point in the ancient history of saws, is the fact that the blade of an open saw, unless extra thick or stiff, might bend or buckle if pushed to cut, but could not so bend if pulled. For which reason we might expect to find that the oldest specimens of these comparatively small and weak blades, as used by one man, with one hand, two thousand years ago, are constructed to cut on the pull and not on the push of the workman. On the other hand, this difficulty of blade buckling is obviated and the superior cutting power of a thin narrow blade attained, if the blade, no matter how thin or narrow and no matter which way worked, is strained upon a frame.

Hence, although ignorant of the teeth construction of ancient saws and without wishing to speculate too much on the interesting subject, we need not be surprised at the statement of Flinders-Petrie, who, though not clearly discriminating in this matter, between open and frame saws, says that the early Egyptian saws (before *c.* 666 B.C. of bronze or hardened copper and thereafter of iron) all cut both ways with no tooth rake; that the first raked saw tooth appeared about 900 B.C., always upon open pull saws; and that there is no evidence of a push saw in Roman times.

But to return to our subject, namely, the shape of the Anglo-American saw teeth under discussion, now so greatly diversified by factory pat-ents, but here considered only in the ancient inherited outlines of one hundred and fifty years ago, we find that they are all raked to act as push saws, with one or two notable exceptions, namely, first, in the remarkable cross-cut saw, previously described (Fig. 31), where the elongated teeth, sometimes set in pairs and interspaced with wide open intervals, are not raked at all and therefore cut both ways. This is because the saw employed for heavy timber cutting is used horizontally, by two men, in which case each sawyer should do half the work. Another exception appears in the horizontal working, two-man veneer saws, just shown (Fig. 145), where, because both men ought again to cut equally, we find that in some cases, the teeth, as in the Korean pit or board saw (Fig. 25), are made to rake, half one way and half the other and therefore to cut both ways.

But who cared a century and a half ago how saws cut, or how, when and where they were made? What old dictionaries pretend to explain how the ancient blacksmith wrought, ground and polished the tool, or produced its teeth? What documentary evidence will show, except by random inference, that the undescribed process of hammering out long or broad saw blades, whether by water-run trip hammers, or by hand, had continued without change for centuries until about 1750, when the job was greatly facilitated by the general establishment in England, of heavy cylinders run by water, called rolling mills, to roll, rather than hammer out, thin sheets of iron or steel?

An inventory in the *Probate Records of Essex County, Massachusetts, 1635-1681, 3 vols., George Francis*

Dow, editor. Salem, Mass., the Essex Institute, 1916-1920, of the stock in trade of Edward Wharton, evidently a merchant, of Salem, Mass., shows that he had for sale in 1677 and 1678: "3 whip saws and tillers, at 5 s. 6 d. a piece, and 15 hand saws of various sizes and prices," all of which must have been hand or trip-hammer-forged in England, either by general blacksmiths or special cutlers.

Advertisements in the *Boston News-Letter,* of May 15 and July 17, 1760, kindly supplied to the writer by George Francis Dow, show that English imported hand and other saws, which must have been either hammered in the old water-run forges, or, by that time, rolled in the earliest rolling mills for the English cutleries, were sold in New England in Mary Johnson's shop in the Cornhill, Boston, and Edward Blanchard's shop in Union Street, Boston.

Bishop also shows that between the close of the American Revolution, *c.* 1785, and the start of the American factories, *c.* 1840, ready made saws or saw blades, were abundantly imported from Europe. Jeremiah Fern, who made axes, near Doylestown, Pa., about 1865, says (1924) that he never made or heard of a blacksmith making saws. Nevertheless, as English saw factories were not probably started on a large scale until after 1750, and as English and European local blacksmiths had made saws for centuries before that, and as Karl Klemp, a German blacksmith in Doylestown, says (1924) that he hammered out the comparatively narrow blades of frame saws in Danzig, as late as 1890, it seems probable, though lacking positive proof, that American local blacksmiths sometimes made saws, as they made axes, in the 18th and early 19th centuries.

A few general facts, as noted in the celebrated *Metallurgy* by John Percy (London, J. Murray, 1864) throw light on this obscure subject, as follows, namely: 1. That from ancient times until the beginning of the sixteenth century, the small blacksmith iron-worker, not yet able to melt iron into a castable liquid, could only soften the lumps of ore and hammer ("forge") them into useable shape. Hence that, though he worked directly on the raw material, he did it on a very small scale. 2. That the art of iron casting, discovered at some unknown date in the fifteenth or sixteenth century, and rapidly developed in the seventeenth century, soon introduced a factory process that revolutionized the blacksmith's work. This was the gigantic blast furnace, which, melting the ore into a white hot liquid in the first place (*i.e.* smelting it), transformed it into workable iron in vast quantities. 3. That this discovery was quickly followed by a great enlargement of the blacksmith's fire apparatus into a huge smithy called the Forge, equipped like the blast furnace with large, water-run bellows, not to melt the iron, but to hammer it into large forms, besides which another highly important operation for widespread production, entirely beyond the common blacksmith's reach, had appeared by the mid-eighteenth century, namely, the invention for squeezing iron into various forms, but particularly into thin plates (tin plates, boiler plates, sheet iron plates), by rolling it between rollers instead of hammering it. 4. That these discoveries and innovations had taken the manipulation of iron ores and all heavy iron work out of the blacksmith's hands by the beginning of the nineteenth century, and finally: 5. That long before the introduction of steam, extensive demands for weapons and mechanical devices resulting in encroachments upon his craft by cutlers, gunsmiths, bell pipe and utensil founders, locksmiths, watch and clock makers, wire drawers, pin and needle makers, whitesmiths (for screws, bolts, and polished ware), etc., etc., more and more preparing the way for the modern factory, had robbed him of his ancient importance, until by the beginning of the 19th century, with allowance for survivals in remote places, like the American backwoods, we find the blacksmith transformed from a master iron-worker into a shoer of horses and a maker of nails, tools, and tool equipments.

While we have no certain proof of the parentage, whether English or American, or of the make, smith or factory, of the saws previously shown, except that they are probably of date earlier than about 1840, abundant evidence shows that American blacksmiths in the 18th century frequently hammered out another highly useful tool of the carpenter, less important than the saw, but continually in his hands in widely distinct parts of the world and since the dawn of history closely associated with the building of the house, namely, the chisel. This is the scalprum of the Romans, a narrow rectangular blade of steel, sharpened at one end, and mounted on a straight handle at the other, used to edge, notch, hollow, and, above all, to mortise woodwork.

Passing over the chisels and chisel-shaped blades of the wood carver, which, though often used by the cabinetmaker to decorate furniture, were rather the tools of special decorative craftsmen, than of the carpenter and joiner, we find that these constructive tools vary greatly in size; that some show flat, some hollowed or saucered, and some mid-pointed, or side-pointed (skew), or side sharpened, or cornered blades; that the handles of some are socketed, of some tanged, that some (for carpenters), are heavier and stronger than others (for joiners), that some are percussion chisels, always used with a mallet, and others pressure chisels, used without a mallet, by shoulder or hand pressure.

If the use of these tools were less simple, their numerous old and new shapes might confuse us, but a study of their construction, rather than appearance, helped by Moxon's little picture and earnest explanations, soon clears up the subject.

The old master mechanic in his lively style describes some of the chisels here illustrated. Others not noticed by him, but exemplified by tools generally about a hundred years old, are shown as follows:

THE FORMING CHISEL OR FIRMER
(Fig. 148)

here appears as the heaviest tool of its class. It is set in a socket for carpenters, and as a lighter tool for joiners on a tang, used with a mallet for preliminary rough edging and also for one of the most important purposes known to the carpenter's craft, namely, the excavating of the mortise or orifice by which one piece of wood is fitted into another. Neither Moxon nor the *Circle of Mechanical Arts,* nor Nicholson, nor Rees' *Encyclopaedia,* nor even Holtzapffel, explain that this all-important wood socket was and is

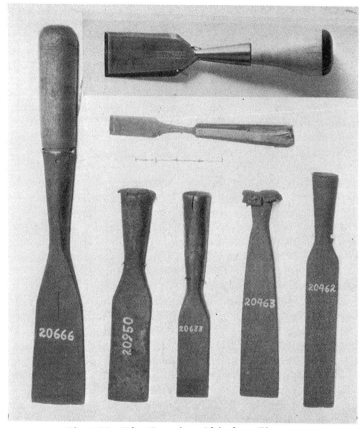

Fig. 148. The Forming Chisel or Firmer

The first chisel used by the carpenter, to roughly side-cut a piece of wood along a line marked with the carpenter's scribe or pencil, probably the scalprum fabrile (Rich) of the Romans. The instrument, grasped vertically by its shank in the left hand, is struck by the carpenter's mallet with the right hand, until, by reaching the line with successive cuts of the blade held basil outward, the handle is tilted slightly towards the workman over the line to avoid undercutting. As described by Moxon and here shown from old Pennsylvania specimens, the forming chisel is of various sizes and of two kinds: (a) comparatively light (No. 2, counting downward), handled on a shouldered tang for joiners, cabinet-makers, etc., and (b) heavy, handled in a socket (left and bottom), socket chisels, for carpenters and joiners, though both workmen use both kinds. Two specimens (left and upper) show their original handles, lost from all the others. The others have been misused, by hammering upon the open socket with an iron hammer or hatchet. The tanged chisel (upper) from the collection of C. J. Wister, Esq., 1820-1860, of Germantown, Pa., is smith-stamped "J. Cam, Cast Steel," and the large socket chisel (left) "Newbould.". It is the forming chisel rather than the mortise chisel, described later (Fig. 153), that was, and still is, used in excavating the large mortises for house and barn framework, in which operation one or more holes bored with the T-handled auger, were inter-cut and squared for the purpose. (Information of David Angeny and Lewis Treffinger, carpenters of Danboro and Doylestown, Pa., to the writer, June, 1926.)

The name mortise axe, occurring eight times in the *Probate Records of Essex County, Massachusetts, 1635-1681, 3 vols., George Francis Dow, editor. Salem Mass., the Essex Institute, 1916-1920,* suggests that the now common axe squaring of auger holes was practiced in the 17th century, and the name "Mortas Wymbyll" for 1407, quoted (from the *Fabric Rolls and Documents of York Minster,* Surtees Edition, p. 207, note) by the *New English Dictionary,* reasonably indicates that the double practice of boring and chiselling, to make a mortise, also prevailed in the 15th century.

Modern price lists show a factory-made forming chisel (top of picture) with bevelled but unsharpened sides, called the bevel edged firmer," no old homemade examples of which, except the ancient Dutch specimen (Fig. 150), have been seen or heard of by the writer.

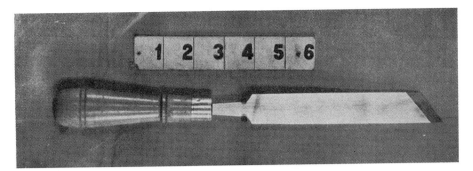

Fig. 149. The Skew Forming Chisel

This old tool, carefully described and illustrated by Moxon (Fig. 67, C. 4.), is a forming chisel, still rarely used by the cabinetmaker, but apparently unknown to the modern carpenter. It varies in the acute angle of its basilled blade and like the forming chisel it is struck, when necessary, with the mallet; but its special use is to penetrate holes in furniture carving or to clean out the corners of angular or mortise cuts. The writer has thus far failed to find an old homemade chisel of this type, and the specimen shown, as the only example seen in a number of recent hardware price-lists, was bought April 1926, under the name of "corner firmer," as a modern factory-made example of the tool shown by Moxon.

made in two ways, *i.e.*, either by the chisel worked alone, or by the chisel and auger worked together, and that in the first place, for small mortises (in soft wood), for door and shutter panels, window sash, etc., the mortise chisel (described later), as Holtzapffel explains with a diagram, did all the work, while in the second case, the forming chisel with several corner and side cutting varieties, presently shown, was and is still used, not alone to cut the orifice, but to intercut and square up one or more holes previously bored with the T-handled auger.

A very rarely surviving kind of forming chisel with diagonal blade

THE SKEW FORMING CHISEL
(Fig. 149)

sharpened on its flat side, which Moxon calls the skew former, used to excavate corners, and which we have failed to find as a homemade tool, is here also shown from a modern, factory-made specimen, still on sale. Another flat bladed variety of this chisel, which neither Moxon nor Diderot show, also here photographed from a modern factory specimen (Fig. 148, top), has its sides bevelled, but unsharpened. And that a flat, side-bevelled chisel is of ancient continental European form is proved by the next illustration,

Fig. 150. Dutch Forming Chisel of the 16th Century

This rusty ancient tool, mounted on a shouldered tang, which is a relic of the Dutch Nova Zembla Expedition of 1596 (cf. Figs. 106 and 112), is either a forming or paring chisel. Whether the basilled sides are sharpened or not, the writer has not learned. Photographed by kind permission of the Rijks Museum, Amsterdam.

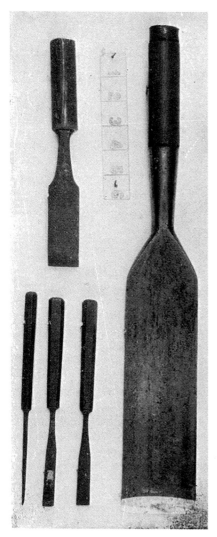

A DUTCH PARING CHISEL OF THE 16TH
CENTURY (Fig. 150)
more than three hundred years old,
and another relic of the Dutch Nova
Zembla Expedition of 1596, previously referred to, although the writer has
not learned from the Rijks Museum
whether its bevelled sides are sharp
or dull.

THE PARING CHISEL (Fig. 151)
is a now rarely used duplicate of the
forming chisel, but is kept sharper
and used without a mallet, by shoulder or hand pressure, for smooth-
finishing edges, with blade varying in
width from 1½ to 3 inches. It is here
shown in its extra large form, now
called, in New York price lists, and by
Pennsylvanian carpenters, a slick; in
this case mounted on a socket, although the modern cabinet-maker,
who uses its smaller varieties, also
here shown, prefers its handle set on
a tang, as less liable to get loose by
shrinkage.

THE GOUGE (Fig. 152)
is a hollow, flat-backed, round-
pointed, cylinder-bladed chisel, basilled on its convex side, used for
rounded excavations. How interesting
the familiar instrument becomes when
we find that its channelled blade,
which will furrow wood without side
tearing it, has always made it indispensable to the turning lathe, described later. How much more so
when we realize, on experiment, that

Fig. 151. The Paring Chisel

This old instrument now sometimes entirely discarded by the carpenter, but still in use by the cabinetmaker, is here shown in various sizes, as sometimes handled in a socket and sometimes on a tang. There is nothing to distinguish it from the forming chisel, except its purpose. It is not or should not be struck with a mallet, but is worked by body or hand pressure and not used to start chisel work, but to follow the forming chisel and to smooth the rough cuts of the latter. Therefore its edge is kept extra sharp. The large specimen mounted in a socket, now called a slick, was loaned for the picture by Jonas Martin, carpenter, of Doylestown, Pa., who still uses it without a mallet. The three small (lower left) instruments are probably pressure chisels, but may have been sometimes struck with a mallet. They were found among the large store of tools pertaining to clock-making and wood-working, used between 1820 and 1860, by Charles J. Wister, Esq., of Germantown. Moxon carefully describes the typical paring chisel as held against the right shoulder with the blade not grasped by the right hand, but inserted under the two middle fingers, for un-obstructed sight of the edge worked upon.

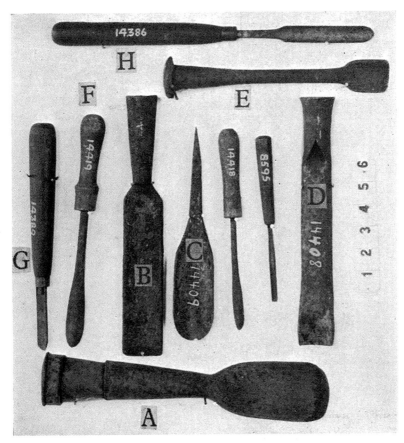

Fig. 152. The Gouge

The tubular shaft of these many sized old tools, variously flattened or elongated, ends in a more or less rounded, but not spooned, point, sometimes basil edged, in its hollow, but generally on its back. The lighter specimens are or were mounted on wooden handles, upon a tang, are all back-basilled, and were probably worked by hand or shoulder pressure while the heavier tools, all basilled in the hollow, are socket chisels used with a mallet and sometimes abused with a hammer or hatchet. The heavy specimens (A, B, D,) and the upper one (E) are certainly hand forged. (C) is stamped "Weldon"; (F) "M. Cox," (G) and (H) are certainly factory-made, and the latter is stamped "J. Tillotson, Sheffield." The gouges (A) and (E) were used until c. 1890, by Abel Swartzlander, wheelwright, at Sandy Ridge, 1½ miles north of Doylestown, Pa.

if held vertically and turned in the hand, it will excavate a round hole in wood. For which reason we need not be surprised at the archaeological evidence which proves that one of the most important of all carpenter tools, in one of its most notable ancient forms, namely the auger, as described later, duplicates this gouge. As here shown in its simplest form, the gouge

is used by the carpenter and cabinet-maker, oftener for ornament than construction, in which latter province it is far outranked by the next and last tool of its class, here considered, namely

THE MORTISE CHISEL (Fig. 153) a master tool incessantly employed by the carpenter, one hundred years ago, as above noted, for excavating the

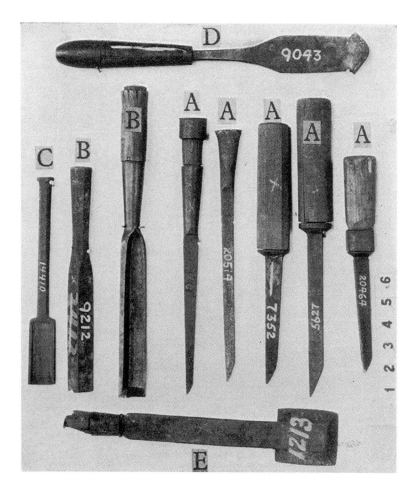

Fig. 153. The Mortise Chisel and Varieties

Although the forming chisel (Fig. 148) will inter-cut and square up auger borings so as to excavate the all-important rectangular socket hole, called the mortise, the so-called mortise chisel, in its commonest form, as described by Moxon, and here shown, (A) extra narrow, extra thick, almost square bladed and deeply basilled, was the once familiar carpenter's instrument for special or soft wood mortising where no preliminary borings were used. It varies greatly in size but is and was generally socket handled for heavy mallet pounding, as appears in the specimens marked (A), the right three of which are mounted on shouldered tangs. In the now called corner chisel, marked (B), in present use by Lewis Treffinger, carpenter, of Doylestown, Pa., the flat shaft is bent longitudinally into a right angle and basil-edged on the inside at the bottom for clearing the corners of mortises.

In the rare (E), for which we have found no name (No. 1213), the stem spreads into a blade, sharpened at the bottom and on both sides, for side and corner cutting of mortises. (D) (No. 9043), with bent up, top-basilled, and rectangular point, was probably used for clearing the bottom of mortises. All these tools, whether tanged, or socketed, are percussion chisels, except (D) the top specimen. The two right specimens are stamped "W. Butcher, Sheffield," over an arrow and cross; the fourth, counting from the left, "Robert Sorby." The top chisel (D) is curiously stamped with a little cross-barred cylinder.

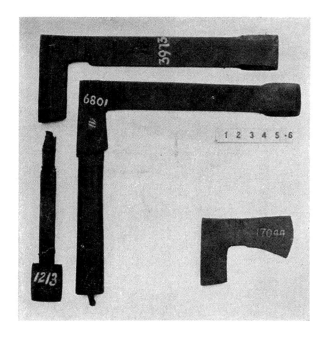

Fig. 154. The Axe Mortise Chisel

Another rare tool, which may be said to be neither chisel nor axe, but a combination of both, is here shown as the axe mortise chisel. This is a chisel-bladed elbow of steel, socketed on a short wooden handle, found in Bucks County, by the writer, among the now obsolete tools of the mill and house builder. Neither Moxon nor Diderot, nor English books show any trace of this remarkable instrument, which the modern carpenter has forgotten. Whatever its origin or history, the evidence shows that with its long, flattened elbow, widened chisel-shaped blade, basilled on its three front sides, it was used with a mallet, until the late 19th century by Pennsylvania German carpenters and mill-wrights, for excavating and squaring deep mortise holes.

Though its blade otherwise resembles that of Fig. 153, No. 1213, here again shown, it is not, like that of the latter, set vertically in its wooden handle, but socketed therein at right angles, like an axe.

David Gehman, a Mennonite minister, of Fountainville, Bucks Co., Pa., told the writer, Jan. 26, 1925, that he had seen this instrument used by Abraham Overholt, a master carpenter, c. 1884, for making mortise holes in constructing the barn now standing on a farm about two miles north of Chalfont, Bucks Co., Pa., marked "Black" on Smith's Centennial Map of Bucks County, 1876. The tool was struck on the flattened elbow with a mallet.

The lower specimen (No. 17044) is probably a polless broad axe or hatchet of German type, as seen lying on the ground in Fig. 32. and should be classed with the hewing hatchets shown in Fig. 83 or in Fig. 80 (No. 6547).

No. 3973 is stamped "E. Scholl cast steel," in letters of the style of about 1840-50. The fact that the name Scholl is typically German, and that it with the words "cast steel" are stamped in letters of 19th century pattern, and that the process of casting steel invented in England by Benjamin Huntsman in 1740 (cf. English Encyclopaedia by Charles Knight), practiced there for tool making in the early 19th century, was not introduced, according to James M. Swank, (cf. his Introduction to a History of Ironmaking and Coal Mining in Pennsylvania, Philadelphia, 1878, p. 80.) into the United States until between 1846 and 1859, and finally that none of the blacksmiths, who only forged with the hammer, without melting steel, could have cast this axe, indicates that it must have been made or repaired in a small Pennsylvania German factory after about 1850.

smaller class of window, door and shutter mortises, generally in soft woods. As described, with a diagram, by Holtzapffel, and according to the information of old carpenters to the writer, the pattern A, here shown in its commonest American form, and as described by Moxon, with handle either socketed or set on a heavily shouldered tang, and with blade

Fig. 155. The Carpenter's Mallet

The wooden form of the malleus, or hammer, of the Romans. The wooden blocks of these old home-made, one-hand Bucks County tools, turned or squared, are penetrated with bored holes, into which the short wooden handle is driven and tightened with a top wedge. The tool, held in the workman's right hand, strikes the chisel, held in his left, without injury to its wooden handle, which an iron hammer would destroy.

sharpened and conspicuously basilled at right angles to its widest diameter, did all the work. In this case no preliminary borings were required. The tool, held in the left hand with flat face towards the workman, was pounded down with a mallet, vertically, to cut the sides, or at a tilt to cut or pry up V-shaped cores, until the hole was deep enough, or until it coincided with another hole cut to meet it from the opposite side of the piece.

Two very different tools not mentioned by Moxon, marked B, with shank L-shaped in cross-section and basil-sharpened at the bottom, inside both angles, form a down-cutting corner blade for cleaning out the corners of mortises. D shows a flat blade broadened at the base into a

turned up rectangular point with an inner basil on both converging sides, a rare tool from Eastern Pennsylvania, and used probably for cleaning the bottom of mortise holes. The heavy form E, with its long, flat shank, abruptly ending in an almost square blade, basilled and sharpened on bottom and side, is now an obsolete and forgotten shop relic of the old Pennsylvania-German carpenter.

A still rarer type of this tool with its sides not only bevelled, but sharpened (*i. e.* basilled), appears in the following illustration as

THE AXE MORTISE CHISEL (Fig. 154)
a now obsolete instrument, but in the memory of persons now living, used by Pennsylvania-German carpenters, for mortise cutting in barn construc-

Fig. 156. The Commander

These two rude mallets, the larger 21¼ inches long from handle top through block, and altogether too heavy for chisel driving, were used with one or two hands, to pound together, as described by Moxon, the newly adjusted mortised and tenoned heavy framework of buildings, doors, etc.

tion, when previously bored auger holes started the work. As in E (Fig. 153), we have a long, flat shank abruptly ending in a square blade, bottom and side-sharpened, but in this case the handle of the instrument is set in a socket, not vertically, but at right angles to the shank, like that of the axe.

Here let us pause for another backward look into the faraway past, suggested by an examination of the next picture, namely

THE CARPENTER'S MALLET (Fig. 155) which is a cylindrical block of wood, with a wooden handle pegged into it at right angles to the grain, used in one hand for driving all chisels except the pressure-paring chisel, above noted. This tool is a wooden variety of the malleus or hammer of the Romans, and archaeological evidence shows that, as distinct from the metal-headed malleus, it was in use in ancient times in two forms, namely:

The club, in ancient Egypt (cf.

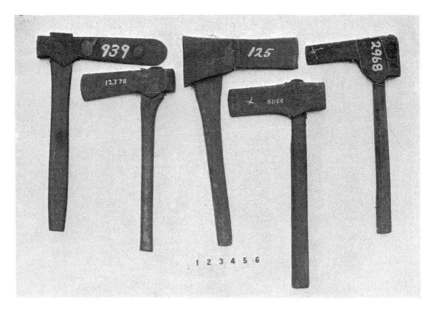

Fig. 157. The Mortising Axe or Post Axe

As old Bucks County farm relics, bought near Doylestown, Pa., between 1897 and 1918, these axes were used by carpenters in the 18th or early 19th century, for cutting large, rough mortises, and were not probably called post axes, until after the invention of the spiral auger, about 1805, when their use was greatly increased to make rail holes in the post and rail fences by cutting out the interval between the two auger holes bored for each rail-hole (*cf.* Fig. 158). Except Nos. 125 and 2968, which were probably imported from Germany, they are all of American homemake, and Anglo-American type, resembling specimens recently found in British American camp sites in New York by the New York Historical Society. The handles are original.

The *Probate Records of Essex County, Massachusetts, 1635-1681, 3 vols., George Francis Dow, editor. Salem, Mass., the Essex Institute, 1916-1920,* without noting the name post axe, mention mortising axe eight times, and refer, in 1676, to "some Post and Rayles as by agreement;" also to a lot of "5 holed posts" sold at 9 shillings a-piece in 1678.

The name post axe appears in a manuscript inventory of sale, dated 1812, of Jonathan Higgins, of Amwell Township, N. J., seen by the writer, in the possession (1925) of W. H. Unger, antique dealer, of Pottstown, Pa.

Flinders-Petrie, *Tools and Weapons*) a short cylindrical billet of wood thinned down at one end into a handle, like the frow club (Fig. 13), which is also the form of mallet found in a tomb at Thebes, where, as if to startle the archaeological grave robber of modern times, the ancient Egyptian carpenter had left it in his tool basket with the Egyptian saw (Fig. 136). The other form, here alone represented, appears in the picture as a rectangular or cylindrical wooden block, mounted on a wooden handle, pegged into it at right angles to the grain, which, according to Flinders-Petrie, did not appear in Egypt till Roman times, and which Rich (*cf. Companion to the Latin Dictionary and Greek Lexicon,* etc., by Anthony Rich, Jr., B.A., London, 1849, article Malleus) shows in two illustrations of specimens constructed exactly like the left two here shown—"copied from tombstone designs of Roman Artisans."

As both the club and the handled block were in use in various trades in England and America in the 18th century, it seems probable, though

Fig. 158. Post Boring Machine

This wide, homemade, four-legged frame consists of two parallel wooden strips, held apart by cross mortised end pieces. In the wide opening between these strips, the fence post, fastened upon a sliding frame (not seen), by means of screw clamps at either end, moves horizontally to the desired distance and is fixed thereat by a ratchet under the frame, not visible. Whereupon, by turning its crank, the spiral auger attached to the vertical side post (left), bored two holes, side by side, for each rail orifice. After releasing the auger and pushing along the post, upon the sliding frame, the operation is repeated four or five times, at spaced intervals, marked on the post, or established by the ratchet. Finally, on releasing the post, each pair of holes is enlarged into rectangular openings, by cutting away the intervening tongue of wood, with the post axe.

As before remarked, it is the spiral auger that made this operation possible and it is this rural machine that greatly increased the use of the post and rail fence in the United States, in the middle of the 19th century. There is sufficient evidence, however, such as a copper engraving of the grounds of Pendhill Court, Surrey, the estate of George Scullard, Esq., from a painting by P. Sandby, R.A., and published by G. Kearsly, 46 Fleet Street, London, in 1776; and another engraving of Felbrig Hall, Norfollk, published by I. Walker, 16 Rosemans Street, London, in 1793; and a landscape wood-cut in the Pennsylvania German almanac, the *Neuer Lancasterischer Kalendar*, published at Lancaster, Pa., in 1798, to show that posts, with rail holes, were planted in the ground, and rails cut to fit them, both in England and America, before the invention of the machine in question helped to devastate forests in the United States.

R. Weems received a United States patent for "a Boring Machine for Fence Posts," March 16, 1801, after which similar patents are listed for 1833, 1837, 1839, the descriptions for which, up to 1836 and 1837, were burned in a fire at the United States Patent Office.

Where available the trunks of the rot-resisting locust tree. (*Robinia pseudo-acacia*, Linnaeus.) were used in eastern Pennsylvania, for post-and-rail fence posts, though sometimes, as near Elizabethtown, Lancaster Co., Pa., about 1875, the borings and blight of this tree's fatal enemies, the"locust borer," the "locust leaf miner," and the "locust rot," (*Fomes rimosus*), stopped the practice. (Information of the Rev. David Gehman, Mennonite minister and artificer, of Fountainville, Bucks Co., Pa., born 1852), to the writer, June 24, 1926).

lacking positive proof, that they must have both survived throughout the Middle Ages.

Today, a modified form of the club, no longer in one piece as a solid club, but as a cylinder or ball-like block, with a handle pegged into it with the grain, is still in use with sculptors and stone workers. Besides these smaller mallets, a large variety of the tool,

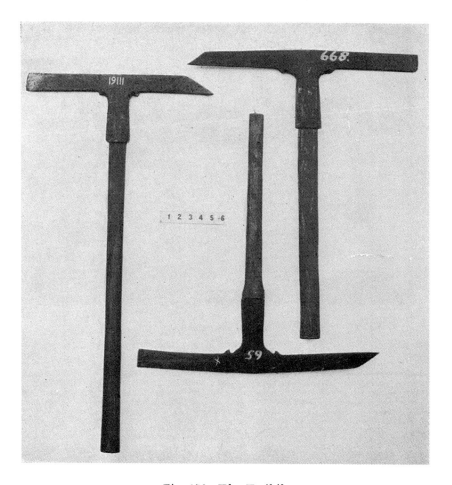

Fig. 159. The Twibil

    This extraordinary mortising instrument consists of a very long iron bladed head mounted like the letter T in a deep socket upon its straight wooden handle. One end of the bladed head is sharpened on the plane of the handle, and the other with a conspicuous basil, at right angles to it.

    The three specimens in their original short handles were found in Bucks Co., Pa., between 1897 and 1910, among the carpenter relics of the Pennsylvania Germans, who used them, with one or two hands, to widen auger borings and cut deep mortises in the timber framing of houses, mills, and barns, until about 1885.

    The twibil was used in New England, according to the *Probate Records of Essex County, Massachusetts, 1635-1681, 3 vols., George Francis Dow, editor. Salem, Mass., the Essex Institute, 1916-1920,* in 1646 and 1675; in old England, by name (*New English Dictionary*), between 1400 and 1465, and in France, in the 18th century (as described and illustrated in Diderot's *Encyclopaedia,* 1768), which calls the axe besaigne and its long bit, with basilled blade set crossways, the bec d'ane, (donkey's nose). No. 65 was given to the writer by Christian Myers, in 1897, and was said by him to have been used by the Stover family, previous owners of his mill, on Tohickon Creek, Pa., between 1830 and 1840. It is stamped by two heart-shaped smith stamps, with a tree-like device. The handle is original.

    No. 668, showing two small smith stamps, was given to the writer by the aged Mennonite minister, Isaac Gross, of Plumsteadville, Pa., in August, 1897.

    No. 19111, bought of Levi Yoder, July, 1923, is from the Cope family of Sellersville, Bucks Co., Pa. The handle is original. The blade is stamped on either side by a fleur de lis, in a shield.

    See Fig. 249, p. 302, for an illustration of the twibil as used during the 16th century.

described by Moxon and called by him

THE COMMANDER (Fig. 156)

is here also shown as used, not to drive chisels but to pound together heavy framework without defacing the wooden surface.

But the mallet and the chisel driven therewith, with or without the help of the auger, did not suffice for cutting the all important and universal mortise, for which ever-pressing need, on special occasions, other tools were used. The chief among these which might have been described with the axes, but which we here classify with the chisels, was

THE MORTISING AXE OR POST AXE (Fig. 157)

a conspicuously long-and-narrow-bitted, short-handled instrument, employed for cutting mortise holes, by hacking out the tongue between auger borings made for the purpose. Judging from pictures and specimens found, the tool, though not noted, either as mortise axe or post axe, in the *New English Dictionary*, probably originated in England, and the words "mortise axe" appearing eight times in the *Probate Records of Essex County, Mass., 1653-1681, 3 vols., George Francis Dow, editor. Salem, Mass., the Essex Institute, 1916-1920*, shows that it was used in or imported into New England in the 17th century. Further evidence proves that it was employed in completing fence post holes in the late 18th century, while still such holes were laboriously bored by body pressure, two by two, with the old forms of auger described later, and about fifty years before the invention of the spiral auger (*c.* 1809), as here explained, immensely facilitated the making of the once common Ameri-

can post and rail field fence of the early 19th century. This result was achieved by means of the homemade

POST BORING MACHINE (Fig. 158)

The illustration shows one of the greatly varying forms of this widespread device, which, increasing the use of the post axe, rapidly became part of the equipment of every farmer in the Middle States, between 1809 and *c.* 1885 to 1890, since which, upon the sudden substitution of wire, for the post and rail fence, it and the post axe have become rare. The ancient side-and down-cutting augers, described later, which do not sufficiently "bite," namely, penetrate without pressure, could not have worked well with this rural machine, but the spiral auger, which in this case does bite without pressure, made it possible, since, while the post, clamped in the apparatus, slides forward or is otherwise adjusted to receive the holes bored in pairs, the latter tool easily penetrates by simply turning its crank. There is nothing remarkable about the appearance of the post axe, except its short handle and long bit, but another rare and double-bitted form of old European mortising axe, imported from Europe, and used in eastern Pennsylvania until about 1890, would challenge attention anywhere from its extraordinary shape. This is

THE TWILBIL (Fig. 159)

It was so named in England, and though not described by Moxon, was used in old New England (*cf. Probate Records of Essex County, Massachusetts, 1635-1681*), and Diderot illustrates the deep cutting tool, with its two very long bits, the narrowest of which, basilled at right angles to the handle, he calls bec d'ane (donkey's nose).

It is the axe handle mounting two chisels that distinguishes this ancient wood-working tool for hacking out mortise holes, from the hammer-headed post-axe, the curved pick-axe, and the adze. The *New English Dictionary* quotes the name nine times, between A.D. 1000 and 1656, and a possibly similar instrument is illustrated in *Blumlein's Kulturleben,* referred to later, as found among relics of the 22d Roman Legion at Mayence.

So much for the homemade tools, which one hundred years ago made the "mortise," namely, the square hole, large or small, deep or shallow, so carefully dwelt upon in old books, which, devoted rather to the theory than to the tools of carpentering, incessantly refer to it as required to receive the tenon necessary in fitting one piece of wood into another. But hardly less important in the woodworker's craft, than this celebrated square hole, is the round hole, made in wood by carpenters for more than two thousand years, which hole, however produced, becomes of immense importance in any worldwide or historic consideration of the subject. The Chinese excavate round holes with the bow or thong drill, or pump drill, as described later, or sometimes by wriggling a long rectangular iron point into wood. The old Anglo-American wheelwright sometimes burnt square holes with a red hot iron, presently shown, but the carpenters of Western Europe and America made round holes, one hundred years ago, by means of another ancient class of master tool, which worked, either (*a*) by squeezing through and pushing aside the fibres without removing them; (*b*) by boring, *i.e.,* by paring the wood away into shavings; or (*c*)

by drilling, *i.e.,* scraping it into dust on the bottom and sides of the hole as the tool goes down; and the simplest of these, as alone representing the first method, is here illustrated by

THE BRAD AWL (Fig. 160)

a thin rod, never much over one-eighth of an inch in diameter, with chisel-shaped point, mounted on a wooden handle and twisted with the right hand, back and forth, so as to perforate the wood. Carpenters often employed it, one hundred years ago, to prepuncture oak or hard wood into which the old malleable wrought nail would not drive without bending, and it is still used by cabinetmakers, joiners and carpenters, to produce preliminary holes for nails or brads (headless or half-headed nails) in easily split wood, or for starting holes for hinge screws. Unlike the round-pointed shoemaker's awl, or the tailor's needle, which pierce by direct thrust, or the auger, or gimlet, which pare away the sides or bottom of the hole with a continuous circular motion, or the variously fluted broach or three- or four-sided tapering hand drill, described later, which pulverize the wood, this little instrument, as here constructed, not workable if larger than about one-eighth of an inch in diameter, and not by continuous revolutions, wriggles back and forth through the wood, by squeezing aside the grain, without producing any shavings or dust.

Moxon, who does not illustrate it, describes what may be it in his "Catalogue of Carpenter Tool Names," as,— "A Pricker, vulgarly called 'awl,' yet for joiner's use it has most commonly a square blade, which enters the wood better than a round blade will, because

Fig. 160. The Brad Awl

This highly effective little one-hand tool, which Knight (1878) describes as "an awl with chisel-shaped point for making insertions for nails," is a short steel shank, set in a straight wooden handle, unworkable in this form if not smaller than a gimlet, or if much larger than a bodkin. How old it is, or how or when it was first used, the writer has failed to learn. Its greatest feature is its blade, which is not tapered to a round point, but is flat and chisel-shaped, and which, when the short tool is wriggled in the right hand, crushes aside and squeezes through the wood-grain very quickly, penetrating all but the hardest woods without making sawdust.

Holtzapffel in *Turning and Mechanical Manipulations*, London, 1846, Vol. 2, page 539, describes two varieties of this tool as employed by English carpenters at that time, namely:—(1) The awl used by wire workers, a square, tapering rod sharpened to a point on all four sides; (2) an awl "sharpened with three facets as a tapering triangular prism," in other words, a tool exactly resembling the Japanese awl shown in Figure 173.

But though both these latter varieties of awl appear in the recent household tool equipments, now (1927) on sale by hardware dealers, the writer has failed to find or hear of old homemade examples of them, called brad awls, or as used by American carpenters in the 18th or early 19th century, while abundant evidence shows that the chisel-pointed tool was continually employed by the old American cabinetmakers to make preliminary punctures for nail driving in delicate finished work or splitable wood, and universally by the carpenter, before 1846, to prepare screw holes for pointless butt-hinge screws.

Diderot does not show the chisel-pointed tool among French carpenter's instruments in 1768, but the word "awl," associated with names for carpenter's tools in the New England inventories, in the *Essex County, Mass., Probate Records*, for 1647, 1659, 1671, and 1678, may refer to it. The *New English Dictionary* first quotes its later and present name as brad awl and sprig bit, for 1823 and 1881.

the square angle in turning about, breaks the grain, and so the wood is in less danger of splitting." But his unfortunate use of the words "square blade," which might refer to a blade square in cross-section (the four-sided hand drill, above mentioned), or a blade chisel shaped in cross-section, seems too doubtful to positively identify the tool as above described or to date it for the seventeenth century.

As here considered, it should not be confused with any other sharp pointed three- or four-sided awl, whether used by carpenters or not, for it is its very distinctive and effective chisel point that gives it its mastery and tempts us to guess at its origin or possible use by the Romans and after a few convincing experiments, to again weigh Moxon's evidence before discarding it.

Far better known, more conspicuous, and indispensable for larger holes, is the primitive boring instrument, of unsettled antiquity in Egypt, but known to the Romans, and according to Rich, referred to as the "terebra gallica," by Pliny, *Historia Naturalis,* 17-25, and by Columella, *De Re Rustica,* 4-29-16, and typified by the auger, here shown in several of its old hand-forged eighteenth-century forms, as an iron shank variously bladed to cut circular holes by hand-twisting in one direction (left to right), its wooden cross-handle.

As archaeologists are continually finding ancient boring bits without their handles, it seems all the more necessary at this point to explain the next illustration

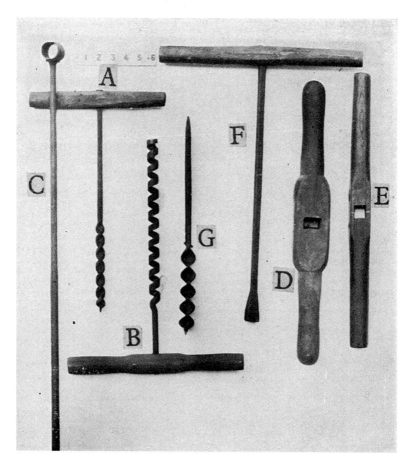

Fig. 161. Augers and Auger Handles

As here shown the homemade handles for twisting auger blades in the 18th and early 19th centuries were variously constructed.

(A, B) Most common. The wooden handle has been made with a draw knife. Through a rectangular tapering hole in its middle, the iron top of the auger shank, tapered to match, has been driven, and top-clenched across the grain.

(C) Rare. A much stronger device, used with very long auger shanks for long borings. The iron shank is topped with a flattened ring through which the wooden cross-handle (here missing) has been driven. The blade, not seen, is that of a spiral auger of the mid-19th century, from Bucks County. Two of the ship's augers of the Dutch Nova Zembla Expedition of 1596 are thus top-ringed (Fig. 180).

(D) Rare. Used by wheelwrights in the 18th and 19th centuries. The middle of the loose wooden handle is perforated with a tapering rectangular (not equi-sided) hole, with its long diameter across the grain. As into this the shank-top, tapered to match, is loosely thrust, the handle is easily releasable. One such handle would serve for several variously-sized auger bits for boring, or reaming, wheel-hub-holes. If the handle hole and shank top are equi-sided, as in the similar specimen (E), the wheelwright, standing on the wheel and boring downward, can ease and steady the operation, by releasing and replacing the handle at right angles, at each half-twist, without changing hands. Information (1927) from Abram Stone, wheelwright, *c.* 1880, Doylestown, born 1854).

(F) Rare. An adjustable twist-handle, sometimes used as a bit-extension, in long borings by carpenters, with variously sized loose auger bits. An iron shank with fixed cross-handle, as in (A), and with tapering equi-sided, "four-square," rectangular socket at bottom, into which the top of the auger-bit, tapered to match, is loosely set without catch-pin, and therefore at any time easily releasable.

(G) A loose spiral auger-bit used in this manner, but which does not fit this particular shank (F). Both specimens are from Bucks County, Pa. Ring-topped, adjustable twist-handles of this pattern, sometimes twelve feet long,

Fig. 162. The Breast Auger

This engraving from an English illuminated manuscript of date earlier than the 15th century, shows Noah boring one of the planks of the Ark with a pod-auger. He twists the handled instrument in the usual way, whiie to increase its downward pressure he leans upon a revolving circular breast plate, set or attached upon the top of its shank above the handles. The picture appears as one of the many interesting illustrations in *Schaffende Arbeit und Bildene Kunst*, Kroner, Leipsig, 1927, and is here reproduced by kind permission of its author, Professor Dr. Paul Brandt, of Gottingen University. Ernest Puter, wheelwright, of Bedminster, Bucks Co., Pa., described to the writer, in September, 1927, a similar auger with loose bottom-dented breast-pad, and top-shank filed to a pivot-point, used by him in boring hub-holes in hard wood, when learning his trade near Breslau, Germany, about 1905.

---

are always used by wooden pump makers to bore and ream freshly cut logs for "pump-trees," with the various heavy unmounted pump bits, as shown in Fig. 169 (E. F). All the specimens shown are from Eastern Pennsylvania except D. E was bought from Samuel Krout, a retired wheelwright, at Bedminster, Bucks Co., Pa., in September, 1927, D with a lot of obsolete tools from Franklin Bigelow at Fall River, Mass., in 1897. (D, E, F, G) may explain the lost mountings of many of the larger top-tapered boring bits excavated at Roman sites in Europe, as those now on exhibition at the Saalburg Museum, Homburg, Germany, at the Swiss National Museum at Zurich and at the Municipal Museum at Saumur, France. (cf. Fig. 165.)

AUGER HANDLES (Fig. 161)
which shows that in the eighteenth and probably for many preceding centuries, auger handles were either fixed or releasable,

(1) by flatttening or squaring the iron shank top and clenching or riveting it over a centre hole in the handle;

(2) by cross-driving the handle through a ring in the shank top;

(3) by flattening or "four-squaring" the shank top to loosely fit into a rectangular hole in the wooden handle, for easy release in certain borings;

(4) by flattening or by "four-squaring" the shank top and setting it releasably with or without a pin in a coinciding iron socket in an extra iron twist shank with a cross-handle as in (1).

The fact that the auger has been sometimes equipped with a breast pad, to increase its downward pressure, is too interesting to be overlooked, and though the writer has failed to find an eighteenth-century tool so constructed, the next picture,

THE BREAST AUGER (Fig. 162)
from a pre-fifteenth century painted manuscript at St. John's College, Cambridge, gives conclusive evidence on the subject.

In the engraving, one of the very interesting and novel series of pictures, illustrating ancient industries, in *Schaffende Arbeit und Bildene Kunst*, by Prof. Dr. Paul Brandt, Kroner, Leipsig, 1927, kindly found for the writer by Mr. J. E. Sanford, the old painter shows us Noah boring one of the Ark planks, with a cross-handled auger equipped, upon ‚its shaft top above the handle, with a breast pad, under which the instrument revolves. Doctor Brandt shows

another similar manuscript picture of similar date, location unnamed, reinforced with the same attachment, which, however, only helping the down pressure of the instrument, in no way changes its construction or increases its velocity.

If the auger had not been so long and so universally necessary to bore axle holes for the wooden wheels of wagons, to start mortise holes, and to peg together furniture; if, as before noted, the planks used in Europe to sheathe wooden ships had not been so generally fastened thereto with unrustable wooden pegs, rather than nails; or if pegs could be driven into place without preliminary openings, then the worldwide necessity of the auger, as an agent in the history of human industry would not compel us to wonder at its origin and distribution, while in comparison with its vast efficiency in the hands of the wheelwright or shipbuilder, its use in other trades, and as here considered, by the carpenter, or joiner, to peg-hole tenons or rafters, or parts of furniture, seems a matter of minor importance.

The difficulty of boring wood with one of these old tools, greatly increased by working in hard wood, or by adding to the depth and size of the hole, was met by iron shanks, expanding into blades, which may be roughly divided into two classes; namely, those which cut downwards, and those which cut sideways; the simplest of which, cutting chiefly downwards, is typified by

THE GOUGE BIT (Fig. 163, A, B)
the blade of which, the so-called "reed," is described and illustrated by Holtzapffel in 1846. It consists of what

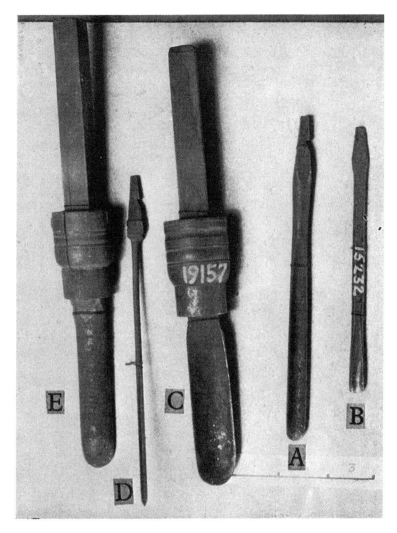

Fig. 163. The Gouge Bit (A, B) and Spoon Bit (C, D, E)

An elongated steel trough (A) with parallel sides and sharp rounded point projecting straight downward on the level of its back without forward bend, or spoon, thus resembling a common form of the carpenter's gouge (Fig. 152). The bottom of the blade is sharpened on its back or convex side like the carpenter's gouge, but unlike the latter, is also sharpened on the inner concave of *both sides* of its trough. Therefore it cuts both ways; but, as in boring, its bottom blade fails to reach the centre of the hole, the tool leaves a small unexcavated core.

Variety (B) is constructed and sharpened in the same way, except that the sharp bottom blade has no down-curve, and is cross-cut at right angles to the cylinder and therefore is a flat semi-circle. Failing still more than form (A) to reach and excavate the centre of the hole, it only leaves a deep circular incision, releasing a full-sized central plug. Both tools will cut both ways, but as both fail to catch and pull out shavings when the tool clogs, neither would be adapted to deep borings. We have failed to find either of these tools in full auger-size mounted with cross-handles, among American carpenter relics, and here show them in smaller form among the bits used with the carpenter's brace, described later.

In construction the ancient spoon bit (C, D, E) exactly resembles the gouge bit, except that its rounded, down-cutting bottom blade is spooned, *i. e.* saucered upward to the level of the trough sides; a fact clearly explained might be compared to a hollow reed or pipe, sawed in half, lengthwise, and, unlike the carpenter's gouge, which it superficially resembles, is sharpened, not only at the bottom, but also generally on its long parallel sides.

Since many books hurriedly mix up this tool with the bit next described, we should pause here a moment to carefully note that the bottom or down-cutting end of the cylinder, in no way saucered or spooned, in variety (B) is flat, *i.e.*, cross-cut at right angles to the cylinder, while in variety (A) it is more or less rounded downwards, and that in both cases, owing to this lack of spoon or inbend, which may be clearly explained by saying that water if poured into the cylinder would run off, the cutting bottom of the cylinder never reaches the centre of the hole and we find after a few boring experiments that the flat-bottomed variety (B) simply cuts a deep, circular incision ,thereby releasing a full-sized central plug, while the round-bottomed variety (A), managing to make more disturbance at the bottom, still produces a central, if smaller core.

There being no bottom spoon or saucer to either tool, neither will hold and pull out the shavings, if the blade should clog therewith, hence, though both would serve without such shaving discharge for the quick perforation of thin boards, neither would do so well in deeper borings as the next tool shown, namely,

THE SPOON BIT (Fig. 163, C, E, D) in which the instrument is constructed in the same way, except that the down-rounded-cutting bottom of the cylinder is spooned, and therefore would pull out some, at least, of the shavings. Besides which in revolving it reaches the center of the hole and hence pares the entire orifice, leaving no core.

Both the gouge and the spoon bit cut chiefly downwards and cease to cut sidewise as soon as the full diameter of the cylinder is reached. Moreover, they will cut both ways, *i.e.*, forwards and backwards, and in all similar specimens seen by the writer the bottom of the blade is sharpened on its convex back, while both sides of the cylinder are sharpened on their inner concave for more than half their length, as if to smooth the hole.

In the eighteenth century (1768), Diderot shows the spoon, with auger handle, as used in France by the carpenter, ebeniste, wheelwright, and other woodworkers, and called "Tarriere" (*cf.* "Charpente," Plate XLIX, Fig. 25). But though the writer has found numerous examples, large and small, of these boring gouges and spoons, which will cut both ways, as smaller equipments of the carpenter's brace, described later, no old American full-sized augers, so bladed, have thus far appeared.

Nevertheless, interesting evidence proves that a large variety of this

---

by saying that water poured in to fill the upturned trough will not, as in the gouge bit, run out. Again the down-cutting tool will work both ways, but as in this case the spooned blade reaches the centre of revolution, it will not only pare out the entire orifice into a round-bottomed hole leaving no core, but also partially pull out its clogged shavings in deep borings. Having failed to find an old example of the instrument mounted on a cross-handle, like an auger, it is here shown in smaller size as one of the brace bits of the 18th century carpenter. The specimens C and E with their old brace, not shown, were obtained in 1923 from the estate of Charles Bryan, an old chairmaker at Dublin, Bucks Co., Pa.

Fig. 164. A Cylinder Auger of the 14th Century

This picture, showing a carpenter using an auger with a gouge or spoon blade from one of the paintings in a French illuminated manuscript of 1362, *Libre des Proprietez Dez Choses*, by Jehan Carbechon, in the British Museum (Bib. Reg. 15-E-11-Folio 99), reproduces an illustration in *The Guilds of Florence*, by Edgcumbe Staley, Methuen, London, 1906. It was found for the writer by Mr. Joseph E. Sandford, and is here republished by kind permission of Mr. Edgcumbe Staley.

elongated untwisted trough, mounted on a cross-handle, represents, if not the oldest, a very old form of the full-sized auger; and the more we compare

the efficient spoon with the less efficient gouge, the more interesting it might seem to trace back, if possible, the comparative antiquity of both

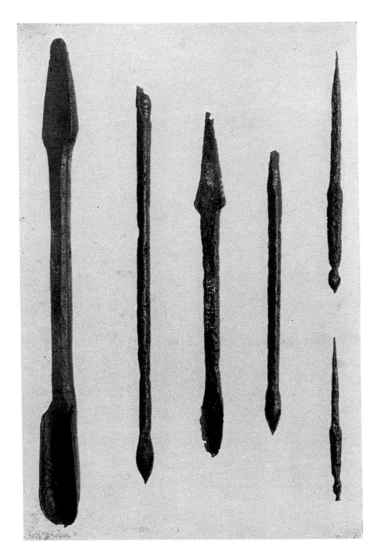

Fig. 165. Boring Bits of the Roman Carpenter

The steel bits here shown were found in Roman camp sites in Switzerland and are now preserved in the Swiss National Museum at Zurich. In 1 (left) found at Wettsweil (Zurich), and 3d (from left), found at Windisch, the blades must be either gouge-shaped (Fig. 163, A. B), or spoon-shaped (Fig. 163, C, D. E). The first is about 24 inches long. Another, 15 inches long, is in the Town Museum, at Saumur, France, and several similar spoon or gouge-bladed boring tools found at the Saalburg Roman fort, near Homburg. Hesse, Germany, 13, 16 and 21 inches long, seem too large for rapid turning. Others, smaller, at Saalburg and elsewhere, are constructed in the same way, but show no signs of top clenching. A striking feature of these larger Roman tools is the resemblance of their lanceolate or pyramidal tops to the tops of the large auger and reamer bits of the modern pumpmaker and carpenter (Figs. 169 and 170). This would suggest that they may have been worked with a releasable wooden cross-handle like the specimens D, E, in Fig. 161. But as yet no Roman bitstock and no handle of any kind has been found for any of these tools. The bits are photographed by the kind permission of the Swiss National Museum at Zurich.

Fig. 166. Down Cutting or Nose Auger

Here the iron shank in full auger size, with cross-handle, appears as a perfect half-cylinder, ending, without taper, in a horizontal nose-shaped inbend of its side, forming a knife; the "nose," seen faintly in the right specimen and clearly in the outline marked A, cuts downward at very nearly the full diameter of the instrument. This auger, therefore, from the start, makes a cylindrical hole, without taper, but as it lacks a screw point, and the "nose" does not center itself, a preliminary hole must be bored or dented in the wood to start it. Neither this tool, nor the pod auger, nor the taper auger (described later) will "bite" sufficiently to penetrate wood without body or hand pressure, hence neither will work on a crank, and as neither automatically discharge their shavings, they must be continually pulled out of the hole, when the shavings enclosed in the cylinder clog the work. Diderot in 1768 (*Charpente*) does not show this tool.

tools. Unfortunately the two bits resemble each other too much to be distinguishable in old pictures and nothing short of actual examination of ancient excavated tools, with unrusted points, could certainly establish dates for either blade form.

A French illuminated manuscript of 1362, in the British Museum, also found for the writer by Mr. Joseph E. Sanford, as seen in the next illustration,

A Cylinder Auger of the 14th
Century (Fig. 164)

clearly shows an auger equipped with
one of these down-paring, untwisted
cylinder blades, which may be either
spooned or unspooned. Another appears hanging on the wall, in the
"Carpenter," one of a series of eighteen etchings, showing workmen at
their trades, by Rembrandt's pupil
Jan Joris Van Vliet, born at Delft in
1610 (cf. reprint by Carl Gerlinghaus,
Munich, 1925). While to prove its far
greater antiquity, the next illustration

Boring Bits of the Roman
Carpenter (Fig. 165)

shows two Roman instruments of this
construction (1) and (3), counting
from left, found at ancient sites (1) in
Wettsweil (Zurich) and (3) Windisch,
in Switzerland.

The blades of these rusty relics of
a bygone age, several more of which
were dug up at the Saalburg Roman
fort near Homburg, Hesse, Germany,
and are now (1927) on exhibition at
the Museum there, appear to be considerably spooned. All lack their original handles. Some, like the left-hand
specimen, here shown, with shank
about two feet long, too heavy for
rapid revolution, must have been
mounted on a T-handle like the modern auger. Others are small, and we
may guess from their socket-shaped
tops, that some device, not yet found,
resembling either a carpenter's brace
or an auger or gimlet cross-handle was
used to turn them.

As before observed, in shallow
board or plank borings, quickly penetrating the wood, and hence where no
outpull of clogged shavings was
needed, the gouge or spoon bit would

do well enough. Otherwise, in the
eighteenth century, the difficulty of
shaving release in deep borings, was
sometimes met by a curious variety of
the spoon bit called the duck's bill or
duck's nose-bit alias brush bit and
cooper's dowel bit, in which the spoon
sometimes ends in a side-sharpened
upcurled point, which, though not
helping the down-cut would, because
of its cross-reach beyond the centre of
the hole, catch and pull out shavings
that the plain spoon, only half grasping the orifice, would miss. The auth-
or has failed to find an old specimen
of one of these rare and interesting
tools, which Knight merely names,
and the careful Holtzapffel describes
without illustrating, as used by brush
and cabinet makers, and by coopers
for boring the dowel holes in barrel
heads. But Diderot illustrates it as
used by the wooden-shoe maker, "sab-
bottier" (cf. Economie Rustique, Vig-
nette Fig. 8). Also, as one of the only
three French carpenter's augers which
he shows for 1768. He calls it in the
former case "grande cuilliere," and in
the latter "laceret," and though poorly drawn, its profile reasonably distinguishes it from the other two carpenter's blades, namely the pod auger and
the spoon auger, shown on the same
plate ("Charpente," Plate XLIX, Fig.
24).

Feldhaus, Technik der Vorzeit, article "Bohrer," shows, without describing, a woodcut of the tool of date
1615, and Daremberg and Saglio (article "Terebra") illustrates a remarkable Roman specimen, which they
call "terebra Gallica," dug out of a
wall at the ancient Uxellodunum,
near Cahors, France.

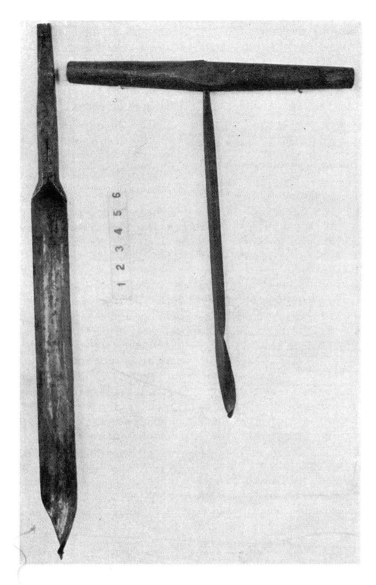

Fig. 167. Twisted Cylinder or Pump Auger and the Pod Auger

This ancient and now almost obsolete instrument is here illustrated in two varieties, that at the left being the loose bit of a pumpmaker's auger mounted, when worked, on a long shank, not shown. The tool is an elongated open cylinder with sides, one of which is sharpened as a blade, somewhat twisted as they taper downward to end in a screw point, and cuts not directly, but diagonally downward, enlarging the hole, until the full diameter of the tool is reached. It engages the wood much more firmly than the untwisted gouge auger, though much less so than the spiral auger, described later. Nevertheless, it does not grasp it sufficiently to enable it to penetrate without occasional man pressure, and hence, will not, like the spiral auger, work freely on a crank. Because the long parallel sides of the cylinder steady the tool and prevent its boring off the line, the instrument was preferred in elongated accurate borings

While the spoon-bit is clearly an improvement upon the gouge, and the duck's bill sometimes upon the spoon, another device of unknown antiquity, appended to this same untwisted boring trough, clearly appears in the eighteenth century, namely the

DOWN CUTTING OR NOSE AUGER
(Fig. 166)

In this now almost obsolete home-made Colonial instrument, the bottom spoon of the spoon-bit has been deeply notched, and one of the spoon projections thus produced has been bent upward to clear the wood, while the other, sharpened all around and round pointed, forms in profile the so-called "nose," which more effectively pares up the entire bottom of the hole as the tool goes round. Meanwhile, the other non-cutting spoon up-bend, still holds the clogged shavings, when the tool is pulled out to discharge them.

While the nose-bit is turned, it is not its sides, but only this revolving nose, which cuts, and only downwards at that, but no longer both ways, therefore only one of the side blades, which may be said to serve only to clean out or to smooth the hole, and steady the instrument, need be kept sharp. Further, as the sides are parallel, the hole, save for its round bottom, is cylindrical, whether the entire instrument penetrates the wood or not. But because this "nose" fails to "bite," at first, the tool, according to Holtzapffel, must be started with a preliminary dent or notch.

The next illustration shows in varied form another boring tool whose origin is lost in antiquity, namely the

TWISTED CYLINDER OR PUMP AUGER
AND THE POD AUGER (Fig. 167)

This ancient instrument appears in two varieties, as here shown— (left) as used by pumpmakers—a long cylindrical trough, tapering at the bottom, with sides (one of which is sharpened) slightly twisted into a spiral ending in a pivot screw, which latter merely "bites" or grasps the wood without cutting it, until, as the tool goes down, one of the spiral blades diagonally side-cuts the hole to the full diameter of the instrument, after which it ceases to cut. Hence the elongation of the cylinder beyond this point of widest diameter, which considerably increases the friction, only serves to steady the instrument, where long, straight holes, as in wooden pump stocks or pumptrees, are required.

The variety (right) also illustrated

(as by the old pumpmakers for wooden pump trees) to the other variety here shown to the right. This is known as the pod auger and is constructed in the same way, except that the cylinder is shortened into a boat-shaped open trough causing less friction, called the pod, from its resemblance to a seed pod. In both instances, the cylinder, however shaped, holds the shavings when the clogged instrument is continually pulled out of the hole to remove them; while both tools, because their diagonally twisted blades will hold fast in penetrating the end of a log, have maintained, in long borings parallel *with the grain*, a superiority over the otherwise more effective spiral auger described later, whose crosscut parings in that case break off. Both specimens here shown are homemade Bucks County farm relics. The left-hand example, smith-stamped "Dubs," was used until about 1890 near Doylestown, to bore out the valve holes in wooden homemade pump-stocks, the so-called pump-trees. According to the information of Edward Haycock, homemade pump-maker of Fountainville, Bucks Co., Pa., given to the writer in March, 1926, who still bores wooden homemade pump-trees, the freshly cut white oak log to be bored, was squared with the broad axe and laid horizontally on blocks, whereupon, when the auger point was centred upon a preliminary hole in the log end and its long shank was firmly steadied on a bracket, the instrument was slowly worked, generally by two men, sometimes by one, who twisted its cross-handle without much forward pressure. Thus, working from both ends, they laboriously perforated a sixteen-foot log endwise in one day, after which the hole had to be enlarged three or four times by various sizes of the taper, side-cutting reamer, shown in Fig. 169—F. E.

Abb. 16. Zimmermann bei der Arbeit (Heilige Familie). Kpfr. von Veit Stoß. 15. Jahrhundert.
Dresden, Kupferstichkabinet. P. II, S. 153, Nr. 4.

Fig. 168. Pod Auger of the 15th Century

From a 15th century German copper engraving of the "Holy Family," by Veit Stoss, now preserved in the Kupferstiche Kabinet at Dresden. (*Monographen Zur deutschen Kulturgeschichte*, Vol. 8, *Der Handwerker*, E. Mummenhoff, Leipsig, 1901.) Saint Joseph is represented boring a plank with a pod auger, the sides of which are twisted more than in the photo-engravings of other examples here shown. A log dog and a cross-cut saw, with the wide-spread twin teeth (in modern outline) appear on the floor.

here, is constructed in exactly the same way, but differs in the shape and length of its cylinder. It is called pod auger in the United States, from the resemblance of said tapered cylinder to a seed pod, whose rounded shorter sides decrease the friction but no longer steady the tool. Again, one of these sides is sharpened and twisted towards the bottom, so as not only to cut but to grasp the wood, as the instrument penetrates, and again, as in the left specimen, this bottom-twist of the cylinder, is helpful in holding the shavings, as the clogged blade is continually pulled out of the hole to discharge them.

A final glance at the two tools laid side by side, and helped by the rapidly vanishing information of men who still use them, clearly shows that both tools cut only one way, *i.e.,* forward in the direction of the spiral twist; that the elongated cylinder must cut more accurately, but with more friction than the short pod; that the little start screw, though it does not cut at first, in both cases holds the instrument to a centre; while the swelling blade-twist of the cylinder, strongly grasping the wood, as it enters the hole, not only greatly reduces the man pressure otherwise necessary, but explains why both tools, now so rarely seen (because entirely superseded in cross-grain boring, by the spiral auger described later), still hold their own for deep borings made endwise into wood.

This is why Edward Haycock, who (1926) with the pump auger (left), bores sixteen-foot white oak logs endwise for wooden "pump-trees," at Fountainville, Bucks County, Pa., does not and cannot use the otherwise more efficient spiral auger for this purpose, because, as he says, its parings

break off across the grain, and so do not hold the tool to its work.

How easy to glance at outline drawings of these master tools in books, or to think we understand them, from the superficial descriptions of writers, who begin and end their explanations with names, or take for granted a knowledge that no one has or can have, without attentive study. If the archaeologist does not understand them, he cannot explain the similar tools dug up at Roman sites in Europe, and if we cannot describe them without wearying the reader, the photographs at least remain. They show, if often too dimly, the trenchant forms, never constructed for show, and whose every variety has a studied purpose.

That the pod auger is also an old European instrument, is shown not only by Moxon's miniature picture of it (Fig. 67K), but also by the next illustration, namely:—

A POD AUGER OF THE 15TH CENTURY (Fig. 168)

from a copper engraving, representing the Holy Family, by the German engraver, Veit Stoss (born *c.* 1447, died 1533), in which the tool, with the blades more twisted than in the specimen above shown, is turned by Saint Joseph, to bore a hole in a plank.

The blade of the pod auger is very clearly drawn in the old English manuscript painting, shown in Fig. 162, and several other examples of these extra-twisted instruments, as clearly distinct from the ancient gouge, spoon or nose auger, whether for two hands or one, appear in another ancient woodcut from a monastic picture book of the fifteenth or sixteenth century, in the Town Li-

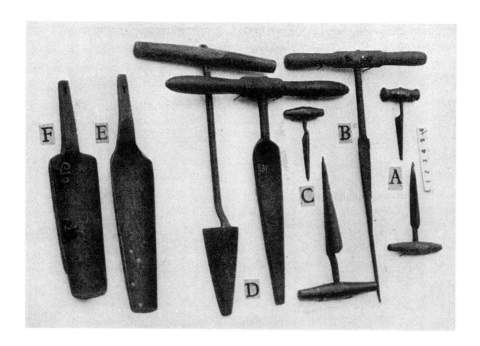

Fig. 169 (A, B, C). The Taper or Tap Auger; (D, E, F). The Reamer

In the four old homemade big and little side-cutting instruments (A, B, C) called tap augers, the cross-handled shank ends, not in an open-sided half-cylinder, but a half funnel, which cuts a tapering hole, unless the blade gces clear through the wood. The blades are not dull-bottomed or open-bottomed, but dwindle into side-sharpened points, more or less twisted, ending in straight screws, like the pod auger. Hence, by diagonal side-parings, they produce a tapered hole, where needed by cabinetmakers or particularly by coopers and others, who still use factory-made dupl - cates of them (A, A, C) with one and (B) two hands, to tap casks for bung and spigot holes. As in the wheelwright's auger, both sides of the funnel are sharpened to cut. The shanks are riveted or clenched fast to the handles through rectangular holes.

The down--tapering, funnel-shaped reamer, sharpened sometimes only on one side and sometimes on both sides, will not bore a hole but only enlarge by side-paring a hole already bored. The two specimens (F, E) are pump reamers, or rather bits therefor, which, when mounted and pegged fast into rectangular bottom-sockets, on very long iron twist shanks (not shown) (*cf.* Fig. 161), enlarge holes previously bored by one of the augers already described. Only one of the blades in each specimen (the right), hollow upward, as here seen, is sharpened towards its bottom. Because the pump-tree lies horizontally and the shavings will not, therefore, drop through the hole already bored, the unsharpened, inbent base of the funnel is desirable as a box to catch them.

In the first specimen (F) a dull-edged iron plate is screw-bolted on the outer, dull, left edge of the funnel, not to cut, but to enlarge the cutting diameter of the said funnel, when the right sharpened edge does the work. (E) lacks this enlarging plate. In the next two wheelwright's reamers, with fixed handles (D), also side-cutting, used likewise to enlarge holes previously bored in wagon hubs, both blades are sharpened; but as they are held vertically by the workman, and the shavings drop down through the already open hole, they lack bottoms.

brary at Nuremburg, as reproduced in *Handwerker der Deutschen Vergangenheit,* edited by C. Mummenhoff, Leipsig, 1901, following page 40, which shows a pod auger being forged on an anvil, with seven finished pod augers and pod gimlets lying before a monkish blacksmith on a table.

Still more interesting, as amongst the rarest relics of ancient industry yet found by archaeologists, and as proving that the Romans had invented and used the pod auger, whether as a full sized auger, or as a bit in a carpenter's brace, described later, are the examples also shown in Fig. 165 (3 specimens right and 2d from left), in which the rusted instrument (2d from left), with shank broken and handle lost, but still nearly 18 inches long, and clearly preserving its twisted pod shaped blade, appears among the tools excavated at one of the Roman camp sites in Switzerland, and here illustrated by the kind permission of the Swiss National Museum at Zurich.

But, as these specimens show, the blade of the pod auger is not cylindrical, but tapers downward, and therefore does not produce a hole entirely cylindrical unless it goes clear through the wood. For this reason another ancient Anglo-American form of instrument, specially constructed to cut a taper hole in the first place, though it would still enlarge by complete penetration a hole already cut, is represented in the next illustration as

THE TAPER AUGER (Fig. 169, A, B, C)

Here we see a long, pointed funnel, more or less twisted, and side-sharpened to cut laterally, ending in a screw point, used by coopers to cut bung or spigot holes in casks, or by cabinetmakers for socketing chair legs, etc.

But because holes too large for the strength of one or even two men were often required, and because it is easier to first bore a small hole and then enlarge it, than to bore a large hole in the first place, another tool, shaped and handled like an auger, but not to be confused with it, because it does not bore at all, is next shown. This is

THE REAMER (Fig. 169, D, E, F) an untwisted, sharp-sided, open half-funnel which only enlarges by side-paring a hole already bored, here illustrated in two varieties (F, E), the pumpborer's reamer, boxed at the bottom to hold shavings, and adjustable as a bit to a long shank, not shown, employed by the old pumpmakers, not to bore holes, but to enlarge holes already bored in pump-trees, or (D) the wheelwright's reamer, a similarly side-sharpened, untwisted but bottomless funnel used by the wheelwright to enlarge wheel-hub-holes. This latter tool as shown in the next picture

THE WHEELWRIGHT'S HOOKED REAMER (Fig. 170, A, B, C)

was sometimes equipped with a round, unsharpened pull hook, which, extending downward from the blade-bottom and attached by a ring or otherwise, to some pulling device, helped in no way to cut, but only to pull the blade through the hole, when the workman standing upon or beside the spoked wheel, laboriously reamed out, i.e., enlarged, a hole already bored through its hub.

That the French cartwright (charron) used the same reaming tool for the same purpose in 1768, is shown by the appended engraving from Diderot (Fig. 170 C), who unfortunately does not describe the method of using its unique hook, while far more interesting is the fact, as further illustrated in the same engraving,

THE ROMAN HOOKED BIT (Fig. 170 E)

that a similar instrument was known to the Romans. The latter, a much-rusted bit, 26½ centimetres (10½

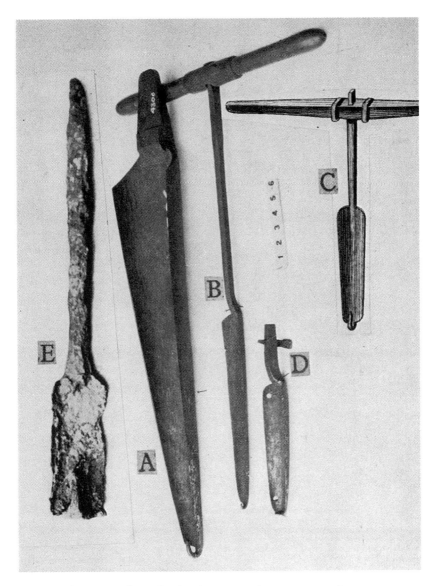

*Fig. 170. The Wheelwright's Hooked Reamer (A, B, C)
and Roman Hooked Bit (E)*

    The gigantic, funnel-shaped steel instrument (A), smith-forged in one piece, 35 inches long, and weighing 26 pounds, sharpened only on the inner concave of its right blade, is equipped at its bottom with a round-sided, unsharpened, down-reaching pull hook, which hook in no way cuts the wood, but when attached to some pulling device, helps to pull downward the blade, while the latter is being twisted through a previously bored hole in a wheel hub.

    Its top tang, for the handle, not an equi-sided, but a broad, flat rectangle, and lacking a peg hole, is not centred by inbending over the point of revolution, but rises directly from the blade's circumference. It is adapted for insert and release upon a wooden cross-handle, here missing, slotted to fit it. According to the information (1927) of Abram

inches) long, kindly photographed for the writer by Dr. H. Jacobi, Director of Excavations, at the Saalburg, near Homburg, Hesse, Germany, was dug up with other iron tools in a well at the Roman fort there. Its hook is very apparent, but as its blade is not tapered, and therefore would not act as a reamer, we must either suppose that its taper has been rusted away, or that its hook has been used not to pull the tool through a previously bored hole, but originally was side-sharpened, as in the duck's bill bit, to down cut and pull out shavings when boring a hole in the first place.

Before leaving the subject of reamers two other interesting varieties of the tool constructed, not to bore, but to enlarge holes already bored, are shown in

Fig. 171. THE TWISTED PUMP REAMER

Fig. 171. The Twisted Pump Reamer

The four bits with long adjustable iron twist handles (not shown), were used to enlarge previously bored holes in pump stocks in Lancaster County, Pennsylvania, in the nineteenth century. Their dull bottoms which will not cut, are constructed either with an open incurl of the right blade corner, or a cross funnelling of the entire blade, designed to catch and pull out shavings. Kindly photographed for the writer by Mr. H. K. Landis of Landis Valley, Pennsylvania, in December, 1927.

Stone, born 1854, who, as a wheelwright, used exactly similar tools for this purpose in Doylestown, c. 1880, the already-spoked wheel, with its hub hole previously bored, was laid horizontally on a trestle, under which a ring-topped iron rod, threaded at bottom through a hole in a fixed iron cross-bar, projects upward so as to encircle the reamer hook, and by action of its screw, pulls down the reamer, when the workman, standing upon the wheel, twists the reamer's cross-handle, like that shown in Fig. 161 E. Mr. Stone says that his reamer handles, made by himself of oak, and releasable on equi-sided rectangular tangs, were lifted and replaced at each half turn, to save the usual right-to left-hand shift necessary with ordinary fixed auger handles. Also, that some of his reamer tangs were centered, while others, as here shown, were side-set, and that in the latter case, the reamer cut better with certain woods.

(B) shows a smaller variety of the same tool with centered shank and fixed handle and (C) a duplicate, used in 1768, for the same purpose, by the French cartwright, with long iron shank and fixed handle, as illustrated in Diderot's *Encyclopedia*, "Charron," Plate 2, Fig. 2, where, unfortunately, no mention is made of the hook and no better description given of the tool than that it was used *"pour accroitre les trous des moyeux,"*—to enlarge hub holes.

(D) is a pumpmaker's reamer bit, with two holes for attaching a side extension plate, here missing, constructed exactly like Fig 169 F, except that its bottom is not boxed to pull out shavings, but more cheaply and easily fitted with a flat, unhooked, iron plug for the same purpose, and in no way intended, like the hook, on A and B, to pull the tool through the hole worked upon.

(E) illustrates a much rusted, but very remarkable hook-bottomed ancient boring bit, dug up at the Roman Fort at the Saalburg, near Homburg, Hesse, Germany, now on exhibition at the Museum there, as described in the text by permission of Dr. H. Jacobi, its Director.

with dull bottom, not boxed, like F and E Fig. 169, but incurled or funneled, so as to catch and pull out shavings. Four specimens are here shown, used by the 19th century pump makers in Eastern Pennsylvania and now in the collection of Mr. H. K. Landis of Landis Valley, Lancaster Co., Pa.

The next picture,

A WHEELWRIGHT'S REAMER OF THE 17TH CENTURY (Fig. 172)

reproduces an illustration from *Het Menslyk Bedryf,* Amsterdam, 1718, an old Dutch picture book showing workmen at their trades, and here represents a wheelwright, in this case boring downwards so as to enlarge the previously bored hub-hole in a wheel, with one of these now almost obsolete, untwisted, side-cutting instruments, which may or may not be equipped with a hook.

At this point, for the sake of clearness, though at the risk of wearying the reader, another boring tool, though too small to be called an auger, ought to be described. This is the celebrated

CENTRE BIT (Fig. 173, A, B)

referred to later as one of the boring adjustments of the carpenter's brace (Fig. 179). It consists of a horizontal blade or router, revolving round a central pin or pivot, which blade horizontally pares off the bottom of the hole as the tool revolves. On the other side of the central pin the upcurved, non-cutting blade ends in a knife-edged outer pin, which circumscribes and clears the corner of the descending hole.

The centre bit is distinctly a down-cutting and not a side-cutting instrument, and like the nose auger, excavates a cylindrical hole from the start, for which purpose, because immediately steadied by its central pin, and because it produces a flat and not a round-bottomed hole, as for shallow socket borings, it must have been very efficient long before the spiral auger (described later) came into general use. Nevertheless, the tool with its open sides and half-open bottom is less adapted than the nose bit or even the spoon or duck's bill bit to pull out shavings from a clogged hole, hence is not convenient for deep excavations, and it is probably for this reason that the writer in many searchings has always found it as here shown, in the form of a comparatively small instrument, with a tapering rectangular plug-tang adapted for insertion in a carpenter's brace, and never mounted on a cross-bar handle like an auger.

That the Romans knew the centre-bit might well have been proved by a remarkable Roman specimen, with fully developed horizontal router, illustrated by Blumner in his *Technologie und Terminologie,* as on exhibition, about 1887, at the Antiquarium Museum at Zurich. But the unique tool has been unfortunately lost or mislaid, and according to information from the curators in 1927, cannot now be found at Zurich, either in the University Museum or Swiss National Museum. Replacing the router with a vertical scrape-blade the centre-bit, with either one or two scribe-points, becomes the so-called

BUTTON BIT (Fig. 173, C, D)

used one hundred years ago to in-

De uitvinding van het wagenwiel
Kan zwaare laften licht vervoeren :

Fig. 172. Wheelwright's Reamer of the 18th Century

This picture from a copper engraving in the Dutch illustrated book of Trades, *Spiegel Van Het Menselyk Bedryf*, by Jan and Kasper Luiken, Amsterdam, 1718, shows a wheelwright enlarging a previously-bored hole in a wheel hub, with one of the side-cutting, bottomless taper reamers as shown in Fig. 169.

The ingenious makeshift, tripod prop-device, by which the wheel was lifted from the ground to let the reamer pass clear through its hub, is here imperfectly illustrated by the old Dutch artist. Three heavy wooden sticks, pushed at equal distances under the tire, were thrust upward not thus directly against the hub, with no down-bearing at all, but crossways, so as to bear down, each upon the inner end of a spoke. Seen by the writer in use by Ernest Puter, wheelwright, at Bedminster, Bucks Co., Pa., September 14, 1927, Puter said he had learned his trade near Breslau, Germany, about 1902.

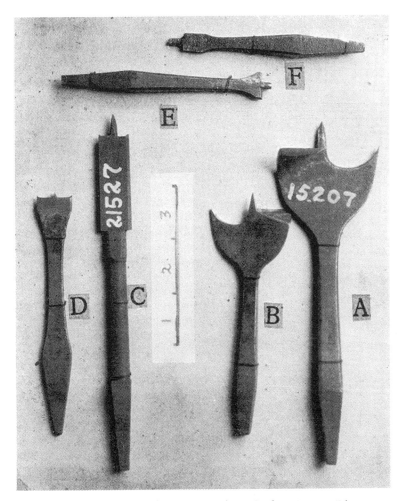

Fig. 173. Centre Bit, Button Bit and Plug Centre Bit

In the celebrated centre bit (A B) the down-cutting, horizontal blade (router) revolves one side only of a central pivot pin, on the other side of which pin, the tool, clearing the wood, does not cut until its outer circumference ends in a thin, sharp point which circumscribes the hole as the tool goes down. The tool is too open to hold and pull out shavings and hence is not adapted to deep borings. It appears among the brace bits of the 18th century carpenter, but the writer has never found it mounted with a permanent cross-handle like the auger. The specimens A and B were found in the amateur workshop of Mr. C. J. Wister (1820-1860), of Germantown, Pa.

The two outer scribe points of the button bit (C, D) revolve around its central pointed pivot, while the remaining bottom of the blade, chamfer-sharpened in opposite directions, on either side of said pivot, smooths the surface worked upon. As the circular incision so made will release discs from thin plates of bone or wood, the tool was used to make bone buttons one hundred years ago.

(D) shows a reproduction in steel of a button bit excavated with numerous bone buttons and the shoulder blade of a sheep, perforated with coinciding holes. Found in 1925 by Mr. W. L. Calver, at a Revolutionary camp site near New York City.

(E and F) called by Holtzapffel plug centre bits, found among the tools in the amateur Germantown workshop of Mr. C. J. Wister (1820 to 1860) previously mentioned, are constructed like the button bit, but lack the outer scribe points and replace the central pointed pivot with a round, blunt plug. When the plug is set in a hole previously bored for the shank of a screw bolt, the bit cuts a cylindral counter-sink or counterbore for the bold head.

scribe, smooth, and cut out, circles through thin bone plates, and thereby produce bone buttons.

Of the two specimens here shown, C was found among the tools, above noted, of C. J. Wister (c. 1820-1860), of Germantown. The other (D) is a reproduction of the button bit excavated, with a perforated bone tablet and numerous buttons, by Mr. W. E. Calver, for the New York Historical Society, at a Revolutionary camp site near New York City, in 1923, almost duplicating the discovery of several bone discs (buttons) and blade bones of sheep, perforated with coinciding holes, found at the Romano-British site at Silchester, near Reading, England, which indicate by inference that the Romans used the button bit to make buttons between the first and fourth centuries, A.D.

Still another variety of the centre-bit, shown in the same illustration, is noted by Holtzapffel as

THE PLUG CENTRE BIT
(Fig. 173, E, F)

The tool may be described as a revolving chisel, in which, as seen in the specimens E, F, the central pivot point is an unsharpened, flat-bottomed plug around which revolves the chisel blade, basilled as in the button bit, contrariwise on either side of the plug, which scrapes rather than pares (routs) the material worked upon.

When, as Holtzapffel explains, the plug is inserted into a hole previously bored in hard wood, bone or metal, to receive the shank of a bolt or screw, the revolving bit, which lacks outer scribe points, will countersink a socket for the bolt or screw head.

That the Assyrians and Egyptians knew a tool thus constructed seems to be proved by two dimly photographed specimens in Flinders Petrie's *Tools and Weapons,* Plate LXXVIII, M. 24 & 25, found, says the writer, in a group of Assyrian implements of date c. 670 B.C., at Thebes.

The Japanese still employs a variety of the centre bit, here shown as

THE JAPANESE ANNULAR AUGER
(Fig. 174)

to bore holes through boards, and we may well pause to examine this remarkable Far-Eastern instrument, with its one inch wide blade, which shows a very long centre pivot and two scribe points sharpened on both sides for back twist. Turned not by a cross-bar handle, like the Western auger, but by extra strength of hand, upon a straight, vertical handle, and probably useless for deep borings, it will, nevertheless, when held to its puncture and worked on one or both sides of a board, cut a round hole therein by releasing a cylindrical plug (as seen on the pivot point in the picture).

Whether or not the Japanese invented this remarkable bit, the fact that the Chinese have no such tool, leads us to suspect, though without proof, that the former derived it from European traders in comparatively modern times.

If we reëxamine the augers, ancient and modern, thus far described, we find that what might be called a serious defect applies to them all, namely, that all, in their operation, fail of themselves to discharge their shavings, hence that they interrupt the workman, who must continually stop, pull them out, and clean the hole. This fact brings us to a differently constructed and far more effective form

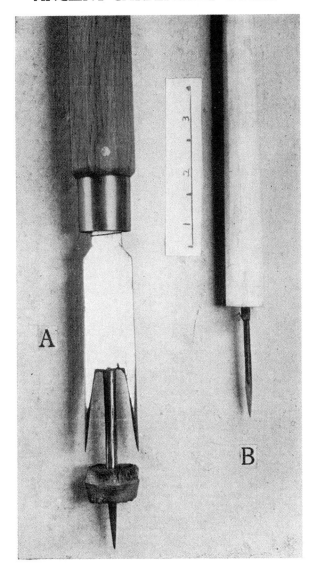

Fig. 174. Japanese Annular Auger

This remarkable auger, without cross-bar, turned by hand strength on its straight, vertical handle, is bladed with a very long central pivot-point around which two thin scribe-points, knife-edged to cut both ways, circumscribe the work. The pivot-point is not chisel-shaped, like the western brad awl, but tapers to a point on its four sides, like a drill. When the pivot point has penetrated a board and the scribe-points have made deep incisions, the instrument may be withdrawn and repivoted on the opposite side of the board in the pivot hole thus made; whereupon, when the revolving scribe-points penetrating the wood meet their previously made opposite incisions, a wooden disc is released, leaving a circular hole in the board. In this singular instrument, constructed not to make deep borings, but only to cut through comparatively thin boards, as for bung holes in a cask, there is no provision for the release of shavings, and the down-cutting, horizontal router blade of the Western centre bit is entirely lacking. The tool, apparently not used by the Chinese, but still surviving in Japan, was bought from a Japanese workman at Kuling, China, by Mr. R. P. Hommel, in 1926.

The smaller tool (right) shows a vertical-handled, Japanese hand drill or brad awl with single point tapered not like the Western brad awl, but to a three-sided drill point. Obtained at the same time and place.

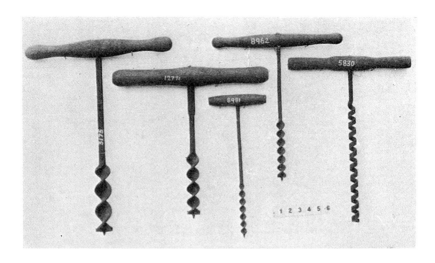

Fig. 175. The Spiral Auger

This very efficient and revolutionary instrument, which generally, early in the 19th century, superseded the old augers, here described, differs from them all in two important points,—in the first place, its shank, twisted in a spiral, is not sharp-sided, and does not cut as in the pod auger, but only discharges the shavings. Secondly, its spiral, centreing in a pivot screw, ends generally in two horizontal blades, facing opposite directions, which so strongly engage the wood that the tool requires no start hole like the old nose auger, and, unlike it, will penetrate if worked across the grain on a crank or by turning its handle without pressure. The blades also cut directly downward, while their sharpened, upturned outer corners, corner-cut the hole as the tool turns. The thin shavings thus pared horizontally, and loosened at the sides, travel up the spiral, above each blade, in two separate channels in the same direction, and fall out at the top of the hole. In the less effective, open spiral, ending in a single bottom-router (right), with upbent outer edge to corner-cut the hole, but lacking a pivot screw, called the "single twist," the shavings travel in one rather than two channels. Like the nose auger, the spiral auger cuts from the start a perfectly ·cylindrical hole. Nevertheless, though otherwise highly efficient, it will not grip the wood sufficiently to bore large and deep holes endways into a log, because, in that case, its thin parings, cut at right angles to the grain, break off. For which reason the old wooden-pump makers continued (in Pennsylvania until about 1890) to use the twisted cylinder auger (Fig. 167), for their laborious purpose.

Neither Moxon nor Diderot describe the tool, which Knight's *American Mechanical Dictionary* says was invented by Lilley, of Connecticut, and afterwards by Gurley, of Mansfield, Conn., about 1800. But the earliest United States patents are for Hoxie (1804), Hale (1807), and L'Hommedieu (1809), and about a dozen other patentees up to 1834, of which Knight says that the instrument invented by L'Hommedieu was the type of its class. It was not introduced among carpenters in Northern Hungary at Gross Lomnitz, until about 1887 (information of Jacob Reptsik, cabinetmaker, of Lansdale, Pa., to the writer, Jan. 2, 1921).

of auger, unknown to Moxon, which came into general use in the United States and England one hundred years ago, namely

THE SPIRAL AUGER (Fig. 175)

in which the horizontal, revolving bottom knife of the tool cuts or "routs," not sideways at a taper, but as in the centre bit, downward at the full diameter of the hole, while the improved spiral twist does not cut at all, as in the pod auger, but manages to lift up and continuously discharge the shavings out of the hole, which the centre bit fails to do. This was an immense improvement, and although the spiral auger will not work in large borings *with the grain*, because its cross-cut parings, in that case, break off, and fail to grip the blade, this novel shaving discharge at once revolutionized the tool for all common side-grain perforations.

To study the United States patented

attempts to vary and improve this instrument, in the form of the spiral, the shape and angle of the routing knives, the screw axis to steady them, or the blade upbend to scratch around the descending hole, is a bewildering task, until, fixing our attention upon the spiral shank, we see not only that said spiral is never sharpened to cut, as in the old auger, but that its twist is much less steep than in the latter, and that in the most improved pattern of the tool, as here shown, the spiral is double, so to speak; that is, that the twisted flange forms two channels for shavings, each ending downwards in a horizontal bottom-router with upturned, sharp outer corner, by which the chips pared off the bottom and cleared off the side of the hole, travel upward in two spiral streams, one above the other, at an easy incline in the same direction.

It is this revolutionary device that L'Hommedieu (1809) and others are associated with in the United States, as a great improvement rather than an invention, since the horizontal router had previously existed in the centre bit, and the spiral shaving discharge had already been devised, as shown by F. M. Feldhaus, in his Technik der Vorzeit, Engleman, Leipsig—Berlin, 1914, article "Bohrer," and illustrated in the next picture

COOKE'S AUGER OF 1770
(Fig. 176)

Throwing light upon the obscure origin of the spiral auger, Feldhaus shows this remarkable auger invented by P. Cooke, in England, in 1770, not noticed by Holtzapffel, and not officially listed among British Patents, but shown by William Bailey in

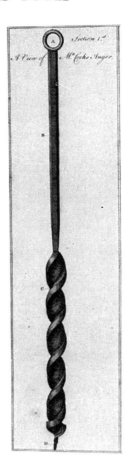

Fig. 176. Cooke's Spiral Auger of 1770

The engraving photographed from Plate XLIX and described on page 276 of *The Advancement of Arts, Manufactures and Commerce*, by William Bailey, London, 1772, shows "Mr. Phineas Cooke's New Constructed Spiral Auger," for the "invention" of which the Society for The Encouragement of Arts, Manufactures and Commerce voted him a bounty of thirty guineas on May 1, 1770.

As explained in the description and here shown, the dull spiral for discharging shavings completely anticipates the same device in the present (1927) tool. But the instrument cuts, like the pod auger, on the bottom-sharpened twist of said spiral and not on the characteristic horizontal bottom router (borrowed from the centre bit) of the modern spiral auger as shown in Fig. 175.

The remarkable picture was brought to the writer's notice by F. M. Feldhaus, who describes and illustrates it in his *Technik der Vorzeit*, Englemann, Leipzig-Berlin, 1914, article "Bohrer."

The Advancement of Arts Manufactures, etc., London, 1772. Superficially resembling the modern spiral auger with long dull spiral for shaving discharge, it cuts, not by means of the characteristic horizontal router, but, like the pod auger, on the sharpened down-twist of its bottom flanges. Hence it is less clearly a prototype of the revolutionary true spiral auger, in question, than the curious router-bottomed auger, with equally perfected shaving discharge shown in the next picture

A Spiral Auger from Madeira
(Fig. 177)

This remarkable instrument, possibly of the eighteenth century, with this same blunt, spiraled shaving-discharge, was dredged up in the harbour of Funchal, Madeira, before *c.* 1900, and is now in the Museum of The Bucks County Historical Society. Here the dull-edged steel spiral following the full length of the shank, flat-twisted and double-channelled, as in the modern tool, makes no pretense at cutting and must solely serve to discharge the shavings. If this striking relic of the sea had a definite date, it would be more significant. But its massive handle socket, lack of central start screw, and above all, the unique clawed shape of its flaring horizontal router blades, which do all the cutting, directly downward, would seem to class it as an European rather than an American tool, and of earlier date than the nineteenth century.

The Gimlet or Wimble
(Fig. 178)

The terebra antiqua of the Romans (according to Rich, who cites *Colum-*

Fig. 177. Spiral Auger from Madeira

In this steel instrument, the long, unsharpened spiral does not cut, but only discharges the shavings, and as in the modern auger, said spiral ends in two horizontal blades turned in opposite directions, which cut only downward, while the shavings travel up the spiral in two separate channels in the same direction. But the tool centering in an open notch lacks a pivot or start screw, and unlike the modern instrument, its bottom blades, projecting beyond the diameter of the spiral, are not turned up and sharpened at their outer corners so as to corner-cut the hole and loosen the bottom parings as the instrument goes around. On one side of the heavy rectangular socket for the blade, the initials R. J. P. have been roughly incised with a chisel.

The remarkable specimen, now in the Museum of The Bucks County Historical Society, was dredged up in the harbor of Funchal, Madeira, in the late 19th century, and given to the writer's father, William R. Mercer, by the Curator of the Funchal Museum, about 1900.

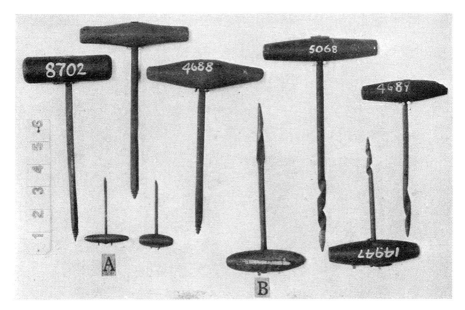

Fig. 178. The Gimlet or Wimble

The gimlet, perhaps the terebra antiqua of the Romans, as illustrated by Rich, and here shown in its 18th century form, is a small auger turned by one instead of two hands. Unlike the brad awl, it does not squeeze, but cuts, a round hole through the wood and therefore makes shavings. All of the instruments here shown have the pivoted-start screw point, which only penetrates and grasps the wood but does not cut. None show the horizontal bottom-blades seen in the down-cutting or "nose" auger (Fig. 166), therefore none cut directly downward. Four of them (left A), representing the oldest type as illustrated by Moxon in 1678, and in the *Circle of Mechanical Arts*, 1813, are bladed with straight-sided open cylinders, which immediately, at bottom, side-cut the hole to its full diameter. The others, called twisted gimlets (probably factory-made, except one [B] which is certainly hand-forged), show blades conspicuously twisted into sharpened spirals, which, unlike the unsharpened spirals of the spiral auger, side-cut the hole to its full diameter, after which they stop cutting.

That the latter, now common, side-cutting tool which Moxon and *The Circle of Mechanical Arts* fail to show, is a German rather than English invention there seems little reason to doubt. Holtzapffel, in *Turning and Mechanical Manipulation*, in 1846, says that it is a good tool, but as it is somewhat more expensive than the common kind (A) it is less used. In a footnote to Volume 2 ,page 544, he doubtfully suggests that though supposed to be an American invention, it was probably derived from the common spiral auger, which he believes to be English. But because the sharpened spiral of this tool, as here seen, particularly in the hand-forged specimen, is constructed to side-cut like the German pod auger, and not like the dull-edged spiral of the spiral auger, only to discharge shavings, and because the old Nuremburg monkish book of trades (*cf.* Mummenhoff *Handwerker der Deutschen Vergangenheit*, Leipsig. 1901, p. 40), apparently shows it is being forged by a monk along with pod augers in the 15th or 16th century, it seems reasonable to suppose that the instrument was brought to the American Colonies by the Pennsylvania Germans in the 18th century, and was there adopted by the Anglo-American carpenter, and that it travelled thence to England.

ella, 4-29-16) is and was a small form of the auger, in which the knife, revolving as it penetrates, gradually deepens the hole. The little instruments here shown and more fully described under the illustration, all cut sideways; none directly downward. In the older Anglo-American specimens, the sharp, untwisted sides of the cylindrical shank are parallel; in others, probably derived, not from the American spiral auger, with its dull spiral, but from the German pod auger, with its sharp spiral (Fig. 167), they are not only twisted, but sharpened. But all, like the augers, work slowly by intermittent twisting of the handle with one or two hands, until at some

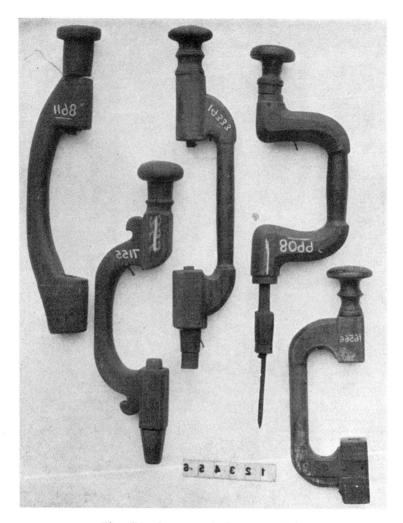

Fig. 179. Carpenter's Brace and Bit

In its 18th century American form, here shown, the instrument consists of the brace, or bit stock, a wooden semicircle, pivoted by means of a locked wooden pin on a discoidal top or breast plate, and the bit described later, a variously-shaped steel blade with rectangular top adjustable by insertion into a rectangular socket hole in the lower brace end. When pressed under the workman's left hand or body, the tool, grasped midway and turned by his right hand, works continuously, and far more rapidly than the common auger. Nevertheless, it never abolished the auger for one-man hand-boring, because, lacking the leverage of the latter, it could not cut large holes. Diderot (1768) illustrates it among the tools of the bowl maker (boisselier), marquetry maker (ebeniste), cabinetmaker (menusier), and boxmaker (layettier), but not of the French carpenter. The old master-tool in the hands of Saint Joseph, clearly appears in a painting of the Annunciation, of date about 1438, by the unknown Flemish painter, known as the Master of Flemalle (a contemporary of Van Eyck), in the Merode Gallery at Brussels, here shown in Fig. 180. It is named in the *New English Dictionary* as stock and bit for 1567, and is illustrated by Moxon (1678) and twice by Rembrandt, as hanging on the wall in two paintings of the Holy Family, one of alleged date 1645, in the Hermitage Gallery, in St. Petersburg, and another of 1640, in the Louvre.

It is noted for 1654 in the *Probate Records of Essex County, Massachusetts, 1635-1681, 3 vols.,* Geroge *Francis Dow, editor. Salem, Mass., the Essex Institute, 1916-1920,* and as a breast wimble, in 1655, and it is again shown here (Fig. 182), as a characteristic relic of the Dutch Nova Zembla Expedition of 1596.

unknown time, in the Middle Ages, or in the Roman period, the speed, not only of these tools, but also of small augers, was greatly increased by the invention of the

CARPENTER'S BRACE AND BIT
(Fig. 179)

in which the brace or bit stock, a shoulder-pressed or hand-pressed swivel, turns, not slowly by hand shifts, as in the common auger, but rapidly and continuously in the carpenter's grasp. As shown in the picture the instrument consists of a wooden elbow, with a large revolving button at one end, and a variously constructed socket for holding the blade or bit, at the other, and should be carefully distinguished from the breast auger, as shown in Fig. 162, where a revolving disc in the form of a breastplate appears as an efficient fixture on the top shank of a mediaeval auger, but while, in that case, the device only helps and does not make the tool, which with or without such down-pressure turns slowly by intermittent hand-release and regrasp, here, the revolving top button is absolutely necessary to the construction of the instrument. When the button is held in the left hand or pressed against the shoulder, and the elbow grasped at its smooth centre, and twirled with the never-released right hand, the bit revolves rapidly, and it is not only the speed of these revolutions, only exceeded by that of the bow drill and pump drill, described later, but the fact that the revolution is continuous and not intermittent, that gives the tool its importance. Nevertheless, as no man is strong enough to bore a large hole at the leverage and speed required, the

brace and bit still yields to the slower and more powerful auger for this latter purpose.

In speculating upon the antiquity of this device, two interesting tools demand attention—one, the raft auger, already illustrated (Fig. 43), a five-foot-long iron rod forged at bottom into a spiral auger, top-elbowed for right-hand turning and held in the left hand without revolving top button. The other, the old smith's brace, not here shown, for drilling holes in cold iron, a heavy iron elbow, with an adjustable bottom drill point, worked again by hand twisting, and revolving on its top point set in a dent in an iron under-plate on a log lever.

But all four specimens of the raft auger, seen by the writer, mount spiral augers, and cannot, therefore, be older than the nineteenth century, and as the antiquity of the smith's brace, which Moxon does not mention, seems doubtful neither tool is here offered as thus far furnishing valuable historic evidence on the subject.

As shown in the next picture

A BRACE AND BIT OF THE 15TH
CENTURY (Fig. 180)

the carpenter's brace clearly appears in an old Flemish panel-painting of Saint Joseph as a carpenter at work, of date about 1438, in the Merode Gallery, at Brussels, by the so-called Master of Flemalle (cf. Alt Niederländische Malerei, Ernst Heidrich, Jena, 1910).

Again associated with Saint Joseph at work, we see it lying on the ground near an open hand-saw and pair of pincers in a woodcut of the fifteenth century attributed to the Carmelite Monks of Vilvoorden, near Brussels, recently shown by Professor Dr. Paul Brandt in his *Schaffende Arbeit im Alterthum and Mittlealter,* Kroner, Leipsig, 1927, p. 280.

It was in full use in the time of Moxon (1678) who illustrates it in his little picture (Fig. 67) showing the carpenter's tools of his day. The *Probate, Records of Essex County, Massachusetts, 1635-1681, 3 vols., George Francis Dow, editor. Salem, Mass., the Essex Institute, 1916-1920,* notes it in 1629, 1630, and 1654. Rembrandt paints it in 1640 as hanging on the wall in his "Holy Family," at the Louvre, and again in 1643 in a similar picture, showing Saint Joseph at work as a carpenter, in the Russian Hermitage Picture Gallery, and the *New English Dictionary* quotes the name in 1657; but whether the Romans knew of it or how or when it first appeared, or by whom it was invented, the writer has failed to learn.

It is by reason of this speed and this construction, that the so-called bits or boring blades of this instrument, adjusted to its brace or bit stock, and illustrated in the next picture as

BRACE BITS OF THE OLD CARPENTER
(Fig. 181)

show a greater variety than those either of the auger or gimlet. Here we see miniature forms of all the old auger bits, except the duck's bill, previously described, on page 186.

Besides, though not properly carpenter's tools, a group of seven bits marked I, require a moment's particular attention since they illustrate a distinct and very ancient method of perforating not yet described, which may be called drilling rather than boring. In other words, they scrape rather than cut or pare the sides and bottom of a hole, either as ovate or triangular, sharpsided drills (upper

Fig. 180. A Brace and Bit of the 15th Century

One of the panels of an altar painting of the 15th century, by the Master of Flemalle in the Merode Gallery at Brussels, Saint Joseph is seen boring one of more than a dozen holes in a small, square piece of board held down in his left hand on the arm of the settle upon which he sits. Before him, on the floor, we see an open-bladed push handsaw, a hewing axe, and on a bench a very wide-bladed gouge, chisel, hammer, nails, pincers, auger, and possibly a spool box for his marking line, before the days of chalk, with an ink bowl and brush to black mark the line in Chinese fashion. The picture is taken from one of the illustrations in *Schaffende Arbeit und*

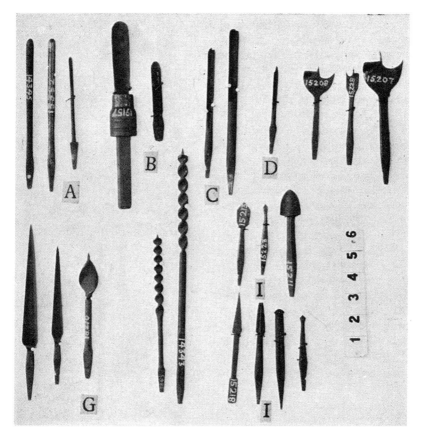

Fig. 181. Brace Bits of the Old Carpenter

(A) Three specimens — The gouge bit, also called quill bit, or shell bit, an open-sided cylinder, sharpened like a carpenter's gouge, but not spooned at the base.

(B) Two specimens of the spoon bit, alias dowel bit, with spooned or saucered base. If saucered to a projecting bill or out-curled point (not shown) it was called the duck's bill bit.

(C) Two specimens — The nose bit, a variety of the spoon bit in which the more or less inbent and flattened spoon blade is deeply notched into a wing called the "nose," sharpened in profile to cut almost horizontally, with the remaining small, dull wing of the spoon bent up above its level (cf. Fig. 166).

(D) The gimlet bit, a duplicate of the old cylinder gimlet, previously described (Fig. 178).

(E) Three specimens (upper right), the celebrated centre bit, adapted to bore short, abruptly-ending cylindrical holes to receive bolt heads in wood, etc., consists of a horizontal blade or router, revolving around a central pin, which blade cuts horizontally and cleans the bottom of the hole. On the other side of the pin, the shank is scalloped up to clear the wood, and ends in another knife-edged pin, which circumscribes the hole so that the router may clean cut its corner, as the tool revolves. The New English Dictionary quotes the name "centre bit," as used in 1794.

(F) The taper bit (two specimens, lower left), — a miniature variety of the tap or taper auger, already described (Fig. 169).

(G) The pod bit, — a pod-shaped, twisted cylinder, with pivot screw, as in the pod auger (Fig. 167).

(H) The spiral bit, — a reduced version of the spiral auger, already described (Fig. 175), as of latest (post-18th century) date, and finally—

(I) Group of seven specimens, showing the drill, three specimens (top) with the leaf-shaped French bit in the middle, properly a drill, generally used in the mandrel lathe, a flat, leaf-shaped blade, lacking screw point, for metal

bildene Kunst by Prof. Dr. Paul Brandt, Alfred Kroner & Co., Leipsig, 1927, and is here reproduced by kind permission of Doctor Brandt and the publishers. See also Alt Niederlandische Malerei, by Ernst Heidrich, Jena, Diedrichs, 1910 (Fig. 20), and for its date, about 1438, Fig. 24 in the same work.

three), which produce the entire hole, or, as broaches or reamers, with fluted or polygonal sides, which enlarge a hole previously made, or, like the fluted conical "countersink bit" (lower right), which produce shallow cavities for the heads of wood screws or bolts.

These tools, with a multitude of varieties not shown, generally employed in making small holes, were worked at considerable speed by continuous rotation, not only in the carpenter's brace but also in the mandrel lathe or bow drill, described later. Except for the carpenter's countersink bit, last named, they are probably metal-working tools and rarely used for wood (unless by musical instrument workers) and therefore we will escape confusion by not dwelling upon them here.

The next illustration

THE DUTCH BRACE AND BIT OF 1596 (Fig. 182)

again shows the carpenter's brace in familiar wooden, 18th century form, as another relic of the unfortunate Dutch Expedition to Nova Zembla in 1596.

While still considering the purpose of these tools, let us glance next, by way of comparison, at a remarkable instrument for burning, rather than boring holes in wood, namely:—

THE WHEELWRIGHT'S BURNING IRON (Fig. 183)

or hard wood. The reamer bit, or broach, appearing in many forms as cones or polygons, here shown as tapered shanks, with fluted sides, two specimens (lower left), made chiefly to enlarge or taper previous borings in metal, or as the abruptly-fluted chamfer bit or countersink bit (lower right), to countersink head-holes for screws or bolts, chiefly in metal, but sometimes by the carpenter in hard wood.

These latter tools, where used in wood, do not conspicuously pare into shavings, but rather grind to dust the sides of the hole.

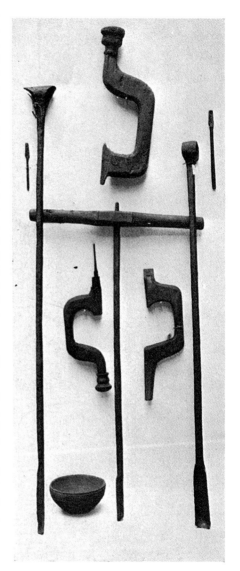

Fig. 182. Dutch Brace and Bit of 1596

These ancient wooden braces or bit stocks, one of which is mounted with a bit, and the cylindrical augers, with down-cutting horizontal, bottom-router blades, are relics of the Dutch Nova Zembla Expedition of 1596. In the three augers, probably ship carpenter's tools, the cylindrical blade, only clearly seen in the right-hand specimen, is unlike any of the other auger blades here shown. Its bottom inbend cuts vertically downward, but is not notched like the nose auger, nor round pointed like the

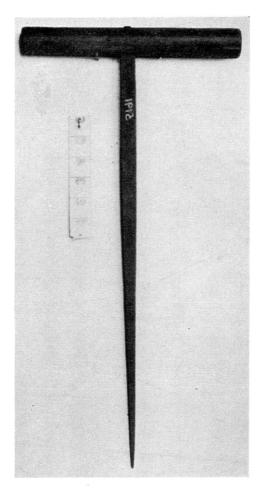

Fig. 183. The Wheelwright's Burning Iron

This tool, a long, tapering, rectangular, wrought-iron point set through a wooden cross handle like an auger, is an old Bucks County, Pa., relic of the early or middle 19th century, made by a country blacksmith. According to the information of David Gehman, born 1852, Mennonnite minister and general craftsman, its point was heated red hot by country wheelwrights and wriggled and pressed through a piece of wood so as to produce a square hole to receive the upper square shank of a screw bolt.

spoon auger. It may be said to form a spoon with flat bottom.

The two cylindrical and unmounted brace bits, shown in this picture, are unfortunately too small for recognition. Photographed by kind permission of the Rijk's Museum, Amsterdam.

As with the modern tools already shown, two of the long auger shanks are ring-topped for handle insertion. The middle one is mounted with a releasable handle as shown in D, E, Fig. 161.

a sharp rectangular spike, with wooden cross handle like an auger, used by the wheelwrights, when red hot, to burn square holes for the insertion of bolt shanks, and then pausing to realize the immense and universal importance of the boring tools in the building of ships and wagons, again reflect

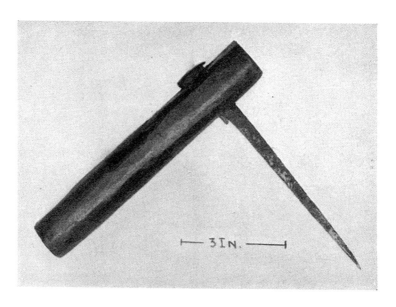

Fig. 184. The Chinese Wood Punch or Reamer

This unique L shaped instrument, a rectangular tapering wrought-steel spike, riveted at right angles through the end of a wooden handle, was photographed in January, 1923, at Lingkiang, Kiangsi, China, from among the tools of a Chinese carpenter, by Mr. R. P. Hommel. According to information from the latter, in 1926, the Chinese use neither the auger, gimlet, nor brace and bit, but otherwise bore all holes in wood (particularly the preliminary holes for the iron nails used in ship planking) with the bow or thong drill or pump drill (Figs. 185 and 186). Besides which they sometimes, though rarely, employ this tool to drill, rather than bore, wooden holes for the insertion of dowels in joinery. The instrument, he learns, is never heated like the American wheelwright's burning iron (Fig. 183) nor worked continuously like the auger, but is pounded down or hand pressed into the wood, and wriggled back and forth by the workman, so as to reduce the fibres to dust, like the reamer, Fig .181 (I), rather than to squeeze through them, without dust or shavings, like the brad awl (Fig. 160).

upon the surprising fact that the Chinese get along without the auger or gimlet. That they should have failed to discover the brad awl, and that they should satisfy themselves with the pump drill and the bow drill and sometimes squeeze large holes in wood by wriggling an iron spike therein, without employing the great boring tool of the West, might well astonish the American carpenter. Nevertheless, abundant evidence from China proves the fact. In the

CHINESE WOOD PUNCH OR REAMER
(Fig. 184)

we see a long, tapering, rectangular iron spike set at right angles through a wooden lever, which spike when wriggled back and forth in the wood, by said handle, does the work rather of a drill than a brad awl on a large scale, because it lacks the wedge-shaped point of the latter, besides which it probably works with far more danger of splitting the wood. According to the information of Mr. R. P. Hommel, to the writer, from Kuling, China, in May, 1926, the Chinese carpenter rarely uses this extraordinary instrument, but as his chief wood-boring tools serving to make

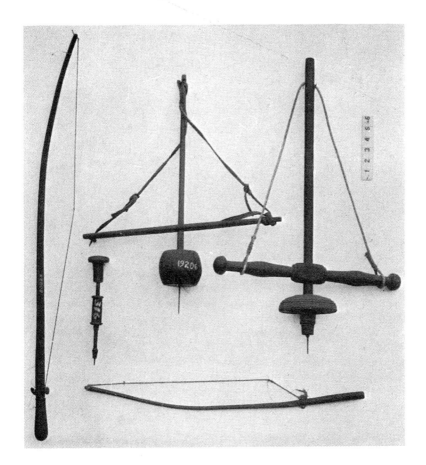

Fig. 185. The Pump Drill and Bow Drill

As described in the text, the two homemade upper right specimens are pump drills, recently used by marble workers and one hundred years ago by blacksmiths and other metal workers, for producing small holes in metal. The spindles and fly wheels are of wood, and the wooden bow or handle is perforated for the spindle, which slides through it, as the bow is raised and lowered. The bow string passes through a hole in the spindle-top. The bits are adjustable, flat, V-shaped blades of steel, not basilled, but sharpened on both sides to work both ways.

The lower and left pictures show a spindle and two bows of the Bow Drill. The top of the spindle is mounted with a loose wooden disc, or swivel, acting as a pivot, upon which the lower spindle, equipped with a steel drill point, fixed in a rectangular bottom socket, revolves. The middle of the spindle is thickened into an immovable wooden spool, around which the bow string is once twisted. When the workman, holding the bow horizontally in his right hand, moves it backwards and forwards against the spindle, held vertically by its top disc in his left hand, the drill point, by pull and push of the string twist, revolves back and forth. Sometimes the top disc was dispensed with and a loose breast-plate used instead, as when, according to Moxon, in boring cold iron, the old blacksmith set an iron plated wooden tablet faced with a dent, or a side-dented hammer, against his breast so as to press down heavily therewith upon the free top point of the revolving spindle.

The bows are of wood and the strings, for the larger, of rawhide, and for the smaller, of twine. Both the bow and pump drills thus work, not continuously in one direction, but both ways, with intermittent back action. They are still sometimes used by marble cutters in cutting and lettering tombstones. (Information of John P. Stillwell, marble cutter, of Doylestown, Pa., in 1926.)

the holes needed for the pegging to-gether of wooden framework and fur-niture, and above all, the innumer-able holes needed for his iron staples in the planking of ships, employs two of the most ancient and interesting perforating and drilling instruments of the world, and although these are not to be classed with carpenters' tools in Europe and America, let us, before leaving the subject of wood boring, on account of their vast archaeologi-cal interest, glance at the next illus-tration which shows them as

THE PUMP DRILL AND BOW DRILL
(Fig. 185)

Here the bow drill appears as a shaft or spindle, equipped at the bot-tom with an adjustable point or bit, and at the top, like a carpenter's brace, with a revolving handle or but-ton, which the workman holds in his left hand, while by means of the bow string wrapped around the middle of the shaft, he causes the latter to twirl rapidly back and forth by the push and pull of the bow here shown, when the latter is held in his right hand. In the more ingenious pump drill the back and forth movement of the tool is increased by a horizontal fly wheel, fixed part way up the spin-dle, while its revolution is caused, not by wrapping the bow string around the spindle, but by setting its middle through a hole in the spindle top. The apparatus is started by twisting the spindle and with it the bow string, so as to lift the bow, whereupon the workman, holding the bow horizontal-ly with one hand at each end, by de-pressing said bow, causes the string to untwist, and then, by the momen-tum of the fly wheel, retwist and relift the bow, when the down pressure is repeated. Both the bow and pump drill are quick, mechanically-twirled rather than direct hand-twisted in-struments; but, as here shown, they will only bore comparatively small holes, and as contrasted with the auger, or brace and bit, act on a different principle, which should be well understood; that is, they do not work continuously in one direction, but, by intermittent back action revo-lutions. Pulverizing the wood into sawdust, they do not pare it into shav-ings as they go down, and hence are drilling, rather than boring tools.

While this fact greatly limits their effectiveness, it extends their range, since, though some of the continuous-boring bits, used in the carpenter's brace, above described, likewise pul-verize rather than pare, the back mo-tion of the bow and pump drill gives them an advantage over the latter, in stone and substances which cannot be pared but must be pulverized; hence the bow drill was used by the black-smith one hundred years ago, while both tools have survived among mar-ble workers until the present time (1926).

Why should archaeologists overlook these facts when unmounted boring tools are found, and important infer-ences as to human culture would de-pend on whether their blades would pare or only pulverize, and whether their handles would turn them con-tinuously like the auger and bit stock, or like the bow and pump drill, back and forth?

In their European forms, as shown above, Diderot (1768) illustrates both the bow drill, called "fut de trepan," and the pump drill, as used by the French cabinetmaker (ebeniste), mar-ble worker, and locksmith (serrurier). Pliny describes the bow drill, and

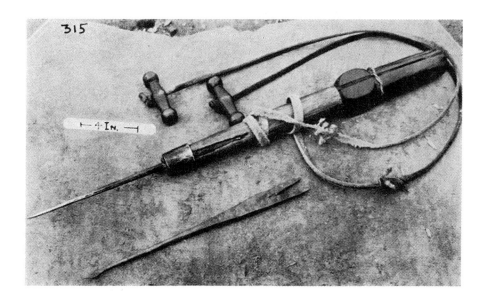

Fig. 186. Chinese Shipbuilder's Thong Drill

The picture shows an efficient variety of the bow drill, resembling in construction the Eskimo one-man fire drill, as presently described, which may be called the thong drill. It was photographed by Mr. R. P. Hommel, at Fuchow, Kiangsi, China, in January, 1924. One of the steel drill bits, with flattened forked ton and V-shaped point, has been adjusted rigidly, under a ferrule pushed over it, in the slotted base of the spindle, which spindle, as with the American bow drill, revolves upon its upper pivot-handle. To work the apparatus, the thong here shown is twisted around the spindle, whereupon one man, holds down the pivot-handle, thereby pressing down the drill bit into the wood, while two other men, each grasping the thong by one of its terminal handles, or one man holding a thong handle in each hand, and pulling the thong to and fro, causes the drill to twirl back and forth, as with the common bow drill.

According to Mr. Hommel, writing from Kuling, China, in April, 1926, the Chinese who do not use the auger or gimlet, but employ the bow and pump drill in their wood-boring operations, continually employ this powerful variety of the former in boring the preliminary holes for the iron, staple-shaped spikes which, unlike the European and Japanese shipwright, they use in building their ships. (*cf*. Fig. 206.)

A variety of this very efficient Chinese, three-man, shipbuilder's thong drill, was used until recently by some of the Alaskan and Greenland Eskimos in making fire. It is worked by one man, who, leaning forward and holding a loose equivalent of the top pivot of the spindle, generally a concaved piece of bone, in his teeth, pulls back and forth a thong, held at either end in either hand, and wrapped around the spindle, thus causing the latter, pivoted under his mouthpiece, to twirl to and fro as before. (*cf*. "A Study of the Primitive Methods of Drilling," by J. D. McGuire, *Report of United States National Museum*, 1894, p. 623, and "Fire Making Apparatus" in the United States National Museum, by Walter Hough, *Smithsonian Report*, 1888, p. 531.)

Rich shows it as used by a bronze worker, from a wall painting at Pompeii, while the pump drill is very clearly shown in the hands of a stone cutter, in a relief by Nanni di Banco, on the wall of the Church of Or San Michele, at Florence, of date *c*. 1408.

The next illustration shows an extraordinary variety of the bow drill, used according to the information of Mr. R. P. Hommel, above noted, by Chinese carpenters in boring the preliminary holes for the iron staple-shaped spikes which they use in ship construction instead of wooden pegs. This is

THE CHINESE SHIPBUILDER'S THONG DRILL (Fig. 186)

in which instrument, known also to

the Greenland and Alaskan Eskimo, the hand bow is dispensed with, and a loose thong is twisted around the spindle. This thong when grasped by two men, one at either end, while a third holds the drill, greatly increases the power of the instrument.

In their simple Anglo-American forms, as shown in Fig. 185, both the bow and pump drills are of worldwide use. But beside their antiquity among civilized races, scientific and historic interest is attached to them from the fact that primitive men in many parts of the world have used them until recently, not only to drill shells and stones, but to make fire. In associating both tools with the momentous discovery of fire on the one hand, and their possible derivation from the bow and arrow on the other, we may well wonder why archaeologists should have classed them together, or dwelt so lightly upon their difference in construction, or why the device of the pump drill should be so much more complex than that of the bow drill, that its mere existence among certain primitive tribes seems to defy explanation. Reflecting upon the unexplained presence of prehistoric races in the New World, we may further ask why the Aztecs and Peruvians, knowing nothing of this device, twirled the spindle between the palms of their hands, while the more primitive Eskimo had learned to hold a pivot block in his teeth and twirl the spindle (Chinese fashion) with a thong held in both hands at either end, or why the Iroquois (or Penobscots, as seen by the writer), came, by the use of the pump drill, to out do in ingenuity so many other native peoples otherwise their superiors.

In examining the two tools with the reverence, and even awe, that they deserve, it appears at once that the more elaborate and weaker pump drill will not work horizontally, while the bow drill, as we learn from Moxon and Diderot, and find on studying the apparatus of the old American clockmaker, or of the Arab woodturner, can be worked sidewise, so as to round out, or "turn," pieces of wood, or metal, when said pieces, fixed upon pivots, and wrapped with the bow string, take the place of the spindle of the apparatus.

In its simplest form as one of the oldest machines known to man, the latter device, though now obsolete among joiners, has survived as

THE BENCH OR HAND LATHE
(Fig. 187)

used by clock and watch makers until the end of the 19th century. The minature apparatus consists of two little thumb-screwable bar-pivots, ending here in sockets, but generally sharpened into points, and called "centres," set face to face in two upright framed posts called puppets, upon which centres the material worked upon, generally a rod or axled disc, with ends pointed to turn in the sockets, by means of a bow string wrapped around it, is made to revolve not continuously, but back and forth, when the little bow is moved forward and backward in the workman's left hand.

Screwed upon the middle of the frame we see the all-important T-shaped prop-fixture, called the rest, steadied upon which he pushes forward his chisel-shaped cutting tool, so as to pare away, incise, or convex the revolving material.

The ancient apparatus, here of

Fig. 187. Bench or Hand Lathe

Though this little apparatus (A), 8½ inches long, used to make the brass axles, wheels, etc., of clocks, is not older than about 1800, and is carefully made of iron, it represents in construction the turning lathe in its simplest and probably oldest form. It consists of two (here socket ended, but otherwise generally pointed) pivot rods, as shown in the reversable right point, set face to face in the tops of two vertical posts called puppets. The left rod is threaded to screw forward or backward. The reversable right rod slides. Both rods are fixable under top thumb screws. When the material to be worked upon, a brass cylinder (the wheel axle of a clock, etc.) with ends filed to points, is inserted in the confronting rod sockets, it is made to revolve back and forth by a bow string twisted around it, when the bow is moved to and fro in the workman's left hand. On the mid-frame slides the adjustable, T-shaped prop, called the rest, upon which he steadies his chisel, held in his right hand, to pare away, groove, or convex the revolving material.

This instrument was found in the amateur workshop, c. 1820-60, of C. J. Wister, in Germantown, Pa.

(B) Reproduced from *Description de l'Egypte. Observations Et Recherches. Etc.*, publie par les ordres de sa majestie l'Empereur Napoleon le Grand, 19 vols., folio, Paris, 1809-28. Vol. 7, Plate XV, fig. 4. It is one of

Fig. 188a. Back Action Pole Lathe

iron, was often made of wood, and sometimes was used by joiners, one hundred years ago, and as we examine its history and follow it about the world, the shape and contsruction of its rest, tightening screw, and pivot points vary. The East Indian may drive his puppets into the ground. The Arab may pivot his work on el-bowed spikes, or use a roller rest. The Chinaman, ingeniously freeing both hands, may replace the bow with the back and forth, right and left, hand pull of a twisted thong, seesawed over the stick by another man. The American watch maker may string his bow with a horse hair. But the principle remains the same. The revolution is

a unique and very instructive series of pictures, illustrating a subject of great archaeological importance, overlooked by Lane (*cf. Modern Egyptians*) and ignored by the modern Egyptologist, namely the Arts and Industries of the Arabs. It shows an Arab turning a wooden cylinder in a similarly constructed lathe. His pivot points (pikes) are elbowed spikes. His rest is a rolling rod, and his right foot helps to steady his chisel. As both of the above lathes are operated with the bow, only one hand is free to work the chisel. But in the similar Chinese lathe of this type, not here shown (two counter-set pivot points in a wooden frame with a loose board rest), the bow is dispensed with and both hands are free, because an extra workman turns the pivoted material, back and forth, by means of a thong held by its ends, in each hand, and twisted around the revolving stuff, as observed and photographed for the writer by Mr. R. P. Hommel, March, 1925, in China.

Fig. 188b. Back Action Pole Lathe

The illustration shows the construction of this ancient apparatus, as figured by Moxon, in 1678; in Rees' *Cyclopaedia, c.* 1800, and as described in the text. The right puppet forming the end of the frame is fixed, while an extra removable puppet for short stuff, seen in the middle, slides upon a long slot, the bed, shown as two heavy cross strips holding the two end posts (puppets) together, to which it is tightened by an under wedge. The stuff to be turned, a wheelbarrow hub, wedged on a broom stick, found in the lathe and here inserted, revolves, not continuously, but back and forth on the greased puppet pikes, scarcely seen, tightened by the screw-crank handle shaft of the right pike. The stick turns rapidly back and forth by means of a string wrapped around it, extending from a flexible pole in the ceiling, which bends down on pressure of the foot treadle and springs up on release of the workman's foot. The rest upon which the workman slides his tools against the turning stick, appears as an adjustable strip of wood, tightened against the puppet posts parallel to the stuff by two wood screw buttons.

Pole, string, rest, and treadle are original and are placed in the illustration in their respective positions, as found, in 1926, by Mr. A. H. Rice, in one of the dilapidated rooms of an old deserted house near Flemington, New Jersey. The lathe pole was wedged under the rafters of the low ceiling upon two long poles extending from wall to wall. The right arm of the foot treadle was hinged, as seen, by a strap nailed upon the floor, while the foot piece, extending therefrom, at right angles, was hinged on a peg, in a slotted post, mortised into a block and board, also nailed upon the floor. This cheap, homemade apparatus, common in England, France and the United States, in the 18th century, with its advantages and disadvantages, as described in the text, was generally supplanted in Pennsylvania by the continuous action mandrel lathe (Fig. 191) in the early 19th century. The specimen was kindly presented to the Doylestown Museum by Mr. Rice. Another like it, in the Museum, but lacking the foot treadle, was bought with some old farm shop relics from Abraham Gross, son of John Gross, a Mennonite farmer, two miles northwest of Plumsteadville, Bucks Co., Pa., April 9, 1890.

J. J. v. Vliet, der Drechsler (verkl.)

Fig. 189. A Pole Lathe of the 17th Century

The picture, one of a series of eighteen small copper engravings, illustrating workmen employed at their various trades, by the Dutch painter-engraver, Jan Joris Van Vliet, born at Delft, Holland, in 1610, shows a man turning the stuff, *i. e.*, the leg of a chair or spinning wheel, as seen in the engraving, with a back and forth action pole-lathe. The two puppet posts, one of which slides in the bed, the rest, or cross-piece on which he holds his chisel, the foot treadle working the thong twisted on the stuff, and with it the spring pole, in the ceiling, are clearly shown. A compass and several chisel-shaped turning tools, are racked against the wall or laid across the lathe bed.

never continuous, but always back and forth, and because the chisel cuts only one way, the workman must pull it off at every back twirl of the material worked upon.

This brings us to a variety of the instrument in common use among wood workers one hundred and fifty years ago called the

POLE LATHE (Fig. 188, A & B)

in which a foot treadle takes the place of the ancient bow. In the home-made, now obsolete apparatus, here shown, found in February, 1926,

standing, as when last used, in a ruined house near Flemington, N. J., the framework, two heavy braced strips, forms an open channel, from which project vertically, the two adjustable posts, above described, called puppets ,each side-pronged at the top with a greased spike, called the pike, forming the two so-called centres. When a previously rough-rounded stick dented at either end, is inserted between these puppet pikes, so as to pivot truly thereon, it is said to be "centred," and is caused to revolve, not continuously, but back and forth, by a thong twisted two or three times around it, and extending from a flexible pole, here shown, in the ceiling to the workman's foot treadle.

The pole lathe is illustrated by Moxon in 1678, and nearly one hundred years later in *L'Art de Turner* by P. C. Plumier, Paris, 1749 (plate 79), who speaks of it as the common lathe of his time, and it is described and illustrated in Diderot's *Encyclopedia*, of 1768, and in Rees' *Cyclopaedia*, c. 1800.

The apparatus at work, is again here illustrated in

A POLE LATHE OF THE 17TH CENTURY
(Fig. 189)

in which an old Dutch woodcut, by Jan Joris Van Vliet, born at Delft in 1610, shows a workman, by means of a foot treadle, thong and ceiling pole, turning a duplicate of one of the legs of a slat-backed, frame-seated chair, standing near him on the floor. In another lathe, for low-studded work shops, the ceiling pole is planted vertically in the floor, with its thong angled on a pulley, and in another, it is supplanted by a suspended bow, like the archer's weapon, from the string of which, the thong, still twisting around the revolving stick, reaches the workman's foot treadle, as before. The latter holds his longhandled, chisel-shaped tools, steadied upon the so-called rest, as explained under the illustration, against the revolving wood, only when his treadle goes down, and withdraws them, when it goes up.

The great advantage of this circular cutting and smoothing foot-worked apparatus, which survived into the middle of the 19th century, among country workmen, was, that it left both hands free; also, that it was cheap, too simple to get out of order, and worked true upon its rigid pike points. But its back action, exacting special skill in the pull off of the tools, was one great objection to it. Another, was that as the wood was pivoted at both ends, the machine would only work uninterruptedly against the side, not against and into the ends, of the revolving material, and hence could not turn globes, decorated board surfaces, or hollow wooden ware, without leaving a central untouched pivoted core for the stuff to revolve upon. Nevertheless, that bowls were thus turned on the pole lathe is proved by the next engraving,

A POLE LATHE OF THE 13TH CENTURY
(Fig. 190)

a very interesting picture from a manuscript ascribed by L. F. Salzman, to the 13th century MS. lat. 11560-f. 84 (1) in the Bibliotheque Nationale, at Paris—shown in *English Industries of the Middle Ages,* by L. F. Salzman, Oxford, 1923, page 172, in which the proposed bowl forms a large central lump on the revolving stick and the workman holds his continuously withdrawn chisel, not at right angles, but parallel to it, over the top of the left puppet, and as in this case, he dare not cut through the solid pivot of his stuff, he cannot turn the full bowl bottom, but must leave it unfinished, with what might be called a protruding axle to be cut off afterwards. To turn the inside concavity he must reverse the stick and proceed exactly as before, leaving another opposite unfinished stub. Whether bowls or globes, etc., were ever thus made,

MAN TURNING A BOWL ON A LATHE. 13th cent.

Fig. 190. Pole Lathe of the 13th Century

With its over-bent pole, thong and foot treadle, the picture clearly shows a pole lathe upon which a man is turning a bowl. The bowl forms a large swell in the middle of the revolving stuff, and the workman holds his tool over the top of the left puppet against the outer bottom of the vessel, to reach the inside of which the work must be released and turned. When finished, two long stubs, necessarily protruding from inside and outside the bowl, must be removed.

The picture is from a manuscript—Latin-11560-f. 84 (1)—in the Bibliotheque Nationale at Paris, and appears, ascribed to the 13th century, as an engraving on p. 172 of *English Industries of the Middle Ages*, by L. F. Salzman, Oxford, 1923. It is here reproduced by kind permission of the author.

upon the pole lathe, in the 18th century, the writer has failed to learn. On the other hand it is well known that the above mentioned difficulties were overcome in the more complicated and costly

CONTINUOUS ACTION MANDREL LATHE
(Fig. 191)

also used in the 17th and 18th centuries and here shown by a simple, home-made, 19th century example. Again we have a treadle, but no pole, and no thong twisted around the stick worked upon, therefore no back action. The treadle, by means of a strap, works continuously a fly wheel, and the fly wheel, a spindle, called the mandrel, axled through the two right-hand puppets, and the left end or face of which mandrel takes the place of the pike, still retained in the other third left-hand puppet. Therefore, while one end of the stick revolves, as before, on this rigid left puppet pike, its other end, being fixed immovably upon, revolves with the revolving mandrel.

Fig. 191. Continuous Action Mandrel Lathe

In this ancient apparatus, described and illustrated by Moxon, in 1678, the action, as explained in the text, is no longer back and forth (intermittent) but continuous. As here seen, the foot treadle turns the large fly wheel, and the fly wheel the mandrel, namely an iron axle, mounting two smaller wooden pulley wheels, fixed rigidly upon it, over which the driving strap from the large fly wheel passes. The axle of this mandrel revolves through holes in the top of the two right-hand puppet posts, and its left projecting iron end is not a round point, but is flattened into a wedge, not clearly seen. When, therefore, a stick of wood (the stuff), is driven at one end into this wedge and centred against the round point (pike), of either the centre (removable) or left fixed puppet, it will revolve continuously in one direction with the mandrel. In this case, the stick is, as turners say, "centred" at both ends, though less accurately than on the "dead" motionless pike points of the pole lathe, because of the wear and wobble of the mandrel. If, however, the adjustable wedge point of the mandrel is replaced by a drill or boring bit, said drill or bit will drill a hole through a piece of material held in the hand and pushed against the revolving instrument. More than this, by means of other attachments, called chucks, described later, variously contrived to hold or clutch a short block or disc of wood, said block, so clutched, is said to be centered only at one end. In that case the other puppets and their pivot spikes, now in the workman's way, are dispensed with altogether, and the block or board revolving freely on the mandrel chuck, by means of the tools described later, can be turned uninterruptedly, not only against its sides, as a globe, but into its ends, as a bowl.

Here the central sliding puppet, adjustable for short sticks, is removable. Both its pike and the pike of the left end puppet are cranked on threaded screws to tighten the stick centred between them and the mandrel clutch. Next to the mandrel, the adjustable, metal-topped rest for steadying the tools is shown fixed by its under wedge upon the frame.

This more expensive homemade machine, would turn bowls, table or Windsor chair legs, or spinning wheel spokes, etc, or bed posts, or decorate the valve boards of old fireside bellows, or drill holes. It was obtained in November, 1908, at the Strouse household sale near the Elephant Tavern, Bucks Co., Pa. A similar lathe, in use by Peter Weierbach, a farmer, in his log work-shop in Haycock Township, Bucks Co., Pa., was seen by the writer in 1920.

Besides the simple thong-turned pole lathe ,previously described, centering the stuff at both ends, the Chinese and Koreans have a mandrel lathe which clutches the stuff, in European fashion, on the revolving mandrel face only. But they do not work the mandrel continuously with a fly wheel, but back and forth, with a twisted thong extending from the mandrel itself, to two treadles, one under each foot of the workman, who sits directly facing the mandrel end. This was observed and photographed for the writer, by Mr. R. P. Hommel, in Nanchang, China, December, 1923. A similarly constructed mandrel lathe, bought in Korea, for the writer, by the Rev. Clarence Hoffman, is now (1927) in the Doylestown Museum.

Two great improvements have thus transformed the machine—first, it revolves no longer in intermittent, back-action jerks, but continuously in one direction; second, the workman while still able as before to fix (center) his work—a long stick—at both ends, can now fix it, if desired ,at one end only; that is, do away with the remaining left puppet pike altogether and by attaching his material (called stuff) fast upon the right or mandrel end

Fig. 192. The Great Wheel

The turner's lathe for heavy work, called "The Great Wheel," described and illustrated by Moxon, in 1698, is worked, not by the turner himself, but by a helper, who turns the big wooden wheel by means of its wrought-iron crank. This runs the apparatus, not back and forth like the pole lathe, but continuously, by means of a leather end laced pulley-strap here seen on the big wheel, which encircles not the stuff worked upon, as in Moxon's picture, but the pulley wheel of the lathe-mandrel.

The big wheel, six feet in diameter, entirely detached from the lathe and resting loosely but firmly by its own weight on the ground, is set at strap-distance from, and at right angles to the lathe. The heavy wooden lathe-bed, eleven feet and eleven inches long, here partly seen, consists of two parallel wooden beams on legs, with an intervening crack, along which, the so-called rest and the two devices, called puppets, for pivoting the stuff, all made of cast iron, can be slid back and forth and adjusted anywhere (to meet different lengths of materials) by means of long, down-reaching, homemade, wrought-iron bolts screwed with nuts on wooden underblocks.

This obsolete apparatus was found near Hartsville, Bucks Co., Pa., stored in a barn belonging to George White, who had inherited it from his father, Samuel White, who had bought it from William Lewis, a wheel-wright, at Horsham, Montgomery Co., Pa., about 1862, and had used it to turn spouts and buckets for wooden pump stocks. After Samuel White's death, his son George, had used it for the same purpose until about 1895 when the general introduction of factory-made pumps spoiled his trade.

The smith-wrought iron and homemade of the wood of the apparatus, date it as probably not later than about 1830-1840.

alone, operate, not against its revolving sides, but, as for globes and bowls, into and against its now unobstructed end.

On the other hand, the apparatus has developed a defect, namely that the work no longer revolves with perfect accuracy on two fixed points, but only on one, because the mandrel face, replacing one of these points is no longer rigid and motionless, but

revolves, and may wobble, as it often did, in the old wooden lathes.

To meet this difficulty, another device, producing continuous action with perfect accuracy, without a mandrel, though not available for globes, bowls, etc., but only for side work on sticks, was frequently used in the 18th century. This was the so called pulley and driver, not here shown, in which the material, as in the pole lathe, was centered directly on two rigid pike points. On one of these, a simple groove-rimmed disc or adjustable pulley-wheel with a centre hole was slid loose, so as to axle freely outside the puppet post.

When turned by the thong from the foot treadle, or otherwise, this wheel communicated its whirl to the material by an elbow extending at right angles from its side over the material, so as to catch an adjustable claw or pin clamped rigidly thereon, called the driver.

But because these simple, one-man, foot-moved machines were too weak for large work, they sometimes had to be operated by power apparatus, impelled before the introduction of steam, by water, or animals, or men.

This brings us to another old form of the continuous turning lathe, for heavy cylindrical turning, which, if not older, is certainly simpler than the foot-worked mandrel lathe. It was called

THE GREAT WHEEL (Fig. 192)

and was illustrated by Moxon and Diderot. In the case, here shown, the frame is equipped with a mandrel as in the common mandrel lathe, but lacks a foot treadle. The tool-holding turner does not operate the machine, for another workman, turning with a crank a large detached fly wheel, runs the apparatus by means of a thong therefrom placed upon the spindle or pulley wheel of the mandrel and in this case by continuous forward revolutions without back action, and with greatly increased force.

In the older variety of this machine described by Moxon, the mandrel is lacking, and the thong, as in the pole lathe, is twisted directly around the stuff, which must be previously rounded, or encompassed with an adjustable roller, to run true at the point of thong-contact. Again, as in the pole lathe, the stuff revolves directly on two rigid pivots and in this case again continuously and without back-action.

Because the great wheel was sometimes worked with a mandrel as here shown and sometimes without it as described by Moxon, the descriptions of old lathes and lathe fixtures have been greatly complicated by writers who, dwelling on details rather than principles of construction, have discussed the form and operation of this powerful two-man apparatus, with the one-man pole lathe on the one hand and the one-man mandrel lathe on the other, besides confusing both the latter with the pulley and driver.

A great deal of attention has also been paid to mandrel-end fastenings, called chucks, described later, which variously hold or clutch the revolving material, and to what might be called wobbling mandrels, which cause the material to gyrate out of a circle and so produce elliptical and eccentric forms. As to these things, and other secondary details of frame construction, fly wheels, puppets, movements, etc., old book descriptions overwhelm the ignorant reader, with a mechanic's vocabulary of contradictory trade names, old and new, a confusion of principles, omitted diagrams, misprints, etc., but if we grasp the action of the turning lathe, in the 18th century forms, here shown, or described, i.e., as either reversed, or continuous, and understand its purpose, as to either work against the sides of a piece of wood revolving on two puppets, as a chair leg, or into the end of a piece of wood revolving on only one

Fig. 193. Mandrel and Chuck of the Great Wheel

The mandrel consists of a heavy cast-iron frame, sixteen inches long, with two upright posts, called puppets, through the top of which is axled the triple-wheeled spindle, on the varying diameters of which, to vary the speed, the strap of the great wheel runs. The protruding, left, axle-end has a square hole, in which the releasable square-shanked wrought-iron chuck (a front-and-back basilled chisel blade, with a central point), here badly photographed, is driven. This chuck clutches the stuff or stick, when the latter is centered tightly between it and the opposing left, screw-cranked, puppet point, and therefore compels the stuff to revolve continuously with the mandrel.

The spindle is made of three heavy wooden discs, wood-pegged together, and driven upon the wrought-iron axle, squared to receive them. The pointed, right, axle-end, does not penetrate the puppet post, but pivots upon a socketed iron block screwed therein. The protruding, left, axle-end, bolted down into a notch in the puppet top, is easily releaseable. It is also threaded outside the puppet to engage various other kinds of chucks. Two long, wrought-iron, homemade screw-bolts, not shown, passing through holes in the frame-bottom, and downward through the lathe-bed-crack, bolted on wooden blocks thereunder, hold fast the mandrel to the apparatus. Hence, the mandrel, like the other left puppet frame and the rest, can be turned about and adjusted anywhere on the eleven-foot-long lathe bed.

puppet, as a bowl, the essential part of the subject, as applied to woodworking would become clear, were it not for another device of immense mechanical importance, long ago applied to the lathe, supposed to have been perfected, if not invented, by Jacques Besson, in France, about 1569. This was to get the mandrel to move forward as it revolved, which was done by threading one of its axle ends in its collar or axle hole, and as this device advanced the mandrel in its other smooth axle hole, a boring bit or drill could be fixed to the working face of the mandrel, which would bore or drill a hole in the material fixed to confront the whirling point.

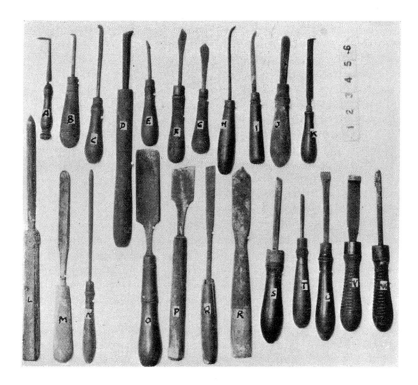

Fig. 194. Turning Tools

These variously-bladed steel shanks, tanged on straight wooden handles, like carpenter's chisels, are held by the workman in both hands with the shank set (to prevent joggling) on the so-called rest, and the blades are pushed at various angles against the revolving wood.

A, B, C, D, E, with elbowed blades, are used for excavating the inside of bowls, boxes, etc.

F, G, H, I, J are various face and side-smoothing tools.

K is a tool used for cutting triangular notches and screw threads in a single spiral incision, or for undercutting bulbs.

L, M, N, O are gouges with concave blades. They represent the first tool used to reduce the whirling surface without tearing it; also to cut grooves.

P, Q are smoothing chisels with blades sharpened on both sides, at an acute angle to the shank.

R is a tool used for cutting triangular grooves. It is worked at right angles to the revolving wood.

S, T are smoothing chisels for reducing the whirling surface to a uniform level.

U, V, W are of the highest importance for cutting screw threads "by hand," on the outside of a wooden cylinder, with the top-notched tools (U. V), or on its inside, with the side-notched (W), as for round wooden boxes, box lids, etc. The operation, also practiced on metal, is called "cutting flying" by Thomas Martin, in *The Circle of Mechanical Arts*, Richard Rees, London, 1813, who notes, how, with great sleight of hand, the master turner moves these tools sideways on the revolving but not advancing material, so as to cut the requisite spiral, rather than a series of parallel grooves which, if held at a fixed point, it would do. This extraordinary and very delicate work, performed both on the back action and continuous lathe, the skilled turned could and did do when he chose, by hand, notwithstanding the fact, previously noted, that long before his time, automatic devices by means of guide screws to advance the chasing tool along the revolving cylinder, or advance the revolving cylinder itself against the fixed chasing tool, had been in use.

All the specimens shown should be dated in the early 19th or late 18th century. They belonged to the turning lathe and apparatus of Charles J. Wister of Germantown, except the specimens L, M, P, R, which were found with the pole lathe (Fig. 188A).

More than this and as explaining the chief principle of the vast variety of screw-making machines now in use, was the further fact that if instead of a drill, or bit, a screw tap was fastened on the advancing mandrel face, it would thread the inside of a confronting hole, or conversely thread the outside of a revolving cylinder, where said cylinder was fixed upon so as to revolve with the mandrel. In the latter case a chisel-shaped tool with a cutting point (described later), was held rigidly by the workman against the revolving side of the cylinder.

As a still further improvement and in order to thus produce several so-called guide screws, on one mandrel, the axle of the mandrel might be threaded not once only on its end bearing, but three or four times on mid-shoulders mounted on adjustable collars, also threaded or notched to engage them, in which case, while the axle ends ran free, each guide screw, by exactly regulating the advance of the mandrel to its own particular threads, would compel the revolving screw tap, or the fixed cutting point, to reproduce said threads on the inside of the fixed hole or the outside of the revolving cylinder above mentioned, while the same automatic result was obtained if the guide screws advanced the cutting point, and the cylinder revolved without advancing.

Though it seems probable that the old carpenters, joiners, or woodworkers sometimes used screw lathe devices of this sort, one hundred years ago, and in Moxon's time, as a substitute for the free-hand chasing of wooden boxes, box lids, etc., described in the following paragraph, or to make the various-sized screw-taps and so-called screw-boxes, also described later, the writer has thus far failed to find an ancient home-made example of this master tool, in any form.

Having thus examined the lathe itself, it is only necessary, in order to end the subject, to glance at the tools used by the old turner to cut, fix fast, and measure his revolving material, beginning with the chisel-shaped instruments shown in the next illustration,

TURNING TOOLS (Fig. 194)

which, as the chief agents of his varied work, the turner steadies by hand upon the sliding support above mentioned, called the rest, and pushes against the revolving wood. Although the instruments are here unfortunately illustrated on too small a scale, a moment's glance at the turning operation explains the use of most of them, as gouged for reducing, flat for smoothing, and hooked or elbowed for side and under-cutting, until we come to the chisels, marked U, V, W, with sawtoothed blades, called by Knight chasing tools. Then we would look half-convinced astonishment at the sleight of hand, which, as described by Holtzapffel and in *The Circle of Mechanical Arts,* enables the highly-skilled turner, helped by eye and touch alone, to hold them against the outside or inside of a piece of revolving wood or metal, thereby producing the accurate spiral incision of the threads of a screw, otherwise more certainly cut on the automatic screw lathes just referred to.

As further described in the label under this illustration (Fig. 194), the evidence shows that the operation, whether thus done free-hand, or auto-

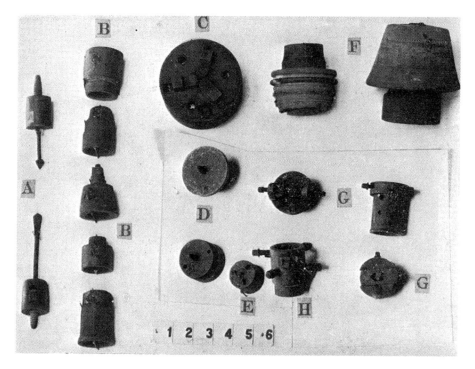

Fig. 195. Chucks

These adjustable devices, threaded inside to screw tight upon the projecting outer threaded axle of the so-called mandrel, of the mandrel lathe, are variously contrived to grip the piece of wood worked upon, so that the latter revolves with the mandrel, either when, as a long stick, it is pivoted (centered) at its other end upon the fixed pike point of the opposing puppet, or when, as a board side or block (for bowl or globe) or a drill boring bit screw tap or grindstone, it is not so centered at the other end, but works free.

(A) Drill chucks — wooden blocks, mounted with steel drills, screwed by means of their wooden screws upon the mandrel.

(B) Open cylinders into which the rough, rounded end of the wood worked upon (stuff) can be driven tight.

(C) Flat discs with concentric sliding arms to clamp a piece of round, flat or hollow-bottomed stuff.

(D) Flat discs with single projecting screws, upon which the stuff can be screwed tight to resist the direction of revolution.

(E) A flat disc with entire point and three wedge points, which centers and holds, so as to revolve with the mandrel, the flat end of a long stick, squeezed against it from the screw-tightened-pike point of the opposing puppet.

(F) Chucks mounted with grindstone for tool sharpening.

(G) Flat metal discs with center holes, collared with screw clamps to grasp pieces of stuff (wood or metal) pushed into the holes.

(H) Open cylinders with six concentric side screws, to not only hold the stuff, but adjust it to the center of revolution.

matically, was by no means always performed on the continuous lathe, but that it was also possible on the pole lathe, whose intermittent back-action did not dislocate the needed accuracy of the thread incision.

A number of adjustable devices also only adapted to the mandrel lathe, called

CHUCKS (Fig. 195)

were and are still used to wedge, nail,

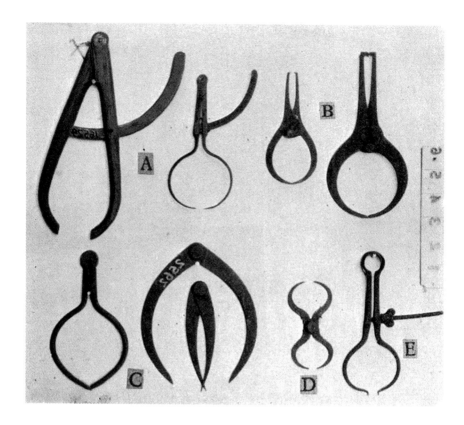

Fig. 196. Callipers

Easily distinguished from the straight-shafted compass, by its semicircular incurved arms, the indispensable callipers are continually employed by the turner, whether with wood or metal, to measure the outer diameter of a solid stick, or the inner diameter of a hollowed cylinder (a bowl, box, or box-lid, etc.) when rounded on the lathe.

In the two specimens (A) hinged on top rivets (left, of wood) — a thin arm fixed to the left shaft, sliding through a slot in the right and stopped by a thumb screw, fixes the open jaws when thrust upon the stuff to meet its diameter. The three top-hinged tools (C) (larger right, of wood) like most callipers, work stiffly enough not to need stops.

In the two middle-hinged, double-jawed specimens (B), the straight top arms, with flat points inturned at right angles, if opened by cross-pressing together the lower jaws, will measure on their outside the inner diameter of a hollow. If themselves cross-pressed, by opening the lower jaws, their inner points would do the same work. The lower jaws act as usual.

In the middle hinged (D), round-jawed both ways, the same operation is performed for inner or outer diameter, by cross-pressing one of the jaws.

In the steel (E), with a spring-top-hinge and hence requiring a stop, the stop is a round threaded wire mounted with a thumbscrew nut. In other forms, not shown, for inside diameter only, the straight arm tops, as at B, turn outwards.

screw, or clamp fast the work upon the mandrel face of the said lathe (Fig. 191), when the material worked upon is held at both ends, or revolves unobstructedly at one end only of the apparatus.

Besides this, a variously constructed instrument, applicable to all lathes and at all times indispensable to the turner, known as

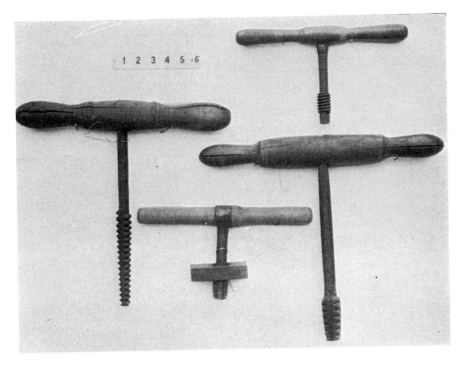

Fig. 197. Screw Taps

As described in the text, these so-called "taps" are for threading the inside of wooden holes. In this case the steel shank of the instrument, handled like an auger, is enlarged into a heavy steel screw, sometimes tapered, sometimes cylindrical, generally filed vertically, into three or more channels, or sometimes side-holed (upper right specimen) so as to open the sides of its threads and thereby transform them into side-cutting knives. When the wood worked upon, previously bored with a hole of required size, is fixed in a vise, the said thread-knives cut the required channel, as the tool inserted into the hole is twisted round by the workman.

The instrument, or its original prototype ,had to be made from a model by hand, in the first place by several processes, as follows:

(1) Filing its threads by hand, by tracing a spiral line marked out first by spiralling a paper band or pasting a right-angled triangle, cut in paper, around a steel rod to get the line, described, according to Holtzapffel, by Pappus of Alexandria, 4th cent. A. D.; or (2) twisting a square, red hot steel bar into a spiral and then deepening the spirals with a file or (3) spiralling and soldering fast a steel wire upon a steel rod; or (4) pushing a knife, set in a slit, diagonally across a steel rod, thereby forced to revolve and advance in a slippery channel; or (5) by turning screw threads against the outside of a steel rod, or inside of a cylinder revolving on the turning lathe, by means of the tools called chasing tools, marked U. V. W. in Fig. 194, either "free hand" (only possible with small screws) or automatically by means of the screw lathe, *i.e.*, by causing the chasing tools to advance by mechanism along and against the revolving work, or by causing the revolving work to advance along and against the fixed chasing tool.

These methods go far to explain all ancient and modern methods of making the original screw or model for producing screws, either in wood or metal, which, according to the very valuable treatise on the subject by Charles Holtzapffel. *Turning and Mechanical Manipulation*, Vol. 2, p. 577, had been long since invented, and as noticed later (*cf.* Screw Bolt, Fig. 713) were practiced in his time (1846) in England.

THE CALLIPERS (Fig. 196) was continually required to measure the outside diameter of the revolving stick, or the inside diameter of the box or bowl, as the work went on.

To end the subject of tools used to shape and fit wood, let us turn again to the operation of thread-cutting, in order to last consider two very important instruments, far oftener used

Fig. 198. The Screw Box Outer Thread

The so-called screw box of the wood worker, for threading the outside of pegs, consists of two rectangular blocks screwed together, handled at either end and perforated with a hole at right angles to the plane of their contact. The hole, smooth at its entrance, is otherwise threaded throughout, and edged with a V-shaped, laterally projecting knife, coinciding with the top of the outermost thread, inserted thereon in a slot between the blocks, and releasable for sharpening by unscrewing them. When the previously rounded peg is held in a vise and the hole thrust upon its point, the required spiral channel is cut by twisting the screw box, by its handles, around the peg, resulting in the wooden screw shown at A.

Otherwise, the box, lacking handles, is held in the vise, and the peg, variously grasped, is twisted into the cutting hole.

If the thread is not cut to full depth at one twisting, another screw box with a hole of the same diameter, but with a longer knife, would be used to complete the operation.

In the screw plate, already described, which is the equivalent of this instrument for making screws in metal, the metal rod is twisted successively into several knifed thread holes of varying diameter, to cut the threads to full depth in the harder material, while in its other metal-working equivalent, also already described called the die stock, the hole's diameter is contractable; that is, the hole is inset with semi-circular threaded blocks, called dies, compressible against the inserted rod by side screws, hence requiring several repeated twistings to complete the screw.

by old carpenters because far less complex and expensive than the lathe devices above noted, which again explain the regulated concave-convex interlock of spiral channels, known as the screw, namely, first

THE SCREW TAP FOR INNER THREADS
(Fig. 197)
resembling an auger with its steel threaded shank channelled vertically or perforated with holes so as to expose the edges of its threads, and so

transform them into spiral-cutting knives, which will counterthread (in intaglio) the inside of a previously bored hole when, by means of its cross handle, the tool is twisted into said hole by the workman.

This highly interesting device, made altogether of steel, and one of the most important instruments known to the mechanic, is a master tool, and has always been worked out in the first place with the greatest care by hand filing a model, as explained under the illustration.

The next picture shows the indispensable converse of the tool, namely, the threaded hole produced by the screw tap, which hole, when also steel-knife-edged, and twisted back and forth on fresh material, enables the screw tap to reproduce itself endlessly. The latter apparatus is known as

THE SCREW BOX FOR OUTER THREADS
(Fig. 198)

It consists of two rectangular, flat, side-to-side placed wooden blocks, perforated by a round, threaded hole, which hole is equipped on its inside, and at the start of the threads, with a V-shaped steel knife, for the insertion and sharpening of which knife, the blocks are releasable on screws.

To work the screw box the peg, previously rounded to size, was held firmly in a vise, and the instrument, grasped by its handles in the right and left hands of the workman, was twisted around the peg, while the wooden threads, already existing inside the hole, immediately occupying the intaglio spiral cut by the knife, guide and steady the operation.

The same result is produced if the screw box, in this case lacking the handles, is held in the vise and the wooden peg is twisted into the hole.

Large and s m a l l holes, each equipped with a special knife, were necessary for thus producing large and small wooden screws, i.e., between about one-half inch and six to eight inches in diameter, under which size the instrument appears not to have been used for wood; and it should be remembered that while with the other celebrated tool for screw-threading metal rods, called the die stock (described later), adjustable threaded semi-circular cutters, called dies, compressed by side screws, are inserted in a single hole in the stock, and several successive readjusted twistings are necessary to cut the hard metal rod to the desired depth, that in this wood-cutting apparatus, no such movable dies are used. The cutter is fixed, and if more than a single twisting in the softer material is necessary to complete the operation, several screw boxes with variously spaced knives are used.

Thus, two operations with the two instruments (screw tap, and screw box), cut the two inter-locking spirals in intaglio in the hole, in relief on the peg, large or small, according to the size of the instrument, which spirals, screwing together in the familiar manner, produced the screw adjustment of spinning wheels, cheese and lard presses, household equipments, bench vises, etc.; and while the one-man lathe was used for very small screws, these tools served well for moderate sized wooden screws and even threaded holes from one-half to about two inches in diameter. But for still larger and longer screws and screw holes, such as the gigantic wood screw of the old cider press, etc., another appara-

Fig. 199. Cider Press Screw Tap

A very rare old shop relic found in 1926, in Berks Co., Pa., by which the hole for the large wood screw of the old cider press, was turned by hand one hundred years ago.

(A) A heavy wooden cylinder perforated at its top for its (missing) turn handle.

(B) A deep spiral incision encircling the shaft of the cylinder.

(C) The guide, a wooden frame enclosing a hole to fit the cylinder, edged inside with a thin iron plate which, as shown, engages the spiral cut in the cylinder as the latter is twisted downward into the hole.

(D) The cutter, a V-shaped, pointed steel blade projecting beyond the full diameter of the cylinder through a socket therein.

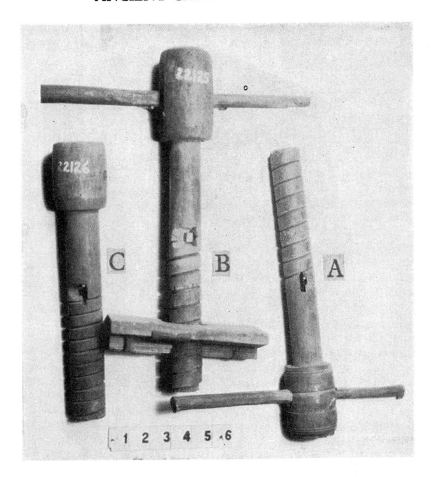

Fig. 200. Wood Worker's Screw Taps

These three old carpenter shop relics from Berks Co., Pa., obtained in 1926, are small examples of the previous Fig. 199, and work in the same way. Two show their original twist handles, but their lost guide frames appear only in a broken fragment in the middle specimen B. This broken guide frame still encloses its iron guide plate, not seen. As clearly photographed, the guide twist spirals of the three specimens differ in spacing and angle.

In this remarkable and very simple and efficient device of unknown antiquity, the great preliminary difficulty of making an original metal screw by hand with a file is escaped and nothing more precise is needed than a spiral saw kerf on a wooden cylinder, a steel point plugged therein, and a piece of sheet iron edged upon a hole.

To work the apparatus the guide frame was probably fixed rigidly upon or against a heavy frame or table. The block or plank to the threaded *i.e.* the so-called stuff, having been previously bored with a hole to fit the cylinder. A, said hole was pushed over the table to coincide with the guide frame hole. When the cylinder was then pushed downward through the block into the guide frame hole, so as to engage with its spiral the guide plate of the latter hole, and twisted downward or sideways by two men, the cutter D excavated the screw thread inside the block-hole worked upon. The projection of the cutter could be varied by hammering and wedging it back and forth in its socket. According to Holtzapffel, who illustrates and describes this in his *Turning and Mechanical Manipulation*, Vol. 2, p. 593, the cylinder was sometimes equipped with two cutters instead of one—the guide frame sometimes enclosed two guide plates, and several repeated twistings, following readjustments of the cutter might be needed to cut the threads to their full depth.

tus, somewhat modified to suit the heavy work, and here shown in one of its parts as

THE CIDER PRESS SCREW TAP
(Fig. 199)

was turned by two men with a cross bar. This ingenious old home-made device, intended not to make the wooden screw, but to thread the inside of the wooden hole therefor, is described and illustrated by Holtzapffel, Vol. 2, page 593. It consists, first, of the guide frame, a heavy framed wooden block perforated with a hole, from the inner side of which hole projects slightly a thin iron guide plate, and second, the tap, a heavy, top-handled, wooden cylinder sized to slide easily through the guide frame hole, and spiralled with a narrow, deep incision, at the top thread of which incision, the cutter, a V-shaped knife, penetrates the cylinder crossways and is adjusted by a wedge. The guide frame is fixed solidly upon the bench top, and the material worked upon is perforated with a preliminary hole sized to admit the cylinder. When said material is pushed over the guide frame and the said hole in the material coincides with the guide-frame hole, the cylinder is pushed downward through both holes. Then the guide plate in the guide frame engaging the spiral incision in the cylinder, exactly regulates its downward progress until the cutter reaches the hole in the material, whereupon as the cylinder goes down through the hole the cutter cuts the spiral screw thread inside said hole.

The next illustration,

WOODWORKERS' SCREW TAPS
(Fig. 200)

shows three old homemade instruments of smaller size, constructed in exactly the same way, which like Fig. 199, produce not screws, but screw holes; that is, threaded orifices for the insertion of wooden screws.

When these tools were in use in the early 19th century, Holtzapffel, who described them in England, in 1831, says that the complementary, outer-threaded screws, to fit these large screw holes (up to four, six and eight inches in diameter), were made by large sizes of the screw box (Fig. 198) then equipped with two cutters instead of one.

But as to the antiquity of these peculiar wood workers' screw taps (Fig. 199 and 200), he says nothing. Whether as wood-working tools they were known to the Romans, who, as shown at Pompeii and at the Saalburg Roman Fort near Homburg, Hesse, Germany, etc., made metallic screws, the writer has failed to learn.

One of the folios of the once celebrated *Theatrum Machinarum Generale*, by Jacob Leupold, variously published in eleven numbers, between 1724 and 1802 (Vol. 1, Plates XIX and XX), shows and explains them, but Moxon (1678), does not notice them. Neither does Diderot, 1768, and whoever would trace back their history into the Middle Ages, is confronted with the difficulty of distinguishing them from the variety of tools often constructed in the same way and used for the same purpose by metal workers, which, for fear of confusion, are not described here.

Tools for Fastening and Unfastening

THIS completes our list of wood-shaping tools and brings us in conclusion to the tools for fastening and unfastening woodwork, among which we have ventured to classify as tools, several important fastening devices used individually but once, yet endlessly employed in duplicate, beginning with the most important of them all, namely, the iron nail, the clavus of the Romans; generally, in the 18th century, a rectangular iron shank tapering to a rectangular point, easily driven into wood with a hammer, until arrested by its expanded top or head; much more used then by the carpenter (for floors, staircases, roofs, washboards, doors, etc.) than by the cabinetmaker, who preferred to glue, dovetail, and to peg together his furniture, and rarely used nails, unless as tacks for upholstery, or as small, half-headed or headless brads, to tack on mouldings, door battens, cupboard backs, etc.

One hundred and fifty years ago, nails were known by a variety of confused trade names, based on (a) their size, (b) cost, (c) purpose, (d) material (iron, copper, brass), (e) mode of manufacture (wrought, cast), and (f) construction (of head, shank, and point).

This explains the nails named in the *Cycle of Useful Arts,* London, Virtue, 1853, in which Charles Tomlinson reduces the old, ill-described catalogue of Richard Neve, *Builder's Dictionary,* London, 1726, to ten varieties here listed, with additions from various sources, under the illustration.

Rather than puzzle over this nail vocabulary of the old ironmonger, we may more profitably glance only at the common and typical varieties found about an old house and sometimes in old furniture and upholstery, namely, (1) nails with convex-hammer-rounded heads, (2) with side-hammered, T-shaped heads, (3) with side-hammered, L-shaped heads, (4) headless (brads), (5) tacks, and (6) spikes.

To avoid injurious wood splitting, or nail bending, preliminary holes were sometimes made for nails with the brad awl, gimlet, or reamer punch, described later, and we find that some nails had hammer-flattened chisel points intended to be driven more safely into splittable wood across the grain, and that to meet the strain of overlapped boards or the joggle of door battens, gates, hinges, latches, bolts, locks, etc., many were clenched, by the carpenter, that is, curled back at the point into the penetrated wood, by hammer blows, for which important purpose, some were specially constructed with flat, lanceolate ("spear") points, which, when thus back-curled in the form of the letter J, would best grip the wood.

For rare uses some nails were made with round, flat-topped, and flat or saucer-bottomed heads, or more properly as rivets, with blunt points, to be riveted through holes upon iron "roves" or "washers"; while for smoothness or looks T- or L-headed or headless nails were punched below

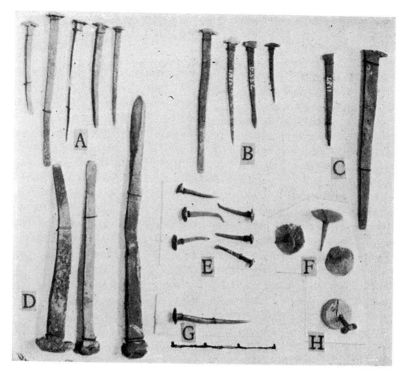

Fig. 201. Wrought Nails

Of the many-named 18th century varieties of wrought nails made for and used by carpenters in the United States until c. 1875, some of the commonest types, as named by Richard Neve, *Builder's Dictionary*, London, 1726, and Charles Tomlinson, *Cycle of Useful Arts*, London, 1853, are here shown. The heads and points vary but, as usual, the shanks formed from nail rods are rectangular and if pointed, hand-hammered to a taper on all four sides. The round-shanked clouts used by wheelwrights are not shown.

(A) Rose nails, large 3 to 4½ inch nails with a flattened rectangular or 4-square (equi-sided) shanks and round heads (18th century).

(A-1) Counting from left, chisel-point Rose, taken by a carpenter from outer cornice at "Monticello"— Thomas Jefferson's house at Charlottesville, Virginia, and given by him to Francis Mireau of Doylestown, Pa., in June, 1925.

(A-2) From left, chisel-point Rose, from Frost Garrison House, Kittery, Maine, of date about 1734. The flat, chisel-point formed by a hammer blow, decreases the danger of splitting when driven across the grain. (cf. Tomlinson, *Cycle of Useful Arts*, London, Virtue, 1854.)

(A-3) Sharp-point Rose, from Frost Garrison House, Kittery, Maine.

(A-4 and 5) Sharp-point Rose, locality unknown.

(B) Clasp nails, alias planching, or plancher, i.e., flooring nails, 18th century nails with T-shaped heads, i.e., round tops hammered flat on each side, for punching below floor levels, etc.

(B-1) Left, from Frost Garrison House (1734) again shows chisel point made by hammer blow. L-headed clasp nails not shown.

(B-2) From left, clasp nail, T-head, sharp point. From Marshall House (18th century) near Mechanicsville, Bucks Co., Pa.

(B-3) Clasp nail, T-head, spear point. No. 7354 from Miss Susan Gentry, Franklin, Tenn.; here the hammer has formed a flat-lanceolate rather than a chisel-shaped point.

(C) Brads (named in *New English Dictionary*, in 1295 and 15th and 16th centuries), large and small nails with L-shaped heads, sometimes headless, for floors, wainscoting, or sometimes small for furniture and cabinet work. Left, No. 1181, flat, rectangular, not "four square" shank point sharp, from Marshall House, Mechanicsville, Pa. Large right specimen, ditto locality unknown chisel-point.

(D) Spikes, heavy, square heads, shanks, four square. Left, from Frost Garrison House, Kittery, Maine.

(D-2) Middle, roof of sail loft Portsmouth, New Hampshire; shows hammer blow forming chisel-point.

(D-3) Right, a copper spike, origin unknown, blunt, spear-point.

the wooden surface level in floors, window and door boxings, cornices, fireplace facings, chair rails, washboards (skirtings), etc., by hammering down their heads with the nail punch, a round blunt-pointed, steel pin, described later.

That nails were classified and sold according to their size, at least five hundred years ago, is shown by the vast historical record of the uses of words in the *New English Dictionary*, which proves by four quotations, that the names, such as "6 penny," "8 penny," "10 penny," and "12 penny," etc., now vaguely applied to nails of different sizes, sold by the pound, are derived from the prices 5 pence, 4 pence, 6 pence per hundred, in the fifteenth century, in England.

While most nails were of forged iron, some few were of cast-iron, some of copper, and some of brass. Of great importance is the further fact that before the general introduction of round-shanked wire nails into the United States from Europe, about 1890, the shanks of all nails were either equi-sided rectangles ("four square"), or flat rectangles, with a few exceptions, namely, the variously pointed, variously headed, so called clouts or clout nails or dog nails, made with round shanks, the better to engage round holes in metal plates, when nailing the latter, as plow or wagon axle plates (by wheelwrights), or as wrought-iron hinge plates (by carpenters) to wood. (*cf.* Charles Tomlinson, *Cycle of the Useful Arts,* London, Virtue, 1853, article, "Nail.")

But above all in importance is a revolutionary change in nail construction that took place at the beginning of the 19th century, namely, that while from the dawn of history, iron nails had been hand forged, i.e., hammered out, one by one, by the blacksmith, and hence comparatively expensive and carefully used until about 1800, after that, in the United States, most of them were "cut," *i.e.,* machine-clipped across the breadth of an iron plate.

Before this revolution in nail manufacture, all old blacksmiths could make nails, and the evidence shows that probably long before the 18th century, many of them, called nailers, made a specialty of the monotonous

(E) Wrought lath nails (not named by Tomlinson), No. 7426, small specimen, lower right, with chisel-point used on Bucks County window shutter.

(F) Scupper nails, large headed, used to fasten leather on blacksmith's bellows. In universal use in Bucks County in the 19th century. Presented by I. J. Stover, New Britain, Pa.

(G) Machine-made wrought nail, probably imported, extra four-faceted cap forged on head, letter "G" stamped on opposite sides of upper shank; late 19th century.

(H) Nail with decorated head, hammer-flattened into two opposite oval projections. From an old table owned by Mr. W. B. Montague, of Norristown, Pa.; a rare example of an iron nail used in old furniture.

Besides nails pertaining to other trades, which do not concern us here, the blacksmith's horseshoe, and frost-horseshoe nails, the shoemaker's sparables and hobs, the mason's cast-iron nails for wall joints, and the wheelwright's round-shanked, round-headed blunt or saucer-bottomed, chisel or spear-pointed clouts, alias "dog" and "jobent" nails, for nailing clouts or iron plates on wagon axles; other common nails, variously headed, shanked and pointed, used one hundred years ago, by carpenters and joiners, but not here shown, were:

The easily clenchable gate, fencing, or hurdle nails, with round, rose-top, flat, rectangular (not 4-square) shank and spear-points.

Rose clench with rose-top, 4-square shank (compare A 5), for clenching directly upon the wood in fastening the overlapping planks of clinker-built boats. Sometimes rivets with points spread upon washers (roves) were used for this purpose. Sprigs, *i.e.,* minute brads. Tacks.

The expression "dead as a door nail" refers in the writer's opinion, either to a nail "deadened" by clenching in the framework of a wooden door, or "deadened" by reverberating blows, when driven and clenched in the wood, under a door knocker.

Round-headed or trunk nails, with varieties of "gimp" and "bullen" (for upholstery and also harness work).

Copper nails (varieties lead, sheathing and deck) for boats, ship-sheathing, and decks, and lead roofs.

Brobs, L heads, heavy, 4-square shank, driven around unmortised post tops under beams, to prevent slipping.

job, and far more in England than in America, in the 18th century, multiplied variations in the trade names and patterns of common nails.

The next illustration

WROUGHT NAILS (Fig. 201)

shows a few typical varieties of iron nails thus wrought by hand, before the machinery of the 19th century, as above noted, revolutionized the nail-making industry. Today, unless rescued from house ruins or made for special purposes or adornment, we rarely see these handmade relics of former days. Nevertheless, abundant evidence shows that they were by no means entirely abolished by the sudden advent of the "machine made cut nail" in 1800, but continued to be made, though restrictedly, for about seventy-five years thereafter. This was because the newly-invented cut nail was for a long time too brittle to clench, and therefore, where clenching was necessary, in the construction of the joggled framework of gates, batten doors, wagon bodies, clinker-built boats, etc., could not compete with its handmade clenchable predecessor. For this reason we find that blacksmiths and nailers went on hammering out the old wrought nail in the old way, particularly in England, until the third quarter of the nineteenth century, after which the successful production of clenchable cut nails in the cut nail machines, at last stopped them. This happened about 1870, or about twenty years before the present round-shanked, clenchable, machine-pressed wire nail introduced from Europe, again revolutionized the nail industry by driving the cut nail itself out of the North American market, about 1890.

The picture should show the human touch in these old hand-wrought

products, which many of us may be able to recognize at a glance. But who knows how a wrought nail was made? And as book after book, dictionary after dictionary, preferring to dwell on the economic or national or statistic importance of nails, fails to properly describe the primeval process of nail forging, we might well stop here to look at, until we understand, the next illustration,

NAIL HEADING TOOLS (Fig. 202)

which shows one of the varieties of the ancient device by which the blacksmith has for centuries helped the carpenter to build houses, by hammering a heated rod of iron to a point, cutting it to the proper length, wedging it into an iron hole, and pounding a head upon it.

The instrument here appears in its commonest Anglo-American form, as a short iron bar, perforated at one or both ends with a bottom-expanding hole, square for common nails, and round for rivets or the round-shanked, so-called clout nails.

Held loose in the left hand over the anvil hole or side, the old nailer, as described under the illustration, having introduced the hot, tapered, nail rod downward as far as it would go, into the square hole in this nail tool, and having expanded its protruding top by hammer blows into a head, had only to tap the instrument upside down over the anvil edge, to release the rapidly cooled and hence shrunken finished nail.

The tool is described by Holtzapffel and Lardner, and still rarely used (1926), by blacksmiths for special nails, rivets or bolts.

The next picture

NAIL HEADING TOOLS (Fig. 203)

shows several obsolete devices for the

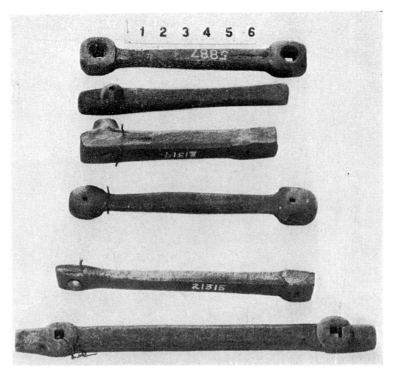

Fig. 202. Nail Heading Tools

These highly important, rarely observed and more rarely described instruments, employed by the blacksmith since Roman times, to head hand-wrought nails, were in universal use in the United States until *c.* 1800, when they were largely superseded by machines to make at first brittle, non-clenchable, cut nails, after which they continued in restricted use until machine-made, clenchable, cut nails abolished them in 1860-80. They consist of flattened bars of iron, from 7 to 12 inches long, with a round or square expansion at one or both ends, which expansion is perforated with a hole, which hole, whether round or square, is never cylindrical, but always expands downward, *i.e.*, is smaller at the top, than at the under side of the instrument.

Karl Klemp and Clarence Davis, blacksmiths, of Doylestown, who still can and do sometimes make wrought nails, describe the process to the writer as follows:

Holding with his left hand, if long enough, or with tongs, if short, the nail rod, a thin rectangular strip of forged iron (furnished the iron worker from forges and rolling mills in existence since the mid-18th century), the smith heats it at one end, tapers it on the anvil with hammer blows on all four sides to a point, and cuts or half-cuts it, to the gauged or guessed nail-length, on the projecting wedge-shaped cutter or hack-iron, called hardy, inserted in a socket in the anvil top (*cf*. Fig. 203 G). Having then placed the hole of the heading tool (small diameter up), held in his left hand, upon the anvil top, immediately over an anvil orifice, or over the anvil-edge, and having thrust the red hot point just made (the nail shank), held in his right hand either with or without the tongs mentioned. Thereupon, because with great skill, by eye, or by a chalk mark on the anvil top, he has gauged the upper thickness of the heated point, so as not to have it drop through the hole, but stick fast and protrude about ⅛ to ¼ inch above it, he can spread, *i.e.*, form, by hammer blows, the protruding metal into the nail head. After which, on turning the heading tool with the finished nail sticking therein, upside down, and tapping it over the anvil edge, or anvil hole, the cooled and shrunk nail drops out of the instrument.

As here shown, by old 19th century specimens, many of the heading tool-ends thicken or swell into bulbs around the nail orifice, so as to give the hammer free side-play in rounding or convexing the head. But because nails were generally square-shanked, only the heading tools with square holes were used to make nails. (2 bottom specimens and middle specimen right end.) Those with round holes (second and third specimens, downward, and fourth, ditto, at its left end) made round-shanked rivets, or the round-shanked, so-called clout-nails used by wheelwrights to nail down wagon axle plates. That shown at top with counter-sunk holes, produced the saucer-bottomed heads of screw bolts, by pounding down (swaging) the hot, protruding metal into the saucer.

No. 21315, from Kutztown, Pa., was obtained in 1925, by Mr. H. K. Deisher. The bottom specimen was bought from Charles Layman, waste iron merchant, Doylestown, Pa., 1898.

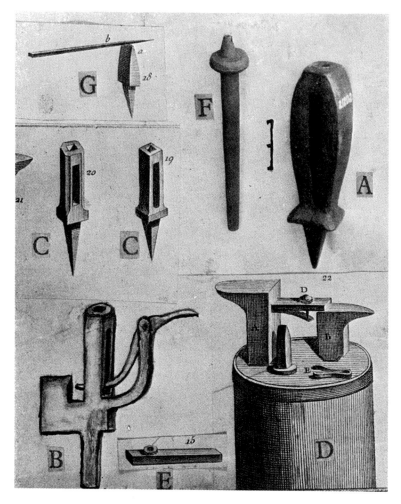

Fig. 203. Nail Heading Tools

(A) Shows another ancient type of nail-heading tool, similar in method, but different in shape from Fig. 202.

The spiked wrought-iron anvil is driven vertically into a heavy wooden block, and the nail is headed as before in the square nail hole seen in the anvil top, which hole, widened at bottom, opens into a large cross orifice in the anvil. When headed, cooled and shrunk, the nail is released by some kind of upthrust (not discovered), under its point, while the latter projects down into this orifce. The tool was found among the obsolete relics of old Pennsylvania German iron workers, by Mr. Charles R. Stauffer of Norristown, and presented by him to the Bucks County Museum in 1926.

(B) Illustrates by a drawing a similar device equipped with a chisel side attachment (hardy) to cut the hot nails to gauged length and a lever hinged under the nail point, which, uprising by an end-tap, released the finished nail.

The original specimen, sold in 1926 by a dealer in Reading, Pa., and recently seen by the writer, from which the drawing was made, was found, c. 1925, among old smith's relics in Berks County, Pa., by Charles D. Schofer of Reading. H. K. Landis of Landis Valley, Lancaster Co., Pa., saw John Carper, a smith of Lancaster County, using a similar apparatus, lacking the hardy, c. 1875, called nageleisen by the Pennsylvania Germans. The tool is poorly described, as formerly in use in Germany, in *Geschichte des Eisens*, Johansen, Dusseldorf, 1925.

(C) Shows a picture of the tool (A) called clouyere a chevilles (heading tool for bolts), given without explanation in Diderot's *Encyclopedia* (1768).

same purpose, generally overlooked in books and now so utterly forgotten that whoever has tried to find or explain them, might look with astonishment at (a) a small hollow anvil tapering into a bottom spike (and therefore drivable into a wooden block) with a down-funnelling nail hole on top, from which the finished and headed nail would have to be released by underthrust of an extra device, possibly spring tongs, not found; (b) a similar anvil with attached lever for nail release from Berks County, Penna.; (c) an illustration from Diderot's *Encyclopedia*, 1768, showing, though without describing, the same tool, there called clouyere a chevilles —nail tool for bolts; (d) another device from Diderot, by which the nail-heading tool shown in Figure 202 is wedged across two anvil tops, over a spring, by tapping which spring, the finished nail springs out of the nail hole; (e) a Chinese nail-heading tool, namely, a heavy iron bar, held vertically in the workman's left hand, while he heads the hot nail-blank in the square, 1½ inch deep, down-expanding, nail hole, on the top of the instrument.

The antiquity of this highly important down-expanding hole, whether in a loose or fixed bar of iron, or an anvil top, which, if found alone in an ancient excavation, would prove the contemporary existence of headed, wrought nails, bolts or rivets, is shown by the next picture,

ROMAN NAIL HEADING TOOLS
(Fig. 204)

illustrating not only (a) the perforated bar, but also (b) a similar nail anvil closely resembling the Pennsylvania specimen, Figure 203), both found at one of the citadels of the Romano-German defense wall, on a hill called the Saalburg, near Homburg vor der Hohe, Hesse, Germany, and (c) another perforated bar, excavated with a number of smith's implements and the iron plane (Fig. 110) at the site of the Roman town of Calleva, near Silchester, ten miles southwest of Reading, Hampshire, England, where it is now (1926) as a great rarity, though perhaps not understood by one visitor in a thousand, on exhibition at the public Museum.

Another picture, illustrating another tool twenty centuries old, too rare and interesting to be overlooked,

A ROMAN NAILER'S ANVIL (Fig. 205)

shows an anvil with a side-overhang perforated by a vertical, down-expanding, side-opened hole, in which the nail was headed, found at the Roman camp site at Kreimbach, near Kaiserslautern, Germany, now (1927) on exhibition at the Museum at Speyer, and kindly photographed for the writer by Dr. H. Jacobi, Director of Excavations at the Saalburg, above mentioned.

That iron nails rust so easily, when exposed to water, is and always has

(D) Shows another instrument illustrated by Diderot, a variety of the common Anglo-American heading tool, Fig. 202. In this case the tool is not held loose in the hand, but wedged fast horizontally upon a spring between two anvil tops. The nail is released by a vibration of the spring caused by a down tap of the hammer.

Very interesting for comparison with all western instruments of the kind, ancient or modern, (F) shows a Chinese nail-heading tool, a bar of iron topped with a little square, 1¼ inch deep, nail hole enlarged at the bottom. The bar encircled with a top rim is held vertically in the left hand on an anvil or block until the hot nail is headed in the hole, after which the instrument is turned sideways and the nail knocked out of the hole, by side hammering its head. Still used (1927) by blacksmiths in China, where imported European wire nails are rapidly coming into use. The specimen now in the Bucks County Museum, was bought for the writer by Mr. R. P. Hommel, at Kuling, China, in March, 1927.

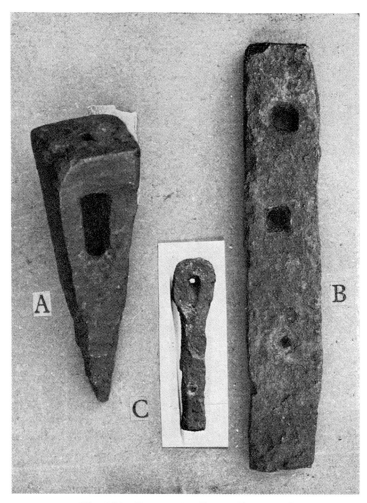

Fig. 204. Roman Nail Heading Tools

(A) A small, wrought-iron anvil-wedge, 4¾ inches (12 centimeters) high, with square-top, nail-hole and side orifice for nail discharge; is constructed like the larger modern American tool (A) Fig. 203, and the French tools C,— clouyere a chevilles, of 1798, shown in the same picture. This specimen was excavated with the Roman iron tools, of c. 200 A.D., at the Saalburg citadel on the Roman defense wall near Homburg von der Höhe, Germany, and is now on exhibition at the Museum there.

(B) 6¾ inches long, a flat, wrought-iron bar, perforated with three square nail holes, though not bulbed around the latter, is otherwise constructed like the modern specimens shown in Fig. 202. It was also found with the Roman tools at the Saalburg fort.

(C) 4¾ inches long, of date, 1st to 4th century, A.D., is also of wrought iron. It is constructed in the same way, with a single nail hole, the enlarged bottom or top of which, as here shown, extends into a side cavity. It was found in 1890-1900 with a hoard of Roman smith's tools at the Romano-British town-site of Calleva, the modern Silchester, near Reading, England.

(A) and (B) Of date before the 4th century A.D., were recently photographed and are here shown by kind permission of Dr. H. Jacobi, Director of the Saalburg Museum, and (C) by that of the Corporate Museum and Art Gallery at Reading, England.

Fig. 205. Roman Nail Heading Anvil

This remarkable, wrought-iron specimen has been kindly photographed for the writer by Dr. H. Jacobi, from a plaster cast in the Saalburg Museum. The original of iron, 9¼ inches high, of date c. 1st century, A.D., was found with other Roman iron tools at Heidenburg, near Kreimbach, near Kaiserslautern, Rhenish Bavaria, and is now (1927) at the Museum Speyer. It is illustrated in *Die Alterthumer unserer Heidnischen Vorzeit*, V Band, Heft VII, plate 46, Publication of the Romano-Germanic Central Museum at Mayence, Von Zabern, Mainz, 1906.

Here, a circular nail hole, with a deep under cavity for nail release, according to the plate description in the above work, penetrates vertically the corner of the anvil top close to its margin, while the remains of two more faintly seen channels for similar holes appear on the broken off original overhang of the anvil side. But the method of nail release, whether by up tap of hammer or tongs, or otherwise, has not been proved.

Jost Ammon shows a nailer at work on an anvil with several nail holes thus constructed penetrating its beak. Unfortunately he fails to picture the method of nail release.

Adam Faust, junk dealer, of Horsham, Bucks Co., Pa., informed the writer, May 20, 1927, that he saw a special blacksmith or nailer named Emory, who worked alone at a small nailery, on Germantown Road and Sixth Street, Philadelphia, there making by hand, to order, nails and rivets, about 1877, on a similar anvil with overlapping side lip with several nail holes. Also, that he saw smiths making nails and bolts by hand in common heading tools (Fig. 202) (for bolts with countersunk head sockets) at Wilson & Child's Agricultural Works, at Second Street and Lehigh Avenue, Philadelphia, shortly before the factory was abandoned, about 1885.

According to tradition and brief documentary evidence, several small forges, devoted only to nail making, existed on farms in Bucks County, Pa., in the 18th and early 19th centuries, i.e., one in a small stone out-building, recently, c. 1924, pulled down on the W. Heacock farm of 1876 (see Smith's Map of that date) one-half mile southeast of Gardenville; another at Furlong (Davis' *History*); and one at New Britain (information David Gehman, Mennonite minister to the writer). A pair of smith's bellows, half the usual size (said to have been used by a smith who only made nails and rivets, was recently obtained by the writer from a smith's sale near Bristol, Pa.

been a great objection to them. Nevertheless, abundant archaeological evidence shows that these headed points, first of bronze, later of iron, were used in ancient Rome, Assyria, and Egypt, and though wooden pegs (trenails) have for centuries largely supplanted them in European shipbuilding, still, several relics of Norse ships excavated from clay burial mounds, or found buried in sand, now on exhibition at the Norwegian Museum at Oslo (see Fig. 211), and at the Museum of Antiquities of Scotland, in Edinburgh, prove clinker-built hulls, nailed, as boats are nailed today, with round-headed iron nails, penetrating the overlapping boards, sometimes with points clenched directly upon the opposite wood, or sometimes as rivets rather than nails (*cf.* Fig. 210) with blunt points, riveted upon iron "roves" (washers) inside the hull, but in any case directly exposed to the water. The next engraving

CHINESE NAILS (Fig. 206)

illustrates the remarkable fact that the Chinese, who prefer wooden pegs for all purposes to iron-headed nails, nevertheless, can and do make nails, not only with an iron heading tool as shown in Figure 203, but also in a highly ingenious manner, apparently unknown to western nations, as here shown, by double-pointing an iron rod, "midspreading" it, and cross-denting the spread. Thereafter when the points are easily broken apart, each point becomes a nail with an iron top wing, which wing bends over into an excellent nail head when the point is hammered down into the wood, as shown in specimen (*c*). Besides this, as if to shock the western shipwright, they use what might be called iron staples, rather than nails

or pegs, as here illustrated, in building their ships, which singular staples (as explained under the illustration) escape water contact by being driven across the plank joints inside the ship.

To conclude the subject and finally explain what has been said about the 19th century revolution in nail manufacture, another more familiar picture,

CUT NAILS (Fig. 207)

illustrates the comparatively modern type of nail above referred to, no longer laboriously hammered by hand from a rectangular rod, but instantaneously sliced by a machine, from a plate of iron, a process unheard of, since iron replaced bronze in human history, until suddenly cheapening nail production, as above noted, it caused the blacksmith to limit the use of his ancient nail tools in 1800, and generally discard them about 1870.

The next illustration,

THE NAIL PUNCH (Fig. 208)

shows the short steel pin, from the point of which, L- or T-headed nails, or headless brads, were often, for smoothness sake, punched below the surface level in wainscoting, chair rails, washboards, etc., but chiefly in floors.

Yet the nail, whether wrought or cut, was not the carpenter's only method of fastening wood with iron in the 18th and early 19th centuries, for numerous examples of old Colonial and Post-Colonial and recent woodwork, show that he then used another of the fundamental products of the blacksmith, of great antiquity and world-wide use, namely

THE RIVET (Fig. 209)

a round, large-headed iron shank

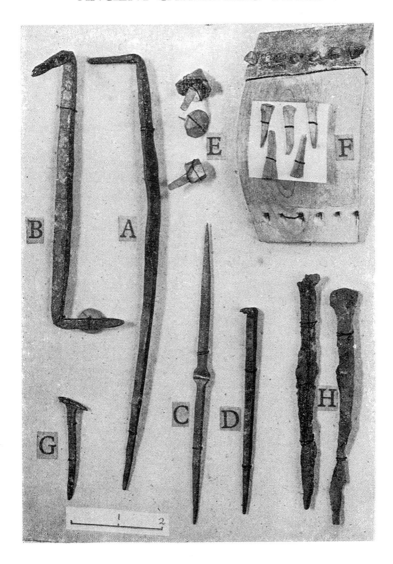

Fig. 206. Chinese Nails

(A) Shows the common form of wrought-iron nail or staple now (1927) used in China, for building boats and ships. Inside the hull, near the crack of two close-fitting boards or planks, an inslanting hole is bored with the thong drill (see Fig. 186); then when the straight staple-point is driven therein, and the shank bent over across the crack, its other sharp, right-angled end is bent slightly outward so as to "draw," and driven tight into the other board. The result is one of the tight, cross-crack staples, set about six to eight inches apart inside the ship, and therefore escaping water contact, which fasten together the Chinese square-ended ships. And it is of further interest to know that these ships are thus planked, not on ribs, but on solid, often water-tight, inside partitions. (Information given the writer by the Rev. Horace Lacquer of Hankow, China, in 1927).

(B) Shows another form of staple similarly used to turn the corner in fastening the side planking to the deck, or the central partitions of cabins which latter serve in China, instead of ribs, to cross-brace the hull.

(C) Shows one of the remarkable Chinese methods for making iron wrought nails without a heading tool. A section of nail rod has been pointed at both ends, hammer flattened or spread in the middle, and deeply cross-dented on

whose blunt point was spread cold by hammer blows upon the penetrated material, *i.e.*, if metal, directly on the metallic surface, or, if wood, upon a loose metal plate, set upon the wood, called a rove or a washer, as described under the illustration. The rivet was often used instead of a clenched nail, to fasten the straps of wrought-iron hinges, where the latter, not mortised into the edges of doors and lintels were set firmly by carpenters on the faces of house and barn doors, as here shown; by joiners upon chests; and sometimes by boat builders, instead of clenched (rose clench) nails, to fasten together the overlapped planks in clinker-built boats.

As a strangely preserved relic of this latter use of rivets by boat builders many centuries ago, the next picture,

SHIP RIVETS AND NAILS OF THE VIKINGS (Fig. 210)

kindly photographed for the writer and here shown by permission of the University Museum at Oslo, Norway, shows a round-shanked nail and two loose rivets with their roves, from the beautiful and romantic Norse burial ship, known as

THE OSEBERG SHIP (Fig. 211)

excavated in 1903, from a clay grave-mound near the mouth of the Oslo Fjord, Norway, and now on exhibition at the University Museum at Oslo; and whoever knows anything of modern shipbuilding would look with amazement at the clay-preserved survival of sea rover's handiwork shown in the succeeding cut,

ANCIENT NORSE BOAT PLANKING (Fig. 212)

which illustrates part of the clinkered side, with the roved rivets in place, and the extraordinary adze-cut rib-sockets from the same historic vessel.

But how trivial seem these comparatively rare uses of the rivet by the woodworker, when contrasted with its universal employment by the blacksmith and metal worker. It is its world-wide importance as a metallic adjustment since Roman times, that might tempt us to turn aside from the carpenter, to trace its history, if possible, in the records of archaeological excavation, and the handbooks of technology, which forget to tell us how the locks and armor of the Middle Ages were fastened together, whether the iron, so-called, nails, as here shown, on these clinkered planks of the Norse ships were actually nails or rivets, or that the scissors of the

---

the spread. The specimen has not yet been broken in half. When it is, two nails are formed with thin top-wings, which wings bend over into heads, when the nail is hammered down into wood. Rare in China, where wooden pegs, except for ships, coffins and shoes, generally supplant nails.

(D) Has been photographed from a finished nail extracted from wood after its wing top has been thus transformed into a head by down pounding.

(E) Shows several Chinese varieties of hob-nails for shoes, headed in a heading tool.

(F) Shows the short, Chinese, wooden, bamboo pegs, knife-cut, with enlarged heads, used to fasten the skin upon drum-tops, as shown in the drum-top section, on which they lie.

(G) Is a wrought-iron nail used for fastening the iron tire to the wheel of a Chinese wheelbarrow. A cross-section of the tire would show an encircling groove therein which protects the nail head narrowed to enter it.

(H) Shows two coffin nails recovered from old graves on the Poyang Lake, near Nankang-Fu, Kiangsi, obtained by Mr. R. P. Hommel, for the writer in 1927.

The other specimens now (1927) in the Bucks County Museum, all representing nails now in use, were bought for the writer in China in 1925, by Mr. R. P. Hommel.

(A), (B), (C) and (D) From shipbuilders at Kien Chang, Kiangsi.

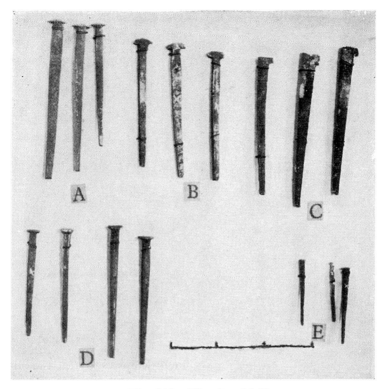

Fig. 207. The Cut Nail

After *c.* 1800, the blacksmith in the United States received as raw material, from the forge, or rolling mill, no longer only the long narrow "nail rod," sheared from the side of a flat plate of trip-hammered (later rolled) iron, but the nail plate, a wide, flat strip of malleable iron, similarly sheared from a similar plate, whose varying width established the length of the nail. The nail-shank, always of the thickness of this nail plate, tapered like a wedge only on its two opposite sides. Sliding the nail plate into the jaws of a horizontal cutter, worked at first by a foot treadle, he cut off, at right angles to said plate, narrow tapered slices of iron (the nails), and then at first dropped each slice, top upward, into a foot-treadle vise, and headed it with a hammer. After *c.* 1820, these two operations were combined in one, and worked at first by water power and later, after *c.* 1840, by steam. Cut nails suddenly and widely replaced wrought nails, between 1798 and 1800, but because they were at first too brittle to clench, did not entirely abolish wrought nails for special purposes, where clenching was necessary, as in shipbuilding, fences, house building, for doors, latches, shutters, etc., until about 1870, *cf.* "Dating of Old Houses," in *Old-Time New England*, April 1924.

A few varieties from old Bucks Co., Pa., houses, are here shown:

(A) Made by two operations with cut shanks and round-hammered heads before 1820, for floors, wainscoting, and general house building.

(B) Ditto, with T-shaped heads, made by hammer blows on either side of the head, before 1820.

(C) Made without such head hammering by one operation, with L heads, or headless, for floors, etc. Made soon after 1800, and throughout the century.

(D) Made by one operation, with square, stamped heads, soon after *c.* 1820, and until *c.* 1890.

(E) Small L-headed, or headless, brads for furniture, panelling, etc. (Heading doubtful.)

Turks and Chinese, or surgical tweezers and compasses, or blacksmith tongs found at Pompeii, were set on rivets.

Still another of the most important of the ancient iron devices known to mechanics, was also used by carpenters until about 1850, on the hook and eye hinges of outer house doors, and (until about 1890) on similar hinges

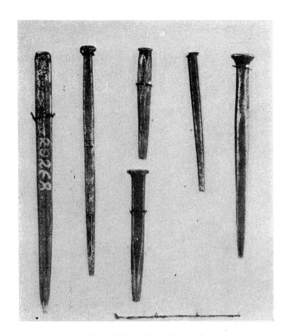

Fig. 208. The Punch

A short, more or less rounded, blunt-pointed, tapering, steel shank. When held in the carpenter's left hand, with its blunt point set upon the head of a nail already driven home it was hammered so as to drive said nail-head below the board surface, where desirable, on floors, to prevent foot scratching, or the catching thereto of mop "thrums," as Moxon says, or where in wainscots or skirtings, etc., the nail top was to be concealed with putty and paint.

No. 20268 (left) was made by Seth Nelson, mountaineer artificer, about 1890, at his remote mountain workshop, near Sinnamahoning, Pa. It was obtained in 1926, by Col. H. W. Shoemaker.

The three middle, upper punches were found in 1925, with a large collection of clock making tools in the amateur workshop (1820-1860) of Charles J. Wister, Esq., of Germantown, Pa.

The right specimen, of date 19th century, is from a set of tools belonging to the late George C. Ruff, of 2512 N. Hancock Street, Philadelphia.

Another similar tool, No. 20391, not shown, is a rivet punch for removing the rivets in strap door hinges, by pounding them through the rivet holes in the iron hinges. Also made by Seth Nelson.

set upon the continually slammed, double-winged entrance doors, or colossal threshing-floor doors of barns, or by cabinetmakers to hold fast the framework of wooden beds. This was

THE SCREW BOLT (Fig. 213) a headed rod of iron, squared at top and threaded at its lower end, to engage the threaded hole of a perforated iron block called the nut, screwed upon its bottom.

Often, in special shifting attachments for domestic or farm apparatus, particularly in the 18th and early 19th centuries, this nut was enlarged into one or more conspicuously forged (later machine-made or cast) side wings, or graceful single-or double-ended, hand-wrought upcurls or "rat tails," as shown in the illustration (lower left corner). But as these variations are not characteristic of the screw bolt as a carpenter's tool, our examination confines itself to the bolt-nut in its most typical rectangular form.

When the screw bolt is thrust through one or more pieces of wood or metal and this rectangular nut screwed upon it, with a wrench, the device holds together the perforated material with tremendous force.

Moxon, in 1678 (cf. *Mechanick Exercises*, above cited), describes the making of screw bolts by top squaring and top heading a rod of iron, and then outer-threading said rod held in a vise, by twisting around it, for small bolts, two or more of the knife-threaded steel holes, in an instrument called the screw plate, namely, a thin steel bar or plate, still in use, handled at one or both ends, and perforated with several of these variously sized screw-cutting holes.

Every mechanic knows further that this ancient operation with the screw plate, in which the diameter of the cutting hole is fixed, applies only to

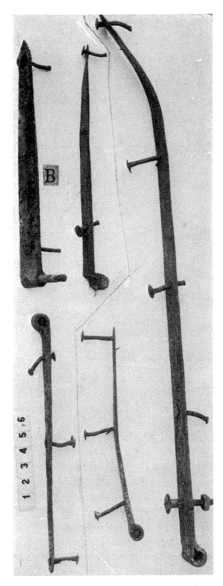

Fig. 209. The Rivet

The picture shows six wrought hinge straps and hinge hooks, with the original rivets attached (except that the right specimen shows a screw bolt in the lower hole), universally used on barn doors in Bucks Co., Pa., until about 1890. The rivets, round, untapered rods of iron, were headed by local blacksmiths in the heading tool with a round hole (Fig. 202) in which operation the rod, first thickened at its end by a hammer blow, to prevent its

falling through the tool-hole, was next, like the nail, cut to a gauged length on the hardy, and then dropped into the tool hole and spread to a head with the hammer, as was the nail. Hinge rivets were attached through a hole in the wooden door, coinciding with a hole in the iron hinge-strap laid thereon, whereupon their malleable ends, penetrating about ⅛ inch above the hinge strap-hole, were spread upon it cold by a carpenter with blows of the face, or the peen of the riveting hammer (Fig. 224) while a fellow workman held an ax-head under the bolt-head, to receive the percussions.

(B) Shows the hook of one of these hinge straps forged upon a long iron plate, also attached with rivets. Such hinge hooks were used in cases where the door frame, as in the small wicket door of the gigantic threshing-floor door, were too light to hold a spike. Otherwise, these large hooks (rarely thus plated, and sometimes set on screw bolts, as shown in Fig. 213) generally ended in spikes, driven into a previously-bored auger hole in the heavy door frame.

It is an interesting fact in house construction, that long after castiron butt-hinges had supplanted wrought hinges on all inner house doors, these massive, homemade hinges continued in use on outer house doors (until c. 1850); on house shutters (until c. 1870) and on barn doors until c. 1890, after which the cheap, sheet-iron, factory-made substitutes now (1926) in use took their place.

Karl Klemp, blacksmith, of Doylestown, Pa., informs the writer that he still uses the heading tool as shown in Fig. 202, for special nails or bolts, and still (1926) for special purposes, sometimes makes rivets therewith.

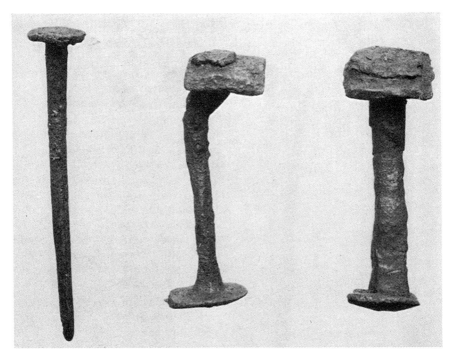

Fig. 210. Boat Rivets and Boat Nails of the Vikings

The specimens of date about the 9th century A.D., all pertain to the Viking burial boat or ship known as the "Oseberg Ship," excavated in 1903 from a clay grave at Oseberg, on the Oslo Fjord, Norway. Kindly photographed for the writer in 1927 by the University Museum of Oslo.

(A) (left) Shows an iron, round-shaped clout or dog nail. (B) and (C) (right) Two loose iron, round-shanked rivets, riveted fast to their roves or washers, as used in the clinker-overlap of the boat planks.

small screw-bolts (and screws) of less than ¼ inch in diameter, while for large bolts or screws, up to two inches in diameter, cutting holes of movable diameter, *i.e.*, composed of segments of cutting holes, called dies, compressible by side screws and inserted in a handled twist-frame called the die stock, produce the same result.

Conversely, to make the nut-threaded orifice which engages the threaded shank, a steel screw transformed into a thread-cutter by fluting its sides across the threads, called the screw-tap, exactly as shown for woodwork in Fig. 197, was twisted into a previously drilled iron hole to spiral the

hole with an internal thread. According to the valuable treatise on the subject by Charles Holtzapffel, *Turning and Mechanical Manipulation*, Vol. 2, p. 615, and notes in Lardner's *Cabinet Encyclopedia*, for Metals, Vol. 1, p. 199, it appears that this tedious and expensive hand-operation for metallic screws, whether with or without nuts, though ancient, was not the only one known for the purpose in 1678, and that before and after Moxon's time, numerous appliances of man and water power (to vary Besson's screw lathe of 1569, or following the inventions in England of Kindley of York, 1641, Grandjean

Fig. 211. The Oseberg Ship

The picture shows the stern of the "Oseberg Ship," of supposed date 835-850 A.D., in its original position as discovered in 1903 on the bank of a stream near the mouth of the Oslo Fjord, Norway. Unearthed under a clay-covered grave, it had been used as the burial chamber of a woman, and contained numerous utensils, tools, bones, etc. It is 70 feet 6 inches long, by 16 feet 9 inches wide amidships, by 5 feet 3 inches deep, nearly equi-ended, with a mast socket, oar rudder as here seen, and oars worked through gunwhale port holes. It has a keel, clinkered planks on each side, and ribs, to which the two top gunwhale planks are bolted and the others lashed, as explained with Fig. 212.

Photographed and here shown by permission of the University Museum at Oslo, where it is now (1927) on exhibition.

in France, c. 1729, or William Wyatt of 1760, Sir Samuel Bentham, of c. 1790-1800, and Maudsley, 1800-1810), had been practiced to produce the highly important metallic device, which became more and more necessary as machines began to supersede hand tools in the late 18th century.

It is because to save time and trouble, the screw bolt, more properly a metal-worker's device, was sometimes used as above noted, in the early 18th century, by carpenters and farmers, in

place of the rivet, to set or reset barn or outer house door hinges, or in special adjustments, when in wooden apparatus a nail or rivet would joggle loose, that it is discussed here; otherwise, though the practice was increased by the cheapening of screw bolts by machine manufacture after c. 1860, and continued until c. 1890, the old carpenter rarely used the iron adjustment.

Not so the wheelwright, who found it more and more necessary in the late

Fig. 212. Ancient Norse Boat Planking

The engraving, from a photograph furnished by the University Museum at Oslo, Norway, shows the exposed inside clinker, or overlapped planking of the shop, with the ends of the roved rivets in place as found. The ribs are gone, but their extraordinary fastenings remain, as spaced rows of heavy wooden welts, left solid upon the inside plank-face, when said plank was hewn (probably with an adze) from the native log. Each welt is cross-notched and cross-bored with two holes, through which holes, it appears that flexible withes, without help of nails or rivets, bound fast the transverse rib strips into the welt-notches.

In the New Bedford whale boat, of late 19th century make, in the Bucks County Museum, the "clinkered" planks are fastened together by square-shanked, cut copper or alloyed metal nails, 1¼ inches long, clenched directly on the inside wood-face, without roves (washers). Larger square-shanked, 2½ inches long, cut, alloyed-metal, unclenched nails, are used to fasten the planks to the ribs without penetrating the latter.

18th and early 19th centuries, and we learn from the *History of the Bolt and Nut Industry in America*, by W. R. Wilbur, of Cleveland, Ohio, 1905, that it was not the advent of steam-run machinery (*c.* 1830), but the early growth of the factory manufacture of wagons in New England, that suddenly started bolt-making in the United States in the 1840's. Then inventive blacksmiths working almost simultaneously (in Connecticut — Barnes & Ruggles; at Marion (1840)—A. H. Plant & Co., 1834-5; in Pennsylvania — William Golcher, Philadelphia, 1840), followed by a host of rivals remodelled the ancient European lathe fixtures, above referred to, or by applying hand or foot or water power

to the old screw tap (*cf.* Fig. 194), or to swages and turning tools, soon enabled one man to more than quadruple his daily work, until meeting the new demand of steam-run machinery, in the 1850's, factory-made screw-bolts, by 1870, sold in packages of assorted sizes (generally 5/16 inch in diameter), were everywhere obtainable at hardware and country stores. Nevertheless, abundant evidence from the information of men now living, shows that country blacksmiths continued to make them by hand for special purposes for some years later, as when David Gehman, Mennonite minister and general artificer, of Fountainville, Bucks County, Pa., tells the writer that he saw

In considering screw-threading devices, it is well to note that Moxon's description only partly explains one of the several methods by which the metallic screw has been threaded for centuries, which, judging from old tools, book references and pictures may be summed up under two processes, namely, first, by moving a V-shaped, steel cutting-point against and along the side of a revolving metal rod, or conversely, by advancing the revolving rod against the fixed V-shaped point; second, by constructing a metallic model screw which will endlessly reproduce itself. This preliminary model is and was produced in several ways, as follows:

(A) By filing a spiral, marked from a slip of paper twisted around a round iron rod; ( ) by twisting a red hot, square iron rod into a spiral and retouching with a file; (C) by soldering fast a spiral wire twisted around a round rod; (D) by cutting a spiral upon a round rod caused to revolve in a trough by pushing a knife held at an angle across said revolving or rolling rod.

Thus made the metal screw must be transformed into a cutting screw, the so-called screw tap, by cross-channelling its threads, or distorting their circumference, so that when twisted into an iron hole they become knives and will thread the hole.

The next step is to again transform said hole, so threaded, into a reverse cutter, namely the so-called screw plate, for small screws, or the die and die stock for large screws.

In the ¼ inch thick screw plate, which is a steel tablet, handled at one or both ends, this transformation is effected in several fixed threaded holes, by channelling the holes vertically inside at least twice, with saw kerfs, which kerfs radiate conspicuously outward into enlarged round punctures. Thus each thread becomes a side-cutting knife, and several twisting operations in holes of varied diameter are needed to complete the thread cut.

In the larger die stock, the threaded hole is circumscribed and cut across the threads into loose sections, which loose sections thus having become sharp-edged will immediately side-cut when twisted laterally. Two or more of these cutting sections, the so-called dies, are set side by side, with intermittent openings, in a circle into the frame of a handled twist-clamp called the die stock, whereupon, being compressed by side screws or otherwise, in repeated twisting, they complete the cut.

As used by carpenters and here shown, the screw bolt sometimes appears as an original termination of the heavy, smith-forged hinge hook (AAA) or more commonly in its typical form (B) as a means of attachment for the heavy wrought-iron straps (D) of old barn door hinges. For the latter purpose, ample evidence shows the rivets (Fig. 209) had been chiefly used since the Middle Ages, and that the screw bolt was never common with carpenters until towards the end of the 19th century when cheap factory-made screw bolts, sold in assorted lots at country stores, met the farmer's frequent need for repairing or rehinging his barn or outer house door.

The lower specimens (C) show several screw bolts, three of which with "rat tail" nuts, can be twisted without a wrench by hand, a hammer blow, or an inthrust rod. All the examples are from the iron refuse of burned or demolished barns or farm shops, and all were bought from Charles Layman and William Darrah, waste iron merchants of Doylestown, Pennsylvania, between 1898 and 1915.

The very ancient key bolt, fastened not by a screw-thread and nut, but by a releasable iron peg (key) like the linch pin of a wagon hub, thrust through a slot near its point, because not properly a carpenter's tool, and only used in rare and special apparatus construction, is not here shown.

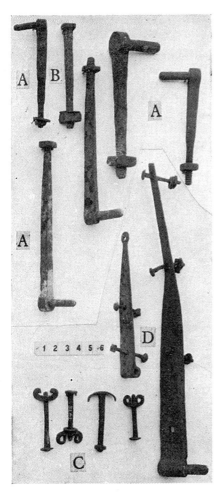

Fig. 213. The Screw Bolt

The screw bolt (B) is a screw-threaded shank of iron expanding into a head at its top and squared thereunder to prevent turning when sliding loosely through the substance penetrated. Its thread engages not the latter, but the nut, a similarly perforated and threaded iron block, screwed tight upon its lower end with a wrench.

Because this nut ceases to work when the thread ends, or would crush soft wood, one or more washers, perforated pieces of metal, are sometimes slipped on the shank under the nut (as here faintly seen and more clearly at (A) (left), to thicken to pressure limit, the substance penetrated, or to protect the wood.

When making the screw bolt by hand, the square head, sometimes under-saucered, was swaged, *i.e.*, the red hot, projecting metal was pounded down in the square or saucered-cavity around the top of the heading tool, specially made for the purpose, shown in Fig. 202.

the blacksmiths, Frank and Reuben Fox, make screw bolts and rivets by hand taps and screw plates, in Douglas Township, Montgomery Co., Pa., about 1862, while he distinctly remembers that rivets continued to be handheaded in heading tools (*cf.* Fig. 202) until about 1890.

But as with the rivet, how insignificant seem these notes on the restricted use of the screw bolt, by the 18th century carpenter and wheelwright, when compared with the wide importance of its history, which the accounts of recent improvements, glorifying modern ingenuity, nations or individuals, have obscured, and which for hundreds of years before the 15th century seems lost.

In considering the construction of the screw bolt as typical of all forms of metal screws designed to engage wood or metal, we may disregard the shape of head, method of twisting, and the presence or absence of a nut, since no matter how the threaded shank operates, what material it clasps, and whether it engages only wood or a little loose metallic block, or any threaded metallic hole anywhere, the principle is the same. If not known in ancient Egypt, it was certainly understood by the Romans (*cf.* screw apparatus found at Pompeii) and according to Rich, is described by Pappus of Alexandria, and Pliny. As kindly shown the writer by Mr. Joseph Sanford, F. M. Feldhaus, in *Technik der Vorzeit, Leipsig*, Engleman, 1914, shows a Roman bell of about 250 A.D. with a screw for handle adjustment, found at the Roman fort-site called the Saalburg, about twelve miles north of Frankfort-on-the-Main, Germany, now in the Saalburg Museum at Homburg,

Hesse, and also a Roman iron bolt-nut shown later (Fig. 227) of *c.* 180-260 A.D., now in the Provincial Museum at Bonn. Turning to comparatively modern times, we learn from the kind information of the Metropolitan Museum, New York, of a screw bolt fixed upon a suit of armor of the 15th century, there on exhibition. But who looks at a screw bolt to wonder how it was made or when and where it was invented, or to realize that the tools used to make it are hardly less interesting than the thing itself? Who taught its principle to the Turks and Arabs? Was it because the Chinese inventors of gunpowder and the gun missed it, that they used gunpowder rather to amuse people by fireworks, than to kill them, and failing to develop the gunlock and thereby the deadly gun, so long lost their battles with Western nations?

Closely allied to the ancient screw bolt, another wood-fastening, threaded device, now very common and conspicuous but rare and expensive before the 19th century, had, by that time, got into common use with carpenters and joiners, namely

THE WOOD SCREW OR SCREW NAIL
(Fig. 214)

This little iron shank, threaded for more than half its length, is equipped with a cross-slitted head sometimes convex-topped and flat-bottomed, but more often, as here shown, flat-topped and under-saucered, to countersink it to the surface level. Though made of metal (chiefly iron, but sometimes of brass), it is generally, in the United States ill-named wood screw, only because it firmly grasps a piece of wood when twisted into the yielding grain of the latter with a screw driver.

This unfortunate name, confusing

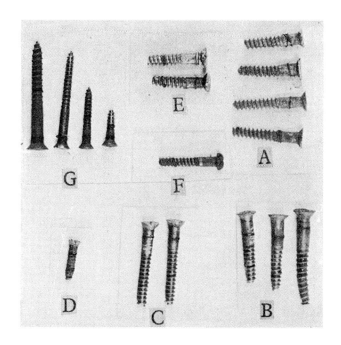

Fig. 214. Wood Screw or Screw Nail

A small, threaded, slit-topped shank of iron (sometimes of brass or other metal) with a flat-topped saucer-bottomed, or round-topped flat-bottomed head (F) which head is slit, and therefore twistable into wood with a screw driver.

Though made of metal and often called screw nail, it is also ill-named wood screw, only because it freely engages wood rather than metal, and hence unlike the metal penetrating screw or screw bolt, requires no threaded metallic hole to receive it. In the 18th century when made one by one, by hand-twisting the screw plate or die and die stock upon its shank, its threads were often finished to a penetrating spiral point with a file. But when made by machinery, in the early 19th century, (as described by Lardner, *Cabinet Encyclopedia*, "Metals," vol. 1, p. 199), though it appears frequently tapered, it was always, unless hand-filed, at the tip, blunt pointed, and therefore required a preliminary gimlet hole, until S'oan's patent superseded the machine-made blunt, with the machine-made pointed wood screw (G) in 1846.

The engraving shows specimens from old houses in Bucks County, Penna.

(A, B, C) Machine-made, pointless, of the early 19th century, before 1846.

(D) Pointless, from brass butt hinges of the door of an old cupboard, owned by the writer; made before 1776.

(E) Pointless, from old "Bartholomew's Tavern" (Colonial Inn with 19th century additions), Montgomery Square, Montgomery Co., Pa.

(F) Round-headed, pointless, wood screw, from broom-making machine in Bucks County Museum. Similar screws used on H L hinges of front doors at "Graeme Park," Montgomery County, Pa., built in 1728.

(G) Machine-made, pointed, wood screws of present type. They superseded the machine-made, pointless screw, after 1846.

As with the similar device used since the Middle Ages to penetrate and grasp metal, a most important feature of the wood screw was the above mentioned slot or kerf cut with a straight handled, metal saw, with wide blade of hard steel, stiffened with a back rib like the tenon saw (Fig. 132) called the screw-head saw in England in the early 19th century and described and illustrated by Holtzapffel, vol. 2, p. 723. Otherwise a knife-edged file, must have slit the convex or flat screw head, to engage the screw driver, described later.

Holtzapffel says that to avoid miscutting with this screw-head saw, the screw head, top-trimmed with a flat file, was often slightly kerfed (notched) with a triangular file, to start the saw cut.

According to Lardner, *Cabinet Encyclopedia*, "Metals," the circular saw had begun to supersede the above instrument for top-slitting wood screws in 1831.

it with the screws made of wood, previously described, obscures its history, which is further mixed up with that of the screw bolt, and the other very ancient metallic metal-worker's screw designed to penetrate and engage metal, and hence requiring a threaded metallic hole for its reception, as shown for 1588 in an engraving of a hand mill in the *Machine Book* of the Italian engineer Ramelli, reproduced by F. M. Feldhaus in *Technik der Vorzeit*, Fig. 484. As used to fasten locks to doors, Moxon notices the wood screw in his paper on "Smithing," published in 1678, but fails to describe it, and evidence for its pre-19th century method of manufacture seems almost entirely wanting. Nevertheless, we may guess that in Moxon's time, when rarely used, it would have been made, as he says the screw bolt was made, by hand, *i.e.,* from hand-swaged shanks, headed by blacksmiths, one by one, in the heading tool (Fig. 202) top-rimmed with a file, top-notched with a file or saw across the head, to engage the screw driver, held in a vise, and threaded by twisting upon said shank one or more threaded steel holes in the iron-worker's screw plate, as previously noted. (*cf.* Fig. 213.)

A hundred years afterwards, towards the end of the 18th century, we may infer, as in the case of the screw bolt, that this slow and expensive, direct hand-process had been generally superseded by hand machines, i.e., numerous lathe devices or hand-cranked, screw-threaded spindles, etc., alluded to by Holtzapffel, until a remarkable apparatus, illustrated and described by Lardner, *Cabinet Encyclopedia,* "Metals," Vol. 1, p. 199, clearly appears, in the early 19th century, as the

chief source of screw manufacture. This was a continuous-action mandrel lathe, axled on a guide screw, and which therefore, advancing as it revolves and clasping at one end the screw shank, threads the latter by twisting it through a knife-edged hole, or, more exactly, between two steel-cutting points compressible by a lever.

That this apparatus, worked by water or man-power in various forms, and another still simpler cylinder turned with a hand-crank, made most of the wood screws for the carpenter in the early 19th century, there can be little doubt.

Nevertheless, the screw so produced was conspicuously deficient in a very important feature, namely that it lacked a point. In other words while the wood screws of the early 18th and 19th centuries, above noted, however made, had been tapered to a sharp threaded point with a file or otherwise, these 19th century screws so much more rapidly machine-made, though often somewhat tapered in the shank, unless retouched by hand, were invariably blunt-ended, and would not, before 1846, penetrate wood without a previously bored or punched hole. Then, by United States Patent, No. 4704, August 20, 1846, T. J. Sloan, of New York, patented a machine to point them, after which, because, when thus pointed, they would more easily grasp the wood, and would screw into it after a hammer tap, they so universally superseded the pointless screw, that their sudden and novel presence, as part of its construction, would very closely date a house, as built after 1846.

These notes, together with the evidence of 18th century guns (one in the Doylestown Museum), with butt

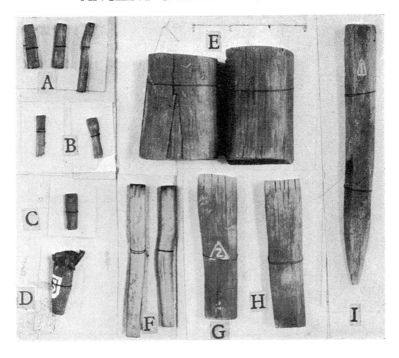

Fig. 215. The Wooden Peg

The typical pegs and parts of pegs here shown, removed from old wooden framework, have been rough cut with pocket knives and hatchets or chisels from sections of oak or soft wood, and driven tight, sometimes top-wedged, in previously bored holes. All were recently obtained and are 19th century Bucks County, Penna., relics of old houses, mills, barns and furniture.

(A) Right — from corner tenon of an old bedstead. (Oliver Holbain, Doylestown.)
(A) Left — 2 specimens from window frame at the Horn house, c. 1840, one mile northwest of Doylestown.
(B-left) From window sash of Horn dwelling house.
(B-right) From window sash of spring house at the Horn farm.
(C) From door panel of the Lovett house, near Pine Run, Bucks Co., Pa., two miles northwest of Doylestown.
(D) From a frame casing nailed upon a window frame of the Horn house.
(E) Sawed off ends of wedged trenails in the dismantled water wheel at Neeley's Mill, near New Hope, Bucks Co., Pa. From an axle framework holding the spokes of the wheel together.
(F) Probably from an old bedstead. (Oliver Holbain, Doylestown.)
G-H) From the corner of a window frame in the Horn house.
(I) Removed from the peak overlap of rafters in the barn at the Horn farm.
All except A and F obtained for the writer by William Woolsey, Doylestown, in 1926-7.

plates fastened by wood screws, quotations for 1622 and 1660 in the *New English Dictionary,* and several other guns, now in the Metropolitan Museum at New York, of the 16th and 17th centuries, indicate that the wood screw must have been continually employed in gun making. But they hardly carry us beyond Moxon's time. What of its earlier history, where books fail us and all depends upon rusty relics twenty centuries old? How unfortunate that the *Short Guide to the Silchester Collections,* describing the remarkable Roman smith's tools there dug up, should make no mention of the unique well-threaded, pointed, wood screw now (1928) on

Fig. 216. The Trunnel or Trenail

(A) Top corner, right, shows three of the large wooden pegs called trunnels, treenails or trenails, taken from the wreck, when the covered wooden bridge across Tohickon Creek, at Point Pleasant, Bucks Co., Pa., was pulled down in 1924. Mrs. Jacob Hahn, of Point Pleasant, now (1926) about 82 years old, who saved the pegs, says that she, as a child, saw them made in a peg cutter, resembling that shown in Fig. 96, in the wood opposite Abraham Meyers, on the turnpike to Doylestown, one mile west of Point Pleasant, when the bridge was built *c.* 1850.

(B) Lower corner, right, shows the trunnels penetrating planks in place, in a rescued, sawed off, section of the side-bracing of the bridge.

(C) Left, ditto, from the demolished Chalfont, Bucks Co. Bridge. Obtained by William Woolsey for the writer. None of these trunnels have been wedged, either inside or outside the perforated wood.

According to information to the writer, of Mr. Israel Snow, of I. L. Snow's shipyard, Rockland, Maine, August 29, 1925, the trunnels still used in 1925, in building wooden ships at said shipyard, are turned by machinery. They are generally made of locust wood, and are always split and wedged, to insure tight work, either at the outer end only,

exhibition at the Reading (Hampshire) Public Museum, or that no notes can be now found to prove whether this epoch-making relic was found in contact with the Roman tools or had been introduced among them in modern times. Its decisive evidence is lost. Not so with the singular iron-forked pulley-frame, ending in a tapered screw point, clearly intended to engage wood, found near the Roman soldiers' well at the citadel fort of the Saalburg, Germany, which may prove, according to Dr. Jacobi, its discoverer, that the Romans, who, after the first century, knew the screw as a metallic movable adjustment, used the same device for permanently engaging wood. (*cf.* F. M. Feldhaus, *Technik der Vorzeit,* Leipsig, 1914, article "Schraube.")

But many centuries passed before a single invention compelled its universal use by Anglo-American carpenters. This happened when the cast-iron butt door hinge was patented in 1775, by Izon and Whithurst, British Patent No. 1102, October 3, 1775, which device, mortised into the edges of doors, where nails would not clench, and nail head projections were not permissible, suddenly resulted in a universal demand for and use of the flat-headed variety of wood screw, although the convex-headed, slit-topped pattern continued to be employed for other purposes.

Far commoner with the 18th century carpenter than the rivet, screw bolt, or wood screw, was the

WOODEN PEG OR DOWEL (Fig. 215) the epigrus or ipirus of the Romans, noted, according to Rich, by Isodorus, Palladio, and Seneca, and used in ancient Egypt (*cf.* Wilkinson's *Ancient Egyptians,* London, 1854, Vol. 2, p. 114) for wood-pinning (dowelling) boards together.

Generally round, sometimes reinforced with glue, sometimes with wedges, described later, the peg or dowel was a headless, wooden, untapered rod from match to broom-stick size. It was roughly or carefully made with pocket knife, hatchet, chisel, draw knife or peg-cutter, and for tight-fitting cut larger than the round wooden hole invariably bored, drilled or punched to receive it. Though several recent furniture books fail to say so, it was continually employed, instead of the iron nail, by the Colonial joiner, who, in dowelling together table tops, inserted these concealed, wooden, headless pegs (dowels) in face-to-face holes bored across the releasable board joints, and though he would *nail* mouldings, legs and backs to chests, desks and cupboards, otherwise, fastened together all kinds of furniture, not with nails, but with these pegs and glue. So the cooper dowelled tight the heads of casks and so, also, the carpenter, though he preferred nails for floors, roofs, staircases, doors, skirtings, cornice mouldings, etc., sometimes reverted to pegs to shingle roofs, as at Ephraim Perkins' barn at Topsfield, Mass., found to be thus pegged when

or, if penetrating the plank, also on the inner end. The holes, auger-bored by hand, require great strength of arm and breast muscles to turn a 1⅜ inch double-lipped auger through oak or hard pine, and the trunnels are turned to fit the auger hole, as the auger gradually wears away because the trunnel must always exceed the hole by 1/16 of an inch for tight work.

Mr. Snow writes: "We have a number of old hand machines (resembling the peg cutter, Fig. 96) on hand, bought by us at old shipyard sales, but to-day everyone turns these trenails by power. In the Chesapeake and Delaware shipyards the builders shave their trenails by hand, thus getting a great deal better trenail, but taking more time to make it water tight. In Nova Scotia the old way was to use limbs off spruce trees."

re-shingled in 1886 (information George Francis Dow); to peg down barn floors (Eastburn barn, Bucks Co., Pa.); or, as all old houses and barns show, invariably used pegs to make wall and partition frames, to cross-lock rafters at the roof peak, to corner-lock window frames, peg door and window frames into log cabins, fasten cross-braces in wooden bridges (*cf.* Castle Valley Bridge, Bucks Co., Pa.) ,and in general to peg fast tenons in mortises. A large variety of the peg is here shown as the unrustable

TRUNNEL (Fig. 216)

otherwise called treenail and trenail, used often in heavy wooden framework, but most of all by the ship's carpenter, instead of iron nails to plank ship's frames. According to the information of Mr. Israel Snow, of Snow's shipyard (1925) at Rockland, Maine, and items in the U. S. Patent lists, it was sometimes, in the early 19th century, made by a hand apparatus, probably resembling the peg cutter (Fig. 96), but in Maine, in 1925, was turned in a lathe, generally from locust wood, by power-run machinery, and is always about 1/16 of an inch larger than the hole bored for it, by hand, with a 1⅜ inch auger. Sometimes, formerly, as in the old Delaware and Chesapeake shipyards, Mr. Snow says it was shaved by hand, and sometimes, in Nova Scotia, made of properly-sized, sawed-off boughs of spruce trees, but in all cases it was split and wedged to make water-tight work on the pounded outside end or water side of the ship's plank sheathing, or inside the latter, if the trunnel penetrated the wood.

If the peg and trunnel are tools, so is the wedge, for it was used, not only as a rough, often temporary makeshift, by the Colonial carpenter, but also thus systematically as a tightening reinforcement, to be driven into the exposed top, or bottom, of the peg, or trunnel (Fig. 210), by the ship carpenter, as noted, or by the cabinetmaker into the exposed end of the peg leg of a Windsor chair, or the projecting tenon of a Pennsylvania German chair-back or the projecting underbracket for an X-leg table. When the peg did not penetrate the wood, then as a "foxtail," that is a little loose sharp-edged block (*cf. Dictionary of Arts and Sciences*, Charles Knight), the wedge was inserted in a slit at the lower end of the peg, or trenail, so as to expand the latter when driven home into the bottom of a hole.

Another implement, no less a tool because made when used one hundred years ago, is

THE KEY (Fig. 217)

a long strip or batten bottom-flared with the grain and driven lengthwise into a bottom-flared channel cut to match it at right angles across the joints of boards, set side-by-side to prevent warping, often thus appearing as two conspicuous flanges on the underside of table tops, designed to clasp the frame, and hold down the top thereto by means of loose inthrusted wooden pins.

A little-noticed and rarer variety of the key was the loose

DOVETAIL KEY (Fig. 218)

again a warp check in the form of a small, thin, flat, rectangular block, flared laterally at both ends and mortised as before across the parallel joints of boards.

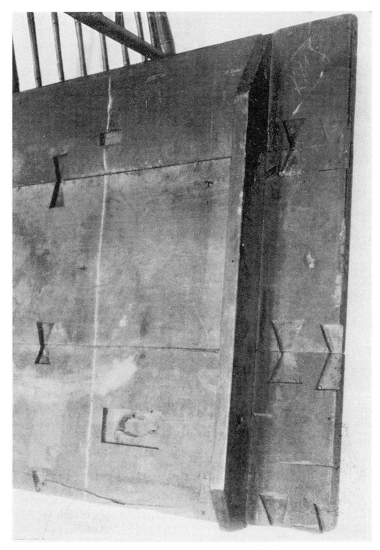

Fig. 217-218. Key and Dovetail Key

The picture shows the boards of a table top, given to the Bucks County Museum by Mr. W. E. Montague, typically held together by a long wooden strip or key (right), wedge-shaped in cross-section, driven so as to slide tight into a wedge-shaped channel, cut across the board ends. Two such keys at either end, form down-extending flanges which not only brace fast the top boards and stop warping, but enclose the table frame and are fixed thereto with removable wooden pegs.

Across the board-joints are seen the smaller, flat, double-fan-shaped sockets for thin wooden blocks (dovetail keys) flared at either end, and driven and glued or nailed therein. The sockets as seen are cut across the joints, on the under side of the table-top boards, less to brace them together, than to stop the cracks from warping open. All the dovetail keys for these sockets are missing except one at the upper right corner, which is held in place by five small nails.

The hull planks of the Egyptian grave-model funeral ship in the Chicago Museum of Fine Arts have been cross-keyed to check warping in this way.

Fig. 219. Carpenter's Glue Pot

The left specimen (No. 20251) shows a homemade glue pot of cast lead, without lid, with a handle made of thick iron wire, hooked through two opposite perforations in the upper rim. Lacking a double bottom it must have been warmed in a kettle of hot water to avoid melting. It was probably cast in the late 19th century, by Seth Nelson, mountaineer, hunter, trapper and artificer, at his remote mountain home, near Sinnamahoning, Cameron Co., Pa. from whom it was bought in 1925, by Col. H. W. Shoemaker.

The right specimen is a modern, store-bought triple-bottomed pot, made of thin cast iron. The glue is heated in the inner kettle by water boiled in the outer receptacles. It was bought from Charles Snyder, carpenter, of Plumsteadville, Bucks Co., Pa., among the carpenter tools inherited by him from his father, who had worked during the middle and late 19th century.

A hundred years ago we sometimes see it as here shown, on the underside of old table tops, and no doubt the contrivance can be traced backwards into the Middle Ages on European furniture. But who realizes that some of the ancient Egyptian ships, not clinker-built, and nailed or riveted together, like the Norse ships, were outwardly keyed, plank against plank, with these warp-checking, flat, wooden dovetails, as is proved by an Egyptian funeral ship, 31 feet, 9 inches long, 8 feet wide, and 4 feet deep, found near the Dashur Pyramids, about twenty miles from Cairo,

Egypt, and now on exhibition at the Chicago Museum of Fine Arts.

Since ancient times, glue, the Roman glutenum, and, as pictured at Thebes, in use by the ancient Egyptian veneer worker (*cf.* Wilkinson's *Ancient Egyptians*, London, 1854, Vol. 2, p. 114), prepared from the heads, hoofs, and bones of animals, had been a joiner's substitute for nails, pegs, and other wood fastening devices. Upon use, in the form of hard, dry, flakes, it had to be first softened over night by soaking, says Moxon, and then carefully boiled in

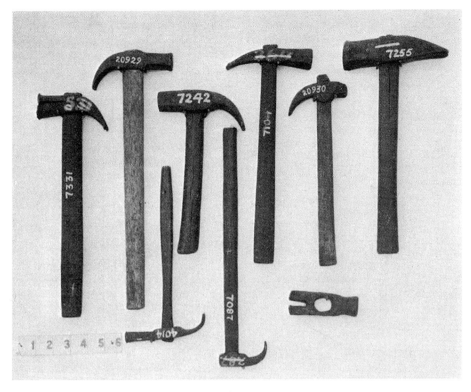

Fig. 220. Claw Hammers

Bought from waste iron dealers in Bucks County, between 1897 and 1925, the specimens, of varying size, shape and claw curve, are all hand-forged by country blacksmiths of the 19th or late 18th century. The old handles in Nos. 7242, 4014, 20930, and 7255 are original. No. 7255 was probably used by carpenters for heavy spike driving; the small specimens by cabinet makers. None show the deepened eye now (1926) universal on the factory-made claw hammer.

a clean skillet, from which it was poured into

THE CARPENTER'S GLUE POT

(Fig. 219)

an original, homemade example of which, constructed of lead for extra heat retention, as described by Moxon, is here shown, No. 20251. Still earlier than Moxon, in the *Probate Records of Essex County, Massachusetts, 1635-1681, 3 vols.*, George Francis Dow, editor. Salem, Mass., the *Essex Institute, 1916-1920*, the carpenter's glue pot is appraised at 1 shilling, in 1644, and at 1 shilling, 6 pence, in 1675. In these cases it seems unlikely that the glue pot could have

been made thus cheaply of expensive lead, neither could it have been double-bottomed, as described in *The Circle of Mechanical Arts*, by Martin, who, writing in 1813, says that the double-bottomed glue pot had just then come into use in England. The illustration also shows one such pot, factory-made, in three compartments, of cast-iron, enclosing an inner receptacle of heat-retaining alloy, of date about 1870, resembling in construction those now in use, in which the glue, in this inner kettle, escapes scorching by being heated by water boiled in the outer compartments.

Except the glue pot, the fastening

devices thus far described, because used but once, and because they leave the carpenter's hands and become part of his work, might not be considered as tools, but are here classed as such, since endlessly reproduced by or for the workman, they are continually employed in duplicate.

Look next at the less doubtful, incessantly-used instruments, which not thus passing out of his hands, have scattered his bench and helped fill his chest from time immemorial.

As conspicuous among these, we here show the carpenter's hammer which one hundred years ago, as now, appears in two distinct forms, the more familiar of which is the non-cutting nail-driving and nail-pulling

CLAW HAMMER (Fig. 220)

known to, if rarely used by, the Romans, with its reduced, generally rounded peen (poll) and unrivalled, very effective, down-curved claw which will pull with irresistible force the head of a partly-driven or bent or exposed nail, not already buried in the wood, or cornered out of its reach, in which case, as described later, unless the said nail head is pried or gouged upward or bared for the operation, the claw hammer becomes useless.

Books fail to follow the history of this efficient tool, which seems highly suggestive, not because it is a hammer, since all carpenters would use a hammer, but because no carpenter would need a nail pull on his hammer unless he used nails. Hence the writer is informed that in China, where pegs generally supplant nails, the claw hammer, though sometimes used as a hob-nail extractor by shoemakers,

does not appear as a carpenter's tool, and this fact would explain what the evidence further shows, that while the claw hammer becomes far more abundant in the 19th century, after the revolutionary multiplication of cut nails by machinery, (c. 1800), it seems to decrease in use as we look backward into the time when cheap pegs were common, and expensive hand-wrought nails were rare.

Its history is also obscured by the fact that the blacksmith had used it for centuries to pull off horseshoe nails in re-shoeing horses.

Without attempting to trace the tool to Pompeii, Egypt, or Assyria, in the elusive notices and confused tool groupings of Flinders Petrie's *Tools and Weapons,* the forgotten record of Rich, *Companion to the Latin Dictionary and Greek Lexicon,* Longmans, London, 1848, nevertheless clearly illustrates it as a Roman carpenter's tool, under the name martiolus, in a woodcut, copied from a stone carving on the tomb of a Roman carpenter.

Blummer *Technologie und Terminologie der Gewerbe und Kunst bei Greichen und Romern,* Leipsig, 1875, Vol. 2, p. 198, illustrates a very rare Roman specimen, about $5\frac{1}{2}$ inches long, which may be a smith's hammer, now at the Swiss National Museum in Zurich, which is here shown from a recent protograph, in the next illustration

A ROMAN CLAW HAMMER (Fig. 221)

And we also, by kind permission of the Provincial Museum at Treves (Trier), Germany, show another specimen,

Fig. 221. Roman Claw Hammer

The picture shows from two angles, one of the very rare surviving examples of a Roman claw hammer, now preserved at Zurich, in the Swiss National Museum, by whose kind permission it is here reproduced from an original photograph taken in 1927. It had been previously illustrated in a woodcut by Blumner, *Technologie und Terminologie der Gewerbe und Kunst bei Griechen und Romern*, Leipsig, 1875, vol. 2, p. 198.

A ROMAN CLAW HAMMER (Fig. 222) there on exhibition, and already illustrated by Albert Neuberger in *Die Technik des Alterthums*, Leipsig, 1919, p. 51. But ancient examples are either very rare or have escaped notice in books.

As to its later use in the Middle Ages, though old pictures and carvings, less and less often show the master tool, a few rare exceptions prove the fact. Mr. William N. Calver, of the New York Historical Society, informs the writer by letter June 7, 1926, that he has excavated in 1926, two "immense iron claw hammers, together with nails and spikes," at the Crusader's Castle of Montfort, in Northern Palestine, taken and destroyed by the Sultan Beyber, of Egypt, in 1271; and we need not be surprised to find several examples of it in an English manuscript painting of the early 13th century illustrating Noah building the Ark, shown by Dr. Brandt in his *Schaffende Arbeit*, Kroner, Leipsig, 1927, p. 240, or in Durer's *Melancholia*, of 1514, lying on the ground, or again, near a ladder, with a bow and buck saw, an axe, and nails, in Tintoretto's great painting of the Crucifixion (1565) at the School of San Rocco in Venice, or in Moxon's illustration of 1678. On the other hand, Diderot (1768) fails to show it, except for the "Farrier," and *The Circle of Mechanical Arts* only illustrates the carpenter's hammer, as shown in Figure 223, without a claw.

Living carpenters inform the writer that the disadvantage of the clawed

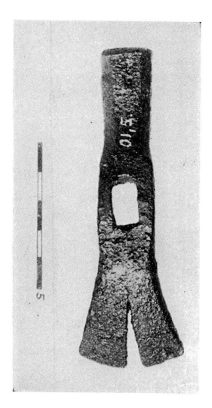

Fig. 222. Roman Claw Hammer

From an original Roman specimen. Kindly photographed for the writer by the Director of the Provincial
Museum at Treves, (Trier), Germany, where it is now
(1927) on exhibition.

*Fig. 223. Claw Hammer with
Reinforced Handle*

The specimen kindly photographed for the writer by
Mr. W. N. Calver, was found, buried together with a
hoard of axes and smith's tools, at Fort Ticonderoga, N.
Y., in 1924, and is now on exhibition at the museum
there. Two loose plates inserted in the eye and now
rusted fast in it, enclosing the original handle (now
gone), were fastened to the latter by two rivets, one of
which still shows. The writer has found an old home-
made adze reinforced in this way, and many recent
factory-made hammers appear to be thus constructed.
But in the latter cases, the reinforcing flanges are not
loose, but from solid, down-reaching extensions upon the
head.

instrument is the tendency of its handle to loosen in the eye, or worse still, break, as the result of continual nail wrenching. This accounts for a significant modern variation in its construction, namely that in all of the late 19th century factory-made claw hammers, the eye has been greatly deepened to meet this disadvantage, while in a few of the old home-made specimens constructed as shown in the next illustration,

THE CLAW HAMMER WITH REINFORCED HANDLE (Fig. 223)

found with a number of military axes and hatchets of date *c.* 1775, excavated at Fort Ticonderoga, and here photographed by kind permission of the museum there, the tool shows two strengthening iron tongues or flanges, as appear in Durer's picture, and again in Moxon's illustration, not forged fast upon the head, but riveted as separate plates upon either side of the handle, and inserted upon it through the eye, to prevent breakage.

Nevertheless, these supplementary iron braces, however constructed, are hard to replace if the handle breaks, and appear rarely on the old Pennsylvania tools. Yet, as if to prove that ancient blacksmiths preferred to occasionally produce them, rather than

Fig. 224. Carpenter's Riveting and Saw Hammer

The specimens in their original handles, all lacking claws, show wedge-shaped peens, for accurately spreading the ends of rivets. The middle hammer, with hand-worn handle, and the top smaller specimens, would have served to set the teeth of saws when the saw blade was held in a clamp (Figures 244 and 245) and its teeth bent alternately to right and left by careful blows with the peen. The iron head (4⅞ inches long) of a similar hammer, lacking claw, was recently excavated from the ruins of the Bull House, of Colonial date, at Providence, R. I. (Information of Mr. Albert H. Sonn.)

The top specimen was made about 1875, by Seth Nelson, mountaineer artificer, near Sinnamahoning, Pa. It and the heavy bottom specimen, also homemade, were obtained by Col. H. W. Shoemaker, of McElhattan, Pa., in 1925.

The two middle specimens were borrowed from a carpenter, Walter Flack, of Doylestown, who had inherited them from his father Oliver Flack, born 1825, died 1914.

deepen the hammer eye, in modern style, or that the old carpenter was in any case willing to get on without the deepened eye, the writer, who has rescued from the melting pot several old hammers and adzes thus handle-braced, has thus far failed to find any pre-19th century examples of the deep eye, above noted, now so universal on all claw hammers.

The other carpenter's hammer referred to and next shown, though also used to drive nails, is constructed not to pull them, but to fasten rivets and set saws. It may be called

THE CARPENTER'S RIVETING AND SAW HAMMER (Fig. 224)

Like the claw hammer, it consists of the pounding or driving face or poll, and the eye for the insertion of the wooden helve or handle. But the claw is replaced by a blunt iron wedge, set at right angles to the handle, called the peen, useful not only in spreading the heads of rivets, but also in setting saws by pounding their teeth alternately to the right and left, so as to ease the moving saw blade by widening its kerf.

Blumner, above cited (Vol. 2, p. 198), shows a Roman hammer about 5 inches long, of this construction, also at the Swiss National Museum, at Zurich. Carlo Ceci (cf. *Piccoli Bronzi*, above cited), shows another at the Naples Museum, from Pompeii, and several appear among the Roman tools dug up at the Saalburg citadel.

Moxon does not illustrate or describe the clawless instrument, which is also used by the metal worker and in other trades, but it appears frequently in German woodcuts of the 16th and 17th centuries, and it may be reasonably inferred that the armorers of the Middle Ages continually employed it, as here shown. Though the writer has not seen the riveting hammer of the modern Arabs, who make frequent use of the rivet in their hinges, pot handles and metal fastenings, the Chinese metal workers, who rivet their scissors, etc., have a similar hammer as photographed in China for the writer by Mr. R. P. Hommel; while *The Circle of Mechanical Arts,* as above noted, illustrates it alone as if no other carpenter's hammer existed in 1813, and abundant evidence of dated hinges found in place, proves that carpenters continually used it in Pennsylvania in attaching the wrought-iron strap hinges, previously shown, to outer house doors and shutters, until about 1850, and to barn doors until about 1890.

According to the information of Walter Flack, carpenter, of Doylestown (son of Oliver Flack, who died in 1914 aged 89), in this operation, the iron rivet, inserted through a hole in the door, bored to coincide with a drilled hole in the iron hinge strap, was held in place by an axe head pushed up under the rivet head by a second work-man, whereupon the malleable rivet point, projecting upward through the iron hinge-strap hole, was expanded by spreading blows with the face and peen of this hammer.

To continue the subject of tools used to fasten and unfasten woodwork, we should turn back to Figure 155, to look again at the mallet, there described, as used for driving the chisels, but also and oftener, a hundred years ago than now, as a fixing tool for driving the once universal wooden pegs, pins, and trunnels already noticed, and in large, two-hand form, the commander (Fig. 156), for driving stakes and pounding heavy framework into place.

THE SCREW DRIVER (Fig. 225)

sometimes called turn-screw, blacksmith-made until about 1840, and though an old, never a common tool, before the 19th century, is a variously-sized, flat blade of steel with rectangular flat working edge thinned on both sides for insertion into the slit, already described, as cut across the top of certain screws, so as to turn the latter into wood or metal.

Some screws have for centuries been turned by the leverage of rods thrust through their head holes; some with square heads by wrenches (Fig. 226); others as thumb screws, between a

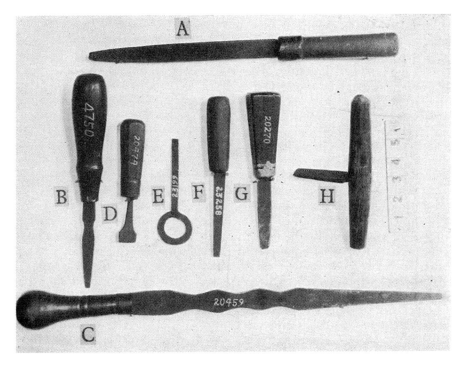

Fig. 225. The Screw Driver

The picture shows eight screw drivers all probably of the 19th century and all hand-forged by country black-smiths, except (B) (probably factory-made after 1850) found (except G) by the writer as old Bucks County farm shop relics. The square-handled specimen (G), No. 20270, with cast lead ferrule, was hand-forged from a "single cut" file about 1875, and worked in the 19th century by Seth Nelson, blacksmith and artificer, at his secluded mountain home, near Sinnamahoning, Cameron County, Pa. It was obtained from him for the Bucks County Museum by Col. H. W. Shoemaker, in 1925.

(D, E, F) Hand-forged by country blacksmiths, are country shop relics, found by the writer in Hilltown and Haycock Townships, Bucks Co., Pa., in 1925 and 1927; (D) with heavy iron ferrule and blade stamped "Wm. Greaver & Son. Cast Steel," in post-1850 letters had been probably worked out of another instrument; (B) with thin brass ferrule, probably factory-made, was bought at Mrs. Schussler's farm sale, near Plumsteadville, in 1917; (C) with blade handsomely forged from a single cut file, among many mill relics at Youngkin's saw mill, Haycock Township, in 1925; (A) ditto, was found in an old deposit of waste iron on E. A. Loux's farm at Hilltown in 1927; (H) with 8½ inch long cross handle, and blade 3¼ inches long and 1 inch wide, too wide for use upon common wood screws by carpenters, was used for releasing and fixing the heavy iron slit-topped screw bolts, called bed screws, used to fasten the rails to the posts of old 18th and 19th century four-post wooden beds.

In this adjustment, not described in the recent furniture books of Cescinsky, Lockwood, Lyon, etc., the 7-inch or more, releasable bolt, screwed through the bed post into the side rail with the grain, engages an iron nut, socketed under a concealing plug, in said side rail. The bed screw was often too tightly set for release by a common screw driver, hence the very powerful cross-handle, workable with two hands on this variety of the instrument. A duplicate was seen in use by Frank K. Swain, near Mechanicsville, Bucks Co., Pa., in 1891; another was made by himself for his own use, by David Gehman, Mennonite minister of Fountainville, about 1895. (Information of Frank K. Swain and David Gehman to the writer, December, 1927.) The specimen was presented to the Museum by V. E. Junette, who had obtained it from the widow of a tollgate keeper at Prospectville.

Though proof of its antiquity fails, the screw driver, as described in the text, must be inferred to be as old as the slit-topped screw for which it is indispensab'e, and hence common to many metal and wood working trades, but the evidence indicates that it was rarely used by the carpenter before the 19th century. It was and is generally worked by him with one hand, when placing the chisel-topped end of its blade in the cross-cut top-slit of an iron wood screw, he twists the instrument forward and backward, thereby inserting or withdrawing the screw.

Another now common form of this tool, not here shown, is an unhandled blade, turned by the carpenter in the bit stock or carpenter's brace (Figure 179) like the tools shown in Figure 181. How long it has been thus used, the writer has failed to learn.

man's thumb and forefinger, by means of fan-like projections, metal circlets or upcurls of the head. But the top of the iron so-called wood screw, or screw nail, of the carpenter, as before noted, whether round or flat, is still, and for an unknown time must have been, top-slitted for twisting, as now, with the common screw driver. Besides which the releasable screw bolt, called the bed screw, often seven inches long, slit-topped like a wood screw, engaging an iron nut concealed in the side rail of beds, used in the 18th and early 19th centuries, to fasten the rails to the posts of wooden bedsteads, had to be sometimes turned with a powerful cross-handled variety of the screw driver, shown in the illustration. But this wide-bladed, auger-handled screw driver is today a rarity, and whatever its antiquity and distribution, we may reasonably infer that until the sudden invention, in 1775, of the cast-iron butt-hinge, the now common screw driver would have been only rarely used by the old carpenter and cabinetmaker to fasten wrought-iron or brass locks, latches, or hinges, etc., that might have required these rare, flat-headed screws rather than nails or rivets.

The writer has failed to hear of any ancient Roman specimens, or to find any mediaeval pictures of the screw driver, as used in other trades, much less by the carpenter, or notices of it in old books or by modern mechanical writers, who, like the gun historians who omit the bullet mould, seem to have conspired to ignore it. Flinders Petrie makes no mention of it in *Tools and Weapons;* neither does the *Probate Records of Essex County, Massachusetts, 1635-1681, 3 vols., George Francis Dow, editor.*

Salem, Mass., the Essex Institute, 1916-1920. Diderot (1768) pictures it (the "tourne vis") for the ebeniste, and mentions it for the gunsmith, but not for the carpenter or joiner, and we find no English quotations for the name screw driver, in the *New English Dictionary,* earlier than 1812, or for turn screw, than 1801. Nevertheless, the hand and factory specimens here shown, though modern in make, must be old in type, and though Moxon overlooks it, it must have existed in 1688, because the wood screw or screw nail, which he mentions as a door lock fastening, inferably slit-topped, and vouched for by words in the same dictionary in 1622, 1660 and 1678, would have been impossible without it.

As a companion to the screw driver,

THE WRENCH (Fig. 226) though generally associated with the blacksmith and metal work, or with the wheelwright, shipwright, gunsmith, etc., may also be called a carpenter's tool. This is because, since the mid-19th century, at least, the carpenter sometimes, in house and barn building, particularly in the hanging of heavy door hinges, used, in place of the common rivet, the screw bolt, which, in many cases, as previously described, would require a wrench.

As we have seen, a screw if its head is slit, may be turned with a screw driver, if ring-topped, up-curled or top-twisted, with the human thumb and forefingers, or if perforated, with a makeshift iron rod. But the block head, or block nut of a screw bolt, generally a plain rectangle, requires a lever (the wrench, as here shown) ending in one or more notches or square holes, for the twisting opera-

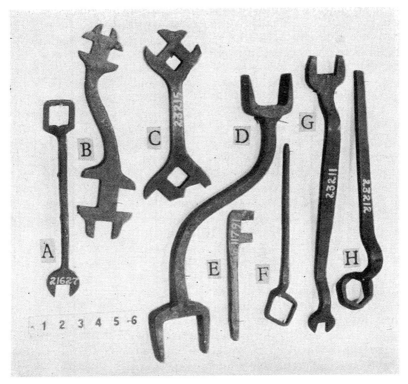

Fig. 226. The Wrench

The stout strips of iron from 6 to 10 inches long, equipped at one end or both ends with one or more rectangular notches (A, B, C) sometimes (A, C, F) expanding into a rectangular hole, are adapted to fit and twist the rectangular nut on a screw bolt or the screw cap or nut supplanting the linch pin on the ends of wagon axles.

(A) and (B) obtained from Heath, junk dealer, of Warrington, Bucks Co., Pa., and (C) of E. Loux, Hilltown, in 1927, are of cast iron. Store bought and factory-made, as here shown, they represent the type common after about 1850.

The others of wrought-iron, hand-forged by country blacksmiths, are all Bucks County farm and shop relics, bought by the writer in 1926 and 1927, except (E) No. 11791, also of wrought-iron, hand-forged, about 1916, by R. D. Roberts, blacksmith, of Big Laurel, North Carolina.

The *Probate Records of Essex County, Massachusetts, 1635-1681, 3 vols., George Francis Dow, editor. Salem, Mass., the Essex Institute 1916-1920,* does not mention the word spanner as a synonym for wrench, and only once notes, the word wrench in 1646, in an inventory, along with blacksmith's tools,—"1 wrench for breech pl."

The word spanner, in this sense, is first quoted for 1790, in the *New English Dictionary.*

Much evidence shows that in the 18th and early 19th centuries wrenches were generally made of wrought-iron and chiefly confined to the use of mechanics, but that after the middle of the 19th century the substitution of screw caps, constructed like bolt nuts, in place of linch pins, on wagon axles, and the introduction of agricultural machinery, resulted in the universal use of wrenches, generally factory-made of cast-iron and sold at country stores, as among the farmers' most necessary tools.

tion. The evidence shows that these wrenches, straight- or angle-handled or S-shaped, often notched or square holed at one or both ends, were homemade, of wrought-iron, by the American blacksmith, in the 18th and early 19th century, but after 1840, by factories, and often, as an exception to all the carpenters' tools here considered, except the glue pot, of cast iron, which circumstance justifies us in here pausing to reflect upon a fact which had not hitherto concerned our study, namely that the art of casting iron, well known to the Chinese, if not to the Romans, was forgotten in the Middle Ages, and reintroduced into Europe in the 15th century; that thereafter, owing to the difficulty of constructing proper moulds in clay or sand, it was, for about three hundred years, confined to the casting of large massive objects, such as cannon, pillars, grave slabs, stove plates, fire backs, etc., until by the middle of the 18th century, Abraham Darby had perfected the art of holding together impressions (moulds) stamped in sand, by means of boxes called flasks. (*cf*. Knights' *A m e r i c a n Mechanical Dictionary*, article "Casting").

This resulted first in the widespread, cheap production of pots, domestic utensils and small objects not subjected to much strain or shock, and finally, in the early 19th century, turned to the complex framework, cog wheels and apparatus of steam-run machinery, but never, owing to the brittleness of cast-iron, to the manufacture of edged tools.

The so-called cast steel, invented in England, by Huntsman, about 1770, and not perfected in the United States (according to H. M. Swank), until *c*. 1850, is no exception to the rule, since, in this case, the misleading term "cast," applies only to the perfection of the raw material, and not to its final shaping. In other words, that the label cast steel stamped upon a blade or tool, indicates that said blade, has been cast, not into the form so stamped, but only into a preliminary ingot, and thereafter made malleable by hammering into said shape.

But to return to the wrench—why have archaeologists paid so little attention to this instrument, which,

though found alone, would no less certainly prove the contemporary existence of a highly important step in the history of mechanical industry, namely the screw, than a claw hammer would prove the nail?

Diderot (1768) shows it (square-holed—not notched) for the blacksmith and farrier. The *Probate Records of Essex County, Massachusetts, 1635-1681, 3 vols., George Francis Dow, editor. Salem, Mass., the Essex Institute, 1916-1920,* only once mentions the word (in 1646), in an inventory along with blacksmith tools —"one wrench for breech plate," and the *New English Dictionary* quotes the word spanner, as a synonym for wrench, first in 1790.

F. M. Feldhaus in his very valuable recent handbook of ancient tools, *Technik der Vorzeit,* Leipsig, 1914, article "Fraser," illustrates (from the *Book of Machines* of the Italian engineer Ramelli, of 1588) two ornate hand wrenches used for twisting square nuts to tighten the jaws of a pipe clamp, and we learn from the Metropolitan Museum, New York, that one of their suits of armor, inferably of the 15th century, shows a screw bolt, useless without a wrench, as one of its plate fastenings. But to go back many centuries, the same work by Feldhaus (article "Schraube") shows a woodcut of a square, Roman, threaded bolt nut, $1\frac{5}{8}$ inches square by $\frac{5}{8}$ inches thick, of iron, now (1928) preserved in the Provincial Museum at Bonn, as a unique relic of the first or second century A.D. By kind permission of the Director, we here show it in the next engraving,

A ROMAN BOLT NUT (Fig. 227) taken from a photograph made directly from the original in March, 1928.

Fig. 227. Roman Bolt Nut

This unique, wrought-iron block, perforated with a hole, threaded to engage the shank of an iron bolt, therefore a bolt nut, proving the use of the screw bolt and bolt wrench by the Romans, has been already illustrated by F. M. Feldhaus, *cf. Technik der Vorzeit*, article "Schraube." It was excavated between 1893 and 1900 with other Roman relics, of date, *c.* 180 to 260 A.D. at the Roman fortified boundary ("Limes") at Niederbieber, near Neuwied, Nassau, Germany, and is now on exhibition (catalogued E, 285) at the Provincial Museum at Bonn. It was photographed at the Museum at two angles from the original, March, 1828, and is here shown by kind permission of the Directors, Doctors Lehner and Hagen.

But how much more does its nineteen hundred years of existence mean than the fact that it would have required a wrench? Can we reflect upon the construction of machines, ancient or modern, without wondering whether any Roman relic less conspicuous or more significant has been thus far found and preserved in any museum?

The next picture,

THE SCREW WRENCH (Fig. 228) for comparison, illustrates one of the now universal factory-made monkey wrenches, so called since about 1860, continually used by carpenters, in which the single jaw sliding against the hammer-shaped head, is adjusted by a handle screw to fit any nut, and which began to supplant the common wrench, as a carpenter's tool, when a sliding jaw, at first adjustable by a wedge, as shown, later by a screw, in various forms, was patented in the United States, under the name screw wrench, in 1835, and 1839, and six times in the 1840's.

This completes the list of fastening tools, and brings us to another class of instruments hardly less important, used for pulling to pieces or unfastening work already constructed. These are well represented by a powerful variant of the claw on the claw hammer, which has already been described and illustrated as a variously pointed instrument called

THE CROW (Fig. 51)

now generally known as crow bar, a name not appearing in the *New English Dictionary* earlier than the 19th century, in some forms of which a heavy, up-curled fork, ending in a massive iron bar, serves not only to pry up ponderous weights, but also to pull spikes, provided the latter are sufficiently exposed to meet its grasp.

Carlo Ceci in *Piccoli Bronzi del Real Museo Borbonico,* Naples, 1858, illustrates two iron crow bars from Pompeii, one with the notched up-bent claw and another with a flat ovate unbent working point.

Moxon (1678) who illustrates it (Fig. 51) with its claw, describes it as a carpenter's lever, pressed over a stick-of-wood-fulcrum, to prize up heavy timbers; but neither he nor

The Circle of Mechanical Arts (1813), which pictures it, nor *A New and Complete Dictionary of the Arts and Sciences by a Society of Gentlemen,* 2nd edition, London, W. Owen, 1763, nor Rees' *Cyclopaedia,* of about 1800, which describes it as an iron lever, with a claw at one end, and a point at the other, for purchasing great weights, say anything of its use for spike pulling. Neither does the *New English Dictionary,* which describes it as a lever or prizing tool equipped not with a claw, but slightly bent-up beak, and named "crow" as early as 1400, 1458, 1555, etc.

The ring-ended crow used by carpenters in the 19th century, particularly adapted for spike and bolt pulling, and also shown in Figure 51, seems to complicate the question, until we learn, according to the *Domestic Encyclopedia,* by A. F. M. Willich, 1st American Edition, Philadelphia, 1803, as kindly found for the writer by Mr. Joseph E. Sanford, that the latter tool was invented by William Rich, of Yalding, Kent, about 1787.

Many modern, so-called crow bars now in use in quarries and mines, and on farms and railroads, are double ended, that is, show a flat, chisel-shaped point at one end, without said upcurl, and a round point at the other, and this conflict of names, shapes, and definitions confuses us, for we realize that the crow, if clawed, is not only a lever, but a spike pull, and hence, archaeologically testifies to the existence of spikes, while if not clawed, it is only a lever and not a spike pull.

Shall we therefore refer the name crow, associating the instrument with the celebrated bird, since the year 1400, to the unnotched upcurl above

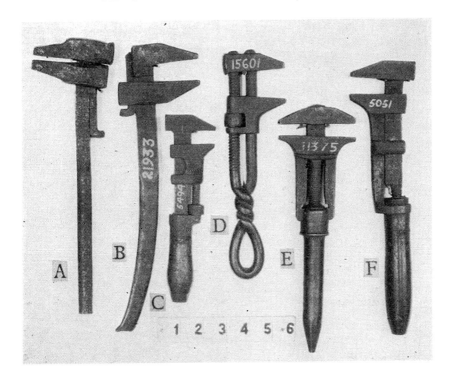

Fig. 228. The Screw Wrench

This very efficient, comparatively modern, adjustable instrument, now (1927) called monkey wrench, is here shown (C, D, E, F) in four of its numerous late factory-made, 19th century varieties, in which a jaw or chop (double ended in [E], slides up on a screw-threaded shank, so as, by varying the tool's grasp, to engage and twist various-sized rectangular nuts upon iron screw bolts. The make up of these four tools, beyond the skill of the common blacksmith, at once betrays their factory origin.

(A) and (B) represent early 19th century, iron, hand-forged attempts to produce the same adjustable grasp, by means of an iron wedge, driven against the sliding lower jaw. (A) bought in 1927, from Miss L. A. Swartz of Point Pleasant, Bucks Co., Pa., was used by her father, a wheelwright, about the time the Delaware Canal was opened in 1832. (B) bought from George Stong, Spring House, Montgomery Co., Pa., in 1926, shows the initials "W. S." in early 19th century style, rudely dotted and chisel-cut, on its lower front, jaw-side, scarcely seen in the engraving.

The idea in various forms was patented in the United States under the name "Screw Wrench," in 1835 and 1839, and six times in the 1840's as "Screw Wrench and Hammer," on May 29, 1866, to L. S. and E. G. Hoyt, of Croton Falls, New York; and as "Monkey Wrench." twice, in 1869, which term, according to the *New English Dictionary*, is used in 1858, in Simmond's *Dictionary of Trades*.

The right specimen was photographed in 1925 through the kind help of Mr. Howard M. Chapin from a specimen in the Museum of the Rhode Island Historical Society at Providence, R. I.

mentioned, as typifying the bird's beak or to the notched upcurl as denoting its claw? And when, in pre-Roman times, did a claw fixed upon the end of an iron hand lever, first adapt it to the carpenter's use?

Diderot throws no further modern light on the subject in 1768, when he illustrates the instrument as a carpenter's tool, both with and without the claw.

A small variety of this device is shown in the next illustration as

THE CLAW (Fig. 229)

a much lighter, shorter bar of iron, sometimes straight, sometimes bent

Fig. 229. The Claw

These old Bucks County specimens, hand-forged by country blacksmiths in the early 19th or late 18th century, with single or double, or back-curved claws (left), were used rather for special spike pulling than like the heavier crow (Fig. 51) for weight uplifting, but are still too heavy to compete with the claw hammer for common nail pulling.

The claw, No. 7671 (left), for pulling heavy nails and spikes, was named goat's foot. It was bought Oct. 23, 1899, of Andrew Stear, Dublin, Bucks Co., Pa No. 4748. for opening boxes etc., was bought May 4, 1916, by Abraham Poulton at the sale of Mrs. Samuel Schisster, Plumsteadville, Pa. No. 20954 (right) was bought by the writer in September, 1925, from Heath, a junk dealer, near Hartsville, Pa.

into a semi-circle at one end, always clawed, either at one or both ends, as shown, adapted to spike pulling rather than to weight uplifting, but still too heavy to be carried about for the pulling of common nails, and therefore as a substitute for the claw hammer.

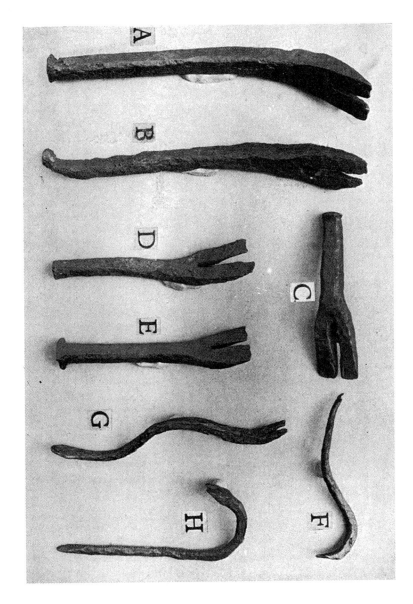

Fig. 230. Roman Carpenter's Claws

These eight well-preserved, wrought-iron specimens, two thousand years old, were excavated since c. 1880, at the Saalburg citadel, on the ancient Roman wall near Homburg, Hesse, Germany, and are now on exhibition at the Museum there. Six of them, A, B, C, D, E and H, resemble in construction the typical 18th century specimens shown in Figure 229. A and B are about 18 inches long.

They were photographed in 1927 and are here shown by kind permission of Dr. H. Jacobi Director of the Saalburg Museum.

Fig. 231. Hatchet Nail Pull

(A) Shows an old homemade shingling hatchet of the early 19th or late 18th century, with its characteristic nail pull, a notch in the lower blade margin, bought from Patrick Trainor, waste iron merchant, Doylestown, July 7, 1898.

(B) Shows the badly engraved nail pull, reproduced from Moxon's picture of 1678, similarly placed in an English plasterer's hatchet of the 17th century.

(C) Shows a double nail pull on the margin of a heavy hatchet or hand axe of date c. 1776, with spiked poll, ploughed up by a farmer near Fort Ticonderoga, New York, now (1927) in the Museum there and kindly photographed for the writer by W. L. Calver.

That this spike-pulling tool was known to the Romans, is well proved by the next picture,

THE ROMAN CARPENTER'S CLAW
(Fig. 230)

showing eight similar ancient specimens of about the 1st to 3d centuries, A.D., found at the Saalburg Roman fort, near Homburg, Hesse, Germany, and now on exhibition at the Museum there.

Far less efficient and familiar, and probably much more modern, is another device, known to the carpenter of the 18th century, namely,

THE HATCHET NAIL PULL
(Fig. 231)

now a universal equipment of his conspicuous hatchet, which hatchet has been already described in its shingling and lathing forms (Figures 84 and 85). Like the claw hammer, the hatchet drives nails, but unlike the latter, also cuts wood, and it is the latter advantage that probably gives it its popularity, rather than this clumsy nail-pull notch on the lower blade margin, as here shown, which is out of the line of leverage, and far

Fig. 232. Pincers

These old East Pennsylvania, hand-forged specimens all show wide, close-fitting, sharp-edged jaws, but vary in the make of their lower handle ends, *i.e.*, double knobbed, single knobbed, with plain (No. 20594) or clawed (No. 5041) pry-points, for use as described in the text. The pry points, plain or clawed, photographed sideways, do not show in the picture. Any of these tools could have been used by farrier-blacksmiths for pulling hoof nails in reshoeing horses or oxen.

less powerful and efficient than the claw of the claw hammer.

As to the origin or history of this now characteristic nail notch, the writer has found little evidence, except that scantily presented in the illustration herewith shown, and already discussed under Figures 84 and 85, namely, that Moxon's picture, here reproduced, would indicate that it is not an American invention; further, that it was rare and not clearly developed on American hatchets before the early 19th century, and that it became common on home-made hatchets between 1800 and 1840, and universal on factory-made hatchets thereafter.

Omitting as a possible piece of blacksmith's decoration, a picture in Diderot ("Charpente," Plate 50, Fig. 34), showing a French carpenter's hatchet (1768) with a corner-notched shoulder on the under blade margin near the handle, the illustration shows (B) Moxon's picture of a lathing hatchet, with a badly engraved nail pull, as used by the English plasterer and bricklayer of 1678; (C) a peculiar, acute-angled, double-notch marking the lower blade margin of an axe with spiked poll, (probably used where found as a military tool), of date about 1776, ploughed up on a farm near Fort Ticonderoga, New York, and now in the Museum there; and (A) an old Bucks County, Pa., notch-bladed, homemade shingling hatchet, representing the large class of shingling and lathing tools of the late 18th and early 19th centuries, thus notched.

While the hatchet as a single tool effects three uses, because it cuts, pounds and unfastens, the next instrument described,

THE PINCERS (Fig. 232) is devoted to only one use, namely, unfastening. This smith-forged tool is equipped with two wide, close-fitting, sharp-edged, jaws, working on a rivet between two handles, which will seize with herculean bite, and pry up, by side or fore-and-back leverage, not only projecting nails and pegs, but also such broken nail stumps, headless brads, tin and wire ends, etc., as the rigid fork of the claw hammer or crow would slip upon.

Abundant evidence shows that in the 18th century it was by no means a special or exclusive carpenter's tool, but used in many trades, particularly by the blacksmith, and by the farrier for pulling hoof-nails in reshoeing horses or oxen; and in attempting to trace back its history, it is necessary to distinguish it from the tongs, tweezers, callipers, forceps, etc., of the blacksmith, shoemaker, gunsmith, watchmaker, turner, doctor, etc., constructed on the same principle, but with different jaws for different purposes. As here shown, one author says that none seem to be known of Roman age, even from Pompeii (Flinders Petrie, *Tools and Weapons*), while another, Neuberger, illustrates in a very small cut what looks like a pair of pincers among the Roman blacksmith tools at Trier, Germany *(Die Technik des Alterthums, p. 51)*.

But highly interesting, conclusive evidence on the subject is furnished by the next illustration,

ROMAN PINCERS (Fig. 233) which shows (c) a clear photograph of the last named original iron specimen now (1927) in the Provincial Museum at Trier, and (A, B) two plaster casts of two unmistakable iron pincers of familiar modern form found at Ober Aden, Lippe, and Weltheim, Westphalia, Germany. The originals of these two latter, rare relics of the 1st and 2d centuries, A.D., kindly photographed for the writer by Dr. H. Jacobi, of the Saalburg Museum, are now in the Museum at Dortmund.

Centuries pass before we find the instrument clearly figured among carpenter's tools in *The Circle of Mechanical Arts,* 1813, and though Moxon does not show or name it as a carpenter's tool in 1678, the word "Pincers" is quoted, without clue as to trade, in the *New English Dictionary,* for the years 1371 and 1410, and five times in the 16th century, while the *Probate*

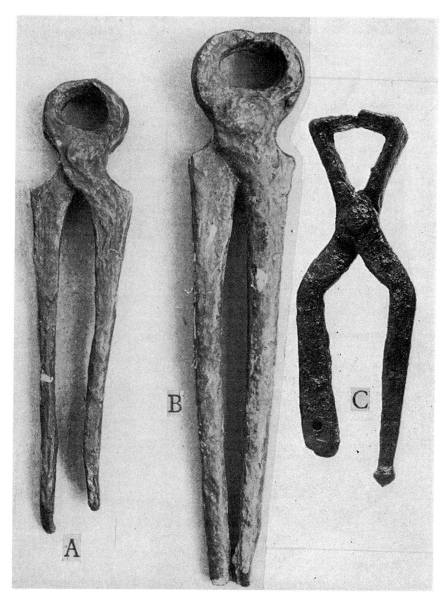

Fig. 233. Roman Pincers

These very rare examples of Roman pincers were found at Roman camp sites in Germany. (A) 18 centimetres long, of the time of Augustus (1st century, A.D.), at Ober Aden, on the Lippe; (B) 22 centimetres long, of the 2d to 3d century, A.D., at Weltheim, Westphalia. The two left specimens here shown, were kindly photographed for the writer by Dr. H. Jacobi, Director of the Saalburg Museum, from plaster casts now on exhibition there. The originals are in the Museum at Dortmund. (C) Shows an original Roman specimen of iron. Kindly photographed for the writer by the Director of the Provincial Museum at Trier (Treves), where it is now (1928) on exhibition.

Records of Essex County, Massachusetts, 1635-1681, 3 vols., George Francis Dow, editor. Salem, Mass., the Essex Institute, 1916-1920, many times lists the names "Pinchers," "Pincers," and "a pair of Pinchers," with carpenter's tools, in old New England inventories of the 17th century, between 1635 and 1681. Diderot, in 1768, illustrates it, in the shape here shown, as a tool of the gardener, beltmaker (centurier), ebeniste, boxmaker (layettier), blacksmith (serrurier), farrier (marechal ferrant), and for the cabinetmaker (menusier), in the latter case with an apparently sharpened, inbent spur on the bottom of each handle.

At this point we should pause a moment to again realize that neither the pincers nor the claw hammer, crow, claw or hatchet nail-pull will work on buried or otherwise obstructed metallic points, unless the carpenter, in some way, lays them bare, hence this master tool, common to many trades, as shown in one of the specimens in Fig. 232, is and was often equipped with a small claw at the end of one of its handles for the purpose of using the instrument like a chisel, when, by pressure, or hammering on the jaw top, the carpenter gouges around, or pries up the buried or obstructed point of seizure.

To end our list of this class of tools, we show three old 18th or 19th century examples of the carpenter's

RIPPING CHISEL (Fig. 234, A. B. C.) as Moxon calls it, with broad, un-basilled blade, and socket for its missing handle, used with a mallet, in demolishing work, not as a true chisel, but as a wedge to start open seams, cut through nail or peg shanks, and force apart pieces of wood nailed, glued, or pegged together. The same illustration shows the more modern, late 19th century blacksmith-made

NAIL CUTTER (Fig. 234 D.) lacking a wooden handle. Another variety often forged since about 1860 for the American carpenter out of one of the plates of a steel wagon spring, but not here shown, was driven with a hatchet, for the same purpose.

Tools for Sharpening

THIS brings us to the end of the tools of the ancient carpenter under consideration, regarded from the point of view of their direct final use. But it does not properly end the subject if we forget the hardly less important sharpening instruments, which as a class, though not the special tools of the carpenter, but pertaining to many other trades, were formerly, and are still, used by carpenters and joiners to keep their tools in edge, and without which their axes, adzes, chisels, saws, augers, planes, etc., would soon become utterly useless. One of the most necessary of these invaluable sharpening devices is

THE GRINDSTONE (Fig. 235)

a heavy disc of fine-grained, specially quarried sandstone, revolving vertically on a wooden frame, and generally worked by two men, one turning a crank and pouring water on the stone, while the other holds the tool very slightly tilted upon the revolving stone circumference.

The illustration shows a factory-made specimen, probably of late 19th century date, with its homemade wooden crank and axle sockets, mounted in primitive pioneer style on a forked tree, obtained by the writer near Revere, northern Bucks Co., Pa., c. 1918.

Charles Holtzapffel, writing in 1830 (*Turning and Mechanical Manipulation,* Vol. 3, p. 1128), says that grindstones of from twenty to forty inches in diameter, or heavy enough to give the required momentum, could be worked by one man with a foot treadle cranked directly on their axle, while if smaller, *i.e.,* from twelve to eighteen inches in diameter, would require either an extra man to turn them with a crank, or if treadled, a flywheel.

Some tools, he says, were sometimes, as by English cutlers, sharpened dry on the grindstone, but as a rule, it was as necessary to apply water to the revolving disc as to drop oil on the whetstone, described later.

Where two men work, the grinder, as noted, pours water on the stone's revolving circumference, from a can held in his right hand. In other cases, a single-treddling workman contrives to have the water dribble from a spigotted water can or tank, or oftener (1928) as a cheap makeshift, through a punctured tin can suspended on a stick over it. In others, the stone skims the water in an adjustable trough, swinging on a rope or chain, under its lowest diameter, which trough can be dropped below the stone to avoid softening, when not in use.

A grindstone apparently thus axled over a water trough, turned by one man with a crank while another sharpens a sword held flat upon its periphery, clearly appears in the *Psalter of Eadwine,* of the 12th century, now in the Library of Trinity College, Cambridge, England, as illustrated by Prof. Dr. Paul Brandt in *Schaffende Arbeit und Bildene Kunst,*

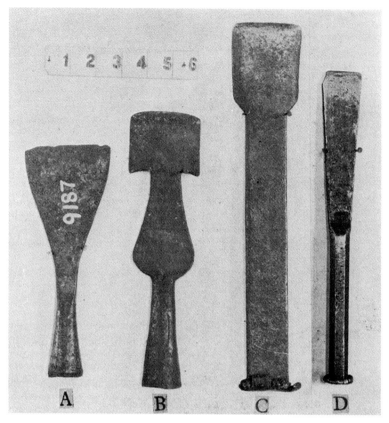

Fig. 234. Ripping Chisel and Nail Cutter

(A) Bought from a Philadelphia antique dealer. Dec. 17, 1908; shows a broad, flaring, blacksmith-forged blade with socket for a wooden handle (missing) of type used with a hammer or mallet, by 18th century carpenters, for ripping apart pieces of wood nailed together, as described by Moxon and in the text.

(B) Ditto, with barbs for back-pull on nail shanks; bought from Henry Worthington, antique dealer, in Doylestown, in 1911.

(C) Ditto, with square, bevel-sided blade; made to work without a wooden handle.

(D) A modern, light, 19th century, factory-made tool, now called a nail cutter, made without wooden handle, now used at the Bucks County Museum, for the same purpose.

Carpenters in the 19th century often had their ripping chisels without wooden handles, made for them, by local blacksmiths, from the steel plates of the springs of demolished wagons. Information of David Angeny, carpenter, of Danboro, Bucks Co., to the writer, in 1925.

Kroner, Leipsig, 1927, Vol. I, p. 216. Feldhaus shows a man turning a foot treadle to sharpen a knife without water on a stationary grindstone, from an engraving of 1485 by Israel Van Meckenen. The *New English Dictionary* dates the apparatus by quotations for the years 1404, 1475, 1573, and 1594, and Captain John Smith speaks of the Chief Powhatan asking him for a grindstone, at Jamestown, Va., in 1607 (*cf. General History of Virginia, New England and the Summer Isles,* III, p. 49; Reprint, James MeLehose, Glasgow, 1907), and again notes a "grindstone or two," as among the needed stores of a ship properly equipped to found an American Colony in 1623, VI, p. 245.

The *Probate Records of Essex County, Massachusetts, 1635-1681, 3 vols., George Francis Dow, editor. Salem, Mass., the Essex Institute, 1916-1920,* between 1635 and 1681, and Bishop's *History of American Manufacturers,* show that grindstones were imported probably first from England and later from Nova Scotia, into the American Colonies, from the time of the earliest settlement, and until American quarried grindstones (factory made at Berea, Ohio, and elsewhere, in the 19th century), generally superseded them, about 1840.

As shown in a celebrated painting by David Teniers, the younger, now in the Louvre, also in Hogarth's laughable print of the enraged musician, the man-turned grindstone, either mounted on a wheelbarrow, or in the form of a large four-legged stool, carried on the back, has been long in use in Europe and America by itinerant knife and scissors grinders, who advertise their coming, in Spain, by elusive notes on pan-pipes of reed or metal, and sometimes, in America by the ringing of a bell, and now, as these old tools are being replaced (in Philadelphia) by gas or electric apparatus, the writer has just bought one of the last of them, from an I t a l i a n-American Philadelphia street grinder, in December, 1926.

To reflect a moment upon the immense efficiency and importance of this revolving sandstone wheel, for sharpening edged-tools, is to wonder at the scanty mention given it by old writers. Yet whoever would describe carpenter's tools without it, only follows the example of histories of architecture, that leave out bricks and stone; of guns, that omit bullet moulds; of ships, that ignore trenails;

of furniture, that leave out pegs; or of descriptions of the decorations of the Alhambra, that overlook plaster of Paris. *Pliny,* H. N. XXXVI - 47, and *Horace Odes,* 2-8-15, briefly refer to a stone called "Cos," used by the Romans for sharpening metallic implements, without explaining whether it is a flat rub-stone (whet-stone) or a revolving stone disc, and if, as suggested by F. M. Feldhaus, in *Technik der Vorzeit* (article "Schleifstein") all evidence of the knowledge of Roman revolving grindstones or foot-treadles rests on one picture, then the next illustration,

A ROMAN GRINDSTONE (Fig. 236) is of unique interest.

The little design appears among the engraved gems in Plate 99 of *Gemmae Antiquae Figuratae,* by the French Antiquary, Michel Ange de la Chausse, published in Rome in 1703, and is copied therefrom by Father Montfaucon in his celebrated work, *Monuments of Antiquity Explained and Represented in Sculptures,* translated into English by David Humphries of Trinity College, Cambridge, London, Tonson and Watts, 1722, Book 3, Plate 58, Figure 7. One hundred and fifty years later, Rich (1848) in his *Companion to the Latin Dictionary and Greek Lexicon,* above noted, shows it without naming his authority. It also appears in Dean Milman's *Horace* (1853). But Feldhaus supposes the gem to be a forgery "ein wohl gefalschtes gemme," and Daremberg and Saglio (*cf. Dictionary des Antiquites Greques et Romaines,* Paris, Hachette, 1877), under the word "Cos," fearing to illustrate the design, say of this picture, "we do not reproduce here an engraved stone, the antiquity of which is at least suspected, which shows us Cupid sharpening his

Fig. 235. Grindstone

This factory-made stone, 19¾ inches in diameter. with mid-axle 22 inches above the ground, is set in primitive pioneer style in the fork of a tree. mounted on three peg-legs, and turned by a homemade wooden axle and crank, running in oiled channels notched on wooden blocks nailed upon the fork. The frame was made by John A. Scheetz, of Tinicum Township, Bucks Co·, Penna., about 1866, axle and crank included, and bought Sept. 3, 1916, by the writer when seen standing in the yard of the former.

Two persons are required to work this primitive farm apparatus, one of whom turns the crank and occasionally pours from a can the necessary water upon the wheel, while the other standing up at the fork opening (left) and leaning forward, presses the blade of the tool, held in both hands (thumbs under) at the desired angle upon the flat rim of the stone, as the latter revolves. generally away from him, or from left to right in the picture.

Holtzapffel says that grindstones were sometimes worked dry in the English cutleries (for forks and needles); that grooved blades, with an outer basil (like the gouge), were rocked upon the revolving stone by the workman; and that, because grindstones generally turn away from the workman and so produce a wire edge, said wire edge was sometimes removed by holding the blade back-handed or tilted away from the workman. and against the direction of the wheel motion.

arrows on a grindstone resembling those used by our knife grinders, illustrating the verse of Horace 'Ardentes acutas sagittas cote cruenta.' "

Where is the little stone now (1928)? Who has seen it in recent years? Must we suppose that some fabricator of antiquities forged it to impose upon gem collectors and deceive LaChausse in the 17th century, and

that though the Romans often made quern stones to pulverize grain by grinding, they always sharpened their weapons on flat rub-stones, and that no Roman grindstone, whole or broken, has been dug up and overlooked anywhere in the excavations of the last forty years?

But however made or mounted, the grindstone soon wore down and not

Fig. 236. Roman Grindstone

The question as to whether the Romans were acquainted with the now indispensable revolving grindstone, or, like the Chinese, ignorant of the device, sharpening all their metal instruments on whetstones and rubbing stones, seems at present to depend largely on this well-known, unique, little picture from a small engraved gem, described more than two hundred years ago, representing Cupid sharpening an arrow on a revolving grindstone, turned in modern knife-grinder style on a wheel-barrow, with a foot treadle. The picture, without special comment, appears in *Gemmae antiquae figuratae*, Rome, 1703, by the French Antiquary, Michel Ange de la Chausse, born in Paris, 1660, died after 1738, and was copied again without comment and republished by Montfaucon, cf. *Monuments of Antiquity, explained in Sculpture*, English translation by David Humphries, London, 1722, Plate 58, Figure 7. One hundred years later it appeared under the word "Cos" in the *Companion to the Latin Dictionary*, London, Longman, 1849, of Anthony Rich, who fails to give his authority. Dean Milman, who illustrates it in his *Horace*, J. Murray, London, 1853 edition, to explain the words "Cote Cruenta" in Carmen VII, p. 90, acknowledges La Chausse. So do Daremberg, and Saglio, who refer to it without illustrating it, *Dictionarie des Antiquities Grecques et Romaines*, Paris 1877, but doubt its authenticity, without telling why. Feldhaus who publishes the picture in *Technik der Vorzeit*, mentioning neither Le Chausse nor Montfaucon, says he gets it from a Paris, 1861 edition of Rich, but asserts in general, without definite proof, that the revolving grindstone and treadle apparatus was unknown to the Romans. He condemns the engraving as a forgery, "einer wohl gefalschten gemme." According to Dr. H. Jacobi, many quern stones, but no grindstones, have yet been found at the Saalburg. On the other hand, the *Proceedings of the Society of Antiquaries of London*, Vol. 18, 2d series, p. 374, refers to, without illustrating, one-half of a small, 5 inch diameter, Roman grindstone, dug up for the Society, with "several whetstones and pounders," at the Romano-British camp site at Birrenswark, Scotland, in 1898.

being easy to replace, the evidence clearly proves that sometimes, until 1840, and often later, the pioneer mountaineer, far removed from the source of supply, chiselled for himself blocks of native sandstone, into heavy discs for grindstones, to prove which the next illustration,

THE HOMEMADE GRINDSTONE

(Fig. 237)

shows a specimen of one of these now rare relics made and used in the 19th century in the mountains near McElhattan, Pennsylvania, kindly found for the writer by Col. H. W. Shoemaker.

In any case, the grindstone, with its crank or treadle, is a cumbersome instrument, and because it was too heavy for easy transport, in some important cases, the less efficient whet-

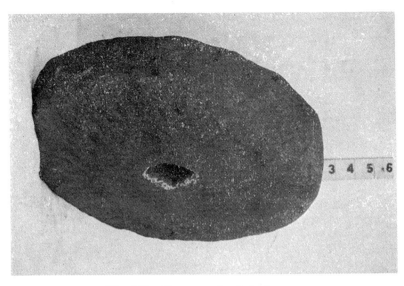

Fig. 237. Home-made Grindstone

The very rare specimen illustrated shows a grindstone, homemade from a piece of natural sandstone. The specimen was described and kindly obtained for the writer by Col. H. W. Shoemaker, of Restless Oaks, McElhattan, Clinton Co., Pa., and given to the Bucks County Museum by Mr. Charles A. Crawford, of Chatham Run, Clinton Co., Pa. It was found in August, 1924, in Thomas Hollow, near McElhattan, by Mr. W. J. Phillips, who was born in 1862, and who said his grandfather had made it of natural rock found in the neighborhood, and had used it about 1820.

stone took its place. This is proved by the next picture,

THE AXE WHETSTONE (Fig. 238) which shows several of the small pocket whetstones, one made by the father of H. K. Deisher, of Kutztown, Pa., and used by him to whet his axe; and others obtained by Col. H. W. Shoemaker (in 1924) from old woodmen in Northern Pennsylvania, who continually, as they told him, until about 1880, made their own axe whetstones from selected sandstones like this, found by them in the woods.

Not all these pocket whetstones, however, were homemade, some, as seen in the illustration, were storebought, factory-made or even imported. But in any case they typify a large class of stones used long before the grindstone was invented, to sharpen metallic blades, either (A), by thus rubbing the stone against the blade, or (B), by rubbing the blade against the stone. Described by several Roman writers as used with oil (cotes oleariae,) or water (cotes aquariae), they have been scantily illustrated and ill explained by archaeologists, who have mixed up blade-sharpening stones with rubbing stones used for other purposes. One of them, however, a true Roman whetstone, upon which a slave sharpens his knife, clearly appears as a flat rectangular slab, in the soul-stirring statue known as the "Knife Sharpener" in the Uffizi Gallery at Florence. A Roman altar, at the Saalburg Museum (*cf. Romische Kastell Saalburg vor Der Hohe,* von L. Jacobi, Homburg, 1897, Plate XXIV) shows abrasions on one of its

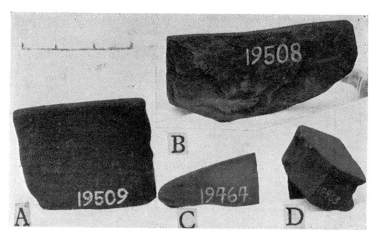

Fig. 238. Axe Whetstones

According to information obtained by Col. H. W. Shoemaker, of McElhattan, Pa., and Mr. H. K. Deisher, of Kutztown, Pa., on long, tree-felling journeys. when the crank grindstones were too heavy to transport, these rare tools, now almost forgotten, were carried in the lumberman's pocket, to keep his carefully guarded axe sharpened. They were held in the hollow of the right hand. moistened with saliva, and rubbed on both sides of the axe bldae.

(A) No. 19509 and (B) No. 19508, are homemade pocket whetstones, obtained by Col. H. W. Shoemaker, Oct. 13, 1924, made and used by Seth Nelson or his father, in the late 19th century.

(C) No. 19464, the broken end of a store-bought whetstone, was used for this purpose, by H. K. Deisher, of Kutztown, Pa., about 1910.

(D) No. 19463 is a piece of native sandstone, found by Mr. Deisher's father. along the road side, near Kurtz's distillery, Kutztown, Pa., and used by the latter, about 1900, for the same purpose.

sides thus produced, and that soldiers thus sharpened their swords against public or sacred walls in later times, is proved by scorings now (1928) visible at the gate of Castle Rushen, on the Isle of Man, and at St. Mary's Church at Thirsk and an old church at North Allerton, in Yorkshire, England.

According to recent information from Mr. R. P. Hommel, the inhabitants of the Kiangsi Province in China, ignorant of the use of the grindstone, were, in 1925, sharpening their knives and tools on convenient street walls, or for common use on farms, upon small sandstone blocks wedged between two bamboo stakes, while carpenters carried to their work their own special whetstones, which they freshly mortised into a fresh wooden

block at each job. But this lavish disregard of time and trouble might well astonish the western wood worker, who, since the sixteenth century, as indicated by Fig. 240, has preferred to keep his whetstone permanently boxed in wood, a fact here illustrated by one of the grimy and greasy specimens familiar to visitors at carpenters' shops, known as

THE CARPENTER'S WHETSTONE
(Fig. 239)

This is a rectangular slab about 3 inches wide and 10 inches long, of very fine-grained sandstone, cemented into a wooden block, often shielded with a wooden lid, to preserve it from dust and injury for very fine sharpening.

From the time of the earliest settle-

Fig. 239. Carpenter's Whetstones

The picture shows two whetstones (Turkey stones) cemented, as usual, in hollowed wooden blocks (the box) with an empty hollowed block used as a lid for one of them. The right hand specimen, with its lid, was bought July, 1916, from Miss L. A. Swartz, of Point Pleasant, Bucks Co., Pa., who had inherited it with the tools of her father, a wheelwright of Point Pleasant, born *c.* 1810, died *c.* 1890.

According to information given the writer, in December, 1927, by Mr. H. K. Deisher of Kutztown, Pa., Christian Schneeberger, about 1800, made and sold whetstones of a fine-grained sandstone, quarried on his property, ¼ mile south of Moselem Church, Berks Co., Pa., and, according to local tradition, sometimes carried loads of his whetstones, 58 miles on foot, to sell in Philadelphia. A partly-worked, splintered, discarded, end-sawed example of one of these stones, 8¼ inches long, by 2 inches wide, found at the old quarry and presented by Mr. Deisher, is now (1927) in the Bucks County Museum.

ment (*cf. Probate Records of Essex County, Massachusetts, 1635-1681, 3 vols., George Francis Dow, editor. Salem, Mass., the Essex Institute, 1916-1920*), and before the numerous substitutes from various parts of England, Germany, and the United States (Arkansas novaculite) had come into use, Turkey stones, *i.e.,* small slabs of black and whitish stone, quarried by the Turks in Asia Minor, in use since the Middle Ages, and long exported from Smyrna, according to Charles Holtzapffel (*Turning and Mechanical Manipulations,* Vol. 3, p. 1081), had been specially cut and furnished readymade not only to the carpenter-joiner, but to all mechanics, to sharpen and resharpen their edged-tools after said tools had been roughly edged or basilled on the grindstone. Then the stone, laid flat in its case on the work bench, was oiled with sperm oil, and the tool held at an angle upon it, in both hands, with thumbs under and most fingers on top, was rubbed upon it to an edge.

Charles Holtzapffel in *Turning and Mechanical Manipulation,* Vol. 3, p. 142, enumerates the angles at which edge tools, used on varying materials, are held and then pushed back and forth to finish their required varying basils. He also tells how some tools like the paring chisel, are sharpened with two hands, and how round-bladed, outside-basilled gouges, are held at right angles to the whetstone, and wriggled in the process, and how the wire edge of tools if flat-edged, thus sharpened, must be removed by rubbing the blade laid flat, face downward, upon the whetstone, or where this is impossible, as in the grooved face of a gouge, retouching it with the whetstone slips described later.

The next illustration,

A CARPENTER'S WHETSTONE OF THE 16TH CENTURY (Fig. 240)

shows (right) a fragment of one of these stones and (left) an empty wood-

hand and shaped to suit the case. To illustrate which the next engraving,

WHETSTONE AND OIL STONE SLIPS
(Fig. 241)

shows several little homemade splinters of selected sandstone or store-bought, imported Turkey stones, or oil stones, as used in the 19th century. They are rough-rounded, single-edged or pointed, or square-cut by lapidaries, to reach, where possible, the blades of augers, brace bits, turning tools, etc.

But this is not enough, since other tools owing to their construction, require a reducing agent still further thinned to suit the case, only possible in metal; hence the file, the "Lima" of the Romans, an instrument of vast importance and range, used since pre-Roman times in all trades for the reduction of metal surfaces, but which, when adapted to sharpen the carpenter's auger, or his greatest instrument, the saw, became a special tool, almost as important in the latter case as the saw itself.

The next picture,

THE SAW AND TOOL FILES (Fig. 242)

is altogether too small to show clearly the chief varieties of this ancient tool, namely the round rat tail file (G), the half round file (C), the knife file (D), or the flat file (E), used for augers, planes, etc. (A) shows one of the most important of them all, the so-called 3 square, an acute-angled triangle in cross-section, and so made in order that its sharp corners may penetrate and sharpen, by cross filing, the notched teeth of a saw, and although the more easily made, thin-edged knife file, or the half round file, had anciently done and still does the same

Fig. 240. Carpenter's Whetstones of the 16th Century

As identical in make and use with the tools used today, the left specimen shows an empty whetstone box, which is a hollowed wooden block, and at the right, a broken whetstone, 328 years old. Both are relics of the Dutch Nova Zembla Expedition, above noted, of 1596. Photographed by kind permission of the Rijks Museum, at Amsterdam.

en whetstone box, both relics of the illfated Dutch Nova Zembla Expedition of 1596, previously referred to.

While nearly all the tools hitherto illustrated and described can be sharpened either with the grindstone or whetstone, or both, others, owing to the peculiar construction of their undercut, furrowed or notched cutting edges, are entirely out of range of a flat, broad, sandstone surface, and therefore require diminutive reducing stones held loose in the

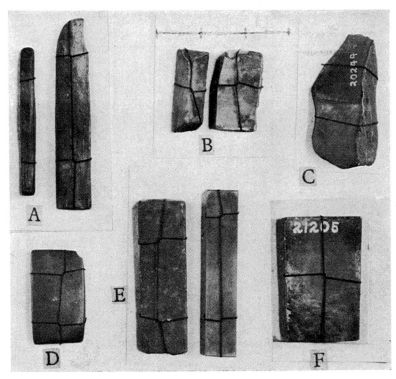

Fig. 241. Whetstones and Oil Stone Slips

Small splintered or sawed pieces of fine-ground sandstone, used by mechanics, with or without the help of files, for sharpening the deep-cornered or undercut blades of edged tools, as by carpenters for the blades of augers and moulding planes, etc., at points beyond the reach of common whetstones or grindstones.

(A. B and D) From the amateur clockmaker's workshop of Charles J. Wister of Germantown (*c.* 1820 to 1865).

(C) No. 20244, bought from Gehrian Lesher, Virginsville, Pa., used by his grandfather, Jacob Lesher, about 1830. Obtained by Mr. H. K. Deisher.

(E) Left, obtained by Mr. H. K. Deisher, is an axe whetstone. *cf.* Figure 238.

(E) Right, marked manufactured by Norton Co., Worcester, Mass., given to the writer by Rev. David Gehman, of Fountainville, Bucks Co., Pa., June, 1926, and used by him in harness making, before 1900.

(F) No. 21205, given by Mr. W. B. Montague. It is an axe whetstone, and was used, *c.* 1885, by John Herman, of the so-called Black Forest, near Williamsport, Pa., to sharpen his double-bitted axe, No. 21204, now in the Museum of the Bucks County Historical Society.

work, this triangular tool, sometimes flattened and side-notched for saw setting, as shown in variety (B), and again, among the Roman files, in Figure 243, continually necessary to repoint and re-edge quickly-dulled saw teeth, had, by the 18th century, become the saw file par excellence.

For two thousand years before the introduction of file making machin-ery in the 19th century, files for saw sharpening and other purposes, had been made by hand. They were hammered out, as described by Charles Holtzapffel, with great skill, by specially trained blacksmiths, from strips of steel forged to shape, filed or ground level, and softened (annealed) to be cut easily. These softened blanks were strapped down cold, upon a slab of lead, and "single cut," *i.e.*, in parallel grooves, or "double cut," with crossed grooves, by chisel strokes, spaced by eye, with exquisite skill, under blows struck with a heavy hand hammer, after which they were rehardened for use.

But whoever supposes that a "file is a file," errs, unless he understands the differently constructed, though similar looking so-called rasps, previously noted, used by carpenters for smoothing wood, or by blacksmiths on horses' hoofs, which not being sharpening tools, are shown, not here, but in Figure 127. These are not thus chisel-cut in parallel grooves, but toothed, *i.e.*, scored with sharp upcurled dents punched upon them with a triangular steel point.

Until about 1850, files, whether hand, or machine-made, were generally imported from Europe, though the evidence shows that a few American smiths had been making files by hand, and like John A. Werner, at Angelica, Berks Co., Pennsylvania, continued to hammer them out, more and more rarely, for half a century later.

Meanwhile modern machinery has, since the mid-19th century, required numerous new makes and shapes of files. But the principle of their construction, either dented (rasps) or channel-cut (files proper), on strips or rods of steel, has remained the same, and we can best grasp the overwhelming variety of the present trade names, by studying the clear scientific classification of files, ancient and modern, given in Knight's *Mechanical Dictionary*, as based first, on their shape, derived from the square (8 varieties), the circle (8 varieties), and the triangle (8 varieties); second, on the character of their teeth, namely, "single cut," with parallel chisel scorings (slow cutting for smooth work), and "double cut," *i.e.*, cross-scored at an angle (quick cutting for rough work), and, third, as classified, according to their relative fineness of teeth (also grouped in various size scales), namely, 1, "rough" (coarsest), 2, "bastard" (intermediate), 3, "second cut" (smoother), and 4, "smooth" (with very fine teeth).

According to Rees' *Cyclopaedia* (c. 1800), and the information (1926) of William Hafler, professional saw sharpener, of Doylestown, Pa., and formerly workman at the Disston Works, Philadelphia, all handsaws were always, with rare exceptions, sharpened with "single cut" files, and although, for saw sharpening, the triangular shape (A) would be the strongest and most effective, any acute edged file would do the work, hence a saw file may be flat on both sides and knife-edged (D), or, sometimes, flat on one side and rounded on the other, like the specimen (C) imperfectly shown in the illustration.

Though rust has as usual destroyed most of the iron evidence for ancient files, it has been generally known from books, and the excavations of the last one hundred years, that the ancient Assyrians, Egyptians, Romans, Greeks, and Chinese, made files either with parallel or with cross-cut grooves for metal working, or with round dents (rasps, Figure 127) for wood, first of bronze, and later of iron.

But definite evidence proving the antiquity of files in scattered proceedings of scientific societies and museum catalogues, has been hard to get at, until the very valuable pamphlet, *"The File in History,"* by Henry Diss-

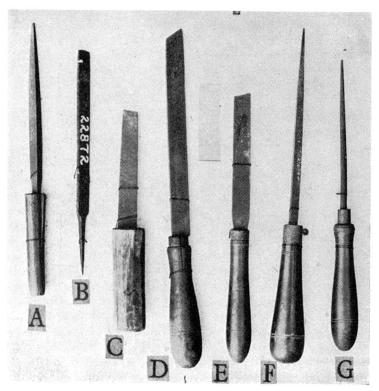

Fig. 242. Saw and Tool Files

The picture shows a series of files, used *c.* 1820-1850, by C. J. Wister, Esq., of Germantown, and represents, not the wood files (rasps), *cf.* Figure 127, but only the common forms of metal-working files used in sharpening carpenters' tools. All except (E) are single-cut, *i.e.*, with the parallel grooves not crossing each other, as described in the text.

(A) A very fine file, the so-called 3 square, is an acute-angled triangle, in cross-section nearly always single cut, except in certain parts of England, *c.* 1840, according to Holtzapffel, generally also smooth cut or nearly so, used in various sizes, one hundred years ago, as now, for sharpening saw teeth.

(B) Found, in 1927, by Mr. J. E. Sandford, in a shed full of obsolete or discarded tools at Centre Bridge, Bucks Co., Pa.; shows the "3 square flat" variety of (A), also single-cut; used for sharpening saws. In this case its top has been hammered flat and a side notch added, in which to insert saw teeth so as to twist them alternately to right and left, in setting saws as described under Figure 247.

(C) Shows the thin round-backed, so-called half round, file which would also serve to sharpen saws. The round back, imperfectly shown in the photograph, supplanted by small whetstone slips (Fig. 241) would also sharpen the saucered basil on the under side of the adze (*cf.* Fig. 89) or some of the curves of moulding planes; and the thinned edge would sharpen the threads of a gimlet or the start screw of an auger.

(D) Shows the knife file, a rarer variety of the flat file, for acute notching, more or less thin-edged, but not here sharp-edged, on one side, like a knife blade.

(E) The flat file, a thin rectangle in cross-section, thin-bladed, flat-edged and variously tapered, or with parallel sides, used sometimes with supplementary help of the small whetstone slips for sharpening pod and side-cutting augers, gouges, pincers, adzes, etc., and tools with gently-curved blades, or in various rectangular sizes, as a cotter file, to side-taper the metal plugs or wedges called cotters used in machinery.

(F) The square file, a rectangular, tapered variety of (D), which might have been used for the inner basil of a corner mortise chisel.

(G) The rat tail, a round, tapered, pencil-shaped file of various sizes, for the inner, short-blade curve of pod augers, or to correct inbendings or dents on the inner, blade-curves of gouges, scorpers, race knives, peg cutters, etc.

David Haycock, wooden pumpmaker, of Fountainville, Bucks Co., Pa., says (1926) that he would sharpen the blades and screw points of his pod and side-cutting pump augers with either single or double cut files, without dis-

tons Sons, Philadelphia, 1920, 1921, and 1922, made available for everybody, such facts as the existence in European Museums of excavated, reasonably dated, ancient files from Thebes, Assyria, Crete, Hallstadt, Hoods Hill (Dorsetshire, England), Silchester, etc., and the making of files in Germany in the 11th century, by the Benedictine Monk Theophilus of Helmarshausen.

The next illustration,

ROMAN SAW FILES (Fig. 243)

shows a number of Roman files of c. 200 A.D., excavated at the Saalburg fort above noted, and kindly photographed for the writer by Dr. H. Jacobi. Many of them are flat knife files, undoubtedly used for sharpening saws, as proved by the fact that in several cases, they are equipped, near the handle end, with a notch for side twisting ("setting") the saw teeth, as is also shown on the modern specimen Figure 242-B.

The next engravings,

SAW CLAMPS (Figs. 244 and 245)

show several homemade examples of the needful device consisting of wooden strips or blocks tightened by hand or thumb screws, or leverage, used to hold the saw blade rigid when filed.

But because the work of filing the teeth of saws does not finish the saw-sharpening process, and because saws, with one or two exceptions, must be "set," as well as sharpened, another group of tools is needed, namely the saw hammer already shown in Figure 224, and the variously constructed devices to give an alternate outward bend (set) to the teeth, one of which, a hammering apparatus, is illustrated in the

SAW SETTING TOOL (Fig. 246)

This, as here shown, is a homemade, spring-hammer device, intended to space and regulate the hammer blows when struck upon the sharpened teeth, so as to spread or bend them apart, alternately to the right and left, and hence diminish the saw's friction by causing the teeth to cut a slit ("kerf") wider than the thickness of the saw blade. Finally,

THE SAW SET OR SAW WREST (Fig. 247)

a side-notched iron plate, variously handled, as described under the illustration, produces the same result, by twisting rather than hammering the teeth.

When we reflect upon the immense technical importance, history and antiquity of the saw, we may well wonder how long man, in Egypt and elsewhere, continued to use saws, by wedging or bending open the saw kerf, without the use of this tool, before necessity forced it upon the toiling sawyer. That archaeologists have missed or overlooked it, that not one person in a thousand who looks at a saw knows or thinks of the saw-set, can in no way diminish its vast historical and technical importance. Pliny, A.D. 79, as quoted by Knight's *American*

crimination, using flat, half round, or rat tail files, fine toothed (2d cut or smooth, in the shape of B, D and F), for the purpose ,and supplementing his work, where possible, with whetstone slips.

David Gehman (general farm artificer), says that he would sharpen gimlet threads with the edge of a half-round file (C), or correct indentations on gouges with the rat tail (G), regardless of whether the tools were single or double-cut.

The *New English Dictionary* quotes early uses of the word "file" in 800 A.D. and c. 1000 A.D., and later in the 14th, 15th and 16th centuries, and in *Probate Records of Essex County, Massachusetts, 1635-1681, 3 vols.*, George Francis Dow ,editor, Salem Mass., the Essex Institute, 1916-1920, the name appears fourteen times between 1635 and 1681, so that it is reasonable to infer that many varieties of files have been used by armourers and metal workers throughout the Middle Ages.

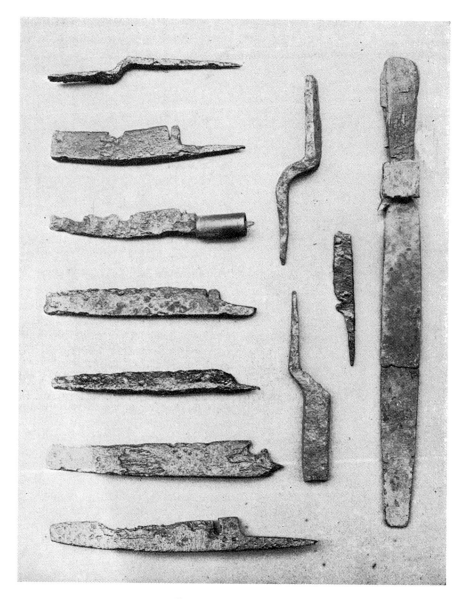

Fig. 243. Roman Files

The picture shows eleven Roman files of about the 1st to 3d century A.D., dug up near Homburg vor der Hohe, Germany, at one of the Roman fort sites on the Great Roman Wall built about the 1st century A.D., from Frankfort on the Main to Ratisbon on the Danube, to protect Gaul from German invasion. Seven of them are knife files, single-cut *cf.* [D] Fig. 242). Six show a notch clearly seen on the tang (handle) end, which enabled the workman who had filed sharp the saw teeth, to set his saw by twisting the teeth in said notch as in the modern saw-wrest file shown in Fig. 242 (B). Three, with their broad, rounded faces bent to clear the workman's hand, resemble the modern coppersmith's file. The right specimen is a flat file of common modern type (*cf.* Fig. 242 [E]). It is 32

Fig. 244. Saw Clamps

No. 7841, an old Bucks County shop relic, bought in 1906, shows a heavy open block, upon which the saw teeth are filed sharp and set when the blade, laid horizontally with teeth upward, is compressed under the iron plate screwed down upon it by the tailed bolt nuts, which as thus formed can be twisted without a wrench, either by hand or by a rod of wood or metal, used as a lever.

No. 11737, another home-made apparatus, bought from the Allum family, of Red Hill, Bucks Co., Pa., about 1917, is designed to grasp the blade of a hand saw, in order to file and set its teeth. It consists of a thin, 3-piece iron frame, bolted upon a heavy, rectangular, wooden block and compressible at the top by two corner, ring-top screws twisted by the point of the flat wrench here seen thrust within the frame. The frame forms a top jaw into which the saw blade, when placed horizontally, is squeezed teeth upward. The square top hole of the wrought iron wrench twists square bolt nuts of the frame fastening, not seen in the picture.

Mechanical Dictionary, refers to the necessity of setting saws, yet positive ancient evidence of the existence of tools for this purpose seems to be entirely wanting, until we come to the remarkable Roman saw wrests, made by notching the blades of files, and shown in Figure 243. But that these notch-bladed files are not the only saw wrests thus far found, which have continued in use for twenty centuries, is proved by the next illustration,

THE ROMAN SAW WREST (Fig. 248)

Look last at this unique iron survival (left specimen), blurred, but not masked by the rust of two thousand years, an iron disc with two side notches forged solidly upon an iron handle, as another relic of the great store of Roman iron tools excavated at one of the Saalburg forts, previously noted, found, well observed and photographed for the writer by Dr. H. Jacobi. No doubt that it is a saw wrest. The fact is proved not only by an illustration from Diderot ("Charpente"), Plate 49, who describes the same device in 1768 among French carpenter's tools, as a "Rainette," "pour donner de la voie aux scies," but also by the other added illustration showing a mid-19th century, now obsolete, wrought-iron specimen, of exactly the same construction, found by the writer in a long undisturbed heap of waste iron, on September 24, 1927, in Hilltown Township, Bucks Co., Pennsylvania.

centimetres long and with its original handle and ferrule, as shown, was preserved in the mud at the bottom of a well. (D) Left row middle, was found at Oberwesel. (A) Left row bottom, at the Feldburg Roman Wall Citadel.

The specimens are now on exhibition at the Saalburg Museum, and were photographed, and are here shown, by kind permission of its director, Dr. H. Jacobi.

Two similar instruments, about 10 inches long, undoubtedly saw-files, thus shaped and thus notched, are described by Sir John Evans, among the iron Roman tools found at the Romano-British town of Calleva (Silchester) near Reading, Hampshire, England,—cf. *Archaeologia,* published by the Society of Antiquaries of London, Vol. 54, Part 1, page 150. One of the instruments is illustrated.

Fig. 245. Saw Clamps

The specimen (bottom) from an old mid-19th century
collection of wheelwright's tools, bought from Miss L.
A. Swartz, of Point Pleasant, Bucks Co., Pa., in 1916,
shows a home-made clamp for holding the blade of a saw
while sharpening or setting its teeth. The jaws, mortised
at an upward angle upon the sides of a board on which
the workman sits, are tightened upon the saw blade by
squeezing up the two handles of the **compressible frame.**
The right, upper specimen (No. 5822), obtained
from Aaron Kratz, of Plumsteadville, Pa., Aug. 29,
1916, and probably used by him in carriage building,

Here ends our list of tools described
tediously perhaps, and with many
omissions, yet it is hoped not without
excuse. A study of them has shown us
that they are nearly all hand tools,
and that while machines, namely
tools operated by mechanical power,
have existed since the dawn of history, it is these more direct allies of
human effort, and not machines, that
have most widely influenced the labour of the woodworker, since man
first made, mounted, or edged them
with iron.

The fact that most of the old
writers from the 15th to the 19th century, absorbed in mechanical novel-
ties, have ignored them, should not
deceive us as to their vast and long
continued importance, for abundant
evidence shows, that throughout the
Middle Ages they held their own
against all mechanical apparatus of
wind, water or animals, and never
yielded to machinery until steam
quickened the latter at the beginning
of the 19th century. Then we find
that the change was affected, not so
much by the manufacture of carpenters' tools, in vast quantities by factories, as by the application of mechanical power to the saw, the plane
and the chisel. As a result of which,
when now (1928) trees fall, turn into
boards, are smoothed, moulded and
mortised as if by magic, not a few of
the master-tools here shown have
gone out of use. On the other hand,
despite these changes, since numerous
occasions for special work still confront the woodworker, we have also

since 1856, is intended to be held in a bench vise. The
long, flexible blade of an old frame saw, as shown, fixed
in the clamp, is held fast between two parallel wooden
strips, irregularly tapered from left to right and held together by releasable screws.

Fig. 246. Saw Setting Tools

In these two homemade machines for setting saw teeth, not only by bending them with wrest (Figure 247), but by hammer blows intended to be very accurate, the apparatus consists of a heavy wooden block, upon which the saw hammer, set on a spring, which spring is lacking in the upper specimen, is hinged with its wedge-shaped peen downward upon two mortised posts. The hammer peen falls close against the top edge of a little iron wedge, shaped like the blacksmith's hardy, or hack iron. When this instrument is screwed down with its two thumb screws upon a fixed surface, the saw blade is held horizontally in the workman's hands, and pushed inward against the vertical wooden rollers framed to revolve at either side of the wedge. One saw tooth then rests upon the wedge while the next is struck and bent downward by the hammer sprung accurately upon it by the workman, and the operation is repeated and reversed for both sides of the blade, as the latter slides along sideways against the rollers.

No. 990 was bought from Henry G. Gross, of Plumstead, December, 1897, and No. 14378 (lower) from Harvey D. Fellman, of Richland Center, Bucks Co., Pa., in 1914.

seen that many of his old characteristic implements, though no longer hand made, still survive in their original 18th century form.

If these tools were of less economic importance, or less ancient, or only American, it might be argued that

they were too insignificant, too modern, too local, to justify this attempt to classify and explain them. But when we again realize that, though continually overlooked by historians, travellers and antiquaries, they pertain to one of the fundamental needs

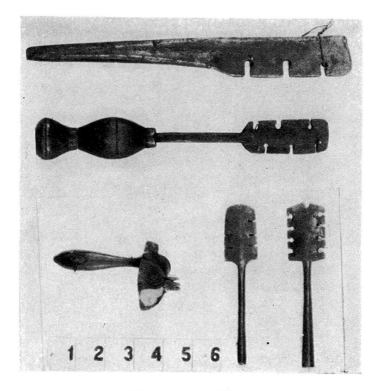

Fig. 247. Saw Wrests

The picture shows the iron blades, with notched rims, called saw wrests, by which the workman sets the teeth of saws, by bending said teeth, so that they lean outward alternately to the right and left of the blade, thus reducing friction in sawing by producing a kerf or cut wider than the saw blade. This tooth-twist is effected on both sides of the saw blade by inserting one of the notches of the tool at intervals between every two teeth, and bending its handle against the saw blade.

The lower, left, specimen, obtained in 1897 from G. B. Fackenthal of Riegelsville, here imperfectly shown, consists of a handled, double-bulbed wooden block, into the top of which, about one inch to the side of the handle, a flat, triangular, steel plate is so wedged, that it faces a notch between two other similar steel plates. In the three projecting notches thus formed, the alternate saw teeth are bent, one by one, by leverage, between the central point, and one of the side points.

In the Roman saw files, and the modern American saw file shown in Figure 242, a single side-notch on the file is used for the same purpose, thus producing two tools, a saw file, and a saw wrest, in one instrument. The tools are all Bucks County, Pa., farm and shop relics of the 19th century.

of human life; that many of them, until the beginning of the 19th century, have remained unchanged in construction for two thousand years; that though made in America, they were not invented here, but represent long-existing types of world-wide use, brought here by the colonists; and finally, that though many are rapidly becoming obsolete, they are still within reach, and in reasonably good condition; it would seem that this investigation, while it ought to be supplemented by research in libraries and museums, could not intelligently have started there, but has begun, not illogically, in the carpenter's tool chest of one hundred years ago.

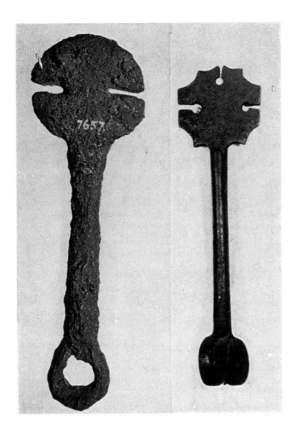

Fig. 248. Roman Saw Set or Wrest

(A) (Right) 5½ inches long, of wrought-iron or steel solidly forged in one piece and of date mid-19th century, shows an iron rod with a forged, double-looped, twist at the bottom of its handle and a thin, circular top-disc set at right angles to the handle, which disc is equipped with three equally-spaced notches, one of which is larger than the others, radiating from start holes. The instrument was found by the writer in September, 1927, in a refuse iron heap in Hilltown Township, Bucks Co., Pa. David Gehman, general artificer, of Fountainville, born 1854, informs the writer that he had owned and used a similar tool for setting his saws, about 1885. Diderot illustrates the same instrument, but without the bottom twist on the handle, and describes it as used by carpenters for sharpening their saws in 1768 ("Charpente," Plate 49).

(B) (Left) Shows a similar tool, 6⅜ inches long, with two notches, of date 1st to 3d century A.D., excavated with many Roman iron tools at Mayence, now on exhibition at the Romano-Germanic Museum there, and kindly photographed for the writer by Dr. H. Jacobi, Director of Excavations at the Saalburg Roman fort near Homburg, Hesse, Germany.

Fig. 249. The Twibil and Broad Axe of the 16th Century

This wood-cut showing the mortising and squaring of timbers for the framing of a new house was executed by the famous artist H. Sebald Beham and printed at Oppenheim, Germany, by Jac. Köbel on March 24, 1518. It is reproduced from Joanne Stoeffler's "Calendarium Romanum Magnum Caesaree Maiestati Dicatum."

For other pictures of the twibil see Fig. 159, p. 174; and of the goose wing broad axe see Fig. 80, p. 83, and Fig. 81, p. 84.

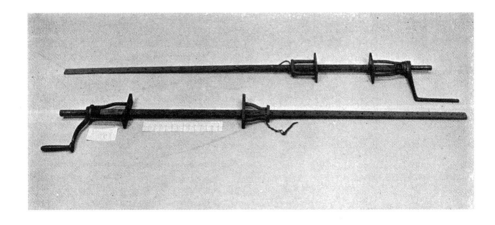

Fig. 249a. Wrought-Iron Clamps

The two carpenter's clamps pictured here are excellent examples of hand-wrought tools which were produced in the early nineteenth century. Measuring six feet in length, they were probably used in preparing panelled doors. A perforated shaft permitted the adjustment of the lower arm while the movement of the upper arm was controlled by the threaded portion of the tool. Both clamps were given to the Society by Mr. Walter Hack of Philadelphia. A carpenter by trade, Mr. Hack used these until his retirement in 1959. (See also Figs. 72, 73, 74, and 75.)

Addenda

Dr. Henry C. Mercer, the author of this volume, planned originally to write a comprehensive, illustrated dictionary or encyclopedia of early tools, machines and utensils patterned after Edward H. Knight's "American Mechanical Dictionary", copyright 1872. Further study of the subject, however, led him to abandon this alphabetical plan in favor of working up separate publications on each individual trade or craft.

While engaged in this research, Dr. Mercer became especially interested in those particular tools that pertained to the construction of houses. He regarded the tools of the carpenter and related wood-working trades as being of unusual importance among all the varied tools of ancient type and universal interest which he had been so instrumental in collecting for the museum of The Bucks County Historical Society.

At a meeting of this Society held January 17, 1925, Dr. Mercer in attempting to show and explain the variety of tools used by the colonial carpenter, realized that the subject selected was so large in scope that any thorough presentation would not only exceed the bounds of a single paper but would preclude reasonable publication in the printed "Proceedings" of the Society.

Therefore, he started to present the results of his original research through the monthly bulletins of the Society for the Preservation of New England Antiquities rather than in the publications of his own Bucks County Historical Society. It was the author's intention to gather these serial articles into book form after the final installment had been issued, and publish them personally for the benefit of the Historical Society under the title, "How Was the House Built, A Handbook of The Tools of the Lumberman, Carpenter and Joiner of the Eighteenth Century."

This contemplated arrangement did not, however, work out as planned. So in 1926 after a half-dozen articles in the "Old Time New England" bulletin had appeared, publication of the Mercer series stopped.* In 1928, Dr. Mercer finished his final manuscript for publication, and in the following year paid the Southworth Press, Portland, Maine, to print an edition of over 400 copies which he gave to The Bucks County Historical Society to sell, the proceeds to go towards the Fackenthal Publication Fund. The title of this first edition of 1929 became, "Ancient Carpenters' Tools Illustrated and Explained together with the Implements of the Lumberman, Joiner and Cabinet Maker, in use in the Eighteenth Century."

During the printing of the first edition, but after it was too late to make the necessary alterations to the text, Dr. Mercer found additional data concerning the spiral auger from Madeira. He presented this information under the heading "Errata" at the end of the volume, saying:

"While these pages are going to press, the writer learns that Fig. 177, page 202, represents a variety of Steel Spiral Auger used by Coal Miners in France and England in the early nineteenth century, to bore horizontally into the coal walls of underground shafts, so as to find and tap subterranean reservoirs of water, and thereby prevent inundations of the mines.

"L. Simonin, in 'Underground Life, or Mines and Miners', translated from the French by H. W. Bristow, N. Y., Appleton, 1869, p. 184, illustrates the tool together with the Taper Auger as here shown (Fig. 169 A, B, C), and

*In fact, nine articles appeared between April, 1925 and July, 1929.

a Nose Auger (Fig. 166), used for the same purpose. Like Fig. 177 Simonin's steel spiral tool, 17½ inches long, is a loose Bit. adjustable to a long twist-handle. But while in Fig. 177, 20 inches long, the 8-twist spiral, of equal diameter throughout, is entirely dull edged; in Simonin's tool, the diameter of the spiral, with only three twists, swells upward to treble size, and therefore must be side-sharpened. The shape of the bottom router blades and lack of pivot screw, is identical in both specimens. Knight's 'American Mechanical Diction-ary' lists the name of 'Coal Boring Bit', without adequately explaining its purpose, construction or history. Mr. R. P. Hommel, writing the author from Tsingtau, Shantung, China, in August, 1928, says that he has recently seen a Boring Bit resembling Fig. 177, sold at auction as part of the equipment of a European coal mining company, and a letter from Mr. Thomas D. Darlington of the Hercules Powder Co., Wilmington, Delaware, received February 12, 1929, informs the writer that Steel Spiral Auger Bits, like the Madeira specimen, are now (1929) and have been for the last fifty years, used to bore horizontal holes, for blasting, into the vertical faces of anthracite coal shafts at the anthracite coal mines near Hazleton, Shenandoah, Mauch Chunk, and Pottsville, Penna. These Bits, he says, up to six feet in length, are turned by a man with a Turn Brace, constructed with a Top Revolving Button, or Breast Plate like a Carpenter's Brace. Their spirals serving only for dust discharge are unsharpened, and of equal diameter throughout. As in the Madeira specimen the router blades lack a central pivot screw, and flaring outward beyond the width of the spirals, do not pare up the bottom of the hole as in a wood boring Spiral Auger, but cut or scrape straight downward. The Bits are some-times mounted solidly on the Turn Brace and sometimes equipped with sockets for the attachment of adjustable lengthening Turn-Rods to deepen the bore.

"Mr. Darlington also says that the shanks of these instruments, above the Auger Spiral, are sometimes extra-threaded, but for a special purpose, i.e., to engage a threaded elbow clamped upon the top of a heavy spike, called the 'Bull Pin', sledged tight into the coal wall, parallel to, and close beside the Auger, which devise, forcing forward said Auger, on simply turning the Brace, does away with man-pressure. He further says that now, 1929, the Miner's Bits used in prospecting for coal veins, i.e., boring or cutting from the open upper surface through earth rock, etc., to find coal veins, are differently constructed and resemble varieties of Bits now used in boring or drilling Artesian wells.

"The specimen dredged up at Madeira (Fig. 177) may also be compared with an ancient class of tools used since the sixteenth century to bore into the earth for various purposes. (Cf. Technik der Vorzeit, F. M. Feldhaus, Berlin, 1914. Article "Bohrer für die Erde"), and though it may have suggested the Spiral Shaving Discharge for the Spiral Wood-Boring Auger to Cooke and later inventors, has nothing to do with woodworking, and should not be classed as a carpenter's tool."

Subsequent to the publication of the first edition of this work, several pertinent articles have appeared which The Bucks County Historical Society think are of sufficient importance to be incorporated as an appendix to the second edition. To the respective authors, Messrs. Dunning, Sandford and Sim, the Society extends grateful acknowledgment for their contributions to the printed history of carpenters' tools.

The Saw*

by

GERALD C. DUNNING, F.S.A.

The iron saw is almost complete except for the point. The blade was originally about 10 in. long and is 3 in. maximum depth, tapering toward the point. The tang is 3 in. long, placed nearer the sawing edge than the back, and is bent slightly out of the plane of the blade. The teeth are cross-cut and very large; there are only four teeth to the inch. Alternate teeth are slightly set to opposite sides, so that the cut made by the saw (the kerf) is wider than the saw itself. The points of the teeth all slope away from the handle, that is, the tool is a push-saw and cuts on being pushed away from the worker. The saw is 0.2 in. wide at the teeth and tapers gradually almost to an edge along the back, so that the tool served the double purpose of saw and knife or chopper.

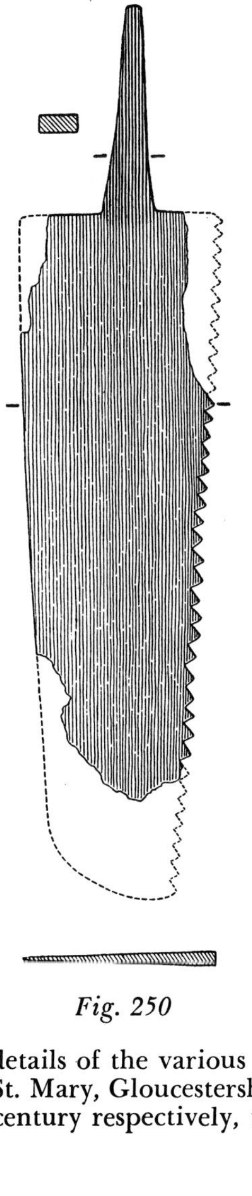

Closely dated medieval tools are very scarce, and since little has been written on the history of the saw in this country, (13) the available evidence may be collated here.

In this country a few saws of the Bronze Age are known, but the tool was not in general use until the latter part of the Iron Age. Complete Iron Age saws have the teeth raked towards the handle, (14) so that they are pull-saws and cut on drawing the blade towards the worker. The pull-saw remained unchanged in the Roman period, (15) and according to Petrie, (16) "there is no evidence of a push-saw in Roman times." It is curious but undoubtedly a fact that the Roman carpenter was content with a primitive form of pull-saw at a time when many other tools were perfected, and lasted almost without change to the present day.

Now comes a long gap in the history of the saw until the medieval period. Indeed the Windcliff 13th-century saw appears to be the earliest dated push-saw known from Britain. The evidence it provides does not, however, stand alone, for occasionally saws are represented in medieval art. In a few churches (17) there are wall-paintings of "Christ of the Trades", inspired by William Langland's poem, The Vision of Piers Plowman, written about 1362. These paintings show the Saviour surrounded by sets of the tools of labour, and although unskilled in execution the details of the various tools are accurately drawn. In two instances, at Ampney St. Mary, Gloucestershire, and Breage, Cornwall, dated late 14th and late 15th century respectively, the saw is depicted, and both tools are clearly push-saws

Fig. 250

with a handle at one end, (18). Another push-saw, in this instance a rip saw for cutting logs into planks, with the handle set at an angle to the sawing edge, is carved on an early 14th century misericord from King's Lynn, now in the Victoria and Albert Museum, (19).

The evidence from these sources is consistent and supports that of the Windcliff saw. It is reasonable to infer that the push-saw was in general if not indeed exclusive use in England from the 13th century onwards. The modern push-saw, then, can be traced back to the 13th century at least, and the only point in doubt is the period or circumstances in which it replaced the primitive pull-saw. The contrast in the performance of these two types of saw is fundamental. The pull-saw cuts on the up stroke, that is, the work is done against the force of gravity. The push-saw, on the other hand, cuts on the down stroke, so that the worker's effort is aided by gravity, and the saw cuts more steadily and is easier to control. The change from pull-saw to push-saw must have been effected at some time between the Roman period and the 13th century. In all probability it happened towards the end of the late Saxon period, when wood was extensively used for beams and planks in the construction of the roofs and doors of churches and houses. But the determination of this point, the only crucial one in the long history of the saw, can only be settled by the discovery of more dated saws.

* This article is reprinted, in part, from a paper entitled, "A Thirteenth-Century Midden at Windcliff, near Niton," which was issued June 29, 1940, as a 10p. separate from the "Proceedings" of the Isle of Wight Natural History and Archaeological Society, Vol. III, part II, pp. 128-137, Newport, Isle of Wight, 1939. On Aug. 10, 1940, Mr. Dunning sent a copy of his complete paper to the library at Fonthill, Doylestown, Pa., where the same may now be seen. The author's seven footnotes which follow are numbered as they are in the original "Proceedings."

13. The only comprehensive account of the saw is a useful booklet, The Saw in History (ninth edition 1926) issued by Henry Disston and Sons of Philadelphia. See also H. C. Mercer, Ancient Carpenters' Tools, pp. 136-62.

14. General account in A. Bulleid and H. St. George Gray, Glastonbury Lake Village, II, 371 ff.; see also Arch. Journ. XCV, 78. The finest Iron Age saw is from La Tene in Switzerland. It is 13¼ in. long including the bonehandle, and the back is edged for use as a knife. P. Vouga, La Tene, p. 112, Pl. XLV, 1-2.

15. A complete pull-saw with antler handle, only 5½ in. long, was found at Newstead. J. Curle, Newstead, p. 289, Pl. LXVIII, 6.

16. Flinders Petrie, Tools and Weapons, pp. 43-4.

17. E. W. Tristram, 'Piers Plowman in English Wall-Painting.' Burlington Magazine, XXXI, 135.

18. I am indebted to Miss H. E. Donovan and Mr. E. M. Jope for kindly sending me full-size tracings of these paintings.

19. Illustrated by F. E. Howard and F. H. Crossley, English Church Woodwork, p. 24.

Carpenters' Tool Notes*

by

JOSEPH E. SANDFORD

The following material is based on marginal notes made from time to time through the years since its publication, in a copy of Dr. Henry C. Mercer's scholarly work *Ancient Carpenters' Tools* (The Bucks County Historical Society, Doylestown, Pennsylvania, 1929). They are largely the result of reading from sources not available to Dr. Mercer while his work was in progress.

The numbers after the subject titles are those of the pages in *Ancient Carpenters' Tools,* to which the notes refer.

Saw (p. 16). The ancient Egyptian wood-worker shown on the XVIII Dynasty tomb wall at Thebes, saws boards with an unframed saw. The vertical balk is lashed at its bottom to the top of a post.

Maul (p. 19). The maul or beetle of wood, the head bound with metal rings to keep the striking surface from splitting, was used by the ancient Romans. See A. Rich's *Companion to the Latin Dictionary* (London, 1849).

Walking Stick Board Measure (p. 50). Not mentioned. An instrument similar to that shown in Dr. Mercer's Fig. 48 but for measuring board-feet, i.e., the number of superficial feet in a board. It is a tapering, eight-sided oak stick fitted with a slightly convex, flanged brass head, one inch in diameter, and a brass ferrule one and one-half inches long. It measures thirty-six inches from the underside of the head flange to the tip of the ferrule. The sides or facets are marked with scales, running from the head to the tip, for finding the surface footage of boards from nine to sixteen feet long, inclusive. The twelve-foot scale can be used as an inch-divided yard-stick. The scale lines make unbroken "circles" around the stick at one-foot intervals. Thus the stick can be used to find the length of the board—after which the proper scale is chosen, and the width of the board measured with it. The reading on the scale shows the number of superficial feet in the board.

This must have been an especially useful tool in the days of random widths.

Race Knife (p. 51). A forerunner of this marking tool was a two-pronged instrument resembling a short crowbar. It was called a roinet by the 17th Century French carpenter. With it he marked wooden morticed and tenoned pieces of wood for assembly. There were four named marks which he made with it—Marc Franc, le contre-marc, le corchet and la patte d'oie. When the pieces were many, he resorted to numerals, Roman numerals in all probability such as the old American carpenter used to help him match his mortised and tenoned joints—the same method by which his grandson marks screen frames.

Chalk Line (p. 53). There are two methods of marking with the snapped line, with wet pigment and with dry. Walter Miller in his *Daedalus and Thespis* (New York, 1929) quotes Sophocles (b. 495 B.C.—d. 405 B.C.) and the contemporary Euripedes, to show that Greek masons used both white and red chalk on their lines, depending on the tone of the material to be marked. This may indicate an early use of the dry method.

*From *The Chronicle of the Early American Industries Association,* New York, N. Y., Vol. II, No. 18. (Sept. 1941) pp. 148, 150, and 152.

The testimony of the Greek Anthology points to the use of wet ochre on the Carpenter's line. The poet Philipus, who is supposed to have written in the second century, A.D. speaks of the "straight running saw that follows the drops of red ochre" and "his taut ochre-stained line". Leonidas of Tarentum who wrote in the third century before Christ mentions "the line and ochre box" among the tools of the carpenter.

Red Ochre was the Rubrica Fabrilus of the ancient Romans, according to Savary, so called because of its use by artisans in wood and stone. In England, red ochre was called "raddle, reddle or ruddle" and in a quote from 1684 in the *Oxford English Dictionary* "Carpenter's Reddle" survives.

Joint Hook (p. 59). Dr. Mercer does not mention this tool by name. Said Peter Nicholson in his *Architectural Dictionary* (London, 1835)—In some cases, where a great number of pieces are required to be wrought to the same angle, a stationary bevel called a "joint hook" is used.

Scriber (p. 61). The traceret of the French carpenter of 1674. It was used by joiners also. Richard Neve in *The City and County Purchaser* (London, 1726) says that the compass point may be used for this purpose. He makes no mention of the scriber or brad awl.

Lead Pencil (p. 61). Conrad Gesner, the celebrated Swiss naturalist, was the first to describe and picture the wood-encased graphite pencil. This he did in his *De omni rerum fossilum genere* published at Zurich in 1565.

While the architect and designer of mid-eighteenth century France made use of the lead pencil, the carpenter marked beams and other members with white chalk or *pierre noire* alias *crayon noire*, a name which seems to have been applied to various black-marking minerals.

The lead pencil was found in the English carpenter's tool-chest as early as 1798. *The Encyclopedia Britannica* (3rd ed.), reprinted at Philadelphia in that year, says that it was made by mixing pulverized black lead with sulphur and was coarser than the pencil used for fine drawings.

The Rule (p. 62). A jointed bronze rule was found among the tools in a Pompeiian mason's shop. It was hinged at the center.

N. Bailey's *English Dictionary* (2nd Ed. London, 1736) tells us that Scammozzi invented the common jointed two-foot rule which was called by his name. Scammozzi's rule is mentioned in John Kersey's *English Dictionary* (2nd Ed. London, 1715). Vincenzio Scammozii, Italian architect and writer was born at Vincenza in 1552 and died in 1616.

From *Chamber's Cyclopedia* (Ed. 1752): "An instrument usually of box, twenty-four inches long and one and one-half broad, each inch being subdivided with eight parts. On the same side with these divisions is usually added Gunter's line of numbers. On the other side are the lines of timber and board measure, the first beginning at 82 (8½ in 1783 edition) and continued to 36 near the other end; the latter is numbered from 7 to 36, four inches from the other end."

"The application of the inches in measuring lengths, breadths, etc., is obvious. . . . The use of the other side is all we need here meddle with."

"1. *The breadth of any surface, as board, glass, etc., being given, to find how much in length makes a square foot.* Find the number of inches the surface is broad, in the line of board measure, and right against it, on the inches side, is the number of inches required. Thus, if the surface were 8 inches broad, 18 inches will be found to make a superficial foot."

"Or more readily, thus. Apply the *rule* to the breadth of the board or glass, that end marked 36 being even with the edge; the other edge of the surface will show the inches and quarter of inches which go to a square foot.

"To find the content of a given surface. Find the breadth, and how much makes one foot; then turn that over as many times as you can upon the length of the surface, and so many feet does the surface contain.

"2. *Use of the table at the end of the board-measure*. If the surface be one inch broad, how many inches long will make a superficial foot? Look in the upper row of figures for one inch, and under it, in the second row, is 12 inches, the answer to the question.

"3. *Use of the line of timber-measure*. This resembles the former; for, having learnt how much the piece is square, look for that number on the line of timber-measure, the space thence to the end of the *rule* is the length, which, at that breadth, makes a foot of timber. Thus, if the piece be 9 inches square, the length necessary to make a solid foot of timber is 21 1/3 inches. If the timber be small, and under 9 inches square, seek the square in the upper rank of the table, and immediately under it are the feet and inches that make a solid foot. Thus, if it be 7 inches square, 2 feet, 11 inches will be found to make a solid foot.

"If the piece be not exactly square, but broader at one end than another, the method is, to add the two together, and take half the sum for the side of the square. For round timber, the method is, to gird it round with a string, and to allow the fourth part for the side of the square. But this method is erroneous; for hereby you lose above 1-5 of the true solidity."

This particular type of carpenter's joint rule is not described in *Ancient Carpenters' Tools*.

The Level (p. 69). "From . . . remarks by Vitruvius . . . it is clear that the ordinary water-level, that is, a glass-tube which is filled with water and contains an air-bubble, was known and used as a leveling instrument."

The Technical Arts and Sciences of the Ancients by Albert Neuburger (New York, 1929). It is unfortunate that the passages in Vitruvius, on which this opinion is based, are not cited.

Iron Square (p. 70). The French glazier of 1674 used a large square of steel, according to *Felibien's Des Principes de L'Architecture* (Paris, 1674).

It is probable that this French work on the building crafts influenced Moxon. Most of the tools from the engraving from Moxon's edition of 1678—which Dr. Mercer says is the earliest known systematic grouped illustration of English carpenter's tools—are to be found in four plates from Felibien. There can be little doubt that Moxon's engraver had these French plates of 1674 before him as he worked.

The Side Rest (p. 73). This is called the "Side Hook" in P. Nicholson's *Architectural Dictionary* (London, 1835). "For cutting the shoulders of tenons."

Tool Handle Clamp (p. 74). This tool was not only used to hold tool-handles while being shaped with the draw knife, it was also used for making trenails.

Draw Bore Pins (p. 75). Not mentioned. These are described in P. Nicholson's *Architectural Dictionary* (London, 1835) as "pieces of steel made in the form of frustum of a cone, but rather taper, and inserted in handles, for drawing through the draw-bores of a mortise and tenon, in order to bring the shoulder of the rail close home to the abutment on the edge of the style; when this is effected, the draw-bore pins, if more than one is used, are to be taken out one at a time, and the holes filled up with wooden pegs."

Axe (p. 86). *The City and Country Purchaser and Builders Dictionary* by T. N. (London, 1703) under the heading "Laths" says that after splitting lengths of timber with wedges, they cleave these split pieces (called Bolts) with their Dowl-ax, by the Felt grain. This is called "Felting". What was the Dowl-ax?

Sand Paper (p. 135). Sand paper was an article of commerce in 18th century America. The *Boston Gazette* (September 10, 1764) contained an advertisement of sand and emery paper and again in November 19th of the same year.

Hand-Saw (p. 136). The hollow grasp hand-saw is shown with other carpenter's tools on a foot-stone in the church yard of St. John, sub Castro, Lewes, Sussex. The head-stone inscription—"In memory of Mark Sharp, Carpenter, Late of this Parish who died 26th November 1741 aged 64 years." If the foot-stone is of that year it pre-dates Hogarth's engraving "Gin Lane" by nine years.

Gruter's Saw (p. 153). Gruter indicates that the saw drawing was in a collection of inscriptions made by Martin Smetius, which was edited by Lipsius and published in 1588. This would be fourteen years before Gruter's work.

The Buhl Saw (p. 155). More correctly spelled Boule, from Andre Charles Boule, a French cabinet-maker who was born in Paris in 1642. He worked for nearly all the sovereigns of Europe. He died in 1732.

Breast Auger (p. 180). One of the earliest examples is found on the Bayeaux tapestry thought to have been embroidered soon after A.D. 1066. The 15th century date given by Dr. Mercer is a misprint for 13th century.

Gimlet (p. 203). "Yankee ingenuity is in a fair way to destroy John Bull's Gimblet trade in this country. The new twist gimblet is almost as much superior to the old English gimblets as the screw auger is to the old pod auger." *New York Post*, August 1, 1833.

Master of Flemalle (p. 205). This painter has been identified as Robert Campin, who settled at Tournai in 1406 at the age of 28. The identification was made in 1900 by M. Hulin.

Mandrel Lathe (p. 221). "Mandrel" the *mandrin* of the French—the word from which mandrel comes. The *Oxford English Dictionary* says that it cannot be traced back of 1690 in France, but it is to be found in the first edition of Felibien's *Des Principes de L'Architecture* published at Paris in 1674.

Screw (p. 254). Although the earliest specimen of screw in the Armor Collection of the Metropolitan Museum of Art, New York, was (in 1928) one in company with three rivets in an Italian 15th century war hammer, and the second oldest in the saddle armor of Jacques Galiot De Genouihac, dated 1527, it was not until after 1550 that examples became more plentiful. Of those 16th century screws examined, all were threaded by the file, and gimlet pointed. It is fairly safe to assume that they were used only by armorers, locksmiths and instrument-makers at that time. Jacques Besson's *Le Cosmolabe* (Paris, 1567) shows screws with gimlet points and thumb grips and a button headed set screw.

The earliest types of screws were not made to be counter-sunk. The earliest surface-applied hinges did not require flat-headed screws for fastenings— nor any screws at all for that matter.

Although the butt-hinge was known in France in 1674, the invention of the cheap cast-iron butt hinge in 1775 (Izon and Whitehurst, British Patent, October 3, 1775) must have done much to stimulate the manufacture of flat-topped screws.

Glue (p. 262). The survival of ancient tools and methods through the ages is well illustrated by glue. The monk Theophilus, writing (c. 1100 A.D.) in his handbook on the crafts associated with church building, gives the receipt for cheese glue—"Soft cheese is cut very small and washed with warm water in a small mortar with a pestle until, being frequently poured in, the water comes away pure. Then this cheese, compressed by hand, is put into cold water until it hardens. After this it is very finely ground, with another piece of wood, upon a smooth wooden table, and in this state it is again placed in the mortar, and is carefully ground with the pestle, water mixed with quick lime being added, until it is made as thick as lees."

"The tablets of altars fastened together with this glue, after they are dry, so adhere together, that neither heat nor humidity are able to disjoin them."

Cennino Cennini, writing an artist's workshop manual in the fourteenth century, speaks of this same glue: "There is a glue used by workers in wood which is made of cheese put into water to soften. Rub it down with a wooden pestle with both hands, adding a little quick lime. Apply it to the boards you wish to join, unite them and fix them well together."

We are told that cheese glue is mentioned in another work in the Byzantine tradition, called the *Lucca MS*, translated at least in part from a Greek original and written in an Italian hand of the eighth century.

Dr. Thomas Shaw in his book of travels, published at Oxford in 1738, wrote of the Moors; "Instead of common glue, the joiners frequently use a preparation of cheese, which is first to be pounded, with a little water, in a mortar, 'till the wheyie matter is washed out. When this is done, they pound it again with a small quantity of fine lime, and apply it afterwards as quick as possible to such boards as are to be joined together, which, after the cement becomes dry, will not be separated, I am told, even by water itself."

Cheese glue in the eighth, twelfth, fourteenth, sixteenth (a quote from 1562: "When stone pottes be broken, what is better to glue them againe . . . like the syment made of cheese") the eighteenth and the nineteenth centuries (Dr. Ure, who wrote in 1843, "The curd or caseum is employed—slices of skim milk cheeses are boiled in a great quantity of water and then incorporated with quick lime on a slab with a muller or in a marble mortar.")

In this twentieth century we buy our cheese glue in powder form at the hardware store. Called a casein glue, it is sold under a trade-marked name. Still used because it is strong and water proof, it is one of the oldest of our modern preparations.

Claw Hammer (p. 264). The modern carpenter, in two instances observed—Brooklyn, N. Y., and Solebury, Penna.,—had a hole drilled in the butt of his hammer handle, which was filled with soap into which he stuck the points of wire nails before he hammered them into hard wood. This makes nails easier to drive.

Screw Driver (p. 268). The first quote in the *Oxford English Dictionary* for "Screw Driver" is dated 1812—but it is mentioned fourteen years earlier in the *Encyclopedia Britannica* (3rd edition), printed at Philadelphia in 1798, where, under *Navigation*, the screw-driver is shown and named. The screw-driver is shown among the tools of the marquetry worker in Felibien's *Des Principes de L'Architecture,* Paris, 1674.

The earliest known reference to screw drivers is to be found in the *Greek Anthology* (Loeb Edition, Vol. 1, p. 405) in a dedicatory epigram written by Leonidas of Tarentum who flourished in the third century before Christ:

"These are the tools of the carpenter Leontichus, the grooved file, the plane, the rapid devourer of wood, the line and ochre box, the hammer lying next them that strikes with both ends, the rule stained with ochre, the drillbow and rasp, and this heavy axe with its handle, the president of the craft; his revolving augers and quick gimlets too, and these four screw-drivers and his double-edged adze—all these on ceasing from his calling he dedicated to Athene who gives grace to work."

The screw-driver was not a common carpenter's tool and screws were rare at an early date, yet in this, the earliest known mention of the screw-driver, we have not one but four! One wonders whether this was poetic license or had the Greeks a similar name for some other bladed tool which has misled the translator? Not being a Greek scholar nor having one handy, this must remain a mystery for the present.

The Barking Axe*

by

ROBERT J. SIM

In Ancient Carpenters' Tools, Dr. Henry C. Mercer illustrates one of these implements among carpenters' hewing hatchets. (Page 87, Fig. 83, No. 306.) But to the shipbuilders down along the Delaware it is the old-time "barking axe" that was used for stripping the bark from logs. Then the logs could be tapered by means of large draw knives and made into masts and spars.

The barking axe, fitted with its short handle, seems to have been a one-hand tool. The thin, rectangular blade is beveled on the right side only; there is no poll for pounding, and the handle bears to the right in order to clear the workman's knuckles from the log.

The half dozen specimens thus far examined are deeply corroded and pitted. One with the blade worn away at one corner was mounted upside down on a long axe-helve and had been used as a turf axe. William Sloane, a marine blacksmith at Greenwich, has a barking axe with the old foot-long handle still in it, the only complete tool of this kind we have seen. A single-purpose implement it seems to be, light but efficient.

* From "Pages from the Past of Rural New Jersey", Robert J. Sim, New Jersey Agricultural Society, Trenton, N. J., 1949. p. 43.

Bibliography

The Figures at the end of each item quoted in the following list are book page numbers referring to the place in this work where the item is used as a reference authority.

Agricola, Georgius. *De re Metallica,* Basil, 1556, trans. from the 1st ed. by Herbert Clark Hoover and Lou Henry Hoover. London, 1912. 78.

Aine, H. Roux. *Herculaneum et Pompeii.* Paris, Librarie de Firmin Didot Freres. 1870. 150 (plate 142), 153, 155.

Almanac. *Neuer Lancasterischer Kalendar,* Lancaster, Pa., published and sold by Johann Albrecht und Comp., Prince Street, 1798. 173.

Amman, Jost. *Stände und Handwerker* (woodcut, 1568). Hirth reprint, Munich, 1888. 80, 104, 109, 243.

Anthon, Charles. Smith's *Dictionary of Classical Antiquities* (Anthon's N. Y. ed., 1843). New York, Harper Brothers, 1844. 152, 153, 155.

Antiquaries. *Proceedings of the Society of Antiquaries* of London, 2 ser., vol. 18, 1899, 1901, 1911, 1912. London. J. B. Nichols & Sons, for the Society. 287.

Archaelogia; or, Miscellaneous Tracts relating to Antiquity, (vol. 54, part 1, p. 150). Oxford, Frederick Hall, for the Society of Antiquaries of London, 1888, 1889. 297.

Augustine, Saint. *De Civitate Dei.* 113.

Bailey, William. *The Advancement of Arts, Manufacturers and Commerce.* London, William Adlard, 1772. 201, 202.

Beauchamp, William M. "Metallic Implements of the New York Indians," in *New York State Bulletin 55.* Albany, N. Y., University of the State of New York, 1902. 1, 8, 91.

Beckman, John. *A History of Inventions and Discoveries and Origins.* London, Bell & Daldy, 1872-1877. 14, 16, 20, 26.

Bishop, J. L. *History of American Manufacturers.* Philadelphia, 1864. 8, 27, 107.

Blümlein, Carl. *Bilder aus dem Römisch Germanischen Kulturleben.* München und Berlin, 1926. (No pages.)

Blümner, Hugo. *Technologie und Terminologie Der Gewerbe und Kunste bei Griechen und Römeren.* Leipzig und Berlin, B. G. Teubner, 1912. 195, 264, 265, 268.

Böckler, George Andreas. *Theatrum Machinarum Novum.* Cologne, 1662. 26, 76, 80.

Brandt, Paul. *Schaffende Arbeit und Bildene Kunst.* Leipzig, Alfred Kroner, 1927. 179, 180, 206, 283.

Browne, John. *Fabric Rolls and Documents of York Minster,* Surtees edition. York, England, 1863. 164.

Bucks County Historical Society, The. *A Collection of Papers read before The Bucks County Historical Society,* 8 vols., 1880-1939. Doylestown, Pa., published for the Society by the Fackenthal Publication Fund. 51.

Carbechon, Jehan. *Libre des Proprietez des Choses.* French illuminated MS of 1362 in the British Museum, London, England.

Ceci, Carlo. *Piccoli Bronzi del Real Museo Borbonico,* (pamphlet), Napoli, 1858. 59, 114, 115, 268, 274.

Cecinsky, Herbert. *English Furniture of the Seventeenth and Eighteenth Centuries,* 3 vols. London, George Rutledge & Sons, Limited, n.d. 18, 20, 94.

Columella. *De re Rustica.* 177.

Croker, Rev. Temple Henry, A.M.; Williams, Thomas, and Clark, Samuel. *Complete Dictionary of Arts and Sciences.* 3 vols. London, printed for the authors, 1764. 52, 61.

Daremberg and Saglio. *Dictionary des Antiqutes Grecques et Romaines,* par M.M. Ch. Darembert et Edm. Saglio. Paris, Librarie Hachette, 1877. 186.

de Hesledin, Simon, and de Coiresse, Nicholas. *Valeur Maxime,* a French manuscript miniature, ca. 1450, now in the British Museum. 148.

Diderot, M., et D'Alembert, M. *Encyclopedie on Dictionnaire Raisonne des Science, des Arts et des Meliers,* 22 vols. text (1751-1777), 12 vols. plates (1762-1772). Paris, Braissons, 1751, 1777. 17, 22, 23, 41, 53, 59, 73, 101, 149, 158, 177, 182, 185, 186, 192, 194, 204, 219, 223, 240, 241, 270, 272, 282, 297, 301.

"Die fahrenden Leute in der Deutchen-Vergangenheit." Leipzig, Diedrich, 1902. (Woodcut.) 84.

Discorides. *Codex Cantazuzene.* (MS. of Discorides.) 152, 155.

Disston, Henry & Sons. (1) *The Saw in History,* Philadelphia, 1916, 1924. (2) *Saw, Tool and File Book,* Philadelphia, 1922. 137, 139, 141, 142, 143, 151, 152, 293.

Dow, George Francis, editor. *Probate Records of Essex County, Massachusetts, 1635-1681,* 3 vols. Salem, Mass., the Essex Institute, 1916-1920. 12, 13, 19, 21, 23, 31, 33, 35, 55, 57, 59, 61, 92, 97, 104, 107, 133, 161, 164, 172, 174, 175, 204, 206, 263, 270, 271, 272, 282, 285, 290, 295.

Dunning, Gerald C. *Thirteenth-Century Midden at Windcliff, near Niton,* published in *Proceedings of* the Isle of Wight Natural History and Archaeological Society, Vol. III, Part II, pp. 128-137, 1939.

"Egypt Napoleons." Observations et Recherches, etc., publie par les odres de sa Majestie L'Empereur leGrand. 19 vols.

Encyclopaedia Britannica, A Dictionary of Arts, Sciences and General Literature, 9th ed., 24 vols. New York, Charles Scribners Sons, 1878-1888. 17.

Feldhaus, F. M. *Technik der Vorzeit.* Leipsig, Berlin, Engleman, 1914. 186, 201, 254, 256, 259, 272, 273, 283, 285.

Flinders-Petrie, W. M. *Tools and Weapons.* London, Constable & Co., 1917. 115, 116, 145, 147, 150, 159, 161, 172, 198, 264, 270, 280.

Fox, George E. *Short Guide to the Silchester Collections,* 6th ed., revised by Mill Stephenson. Reading, Eng., Bradley & Son, 1920. 257.

Greuter or Gruytere, Janus. *Inscriptiones Antiquae totius orbis Romani,* (1) second edition, 2 vols., with plates, Heidelberg, 1602-3, (2) 4 vols., Amsterdam, 1707. 150, 152, 153, 154.

Heidrich, Ernst. *Alt Neiderlandische Malerei,* 200 Nachbildungen von Ernst Heidrich, 1-15 Tausend, Jena, verlag bei Eugen Diedrichs, 1910. 205, 207.

Holzapffel, Charles. *Turning and Mechanical Manipulations.* London, 1846. 22, 24, 26, 70, 71, 72, 76, 92, 95, 98, 101, 102, 103, 108, 113, 149, 155, 156, 157, 158, 159, 169, 177, 186, 197, 198, 203, 233, 234, 250, 283, 286, 290.

Hough, Walter. "Fire Making Apparatus in the U. S. National Museum," *Smithsonian Report,* 1888. 213.

Jacobi, L. *Romische Kastell Saalburg vor der Hohe.* Homburg, Germany, 1897. 194, 241, 242, 259, 277, 280, 281, 287, 288, 295, 297.

Johansen. *Geschichte des Eisens.* Dusseldorf, 1925. 240.

Knight, Charles. *English Cyclopedia.* 8 vols. London, Bradbury, Evans, etc., 1866-1868. 169, 260.

Knight, Edward H. *American Mechanical Dictionary.* 3 vols. New York, 1877; Cambridge, University Press, Hurd & Houghton. 119, 139, 151, 152, 153, 155, 200, 295.

Lardner, Rev. Dionysius. *Lardner's Cabinet Cyclopedia of Useful Arts and Manufactures in Metal.* London, Longmans, 1831-1834. 250, 255, 256.

Lasinio, C. Engraving in *Pitturi del Campo Santo di Pisa.* Firenze, 1813. 24.

Leupold, Jacob. *Theatrum Machinarum Generale.* (In eleven numbers from 1724 to 1802.) 234.

Lucretius. De rerum Natura. 65.

Martin, Thomas. *The Circle of Mechanical Arts.* London, Gale Curtis and others, 1813. 52, 56, 59, 62, 66, 80, 92, 95, 103, 113, 124, 133, 135, 141, 203, 225, 226, 263, 265, 268, 274, 280.

McGuire, J. D. "A Study of the Primitive Methods of Drilling," in *Report of the United States National Museum,* Washington, D. C., 1894.

Michel Ange de la Chausse. *Gemmae Antiquae Figuratae* (engraving). Rome, 1703. 285, 286, 287.

Milman, H. M. *Dean Milman's Horace Odes.* London, Murray, 1853. 285, 286.

Montfaucon, Father. *Monuments of Antiquity Explained and Represented in Sculptures,* 5 vols., trans. by David Humphreys. London, J. Tonson and J. Watts, 1722. 152, 153, 285.

Moxon, Joseph. *Mechanic Exercises, or Doctrine of Handy-Work.* London, Midwinter and Leigh, 1703. 20, 52, 53, 55, 57, 58, 59, 60, 61, 62, 63, 65, 69, 70, 75, 77, 78, 80, 88, 97, 139, 141, 145, 149, 166, 168, 169, 176, 190, 203, 204, 217, 219, 221, 222, 223, 249, 274.

Mummenhoff, E. *Monographen zur deutschen Kulturgeschichte,* vol. 8, "Der Handwerker". Leipzig, 1901. 189, 191, 203.

Murray, Sir James, and others. *New English Dictionary on Historical Principles,* founded mainly on materials collected by the Philological Society. 11 vols. Oxford, 1888-1928. 12, 19, 20, 33, 35, 52, 61, 103, 104, 113, 123, 135, 139, 148, 164, 174, 175, 176, 177, 206, 207, 237, 270, 272, 274, 280, 295.

Neve, Richard. *Builder's Dictionary.* London, 1726. 235, 236.

Nicholson, Peter. *Mechanics Companion,* American ed. Philadelphia, Lacken, 1832. 157.

Neuberger, Dr. Albert. *Die Technik des Alterthums.* Leipzig, Voigtländers, 1919. 152, 153, 155, 265, 280.

Owen, W. *A New and Complete Dictionary of the Arts and Sciences,* 4 vols. London, by a Society of Gentlemen, 1763. 274.

Patents for Inventions by U. S. Patent Office from 1790 to 1873, incl., vol. 1. Washington, Government Printing Office, 1874. 42.

Percy, John. *Metallurgy.* London, J. Murray, 1864. 162.

Pliny, the Elder. *Historia Naturalis.* 1682. 113.

Plumier, P. C. *L'Art de Turner,* (plate 79). Paris, 1749. 219.

Publico, Jocopo. *Oratoriae Artis Epitomata* of the Florentine Jocopo Publico. Venice, Erhard Ratdolt, 1482-1485. 149, 151.

Rees, Abraham, D.D., F.R.S. *The Cyclopaedia; or Universal Dictionary of Arts, Sciences, and Literature,* 1st American ed. adapted to this country. 43 vols. text, 4 vols. plates. Philadelphia, Samuel F. Bradford and Murray, Fairman and Co., probably 1807. 52, 61, 91, 113, 133, 217, 219, 274, 293.

Rhodes, J. H. *Exact Dealer Refined,* 5th ed., enlarged. London, printed at the Star by J. H., author of The Secretary's Guide, 1702. 136.

Rich, Anthony, Jun., B.A. *Companion to the Latin Dictionary and Greek Lexicon.* London, Longmans, 1849. 57, 113, 114, 152, 155, 172, 202, 264, 285.

Salzman, L. F. *English Industries of the Middle Ages.* Oxford, 1923. 219, 220.

Sandford, Joseph E. *Carpenters' Tool Notes,* printed in *The Chronicle of the Early American Industries Association,* Vol. II, No. 18 (Sept., 1941).

Sims, Robert J. *Pages from the Past of Rural New Jersey,* New Jersey Agricultural Society, Trenton, N. J., 1949.

Smith, Captain John. *General History of Virginia, New England and the Summer Isles,* 3 vols., 1607. Reprint, Glasgow, James McLehose, 1907. 284.

Staley, Edgcumbe. *The Guilds of Florence.* London, Methuen, 1906. 148, 183.

Stoeffler, Joanne. *Calendarium Romanum Magnum Caesaree Maiestati Dicatum,* Opponheim, Kobel, 1518.

Stokes, J. *Complete Cabinetmaker's and Upholsterer's Guide.* London, Dean and Munday, 1829. 135.

Tertullian. *Apologeticus Adversus Gentes.* 113.

Tomlinson, Charles. *Cycle of Useful Arts.* London, Virtue, 1835. 235.

Tryon, Rolla Milton. *Household Manufactures in the United States,* 1640-1860. Chicago, Ill., University of Chicago, 1917. 56.

Van Der Lys, Van Kornelis; Luiken, Jan und Kasper. Spiegel Van het Menselyk Bedryf. Amsterdam, 1718. 80, 138, 195, 196.

Vitruvius De Architectura. Venetii, Fr. Sensensem et Joh. Crugher, 1617. 9.2. 55.

Wilbur, W. R. *A History of the Bolt and Nut Industry in America.* Cleveland, Ohio, 1905. 252.

Wilkinson, Sir J. Gardner. *The Ancient Egyptians,* 2 vols. London, John Murray, 1854. 160.

Zabern, Victor von. *"Die Alterthumer unserer Heidnischen Vorzeit,"* v. band, heft vii, in Publications of the Romano-Germanic Central Museum at Mayence. Mainz, Von Zabern, 1903. 243.

Index

The light face numerals refer to the page numbers of the text. The bold face numerals refer to the page numbers of the illustrations.

317

INDEX